THE ORTHODOX BI

MW00582649

THE GOSPEL
OF LUKE

GOOD NEWS FOR THE POOR

by Fr. Lawrence R. Farley

Ancient Faith Publishing
Chesterton, Indiana

THE GOSPEL OF LUKE:
GOOD NEWS FOR THE POOR
© Copyright 2010 by Lawrence Farley

One volume of *The Orthodox Bible Study Companion Series*

All Rights Reserved

Published by   Ancient Faith Publishing
                A division of Ancient Faith Ministries
                P.O. Box 748
                Chesterton, IN 46304

Printed in the United States of America

ISBN: 978-1-936270-12-5

Dedicated to
The Very Reverend Larry Reinheimer,
priest, friend, inspiration

Table of Contents and Outline

❧ Introduction to the Series ❧

A Word about Scholarship and Translation

This commentary was written for your grandmother. And for your plumber, your banker, your next-door neighbor, and the girl who serves you French fries at the nearby McDonald's. That is, it was written for the average layman, for the nonprofessional who feels a bit intimidated by the presence of copious footnotes, long bibliographies, and all those other things which so enrich the lives of academics. It is written for the pious Orthodox layman who is mystified by such things as Source Criticism, but who nonetheless wants to know what the Scriptures mean.

Therefore, it is unlike many other commentaries, which are written as contributions to the ongoing endeavor of scholarship and as parts of a continuous dialogue among scholars. That endeavor and dialogue is indeed worthwhile, but the present commentary forms no part of it. For it assumes, without argument, a certain point of view, and asserts it without defense, believing it to be consistent with the presuppositions of the Fathers and therefore consistent with Orthodox Tradition. It has but one aim: to be the sort of book a busy parish priest might put in the hands of an interested parishioner who says to him over coffee hour after Liturgy, "Father, I'm not sure I really get what St. Paul is saying in the Epistles. What does it all mean?" This commentary tries to tell the perplexed parishioner what the writers of the New Testament mean.

Regarding the translation used herein, an Italian proverb says, "All translators are traitors." (The proverb proves its own point, for it sounds better in Italian!) The point of the proverb, of course, is that no translation, however careful, can bring out all the nuances and meanings of the original, since no language can be the mathematical equivalent of another. The English translator is faced, it would seem, with a choice: either he can make the translation something of a rough paraphrase of the original and render it into flowing sonorous English; or he can attempt to make a fairly literal, word-for-word translation from the original with the resultant English being stilted, wooden, and clumsy.

These two basic and different approaches to translation correspond to two basic and different activities in the Church. The Church needs a translation of the Scriptures for use in worship. This should be in good, grammatical, and flowing English, as elegant as possible and suited to its function in the majestic worship of the Liturgy. The Church also needs a translation of the Scriptures for private study and for group Bible study. Here the elegance of its English is of lesser concern. What is of greater concern here is the bringing out of all the nuances found in the original. Thus this approach will tend to sacrifice elegance for literality and, wherever possible, seek a word-for-word correspondence with the Greek. Also, because the student will want to see how the biblical authors use a particular word (especially St. Paul, who has many works included in the canon), a consistency of translation will be sought and the same Greek word will be translated, wherever possible, by the same English word or by its cognate.

The present work does not pretend to be anything other than a translation for private Bible study. It seeks to achieve, as much as possible, a literal, word-for-word correspondence with the Greek. The aim has been to present a translation from which one could jump back into the Greek original with the aid of an interlinear New Testament. Where a single Greek word has been used in the original, I have tried to find (or invent!) a single English word.

The result, of course, is a translation so literally rendered from the Greek that it represents an English spoken nowhere on the planet! That is, it represents a kind of "study Bible English" and not an actual vernacular. It was never intended for use outside the present commentaries, much less in the worship of the Church. The task of producing a flowing, elegant translation that nonetheless preserves the integrity and nuances of the original I cheerfully leave to hands more competent than mine.

Key to the Format of This Work:

• The translated text is first presented in boldface type. Italics within these biblical text sections represent words required by English syntax that are not actually present in the Greek. Each translated text section is set within a shaded grey box.

> ॐ ॐ ॐ ॐ ॐ
>
> 9   According to the custom of the *priestly* office, he was *chosen* by lot to enter into the sanctuary of the Lord and burn incense.

• In the commentary sections, citations from the portion of text being commented upon are given in boldface type.

Zachariah's lifetime dream was fulfilled. **According to the custom of the *priestly* office**, lots were cast to decide which priest should **enter into the sanctuary of the Lord and burn incense** on a given day, and the lot fell to Zachariah.

• In the commentary sections, citations from other locations in Scripture are given in quotation marks with a reference; any reference not including a book name refers to the book under discussion.

The priestly clan of Aaron since the days of King Solomon was organized into twenty-four divisions (see 1 Chr. 24:1–18), and Zachariah was "of the division of Abijah" (v. 5).

• In the commentary sections, italics are used in the ordinary way—for emphasis, foreign words, etc.

The word translated *mute* is the Greek *kophos*, which means "deaf" as well as "mute" (compare its use in 7:22).

❧ Introduction ☙

The Characteristics of Luke's Gospel

The Gospel of St. Luke has been described as "the loveliest book in the world," and while intending no disrespect for the other canonical Gospels, one scholar (Donald Guthrie, in his *New Testament Introduction*) has written, "there is something especially attractive about this Gospel." What is it about this work that has so touched the hearts of men?

It is important to recognize that St. Luke wrote for the very purpose of touching the hearts of men. He did not write his Gospel for the Church alone, but also as an *apologia*, a defense of the Faith, a commendation of the Church's message and life to the world at large. The world was beginning to be very curious about this strange new Faith, and some knew little about it, only that "it was spoken against everywhere" (Acts 28:22). Educated Romans (such as Luke's friend Theophilus) wanted to know about this new sect, the Christians. Where did it come from, and what was its message? Was it really politically subversive, as some were saying?

St. Luke wrote his Gospel and his history of the Church (the Acts of the Apostles) in response to such questions. He wrote not only to tell the historic truth about Jesus and His Church, but also to present the new Faith in such a way as would commend it to the world. If his Gospel was indeed "the loveliest book in the world," it was thus because Luke took care to make certain points about the Faith of the Church.

What were these points?

1. Luke stressed that *joy* is the signature of the Kingdom of God, the sign that God is truly active in the world of men. This world

with all its sorrows grinds wearily on. It was a hard world into which the Gospel came, full of oppression and slavery, suffering and injustice. What was crooked could not be straightened, and what was lacking could not be counted (Eccl. 1:15). There was some happiness (especially for the rich and powerful), but for the mass of humanity, there was little hope. They tried only to snatch what little happiness they could before they died (or before someone else robbed them of it or took it from them by force).

Into this grey world of tired men, the Kingdom came as a cry of joy, as a proclamation of release to the captives, of liberty to the downtrodden, of good news to the poor (Luke 4:18). Such joy had never before been seen under heaven. But wherever Jesus was, there was joy: joy over His Birth and the birth of His Forerunner (1:14, 44, 47, 58); joy for His disciples when they cast out demons (10:17); joy from the people at Christ's miracles (13:17). There was joy in heaven over returning sinners (15:7, 10, 32; 19:6); joy at Christ's entry into Jerusalem (19:37); joy when He rose (24:41, 52). This joy meant that something new and supernatural was happening on the earth.

2. St. Luke emphasizes *the poor*. The poor had been universally despised, and many thought of poverty as a curse. To be poor meant in some way that one had been rejected by God, for wealth was the blessing He bestowed upon His favorites. The Scripture commended almsgiving to the poor as a pious duty, but the poor remained disdained by the world. Over against such thinking, Christ proclaimed that the poor were now being blessed by God, and He offered them the Kingdom freely. Indeed, God had chosen the poor of the world to be rich in faith, and His heirs (Jas. 2:5); He had filled the hungry with good things, but sent the rich empty away (Luke 1:53).

Thus Luke records many of Christ's words about the spiritual dangers of wealth. He records His words about the poor being blessed, and about the rich inheriting woe (6:20f); His parables about how wealth weighs down the soul (12:13f; 16:1f, 19f); the story of how rich Zacchaeus gave away wealth and inherited the Kingdom (19:1f). He records Christ's counsel to sell one's possessions (12:33), to share one's bounty with the poor (14:12f), and to renounce one's wealth and status in this world (14:33). This indeed came as good news to the poor (4:18; 7:22).

More than that, Luke focuses on *the marginalized and the powerless*—outcasts (7:36f; 19:1f), women (8:1f; 23:27), children (18:15—Luke alone mentions even the "infants"), Samaritans (9:52f; 10:33f; 17:16). Here again was something new in the world. Never since the world began had such love and care been lavished upon such as these. This love was a sign that the Kingdom of God had come.

3. Luke emphasizes *prayer*. Prayer is the hallmark of holiness, and therefore a sign of the Kingdom. Luke stresses that the people were praying when the angelic announcement was made to Zachariah (1:10, 13) and that Anna the prophetess spent her days in prayer and fasting (2:37). Luke alone mentions that Christ Himself was praying when the Spirit descended upon Him after His Baptism (3:21), and that He prayed after His miracles (5:16), before the call of His apostles (6:12), before the confession of apostolic faith at Caesarea Philippi (9:18f), at His Transfiguration (9:29), and before teaching on prayer (11:f).

4. St. Luke stresses the work of *the Holy Spirit*. This is especially seen in the Acts of the Apostles (which some have dubbed "The Acts of the Holy Spirit"). After His Baptism, Jesus is said to be "full of the Holy Spirit" (4:1), and after His Temptation in the wilderness, He begins His ministry "in the power of the Spirit" (4:14). Luke alone records that Jesus "exulted in the Spirit" (10:21); Luke alone records Christ's counsel to His disciples to wait in Jerusalem until they are "clothed with power from on high" (24:49).

5. Luke also has a special interest in *healing*—perhaps not surprisingly, since Luke was a physician himself. The Gospels of both

Matthew and Mark also mention Christ's miracles of healing, but these events seem to have had a special resonance for Luke. He stresses that the power of God was present to heal wherever Christ was (5:17; 6:18–19; 7:21); he stresses that Christ healed the multitude that He would later feed with the loaves (9:11; compare Mark 6:34); he mentions that Christ sent the Seventy to heal (10:9); he quotes Christ's characterization of His ministry as one of "casting out demons and performing cures" (13:32); he alone mentions that Christ healed the person whose ear Peter struck off in the Garden of Gethsemane (22:51). For St. Luke, Christ was the Great Physician, the Healer of our souls and bodies, the One "anointed with the Holy Spirit and power" who "went about healing all who were oppressed by the devil" (Acts 10:38).

6.   Luke emphasizes the Gospel's *universalism*. St. Luke (himself a Gentile) stresses that Christ came not just for the Jews, but also for all men. The angelic announcement at Christ's birth is directed toward all men on earth (2:14); St. Simeon foretells that Christ will be "a light of revelation to the Gentiles" (2:31–32). St. Luke's citation from Isaiah describing the ministry of St. John the Baptizer includes the reference to "all flesh seeing the salvation of God" (3:6). Luke traces Christ's genealogy back to Adam, the father of all men (3:38); he records that in Christ's initial sermon in the synagogue at Nazareth, He spoke of God's salvation of the Gentile woman of Zarephath and the Gentile Naaman (4:26–27); and he records Christ's final word to the apostles before His Ascension that His message was to be heralded to all the nations (24:47). Though Jesus was a Jew, and though this was a Jewish faith, it was meant for all the world.

These are the main distinctive characteristics of Luke's Gospel. St. Luke portrays Christ as the One who came to bring heavenly joy into all the world, a joy that will lift up the poor from the ash heap and make them heirs of the Kingdom. In this Kingdom, the poor and downtrodden of all nations will be rich in faith, rich in prayerful communion with God. They will receive the Holy Spirit for the healing of their hearts and lives. Christ has come to seek and to save the poor and lost, bestowing on them a dignity of which the world has never dreamt.

Luke portrayed Christ in this way not only to win over his fellow Gentiles, such as Theophilus. He also was concerned to show that Christ and His movement were not seditious.

For many suggested that He was seditious, and that His movement continued to be politically dangerous. After all, Jesus had been crucified by the Romans under Pontius Pilate, condemned after a Roman trial on charges of high treason (that is, of making Himself a king in defiance of Caesar; see 23:2). The Christian movement seemed to provoke riots wherever it went (Acts 16:20–21; 17:6–8). Luke therefore is insistent that Jesus' crucifixion was engineered by the Jews (Luke 22:66–71; 23:23), and that Pilate at the trial thrice declared Him innocent (23:4, 14, 22). Herod also found Him politically harmless (23:15). Even the centurion who presided over His execution declared Him to be innocent (23:47), as did the mourning crowds there (23:48). The Christian movement harbored nothing intrinsically politically subversive, and a Roman like Theophilus need not fear to support it.

The Writing of Luke's Gospel

Who was Luke, and when did he write his Gospel? The Luke who wrote this Gospel was the companion of St. Paul, one of those who accompanied him on some of his journeys. (In the Acts of the Apostles, these journeys are referred to in the first person plural; compare Acts 16:10–17; 20:5–15; 21:1–8; 27:1—28:16.) Unanimous Church tradition identifies him with the beloved physician referred to by St. Paul in Colossians 4:14. (That he was a Gentile may be concluded from Col. 4:10–11, which lists Paul's Jewish companions—of which Luke was not one.) Eusebius describes Luke as "by birth an Antiochene and by profession a physician, [who] was for long periods a companion of Paul and was closely associated with the other apostles as well" (*History of the Church*, 3,4). He also ascribes authorship of this Gospel and of the Acts of the Apostles to Luke. This latter judgment Eusebius says was shared by Irenaeus (cited in Eusebius' *History*, 5,8) and by Origen (cited in Eusebius' *History*, 6:25).

When Luke wrote his two-volume set consisting of this Gospel of St. Luke and the Acts of the Apostles is more difficult to determine. We may assume that he wrote them at approximately the same time, and that the Gospel was written first, for both are addressed to the same Theophilus, and the introduction to Acts refers to the previous volume of the Gospel (Luke 1:3; Acts 1:1). This two-volume set must have been written after AD 63, for Paul was first imprisoned in Rome about AD 61, and Luke mentions that he remained there preaching openly for over two years (Acts 28:30–31).

It would seem that Luke used St. Mark's Gospel—or at least the draft notes from Mark of what would later become known as St. Mark's Gospel. If we are correct in saying that Mark's Gospel was written in the late 60s (with Mark making notes throughout the early 60s while Peter was alive, producing a final draft after Peter had died and publishing it abroad from Alexandria), then the following possibility emerges.

I would suggest that Luke began writing Luke-Acts during Paul's second imprisonment in Rome in the autumn of 65 (assuming Paul's martyrdom in the summer of 66). During this imprisonment, Paul requested that Mark come to visit him, joining Luke, who then was the only one with him (2 Tim. 4:11). I would suggest that Mark did indeed come to join Paul and Luke, and that this visit allowed Luke access to Mark's draft of what would later become the Gospel of St. Mark. Using this Markan material along with other sources and his own interviews with eyewitnesses (Luke mentions such eyewitnesses in Luke 1:2), Luke produced his Gospel around the middle of 67 or sometime later.

Other material regarding the life of St. Luke is sparse. Some say that he painted a portrait of Mary the Mother of the Lord. There is nothing surprising in this. After the crucifixion she lived with John in Palestine, where Luke would have come to know her (compare John 19:27); and His Gospel shows he did know her, for she was the only possible source for material in the first two chapters. It would have been natural for Luke to have wanted to preserve her historical likeness. A sixth-century tradition says that Luke sent the image to Theophilus, to whom he dedicated Luke-Acts.

Tradition says that Luke preached the Gospel in many places, including Egypt. It is commonly believed that he ended his days as a martyr. His feast day is October 18.

❧ I ☙

INTRODUCTION
(1:1–4)

☙ ☙ ☙ ☙ ☙

1 1   Inasmuch as many have set their hand to compile a description of the matters fulfilled among us,

2   just as those who from the beginning have become eyewitnesses and attendants of the Word have delivered them to us,

3   it seemed *good* for me also, having from the beginning followed everything accurately, to write *it* for you successively, most-excellent Theophilus,

4   that you might really-know the certainty of the words about which you have been instructed.

This introduction stands apart somewhat from the rest of the Gospel in that it is written in very elegant and literary Greek. (The opening word **inasmuch**—Gr. *epeideper*—is not found anywhere else in the New Testament nor in the Septuagint. Like the rest of the introduction, it is a refined and classical word.) It is as if St. Luke wants to secure a hearing for his message, and so puts his best literary foot forward, making his prefatory remarks as eloquent as he can.

In this introduction, St. Luke refers to **many** others who have **set their hand to compile a description of the matters fulfilled among** the followers of Jesus. These descriptions are not inaccurate—Luke acknowledges them as based on the work of **those who from the beginning** of the Christian story **have become eyewitnesses and attendants of the Word** or message **delivered** as reliable Tradition to the Church. But these descriptions are not adequate for Luke's purpose.

What were these compiled descriptions? It is difficult to say. The Markan material that we think Luke had access to in writing his own work was undoubtedly one of them. There were probably other collections of stories about Christ and His parables circulating in the Church as well. These might have been intended for internal Church use. Luke wanted something different—not just a collection of stories written for Christians who already knew the basic story of Christ, but rather a recitation of the entire story itself, together with a generous sampling of the stories of Christ's miracles and parables. He wanted to set such stories and teachings within a comprehensive framework, and do it in such a way as would commend the totality to his inquiring friend Theophilus. Luke stresses his credentials: he **from the beginning** of the Christian movement **followed everything accurately**, taking care to investigate all with thoroughness (Gr. *akribos*). He is now in a position to **write** it out for Theophilus **successively**.

By **successively** (Gr. *kathexes*) Luke does not mean in strict chronological order. Such is not the case in the fine details. Rather, Luke means to assure his reader that he has not omitted any significant events or covered anything up. He has given Theophilus a complete narrative of Christ's life from beginning to end, through which he can understand the meaning of all the details. By reading this, the inquirer can **really-know** (*epignosko*, a stronger verb than *ginosko*, "know") **the certainty of the words about which** he was **instructed** and informed. He has heard rumors and received reports about Christ and His followers. Now he can know the truth about them.

Who was this **Theophilus** (lit. "God-lover")? Was the instruction he had received formal Christian instruction such as a catechumen would receive? (The word translated here as *instruct* is the Gr. *katecheo*, from which the term "catechumen," "one who is being

24

instructed," is derived.) And was he a governor, perhaps of Luke's own province? (The title **most-excellent**—Gr. *kratiste*—is that used to address Roman provincial governors; compare Acts 23:26; 24:3.)

I would suggest that Theophilus was not yet a Christian, and that the "instruction" he had received was of an informal kind. Certainly a man in the process of preparing for Christian baptism would have known the basic outline of the life of Jesus, and the apologetic note of assuring him about the Christian movement (one of Luke's aims in writing) would have been unnecessary. I suggest that Theophilus was a highly placed friend of Luke's, possibly holding some state position, who had heard many reports about the new Faith, from Christian and pagan alike. Christians had perhaps spoken to him, as well as the foes of the Church. Luke dedicates the work to him, and hopes thereby not just to secure Theophilus's support for the Christian Faith, but also to commend it to pagan society at large.

✂ II ✄

THE BEGINNINGS OF CHRIST
AND HIS FORERUNNER
(1:5—2:52)

Luke interweaves the birth narratives of Jesus and John in a way that shows John was neither a rival to Christ (as John's latter-day followers, mentioned in Acts 19:1f, may have thought), nor His mentor (as many contemporaries may have thought, seeing that John baptized Jesus). Rather, John was Christ's Forerunner. This was evident in the angelic announcements that preceded their births (1:17, 32), as it was in the visit of Mary to Elizabeth, when the baby John leaped in Elizabeth's womb in recognition of his Lord within Mary.

These narratives are not just a kind of literary prelude to the main symphony to follow; they are intrinsic parts of that symphony. They form its opening notes and lay the foundation for events to come. Neither Zachariah nor Mary expected the announcements of the angel Gabriel. The initiative in all these things belongs to God. God was the One who decided that His eternal Son would be born to the holy Virgin of Nazareth as the Messiah of Israel. God was the One who decided that John should be born to Zachariah and Elizabeth as His Forerunner. The rise of John and Jesus in Israel is thus revealed beforehand as the will of God, and not (as their foes alleged) as the result of their own deluded ambition.

§II.1. Announcement in the Sanctuary of John's Birth

> ✄ ✄ ✄ ✄ ✄
>
> 5   It happened in the days of Herod, king of Judea,
>   *that* there was a certain priest by the name of

> Zachariah, of the division of Abijah, and he had a wife from the daughters of Aaron, and her name *was* Elizabeth.
> 6 And they were both righteous before God, walking faultlessly in all the commandments and requirements of the Lord.
> 7 And they had no child, because Elizabeth was barren, and they were both advanced in their days.

Zachariah and **Elizabeth** are first described as models of piety. This is an important part of Luke's apologetic purpose, for it was popularly held that godless parents could not produce a godly offspring. To show that John was a true man of God, it was necessary also to show that he sprang from godly stock.

It was during **the days of Herod** the Great, **king of Judea** (who ruled the Roman province of Judea 40–4 BC), that God broke into their lives. Zachariah was a **priest**, and his wife Elizabeth was **from the daughters of Aaron**—that is, from the priestly tribe as well. There was no necessity for a priest to marry within his own tribe, though this was thought to be preferable. Zachariah and Elizabeth were **righteous before God, walking faultlessly in all the commandments and requirements of the Lord**. They did not merely conform to outward rules of the Law, but sought to please Him from their hearts. Though **they had no child, because Elizabeth was barren**, this was therefore not the result of God's curse upon any disobedience. Childlessness was popularly thought to be a judgment from God (compare such a judgment on David's wife Michal in 2 Sam. 6:23), but this was not the cause of Zachariah and Elizabeth's childlessness. They were **both advanced in their days**, and their many prayers to God for a child had evidently gone unanswered.

> ॐ ॐ ॐ ॐ ॐ
>
> 8 Now it happened, while he was performing his *priestly service* before God in the order of his division,

9 according to the custom of the *priestly* office, he was *chosen* by lot to enter into the sanctuary of the Lord and burn incense.

10 And the whole multitude of the people were praying outside at the hour of the incense-offering.

11 And an angel of the Lord appeared to him, standing on the right of the altar of incense.

12 And Zachariah was shaken when he saw him, and fear gripped him.

13 But the angel said to him, "Do not be afraid, Zachariah, for your supplication has been heard, and your wife Elizabeth will bear you a son, and you will give him the name John.

14 "And he will be a joy and exultation to you, and many will rejoice at his birth.

15 "For he will be great before the Lord, and he will never drink wine or liquor, and he will be filled with the Holy Spirit while in his mother's womb.

16 "And he will turn back many of the sons of Israel to the Lord their God.

17 "And he himself will go on ahead before Him in the spirit and power of Elijah to turn back the hearts of the fathers to the children, and the disobedient to the mindset of the righteous, to make ready a people prepared for the Lord."

The priestly clan of Aaron since the days of King Solomon was organized into twenty-four divisions (see 1 Chr. 24:1–18), and Zachariah was "of the division of Abijah" (v. 5). In the days of Zachariah, there were some 18,000 priests in Israel, and their duties were assigned according to their tribal divisions. Each day, a morning and an evening sacrifice were offered in the Temple, along with an offering of incense within the Holy Place. Because of the great number of priests, their duties were assigned by casting lots, and the opportunity to enter the Holy Place to burn incense would fall to a man but once in his life.

Zachariah's lifetime dream was fulfilled. **The order of his division** had its assigned week to serve at the Temple. **According to the custom of the *priestly* office**, lots were cast to decide which priest should **enter into the sanctuary of the Lord and burn incense** on a given day, and the lot fell to Zachariah. Fresh coals would have been placed on the golden incense altar by assistant priests, who then withdrew, leaving Zachariah alone in the Holy Place. He was to await the signal from the presiding priest, then burn the incense upon the coals, prostrate himself in prayer, and leave the Holy Place. While all this was happening, the people assembled outside awaited his return from within the Holy Place. (Luke notes with his characteristic interest that the people were **praying**.) This was probably the evening incense offering, about 3:00 in the afternoon (compare Acts 3:1).

It was then that **an angel of the Lord appeared to him, standing on the right of the altar of incense**, as if he had just come from the Presence of the Lord in the inner Holy of Holies. This was quite unexpected, and **fear gripped him**. Just as people in former days were stricken upon suddenly encountering the supernatural (Jdg. 13:20; Dan. 10:5–8), so the old man **was shaken when he saw him** as well.

The angel spoke to quickly reassure Zachariah that he had not come with words of judgment, nor to strike him down as if his offering were not acceptable to God. **"Do not be afraid,"** the angel told him, **"for your supplication** which had been offered for so long **has been heard, and your wife Elizabeth will bear you a son."** Throughout the long years of waiting for a child, they had asked God for this blessing, and now their old prayer, the answer to which they had despaired of seeing, was about to be answered. They would have a son, and were to **give him the name John** (Heb. "the Lord has been gracious"). He would not only be **a joy and exultation** to his parents, but **many** others would **rejoice at his birth**. (Luke here first sounds the note of joy, which is a sign of the coming Kingdom.)

The people will rejoice because John is destined to be no ordinary child. Rather, **he will be great before the Lord**, as His chosen vessel. Just as Nazirites are consecrated to God, and as a sign of their dedication **never drink wine or liquor** (Num. 6:2–3), so John also (while not necessarily a Nazirite) will remain in a state of consecration to God. As the greatest of His prophets, John will **be filled with the Holy Spirit while in his mother's womb**. The prophets were filled with the Spirit for their task. Isaiah received his call in the Temple (Is. 6:1f); Jeremiah was marked by God for his office before he was born (Jer. 1:5). John too will begin his prophetic calling while yet within his mother's womb.

For he will have an important task to do. It is his work to **turn back many of the sons of Israel to the Lord their God**. (We note in passing how Jesus is described as the Lord God: John is to go as a Forerunner to *Jesus*; yet here John is said to **go on ahead** before *God*; for the pronoun **Him** in v. 17 has as its antecedent **the Lord their God** in v. 16.)

Israel was in a state of spiritual decadence and was not ready for the Messiah to appear. If He were to come at that time and find His people in such a state of apostasy, they would be smitten with a curse, as the prophets had threatened. John's task was to go on ahead before the Lord their God as a new **Elijah**, working in his **spirit and power**. As Elijah preached without compromise in a time of apostasy and recalled Israel from idolatry (1 Kin. 18:24), so John will recall Israel from hardheartedness. The **disobedient** men of his day will **turn back to the mindset of the righteous**, and thus **the hearts of the fathers** of old, their ancient ancestors, will regard them with satisfaction when they see them repent. Thus Israel will be **made ready** for the messianic Kingdom as **a people prepared for the Lord**. (See Mal. 4:5–6, which underlies this whole passage.)

The angel thus announces that the old prayer of Zachariah and Elizabeth for a child (which they doubtless had long ceased to pray) is now to be fulfilled for the greater salvation of Israel. When the priests offered incense in the Holy Place and prostrated themselves in prayer, that was not the time to offer personal petitions; it was the time to pray for the redemption of God's people, and it is this which Zachariah intended to do. But God is now to do both: He will answer Zachariah's old prayer for a child and work redemption for Israel.

ॐ ॐ ॐ ॐ ॐ

18 And Zachariah said to the angel, "How will I know this? For I *myself* am elderly, and my wife is advanced in her days."

19 And the angel answered and said to him, "I *myself* am Gabriel, who has stood before God; and I was sent to speak to you, and to preach to you this *good news*.

20 "And behold, you will be silent and unable to speak until the day when these things happen, because you did not believe my words, which will be fulfilled in their *proper* time."

Zachariah finds such wonders difficult to believe. He is here an image of the Old Covenant: he is centered on the Temple, he is old and without strength. Like all Jews, he seeks signs (1 Cor. 1:22). He embodies all that is good in Israel, as well as its limitations. He therefore asks the angel, **"How will I know this? For I *myself* am elderly, and my wife is advanced in her days."** Apparently the supernatural appearance of an angel is not enough!

The angel answers him, **"I *myself* am Gabriel, who has stood before God."** Zachariah's self-description is emphatic (**I *myself* am elderly**; Gr. *ego eimi presbutes*), and the angel's reply and self-description is equally emphatic (**I *myself* am Gabriel**; Gr. *ego eimi Gabriel*). Zachariah's protest of elderliness is abundantly answered by Gabriel's angelic nature! For Gabriel is one of the archangels, one who **stands before God** as one intimate in His counsels. Intertestamental Judaism knew very well of Gabriel's exalted position. Not only is Gabriel mentioned in Daniel 8:16; 9:21; he is also prominent in the Book of Enoch (e.g. 9:1) and in other apocalyptic literature.

Gabriel is therefore in a position to know and declare God's will. In fact, Gabriel has been **sent** by God **to speak** to Zachariah and **preach to** him **this *good news*,** declaring this gospel (Gr. *euaggelizomai*, used by Luke for any proclamation of good news;

compare its use in 4:43). Because Zachariah has met this Gospel with unbelief, he will suffer divine punishment: he will **be silent and unable to speak until the day when these things happen**. Zachariah demanded a sign—here is his sign! He himself will be a sign to the people of the **words** of Gabriel, which will **be fulfilled in their *proper* time**. (By using the term *euaggelizomai*, "to preach the gospel," to describe Gabriel's message, Luke calls attention to how the Christian Gospel will likewise be attended by divine punishment for those who reject it.)

ॐ ॐ ॐ ॐ ॐ

21 And the people were expecting Zachariah, and were marveling at his delay in the sanctuary.

22 But when he came out, he was not able to speak to them, and they really-knew that he had seen a vision in the sanctuary, and he *himself* was beckoning to them, and remained mute.

23 And it happened, when the days of his offering were fulfilled, that he went to his house.

This exchange took time. **The people** outside in the courtyard **were expecting Zachariah** to return before this time and **were marveling at his delay**. The priest whose job it was to offer incense customarily prostrated himself and prayed, but he did not prolong his prayer, lest the people worry that he had been struck down. Had Zachariah been smitten by God for some secret impiety when he entered His Presence? Eventually Zachariah **came out**, but **he was not able to speak to them**. Rather, he **was beckoning to them** insistently and **remained mute**, as the angel had said. The word translated *mute* is the Greek *kophos*, which means "deaf" as well as "mute" (compare its use in 7:22). It appeared that Zachariah was deaf also, for people needed to nod and gesture to communicate with him (1:62).

Thus the crowd in the outer court **really-knew** and recognized that **he had seen a vision** while he was **in the sanctuary**. For the time, however, he could tell them nothing about it. After the

33

conclusion of the week, when the time for his division's service had ended, **he went** back **to his house**.

> ঌ৶ ঌ৶ ঌ৶ ঌ৶ ঌ৶
>
> 24 And after these days Elizabeth his wife con-
> ceived, and she was hiding herself away for five
> months, saying,
> 25 "Thus the Lord has done to me in the days when
> He looked *upon me*, to take away my reproach
> among men."

As the angel promised, **after these days, Elizabeth conceived**, after normal relations with her husband Zachariah. She responded by **hiding herself away for five months**, meditating on the goodness of God and glorifying Him for His mercy. Elizabeth was not hiding from her neighbors so that none would know she was pregnant. During those first months none could know she was with child anyway, unless she told them. Rather, Elizabeth retired to prayerful communion to prepare herself for the immense task of raising one who would be God's Forerunner. Her whole life was going to change in a way she had never imagined, and she naturally sought solitude to come to terms with it.

It was a great joy to her, an unhoped-for consolation for one in her old age. She said to herself, **"Thus the Lord has done to me"**—this is the way in which God has vindicated me and heard my prayers. He had finally **looked *upon*** her with mercy, to **take away** her **reproach** of childlessness from among men.

St. Luke mentions this time of seclusion because it accords well with his picture of how God works quietly in the midst of His people. In Elizabeth God had worked mightily in the midst of His people, and they were not aware of it because she was hidden from them. In the same way God would work in Christ—Christ would be hidden from public gaze during His youth, and Israel would not know the Messiah was in their midst until He was revealed at the time of His Baptism.

§II.2. Announcement in Galilee of Jesus' Birth

ॐ ॐ ॐ ॐ ॐ

26 Now in the sixth month the angel Gabriel was sent from God to a city in Galilee, called Nazareth,

27 to a virgin betrothed to a man whose name was Joseph, of the house of David; and the name of the virgin *was* Mary.

28 And having entered toward her, he said, "Rejoice, graced one! The Lord *is* with you!"

29 But at this word she was greatly-shaken, and was questioning what kind of greeting this might be.

The narrative continues without a break, even as the Old Covenant finds its seamless fulfillment in the New. **In the sixth month** of Elizabeth's pregnancy, **the** same **angel Gabriel was sent from God to a city in Galilee, called Nazareth**. The location is significant. The story of redemption began in the Temple in Jerusalem, at the covenanted heart of Israel. God had worked among His people through the long centuries and had established Jerusalem as the place where He had promised to meet with them. Where else could the sacred drama begin but in the Temple?

But God was about to do a new thing upon the earth—a woman would encompass a man (Jer. 31:22). In this newness, old patterns were transcended, and **Gabriel was sent** out again, not to the public courts of the Temple this time, but to a private and humble dwelling in despised **Nazareth**, in "**Galilee** of the Gentiles." God was to be revealed through Christ in humility, not in power and privilege, and so His providence bypasses the famed and exalted Temple to find a humble maiden in a small town.

The contrast between the two geographical locations witnesses to the newness of this work of God. It is the same God that worked in the Law and the Prophets and the Temple who works in Christ—for the same Gabriel was sent both to Zachariah and to Mary. But God chose to come in humility, and so the angel was sent to Mary as she dwelt in Nazareth, not during one of her visits to the Temple. The Temple was the starting place, even as the Old Covenant was the starting place. But the Temple location was bypassed for this Annunciation, even as the Old Covenant would be transcended in the New.

Gabriel found a **virgin** who was **betrothed to a man whose name was Joseph, of the house of David; and the name of the virgin *was* Mary** (Gr. *Mariam*). Because of Mary's betrothal to Joseph, her child could be heir to the Davidic throne; it was through Joseph's legal (though not biological) paternity that Christ was the legal descendant of David and was David's messianic heir (compare God's promise to David in 2 Sam. 7:12). That is why Mary is defined here in terms of her betrothal to Joseph, even though Joseph was not to be the Child's biological father. Mary was perhaps fourteen years old at this time, for girls in Israel were normally betrothed at such an age in those days.

Gabriel **entered toward** Mary and said, **"Rejoice, graced one! The Lord *is* with you!"** (Some manuscripts add the words, "Blessed are you among women," though this seems to be a later addition to the text, based on later liturgical practice.) The salutation, **"Rejoice, graced one!"** has an alliterative poetry in the Greek not easily rendered in English—*chaire, kecharitomene.*

The word "rejoice" need mean only "hail," the standard form of greeting (compare such a use in Matt. 26:49). But here the more literal meaning of "rejoice" seems to be intended as well, for Luke is concerned to stress joy as a sign of the Kingdom. Moreover, the angel's greeting has echoes of the prophet's word to the daughter of Zion in Zechariah 9:9. There the "daughter of Zion" is told to "rejoice" because "God is coming" to her, and in the same way, God is now coming to Mary, the true daughter of Zion.

Mary should rejoice because she is **graced** by God. The word rendered *graced* is the perfect passive participle of the Greek *charitoo*, "to be the recipient of God's *charis*," or grace. (The word is used in Eph. 1:6 to describe the grace God freely bestows on His Church.)

Mary is given the *charis* or favor of being chosen to be the Mother of the divine Messiah. **The Lord** is **with** her in that He is about to act powerfully in her life to bless her. (This does not of course deny that He has been with her since she was conceived in the womb and from her childhood.)

This is as unexpected to Mary as Gabriel's previous announcement was to Zachariah. In humility she did not expect such veneration from a suddenly arriving angel, and she **was greatly-shaken** at such a word (Gr. *diatarasso*, a more intensive form of *tarasso*, "shaken," which was used of Zachariah in 1:12), as she tried to **question** and discern what such a **greeting** might mean.

৯৯ ৯৯ ৯৯ ৯৯ ৯৯

30 And the angel said to her, "Do not be afraid, Mary, for you have found grace with God.
31 "And behold, you will conceive in your womb, and bear a son, and you will call His name Jesus.
32 "He will be great, and will be called the Son of the Highest; and the Lord God will give Him the throne of His father David;
33 "and He will reign over the house of Jacob forever, and of His Kingdom will not be an end."
34 And Mary said to the angel, "How will this be, since I do not know a man?"
35 And the angel answered and said to her, "The Holy Spirit will come upon you, and the power of the Most High will overshadow you; therefore the offspring will be called holy, the Son of God.
36 "And behold, your relative Elizabeth, she *herself* has also conceived a son in her old age, and this is the sixth month for her who was called barren.
37 "For no word will be impossible with God."
38 And Mary said, "Behold, the slave of the Lord! May it be done to me according to your word." And the angel departed from her.

The angel spoke quickly to reassure Mary, saying to her also, **"Do not be afraid"** (compare the identical assurance given to Zachariah in 1:13). Gabriel came with good news—she had **found grace** and favor (Gr. *charis*) **with God**, for she had been chosen to be the Mother of the Messiah. She was about to **conceive** in her **womb** and would **bear a son**, whom she would **call** by the **name Jesus** (Aram. *Yeshua*, meaning "Yahweh saves"). **He will be great, and will be called** and recognized by all men as **the Son of the Highest**, the Ruler over the nations (compare Ps. 89:27). God will give Him all the authority of His Messiah, so that He will sit upon **the throne of His father David, and He will reign over the house of Jacob forever, and of His** messianic **Kingdom will not be an end**.

It is important not to import all the later Christological insights of the ecumenical councils into these words. Gabriel was announcing to Mary that her Child would be given authority by God as His Messiah, the One who would rule over Israel and over the nations of the world. The preexistent nature of the Son and His consubstantial equality with the Father were yet to be revealed.

One must be clear: Gabriel was not announcing simply that one day in the future Mary would conceive. If that were the case, she might have assumed that Gabriel meant she would conceive in the normal way in due time after she was married, and that Joseph would be the father of the child (even as Abraham was the father of supernaturally conceived Isaac).

But that was not what Gabriel was announcing. He was not saying that Mary would *at length* conceive, but that her conception was *imminent*, that it was *at hand*. That was why Mary was puzzled and asked, **"How will this be, since I do not know a man?"** That is, she was as yet virginal—how then could she conceive? Mary was not asking this with an attitude of skepticism, as Zachariah asked a similar question in 1:18. For Zachariah was punished for his unbelief, but no word of rebuke is offered to the Virgin of Nazareth. Her question came not from unbelief or incredulity, but from a desire to know how God would fulfill His word.

The angel is explicit in his answer: **"The Holy Spirit will come upon you, and the power of the Most High will overshadow**

you." This was to be no natural conception, no non-miraculous birth. As the Church sings, where God so wills, the order of nature is overthrown. Just as the divine Presence overshadowed the Ark (Gr. *episkiazo*; compare its use in Ex. 40:35 LXX), so **the power** of the **Most High** God, **the Holy Spirit**, would **come upon** her to **overshadow** her as well. That is why her **offspring** would be no normal Child, but **holy,** the divine Messiah, **the Son of God**. As proof of this, Gabriel offered the case of her relative Elizabeth. This was **the sixth month** of pregnancy **for her who was called barren.** Surely **no word** was **impossible with God**, nothing too difficult for Him to proclaim and perform.

Mary knew only too well what the immediate consequences of such a conception would be: it would be the end of all her hopes for honorable marriage, for earthly happiness, and for a peaceful life. And it almost was, for Joseph was resolved to cancel the wedding and divorce his betrothed wife upon hearing this news; only the intervention of God persuaded him to do otherwise (Matt. 1:18–24). But this future intervention was unknown to Mary at the time of the angelic annunciation. For all Mary knew, she would have to live her life disgraced and alone.

Yet still she submitted to the divine will, humbly bending her holy neck to the divine word. It must have seemed as if all hopes for earthly reputation and happiness were slipping away like sand through her fingers, but still she said, **"Behold, the slave of the Lord!"** (Gr. *doule*, "maidservant, handmaid"; compare its cognate use in Eph. 6:5). **"May it be done to me according to your word."** In that moment of submission and decision, it is said that the eternal Son was conceived in her, and the holy maid of Nazareth became the Mother of God. His work done, **the angel departed from her.**

❦ EXCURSUS
ON THE TWO ANNUNCIATIONS

Luke deliberately juxtaposes the annunciation of Gabriel to Zachariah with the annunciation to Mary so as to make the contrast the more striking. Zachariah's priestly lineage is stressed in the introduction, and the annunciation to Zachariah takes place in the holy city, in the Temple, at the time of sacrifice. The setting of this annunciation narrative is heavy with history—all the sacred history of Israel, with its power, prestige, and glory, is present. We see the pomp and splendor of the Temple with its long history, its teeming crowds, its music, its chanting priests surrounding the holy altar with the praise of the God of Israel. In a word, we see *religion*.

In an obvious and intended contrast, the annunciation to Mary takes place in the humility of the everyday. Gabriel could have found her when she was in the Temple, or at least in Jerusalem. He could have found her when she was saying her prayers. But if she was saying her prayers at the time of Gabriel's annunciation to her, this is passed over in silence. (Orthodox iconography often presents her as holding a spindle during the annunciation—that is, engaged not in prayer, but in a woman's daily chores.) Gabriel found her far from the holy city and its sacred Temple—in humble Nazareth, of which one would say, "Could anything good come from Nazareth?" (John 1:46). He found her at home, in a simple setting. That is, Luke pictures the annunciation to Mary as taking place in a *secular* context, contrasting it deliberately with the sacred and religious setting of the annunciation to Zachariah.

This is meant to mirror the perceived contrast between Judaism and the new Christian movement. Judaism was attractive because it possessed all the trappings of religion: it had a Temple, a vast and functioning priesthood, an altar and countless sacrifices. It was the center of worldwide Jewry, and all adult male Jews paid a tax to support the Temple. It had synagogue buildings and paid functionaries there. All this religiosity gave it credibility in the eyes of the world. By contrast, the Christians had little going for them: they had no buildings, no Temple, no altar, no priesthood. They gathered in people's homes to pray and sing and read the Scriptures and to eat a piece of bread and drink wine from a cup. Compared to the public pomp and glory of the Temple, it looked—well, secular, and not a real religion at all. The Christians' claim that all Israel's religion and Temple and sacrifices prefigured them and their movement looked to many simply incredible.

Luke shows that this contrast was present from the beginning, and moreover that it was the "secular" and hidden and humble Mary, not Zachariah, who possessed the real power—even as the Christian movement possessed the real spiritual power, and not religious Judaism. Zachariah, for all the prestige of priesthood and religion he possessed, did not (initially) please God, but was judged by God for his unbelief. In this, Zachariah embodies Israel, for Israel had the prestige of the Temple, yet was judged by God for not accepting His Word. Mary, on the other hand, despite her humble and "secular" condition, proved to be the faithful one, the one who ultimately enjoyed God's favor. Elizabeth's blessing of Mary (1:42) not only shows how Zachariah and Elizabeth came to acknowledge Mary as central to God's purposes. It also reveals that Israel's religion is subordinate to God's work in Christ, and that it finds its fulfillment in the Gospel and the Church.

§II.3. Visit of Mary to Elizabeth

ॐ ॐ ॐ ॐ ॐ

39 Now in these days Mary arose and went eagerly to the hill country, to a city of Judah,

40 and entered into the house of Zachariah and greeted Elizabeth.

41 And it came about that when Elizabeth heard

> the greeting of Mary, the infant in her womb leaped, and Elizabeth was filled with the Holy Spirit.
>
> 42 And she shouted out with a great yell, and said, "Blessed *are* you among women, and blessed *is* the fruit of your womb!
>
> 43 "And how *has* this *happened* to me, that the mother of my Lord should come to me?
>
> 44 "For behold, when the sound of your greeting came into my ears, the infant in my womb leaped with exultation.
>
> 45 "And blessed *is* she who believed that there will be a fulfillment of what was spoken to her by the Lord."

After hearing the message of the archangel with its news that her relative Elizabeth was in her sixth month of pregnancy, **Mary arose** from her place in Nazareth and **went eagerly to the hill country** of Judea, to the **city** or town where Elizabeth lived. Mary took this trip not to discover whether the angel's word was true, but rather to rejoice with her cousin Elizabeth. The location of the town is not known, but it is possible that it is the modern Ain Karim, five miles from Jerusalem. Whatever the location, Mary's journey was one of about ninety miles, and would have taken her about three or four days.

She **entered the house of Zachariah and greeted Elizabeth**. Then came a supernatural event, the first of a series of acts of the Holy Spirit. When Mary spoke to her cousin Elizabeth, the child within Elizabeth recognized the voice of Mary as the voice of the Mother of God, and he **leaped with exultation**. John was filled with the Spirit while yet in his mother's womb (1:15), and as such he was able to discern the divine presence within Mary, who came near to him. At the same time, before she could respond to Mary's formal greeting with one of her own, **Elizabeth** herself **was filled with the Holy Spirit**, and cried out in prophecy. Indeed, she **shouted out with a**

great yell ("yell" being the Gr. *krauge*; the cognate verb *kraugzo* is used in Acts 22:23 for the yelling of a hostile crowd). Inspired by the Spirit, she pronounced a blessing upon Mary and her offspring: **"Blessed *are* you among women, and blessed *is* the fruit of your womb!"** Both Mary and her Son were recognized by this prophetic utterance to be key to God's coming messianic redemption. Whether or not Elizabeth knew Mary's offspring to be the Messiah to come, she knew that Mary was to give birth to someone who would bring in the Kingdom of God.

But who is she, Elizabeth asks, that she should receive such a privilege? Who is she **that** such an exalted person as **the mother of** her **Lord should come** to visit her in her lowliness? Sharing with Mary how she knew these things (namely, by **the infant in** her **womb leaping** with joy), Elizabeth then pronounces another blessing upon her relative: **"blessed *is* she who believed that there will be a fulfillment of what was spoken to her by the Lord."** This refers to Mary's humble acceptance of the word of the angel in verse 38. Elizabeth, filled with the Spirit for the moment, has prophetic knowledge of Mary's acceptance of the angel's annunciation.

Luke relates this exchange between Mary and Elizabeth not simply as a biographical item in the life of the Blessed Virgin, or to link the two stories of John and Jesus. He also relates it to show how the Kingdom of God begins to break into human history. For long ages, the voice of the prophets has not been heard in Israel, but now at last the time is at hand. The Spirit is moving among the chosen people once again, and the Forerunner and his mother are the firstfruits of it. The Spirit, active in the Church, began His work among men with the conception of Jesus and His Forerunner.

> ॐ ॐ ॐ ॐ ॐ
> 46 And Mary said, "My soul magnifies the Lord,
> 47 "And my spirit has exulted in God my Savior,
> 48 "that He has looked upon the humiliation of His slave; for behold, from now *on* all generations will *count* me blessed!

49 "For the Powerful One has done great things for me, and holy *is* His Name.

50 "And His mercy *is* to generations and generations to those who fear Him.

51 "He has done a mighty *deed* with His arm; He has scattered out the arrogant in the thoughts of their heart.

52 "He has brought down the sovereigns from *their* thrones, and has exalted the lowly.

53 "He has filled the hungry with good *things*, and the rich He sent away empty.

54 "He has helped His child Israel in remembrance of His mercy,

55 "just as He spoke to our fathers, to Abraham and his seed forever."

Mary's reply is itself a kind of lyrical prophecy. In an utterance reminiscent of Hannah's song in 1 Samuel 2:1–10, Mary declares that from her innermost being, her **soul** and **spirit**, she **magnifies the Lord** and declares His greatness; she **has exulted in God** her **Savior**. For God **has looked upon His slave** and maidservant in her **humiliation** and low estate. Though she is but of the poor of the earth, one who shares the humiliation and lowliness of God's people, **the Powerful One has done great things** for her, and chosen her to be His vessel to bring salvation to Israel. He has bypassed the rich and privileged of the world and has chosen her, in all her powerlessness, to open the Kingdom.

In praising God as her **Savior**, Mary stands in a long succession of those who have received divine aid. The term "Savior" does not here mean "one who forgives sin" so much as it means "one who brings rescue," and Mary's use of the term does not illumine the question of whether or not she was sinful. The Hebrew concept of salvation, while not always excluding the idea of needing forgiveness, is more about deliverance, and it smacks more of the victories of the battlefield than the verdicts of the courtroom. Yahweh gives

Israel "salvation" in that He gives them victory in battle over their enemies (Mic. 7:7); and a "savior" was first and foremost one who brought deliverance (compare its use in Obadiah 21: "saviors will ascend Mount Zion"—i.e. those who will rescue and deliver Zion from the Edomites). In Christ, God has moved to save Israel from their foes, **bringing down** their **sovereigns** and oppressors **from *their* thrones** and **exalting** His **lowly** people.

Because of God's choosing Mary to accomplish this salvation, **from now *on* all generations will *count*** her **blessed**, and will acknowledge the greatness of the work that He has done through her. In declaring that **all** future **generations will *count*** her **blessed**, Mary is not thinking so much that people will *praise her* for herself as that people will *praise God* for what He has done through her. Mary is not delighting in her own future reputation and fame; she is delighting in God, knowing that all men will exclaim how blessed is the one through whom God has done such wonders. (This is not to deny, of course, that people will rightly praise her as well for her role in this work of God.) Elizabeth declared Mary **blessed** (Gr. *makaria*) for her acceptance of the divine will (v. 45); in her humility Mary declares that all the world will also ***count*** her **blessed** (Gr. *makarizo*), for they will see the salvation of God and recognize what **great things the Powerful One has done** for her and how **holy *is* His Name**. God's **Name** is His manifested power (see Ps. 20:1; 54:1), and in Mary God has acted powerfully to manifest His holiness in the sight of all.

God has not just chosen to exalt Mary, lifting her from lowliness. Through her He has chosen to exalt all the poor of the earth and to make them blessed, enriched with the universal Kingdom (compare 6:20). **His mercy** and salvation is thus **to generations and generations, to** all those **who fear Him** and trust in Him. The rich of the earth oppressed the poor; kings of the Gentiles lorded it over them (22:25), and trod underfoot the people of Israel also, enslaving **Abraham and his** holy **seed**. But God will overturn them and **do a mighty *deed*** for His people, winning the victory for them **with His arm** and His power. **The arrogant** of the world God has

scattered out (Gr. *diaskorpizo*, a more intensive verb than *skorpizo*, "to scatter"), sending them running in terror. Though **in the** proud **thoughts of their heart** and their inner plans, the arrogant intended to rule forever, God **has brought** them **down**. The **sovereigns** and privileged of the earth are cast down from their thrones whereon they sat, and in their place God has exalted the humble.

This was ever His way. He is the God who "raises the poor from the dust to make them sit with princes" (Ps. 113:7–8); He is the God who "pours contempt upon princes but sets the needy securely on high" (Ps. 107:40–41). Those who exalt themselves, He humbles, and those who humble themselves, He exalts (18:14). **The hungry** He **has filled with good** *things*, so that they stuff themselves full with joy, while **the rich He sent away empty** and hungry.

Thus in Christ God **has helped His child** (Gr. *pais*, also translated "servant") **Israel in remembrance of His mercy. He spoke to** the **fathers, to Abraham and his seed** and descendants, promising them through the Prophets that He would rescue them and exalt them **forever**. Now through Mary He has moved to **remember** His promised **mercy**. Through her Son, the proud will fall, the humble will rise (see Simeon's prophecy in 2:34), and God's salvation will be prepared before the face of all peoples (2:31).

ॐ ॐ ॐ ॐ ॐ
**56 And Mary remained with her about three
months, and returned to her house.**

After these wonders, Mary **remained with** Elizabeth **about three months** and then **returned to her house**, in preparation for the remainder of her own pregnancy. It would seem that Mary stayed until the eve of John's birth, but was not there for that event, for if she was present for it, Luke's silence regarding it is difficult to explain. It is possible that Mary left immediately before the birth of John to avoid the large crowds that would attend such an event, motivated in part perhaps by a desire to conceal her own pregnancy until she had spoken with her betrothed husband Joseph.

ꙮ EXCURSUS
ON MARY AS THE DIVINE ARK

Though it is not stressed by St. Luke in his reportage of the Annunciation and the Visitation to Elizabeth, a comparison of Mary with the divine Ark of the Covenant can still be discerned, for the points of comparison are too numerous to be entirely coincidental.

The word used to describe the action of the Holy Spirit upon the Blessed Virgin is the Greek word *episkiazo*, which we noted is the same word used in Exodus 40:35 LXX to describe the overshadowing of the Ark with the divine Presence.

Also, the coming of the Ark to Jerusalem by the hand of David provides a number of parallels to the coming of Mary to Elizabeth. Just as David said, "How can the ark of the Lord come to me?" (2 Sam. 6:9), so Elizabeth also said, "How has this happened to me, that the mother of my Lord should come to me?" Both David and Elizabeth were in awe that the Bearer of the Divine Presence should come to them. And when this Divine Presence came to David, he responded with a shout of joy (2 Sam. 6:15)—as did Elizabeth when the Living Ark came to her also (1:42), "shouting with a great yell," a spontaneous cry of ecstasy. David leaped and danced in the Presence of his Lord (2 Sam. 6:14, 16), just as Elizabeth's son John leaped in her womb at the Presence of his Lord (1:41). It is perhaps also not coincidental that 2 Samuel 6:11 records that the Ark stayed three months in the house of Obed-edom prior to coming to Jerusalem, and Luke 1:56 records that Mary stayed about three months with Elizabeth.

It seems clear that the coming of the Ark to Jerusalem provides an illuminating foreshadowing of Mary's visit to Elizabeth. St. Luke is not uninterested in the Mother of

God. Indeed, he writes more about her than any of the other Evangelists. For him, this is her significance—that as the Mother of the Messiah, she is the true Ark, the Bearer of the divine Presence, for in Christ, the God of the Old Covenant has drawn near to His people.

For later generations of Christians who have come to know her, this is no surprise. The Ark of the Covenant, as the bearer of God's Presence, was holy, and to touch it with an impious and unauthorized hand was to court disaster (see the example of Uzzah in 2 Sam. 6:6–7). In the same way, the Mother of God is holy. As the hymn for her Annunciation says, "let no impure hand touch her"! For as God's Ark, she too partakes of the holiness of heaven.

§II.4. Birth and Early Years of John

57 Now the time was fulfilled for Elizabeth to give birth, and she brought forth a son.
58 And those around *her* and her relatives heard that the Lord had magnified His mercy toward her; and they were co-rejoicing with her.
59 And it happened that on the eighth day they came to circumcise the child, and they were calling him after the name of his father Zachariah.
60 And his mother answered and said, "No, but he will be called John."
61 And they said to her, "There is no one from your relatives who is called by this name."
62 And they nodded to his father as to what he wanted him to be called.
63 And he asked for a tablet and wrote, saying, "John is his name." And all marveled.

After Mary's departure, at length **the time was fulfilled for Elizabeth to give birth and**, as the angel predicted, **she brought forth a son**. Those around her, the neighbors who lived close by, along with her relatives, all **heard that the Lord had magnified His mercy toward her** in the safe birth of a child, and **they were co-rejoicing with her** and congratulating her (Gr. *sug-chairo* can mean both "to rejoice-with" and also "to congratulate"). On the eighth day they came to circumcise the child according to the Law, and custom dictated that such a son be **called after the name of his father Zachariah**. This would be their only child, their only son, and it was unthinkable that the boy should not be named after such a notable father, for in this way were family members honored. His mother, however, was adamant, saying, **"No, but he will be called John,"** and this despite the fact that there was **no one from** her **relatives who** was **called by this name**. Why pick this name?

It is possible that Elizabeth insisted on the name John because her husband Zachariah had communicated the sum of the angelic message to her. But St. Luke tells the story in such a way as to suggest that Elizabeth's insistence on the name John was a part of the larger miracle. Otherwise, why did Elizabeth not simply reply to her relatives that the child must be called John because they were instructed by God to do it? (See 1:13.) Elizabeth had been filled with the Spirit when Mary came to visit her, and knew information about Mary's encounter with the angel through supernatural prophetic insight (1:41f). This would seem to be another instance of such prophetic insight.

So when the neighbors and relatives **nodded** and gestured **to his father** Zachariah in such a way as to ask him what he wanted to name the child, Zachariah **asked for a** small wooden **tablet** for writing, and on its wax-covered surface **wrote** the words, **"John is his name."** (The name **John** comes at the head of the sentence for emphasis in the Greek.) Note the verb tense: not "John *will be* his name," but rather "John *is* his name." The name had already been given months before by the angel. **All marveled** at this, presumably because of the miraculous coincidence of both mother and father independently insisting on the same name. (If Zachariah had previously conveyed his choice of name to his wife, there would be no miracle to marvel at.)

> ৯৯ ৯৯ ৯৯ ৯৯ ৯৯
>
> 64 And at once his mouth was opened and his tongue *was loosed*, and he was speaking, blessing God.
> 65 And fear came on all those around them; and all were talking about these words in the whole hill country of Judea.
> 66 And all who heard kept them in their heart, saying, "What then will this child be?" For indeed the hand of the Lord was with him.

This miracle was followed and confirmed by another one. As soon as Zachariah had obeyed the voice of the angel and named his son John (1:13), his obedience brought the fruit of healing. The angel had pronounced a sentence of muteness until the child was born (1:20), and now Zachariah's deed brought the lifting of the sentence. **At once his mouth was opened and his tongue *was loosed***, and he began **speaking**, as he had not done in the past nine months, **blessing God**.

The combination of the miraculous agreement of both mother and father in choosing the name John as well the miraculous opening of the father's mouth at this moment overwhelmed the hearers. They knew that they were in the presence of God's power, and **fear came on all those around them**. **All** in **the whole hill country of Judea were talking about these words** and events (Gr. *rema*, which can mean both "word" and "thing" or event). **All** who heard this story **kept** the events **in their heart** throughout the years that followed, and asked themselves, **"What then will this child be?"** What does God have in store for him?—**for indeed the hand of the Lord was with him** as he grew.

ॐ ॐ ॐ ॐ ॐ

67 And his father Zachariah was filled with the
Holy Spirit and prophesied, saying,

68 "Blessed *be* the Lord God of Israel, for He has
visited us and done redemption for His people,

69 "and has raised up a horn of salvation for us in
the house of David His child—

70 "just as He spoke by the mouth of His holy
prophets from of old—

71 "salvation from our enemies, and from the hand
of all who hate us,

72 "to do mercy toward our fathers, and to remember His holy covenant,

73 "the oath which He swore to Abraham our
father, to grant us

74 "that being rescued from the hand of our
enemies, we might worship Him fearlessly,

75 "in holiness and righteousness before Him all
our days.

St. Luke then says that **Zachariah was filled with the Holy
Spirit and prophesied**, even as his wife Elizabeth did (1:41f). It
would seem that the prophecy that follows in verses 68–79 is what
Zachariah uttered when his mouth was first opened and his tongue
loosed in verse 64, and this prophetic hymn is what he said when
he spoke, "blessing God." Luke saves the substance of the prophecy
until now so that it can form the climax to the story of John.

In his prophecy, Zachariah proclaims that God is sending Messiah to save Israel, and thus fulfilling the words which **His holy
prophets spoke** from time immemorial (Gr. *ap'aionos*), **from of
old**. John was to go before Him as His Forerunner.

Zachariah begins by crying, **"Blessed *be* the Lord God!"**
(Gr. *eulogetos kurios o theos*; compare the "blessing" of God—Gr.
eulogon—in v. 64). God is blessed because He has **done** and worked

redemption for His people and **visited** them with His mercy. In the coming Messiah, God has **raised up a horn of salvation** for Israel (that is, a mighty salvation, a **horn** being an image of power; compare Ps. 132:17; Ezek. 29:21).

This Messiah will arise from among **the house** or descendants **of David**, God's **child** or servant (Gr. *pais*; compare 1:54). He will bring **salvation** and deliverance **from** Israel's **enemies and from the hand of all who hate** them. Once **rescued from the hand of** their **enemies**, Israel will be able to **worship** God **fearlessly**, safe from invasion or tyranny. They will be free to worship **in holiness and righteousness before** God **all** their **days**. During the days of the Maccabees, the foreign tyrant Antiochus Epiphanes forbade Israel to worship God according to His Law, and persecuted those who tried to do so (1 Macc. 1:20–50). During the days of the Messiah, Israel will be safe from such tyranny and can worship God in peace. God had promised such mercy by **the oath which He swore to Abraham**, for He assured Abraham that Israel would know His blessing. Through Messiah, God was about to **remember** this **holy covenant** which He made with the **fathers**, with Abraham, Isaac, and Jacob, and would pour out His mercy upon Israel.

ॐ ॐ ॐ ॐ ॐ

76 "And you, child, will be called a prophet of the Most High, for you will go on before the Lord to prepare His ways,

77 "to give to His people knowledge of salvation in the forgiveness of their sins,

78 "through the heartfelt mercies of our God, with which the Rising *Sun* from on high will visit us,

79 "to appear to those who sit in darkness and the shadow of death, to direct our feet into the way of peace."

Zachariah concludes his prophecy with a hymn honoring the birth of his son John. He addresses the child he has just named and declares to him that he **will be called** and recognized by all as a true **prophet of the Most High**, for he **will go on before the Lord to prepare His ways**. (The reference to the prophecy of Mal. 3:1 about God's messenger being sent out before Him to prepare His ways should not be missed.) The Kingdom of God, brought by the Davidic Messiah, is about to come, and John will have his part to play in it. Gabriel has already told Zachariah that his son is to go on ahead before the Lord as a new Elijah (1:17), and given the prophecy of Mal. 4:5–6 to which this alludes, Zachariah knows that his son John is to be the Forerunner to the Messiah.

John is **to give** God's **people knowledge** and experience **of salvation**. And this salvation is rooted in **the forgiveness of their sins**. Until now the nation's sins have kept the blessing of God from them, but John will lead them to repentance (1:16) so that they will know God's forgiveness, and then His blessing can descend upon them. All this is through **the heartfelt** and tender **mercies of** their **God** (Gr. *splagchna eleous*). God yearns for His people and longs to bless them. Now He will do so!

Israel had for centuries **sat in darkness and the shadow of death**. Sitting in the darkness of suffering and mortality, they could not see the way forward, for "the one who walks in darkness does not know where he goes" (John 12:35). All they could do was sit in despair and wait for death. But now **the Rising *Sun*** (Gr. *anatole*, literally "rising") **from on high will visit** them; it will **appear to those** who sat waiting for it and banish the darkness, **directing their feet** to walk safely **into the way of peace** and prosperity and life. As the prophecy of Malachi had promised, the Sun of Righteousness will arise (Mal. 4:2) and will disperse all the shadows of night.

(We note in passing that the word *anatole* may also be translated as "the East," or "the Orient," and it is so translated in 13:29. It is this translation which is reflected in the Orthodox hymn used in weddings and ordinations: "Rejoice, O Isaiah, a Virgin is with Child and shall bear a Son Emmanuel; He is both God and Man and *Orient is His Name*.")

In his prophecy, Zachariah refers to Israel's enemies (vv. 71, 74), as had many prophets before him (e.g. Is. 42:13; Mic. 4:10; Zeph.

3:15). It is possible to read Zachariah's prophecy as predicting a national and political deliverance and kingdom—just as it is possible to read the other ancient prophecies that way. Zachariah himself may have thought of the Kingdom in such earthly terms (the Lord's disciples certainly did; compare Mark 10:37f). But Zachariah was not expressing his own ideas of what the Kingdom would be like. He was prophesying and conveying the words of God. And just as the words of the other prophets, recorded in the Scriptures, need to be interpreted in a spiritual way, so with these words of Zachariah.

The enemies from which God's people are saved are spiritual enemies, for the Kingdom of God is not national and political, but transcendent and spiritual. Our worship is in the Spirit, not in the earthly Temple; the foes who hate us are the demons, not just men; and our struggle is not against flesh and blood, but against principalities and powers in the heavenly places (Eph. 6:12).

> ॐ ॐ ॐ ॐ ॐ
>
> 80 And the child was growing, and was becoming mighty in spirit, and he was in the wilderness *places* until the day of his revelation to Israel.

St. Luke concludes his account of John's birth with the note that **the child** continued to **grow** and become **mighty in spirit**, as befitted one who was to become the Forerunner to the Messiah. As he grew, John frequented **the wilderness *places***, constantly visiting the desert for communion with God **until the day of his revelation** as a prophet **to Israel**. The word of the Lord would not come to him until later (3:1), but throughout his childhood and early years, God had His hand upon him and was drawing him to Himself.

§II.5. Birth of Jesus and His Circumcision

> ॐ ॐ ॐ ॐ ॐ
>
> **2** 1 Now it happened in those days that a decree went out from Caesar Augustus that all the

> world should be enrolled.
> 2   This enrollment first happened *while* Quirinius was governing Syria.
> 3   And all were going to be enrolled, each to his own city.
> 4   And Joseph also went up from Galilee, from the city of Nazareth, into Judea, into the city of David, which is called Bethlehem, because he was from the house and family of David,
> 5   to be enrolled with Mary, who was betrothed to him and was pregnant.
> 6   And it happened that while they were there, the days were fulfilled for her to give birth.
> 7   And she gave birth to her firstborn son, and she swaddled Him and laid Him in a manger, because there was not a place for them in the lodging-house.

St. Luke then narrates the birth of Jesus and His circumcision, in conscious parallelism with those of John, His Forerunner. As a providential preparation for Jesus' birth, **a decree went out from Caesar Augustus that all the world should be enrolled**, and so all those to be thus enrolled went to register themselves, **each to his own city**. That was how Joseph and Mary happened to be in Bethlehem when Jesus was born, even though they formerly lived in Nazareth. The ancient prophecies foretold that the Messiah would be born in **Bethlehem, the city of David**, since Messiah was to be heir to David's throne (Micah 5:2). Caesar's decree was the catalyst for Joseph and his **betrothed** wife, who **was pregnant,** to be in that Davidic town far away from their homes when the time came for Mary to give birth, and thus to fulfill the old prophecy. Though Caesar knew nothing about such Jewish prophecies and details of the Messiah's birthplace, God used Caesar's decree to accomplish His own will.

This was fitting, for Christ came to save **all the world**, not just the Jewish nation. It was fitting that God should use a universal ruler such as Caesar to (unwittingly) fulfill His will, for God's salvation was meant for all of Caesar's subjects, not just his Jewish ones.

Bethlehem in that day was a small town, despite its noble historical importance as King David's birthplace. It was about four and a half miles from Jerusalem, and about ninety miles from Nazareth. The trip there would have taken several days. It is possible that many people descended upon the town to be enrolled in the census, and this multitude made it impossible for Joseph and Mary to find **a place** in the local **lodging-house**. The word rendered here *lodging-house* is the Greek *kataluma,* which can also mean "lodging-room," its meaning in Mark 14:14. But the word has some elasticity and was used to designate a separate inn or khan in the Greek translation of Exodus 4:24. Certainly both verse 7 and the story of the visitation of the shepherds in verses 8 and following give the impression of the Holy Family's isolation. But whatever the nature of the *kataluma,* such a place was not available for Joseph and his pregnant wife.

Luke's recording of this detail is not accidental, for it foreshadows the future rejection of Jesus by His people. There was no room for Him in the lodging-place when the time came for Him to be born, just as there was no room for Him in the hearts of His people when the time came for them to acknowledge Him as Messiah. From the time of His birth, there was no place of welcome among the Jews where the Son of Man could lay His head (9:58).

The only spot Joseph could find for them when it came time for Mary to give birth was a lowly stable (that is, a cave used as a stable; its location was remembered by the early Christians, and there is now a church built over it). Thus after Jesus was born, He was **swaddled** (that is, wrapped tightly in swaddling bands, pinning His arms to His sides and keeping Him warm, as all babies were), and **laid in a manger**, or feeding trough, to keep Him from being trampled by the beasts.

This detail too is not accidental, for it shows the humility the Son of God embraced at His Incarnation. He who would not shrink from the indignity of the Cross did not shrink from the indignity of being born in a stable among dumb beasts and laid in their feeding trough. Thus Mary's **firstborn son** came into the world.

He is called her **firstborn**—Greek *prototokos*—not because Mary would later have other children, but because of the status of the firstborn son in Judaism. The firstborn male was the head of the family and inherited a double share of the ancestral property. He was also thought of as belonging to God in a special way (Deut. 15:19). The firstborn son would thus be so-called even if he were the only child. Luke describes Jesus as the **firstborn son** in order to prepare us for the story of Mary's presence in the Temple, where she would meet Simeon (2:22ff), for the sacrifices she had to offer there were only offered after the birth of the firstborn male (see Ex. 13:1ff).

Some of the details of enrollment are not altogether clear from contemporary secular history. What was this universal census? It is possible that Luke means not that Caesar decreed that all his subjects were to be registered in the same census (of which history has left no other record), but simply that Caesar was reforming the administration of the whole Empire, and that local censuses were part of this overall project of reform and taxation. Herod could well have been required to register his population with a view to this Roman taxation.

Why did Joseph have to return to Bethlehem for the census? It was contrary to usual Roman custom to require that people return to their ancestral home to be enrolled. But it was customary for absentees to return to their hometowns where they owned property (as was done for Egypt in AD 104), and possibly Joseph had a joint share in some property in his ancestral Bethlehem (even though the property was now inhabited by others). If that is so, it is possible that he was required, as a law-abiding subject, to return there for the census.

Luke further says that **this enrollment first happened** *while* **Quirinius was governing Syria**. (Luke speaks of this as **first** happening to differentiate it from the later enrollment in AD 6, mentioned in Acts 5:37.) This reference to Quirinius again has occasioned scholarly debate, for he was governor of Syria only after the death of King Herod, and since Jesus was born during the reign of King Herod, Quirinius could not have been governor prior to His birth. Surviving historical data is rarely complete, and some have suggested an earlier period of governorship for Quirinius prior to this term in office in AD 6. The text, however, does not say that Quirinius was "governor" (Gr. *egemon*), only that he **was governing** (Gr. *egemoneuo*), and it is possible also that the verb allows for a more general ruling function. Some have suggested that prior to being made governor in AD 6, Quirinius exercised a sort of roving authority in the east, having charge of Syria.

It may be asked why Mary accompanied Joseph during his journey to Bethlehem, especially since she was so far advanced in her pregnancy. No one can say with certainty. It is possible that, as a subject who was liable to pay the poll tax (in Syria women were thus liable), Mary was legally required to appear and be registered too. But it is possible that she accompanied Joseph because it was too socially difficult for her to be left alone without him in her native Nazareth. Being found to be pregnant prior to marriage may well have had disastrous social implications for her, leaving her ostracized by all in the town. In this vulnerable time, it is possible that she was unwilling to face such public scorn without the support of Joseph, and so went with him because she felt that she had no choice.

For whatever reason, she did accompany him southwards to his ancestral home, arriving there to face the onset of labor. It was but one more test of her courage in what would be a series of such tests for the young Mother of God.

> ॐ ॐ ॐ ॐ ॐ
>
> 8 And shepherds were in the same region, living outside and keeping watch by night over their flock.
>
> 9 And an angel of the Lord stood before them, and the glory of the Lord shone around them, and they were greatly afraid.
>
> 10 And the angel said to them, "Do not be afraid; for behold, I bring you good news of a great joy which will be to all the people;
>
> 11 "for a Savior who is Christ the Lord was born for you today in the city of David.

> 12 "And this *will be* a sign to you: you will find an infant swaddled, and lying in a manger."
>
> 13 And suddenly there was with the angel a multitude of the heavenly army, praising God and saying,
>
> 14 "Glory to God in the highest, and on earth peace among men of *His* good-pleasure!"

In the fields nearby, there were **shepherds**, who were **living outside and keeping watch by night over their flock**. Shepherds usually kept their flocks outdoors in this way from April to November. The shepherds would take turns **keeping watch over their flock**, some sleeping while others watched. Suddenly, **an angel of the Lord stood before them**. The Greek verb used, *ephistemi*, literally means to "stand by" and can mean "to approach" (its meaning in 2:38 and 10:40). Here it seems to denote a sudden appearance—the shepherds simply looked and beheld an angel standing before them. More than that, **the glory of the Lord shone around them**, as the angels reflected the glory of heaven from which they had come. The unexpectedness of the Presence, with its unearthly brilliance blinding their nighttime vision, left the shepherds terrified. No wonder **they were greatly afraid**!

The angel had not come to fill their hearts with fear, however, but rather with joy. **The angel** bade them **not** to **be afraid** any longer, for he came to **bring** them **good news of a great joy**—a joy which was not just for them but also for **all the people** of Israel. (The word rendered *bring good news* is the Gr. *euaggelizomai*, used for the preaching of the Gospel, the *euaggelion*.) A **Savior**—a Deliverer—was born to rescue God's people from their oppression (see the discussion of the term "savior" in the commentary on 1:47). And this was no ordinary savior, no mere military hero—it was to be the Lord Messiah, **Christ the Lord**, Himself. Here was a cause for **joy** indeed! He had been **born** for them **today in the city of David** (in this context, as in 2:4, David's hometown of Bethlehem, rather than David's capital city of Jerusalem—and perhaps indicated by the angel by a wave of his hand in the direction of Bethlehem?).

They could know which of the newborns of Bethlehem the angel meant by this **sign**: they would **find** the **infant** referred to by the angel **swaddled** (as all newborns were), but **lying in a manger** (which no other newborn was). This extraordinarily humble setting was the sign that the Child was indeed the designated Messiah. The exalted Messiah came, but was to be characterized from the first by the humility of His surroundings and origin.

Bethlehem was a small town, with a small town's network of fast-traveling gossip and news. The story of the young woman from Galilee who was about to give birth and who had found shelter in the cave nearby would not be difficult to discover, nor would her present whereabouts.

The angelic announcement to the shepherds is significant. That the angel made the announcement at night is not accidental. No doubt Christ was born after dark, and that was why the angel appeared to the shepherds with the announcement by night, unable to wait (as it were) and keep the joyful news a secret. But the darkness outside was also an image of the darkness that lay heavy upon the heart of the world. All men sat in darkness and in the shadow of death (1:79), and the word of Christ's Nativity came as light in the darkness, to banish the shades of mortality and bring life and light (2 Tim. 1:10).

It was not accidental either that the angel chose shepherds as the recipients of his message. No doubt the shepherds were told of the birth because they were **in the same region** and were the only ones awake at that hour of the night. That is, they were the ones told because they were the nearest available bystanders. But it is difficult to accept that such a monumental announcement was characterized solely by random chance. I suggest that Heaven chose shepherds as the first recipients of the Gospel because they of all people would know what it was like to search for lost sheep. All Israel were such lost sheep and had been scattered and oppressed, with no one to care for them (Mark 6:34). Shepherds would truly appreciate the coming of the Shepherd.

After this announcement, **suddenly there was with** that lone **angel a multitude of the heavenly army**, all of them **praising**

God and saying, "Glory to God in the highest heaven above, **and on earth** below, **peace among men of *His* good-pleasure!"** At the announcement of Messiah's birth, the heavenly army of angels could not forbear bursting into the praise of God (and thereby setting the tone for the Church's worship, for the priest begins each Liturgy by quietly chanting these very words). Praise is a sign of the Kingdom, and therefore Christ's Birth is accompanied by this ecstatic outburst.

This is what the Birth of Messiah meant—that God in heaven would be glorified, and that men on earth would have **peace** and prosperity (Gr. *eirene*, doubtless translating the Heb. *shalom*, which denotes prosperity and abundance as well as peaceful tranquility; compare "peace like a river, like an overflowing stream" in Is. 66:12). Through this Child all God's will would be done, and all the cosmos, both in heaven and earth, would be blessed.

The phrase **among men of *His* good-pleasure** requires further comment. Some Greek manuscripts read *en anthropois eudokias*, with the *eudokias* as a genitive describing the men—"men *of* good-pleasure." Some Greek manuscripts read *anthropois eudokia*, with *eudokia* as a nominative—"good-pleasure *to men*." The former reading is to be preferred. It is a Semitism, and means men of *God's* good-pleasure—that is, men upon whom His favor rests. Through the Birth of Christ, God was well-pleased to bless the children of men (compare 10:21, where the word *eudokia* recurs) and to give them His peace.

ॐ ॐ ॐ ॐ ॐ

15 And it happened that when the angels had gone away from them into heaven, that the shepherds were saying to one another, "So let us go to Bethlehem, and let us see this word which has happened which the Lord has made known to us."

16 And they came eagerly and found both Mary and Joseph, and the infant lying in the manger.

17 And when they had seen *them*, they made

known about the word which had been spoken
to them about this Child.

18 And all who heard it marveled about the things
spoken to them by the shepherds.

19 But Mary was keeping with her all these words,
conversing in her heart.

20 And the shepherds returned, glorifying and
praising God for all that they had heard and
seen, just as was spoken to them.

21 And when eight days were fulfilled to circumcise Him, His Name was called Jesus, the name
called by the angel before He was conceived in
the womb.

After the angelic army had **gone away from them into heaven**,
the shepherds were saying to one another (possibly throughout
the rest of the night?) that they should indeed **go to Bethlehem** to
see for themselves **this word**, this event (Gr. *rema*, which can mean
both) which **the Lord had made known** to them. They thus **came
eagerly** (waiting until dawn's light, as the earliest moment for making
inquiries?) and at length **found Mary and Joseph and the infant**
still **lying in the manger**, perhaps less than twenty-four hours old.

As the Vesperal Christmas hymn says, they offered the Child their
wonder, rejoicing that the One designated to be Messiah had been
born, and their deliverance would soon be at hand. After leaving the
Holy Family, they in turn **made known about the word** and event
which had been spoken to them by the angel **about this Child**
and His destiny. That is, they told all they met in the town, and **all
who heard it marveled** at their news, to think that Messiah had
been born (even as Zachariah's neighbors had marveled at the birth
of John; 1:63f). **The shepherds returned** from the town to their
flocks, **glorifying and praising God for all that they had heard**
from the angel **and seen** with their own eyes. As said above, the
praise of God is one of the signs of the Kingdom, and the ecstatic
praise of the humble shepherds is one more sign that the Kingdom
of God was breaking into history.

The people of Bethlehem who heard the shepherds' tale marveled, but the Mother of God herself did not marvel, for she had known such things since the Annunciation by the angel Gabriel. Rather, she was guarding and **keeping with her all these words** and events, **conversing in her heart**. The word rendered *keep with* is the Greek *suntereo*; it is used in Sirach 39:2 for preserving within one's memory, and in Mark 6:20 for keeping a person safe (in prison!). A similar verb—the Greek *diatereo*—is used in 2:51 to describe how Mary later kept within her heart the events of her Son's visit to the Temple at the age of twelve. The thought here is of Mary treasuring up securely all these works of God within her heart and pondering the significance of them all in an inner dialogue with herself.

It may be asked, however, why St. Luke mentions this inner pondering of the young Mother of God. I would suggest that the blessing Christ pronounces in 11:28 provides the key. There a woman from the crowd cries out with a thoughtless bit of flattery, "Blessed is the womb that bore You, and the breasts which nursed You!" That is, a blessing was pronounced upon His Mother for the mere fact of her biological maternity. Christ saw in this well-intentioned utterance a hidden danger, for Israel too easily thought that blessedness came from biology—that is, their biological link with Abraham (compare 3:8). So He pronounced a counter-blessing: "Blessed are those who hear the Word of God and keep it [Gr. *phulasso*]!"

It is this keeping, guarding, and observing the Word of God which is saving, and Luke is concerned to show how Mary fulfilled this as well. Her blessedness thus did not derive from the simple fact of her having given birth to the Messiah; it derived from her faithfully keeping and treasuring those sacred events within herself. At every step along the way, she treasured up the words and works of God within her heart. Like the scribe who kept the words of the sages of Scripture within his heart and sought out their hidden meanings (Sir. 39:2–3), so Mary also meditated on the works of God she had witnessed. Luke thus offers her as an example of God's humble disciple whom He delights to exalt (see 1:52).

A week or so later, **when eight days were fulfilled to circumcise** Jesus, He was indeed circumcised, as John had been. Like the circumcision of John, this rite would have been accomplished at home. (It is possible that by this time Joseph had found for them a proper house to live in; compare the "house" of Matt. 2:11.) Like John's, this circumcision was the time for the child's name to be officially bestowed, and **His Name was** then **called Jesus, the name called by the angel before He was conceived in the womb**. By calling attention to the heavenly origin of His Name, Luke reinforces Christ's heavenly origin itself.

§II.6. The Meeting in the Temple

> ৵ ৵ ৵ ৵ ৵
>
> 22 And when the days for their cleansing according to the Law of Moses were fulfilled, they brought Him up into Jerusalem to present *Him* to the Lord
> 23 (as it is written in the Law of the Lord, "Every male that opens up the womb will be called holy to the Lord")
> 24 and to give a sacrifice according to what was said in the Law of the Lord, "A pair of turtle-doves, or two young doves."

In **the Law of Moses** it was stipulated that for forty days after the birth of a boy, the mother of the newborn was ritually unclean (the period of ritual uncleanness was twice as long if the child was female), and that after this period, the mother must offer a sacrifice for the cleansing of her ritual impurity (Lev. 12:1–8). The required sacrifice was a year-old lamb and a turtledove, though if the family was poor, they were allowed to offer **a pair of turtledoves** as a more inexpensive sacrifice.

Coupled with this sacrifice for cleansing was the sacrifice offered to God for the redemption of the firstborn male. **Every** firstborn **male that opened the womb**—whether of man or beast—was **holy to the Lord** and belonged to Him. If the firstborn was that of a clean animal (such as a lamb), it was sacrificed; if the firstborn was one's son, it was redeemed with money (Ex. 13:1–15). It would seem that this redemption of Jesus as the firstborn was done at that time also.

Mary and Joseph came into Jerusalem and her Temple to fulfill these sacred rites. (Even though it was the ritual impurity of the mother that was the main focus of the rite, the rites are described as for **their cleansing**—in the plural—probably mother and Son were considered as a unit.) The Holy Family would have stood at the Nicanor Gate, peering from the Court of Women into the Court of the Israelites with its altar within. After the morning offering of incense, an officiating priest would have approached them, received the turtledoves from their hand, and offered them in sacrifice, afterward receiving from them the customary five shekels paid for the redemption of the firstborn.

St. Luke mentions these details (the phrase **the Law** is mentioned three times in as many verses) to emphasize the piety of Christ's parents (compare a similar emphasis regarding the parents of His Forerunner in 1:6) and to show how Christ fulfilled the Old Covenant. The firstborn was always considered as "holy to the Lord," and this was a prophecy of Christ, the Firstborn of all creation. He truly was holy to the Lord, and it was His holiness and priesthood that were foreshadowed by all the holy priests and firstborn who had gone before Him.

ॐ ॐ ॐ ॐ ॐ

25 And behold, a man was in Jerusalem whose name *was* Simeon, and this man *was* righteous and reverent, anticipating the encouragement of Israel, and the Holy Spirit was upon him.

26 And it had been *divinely*-pronounced to him by the Holy Spirit *that he would* not see death until he had seen the Lord's Christ.

27 And he came in the Spirit into the Temple, and when the parents brought in the Child Jesus, to do for Him according to the custom of the Law,

28 he welcomed Him into his arms, and blessed God, and said,

29 "Now You dismiss Your slave in peace, Master, according to Your Word,

30 "for my eyes have seen Your salvation,

31 "which You have prepared before the face of all peoples,

32 "a light for *the* revelation of the Gentiles, and the glory of Your people Israel."

33 And His father and Mother were marveling at what was being spoken about Him.

34 And Simeon blessed them, and said to Mary His Mother, "Behold, this *One* is appointed for the falling and rising of many in Israel, and for a sign to be contradicted—

35 "and a sword will go through even your own soul—that the questionings from many hearts may be revealed."

It was in the Court of Women that they met two others, who recognized the infant as the designated Messiah. In their acclaim one can discern the true voice of Israel. As Messiah, Jesus fulfilled the Old Covenant, and this messiahship was recognized by representatives of the chosen people.

One was **a man** whose **name *was* Simeon**. His age is not stated, but we can conclude that he was very old, since he proclaimed himself ready to die now that he had seen the Messiah. He was **righteous and reverent** (Gr. *eulabes*, "careful" in the performance of all God's commandments). He lived **anticipating the encouragement of Israel**, the time of messianic glory when Israel would be consoled and compensated for its past suffering. He (with others) thought that time must be close at hand, and **the Holy Spirit was upon him**.

In fact, **it had been *divinely*-pronounced to him by** that same **Holy Spirit *that he would* not see death until he had first seen the Lord's Christ**. The word rendered *divinely-pronounced* is the Gr.

chrematizo, used elsewhere to denote divine oracles and warnings (compare Matt. 2:12, 22; Heb. 12:25; and the cognate noun in Rom. 11:4). Simeon lived close to God and had received a revelation from Him that his lifelong desire to see the days of the Messiah would be fulfilled.

That day **he came in the Spirit into the Temple**, led in a kind of prophetic ecstasy, and divinely sensitive to the voice and leading of God. **When the parents** of Jesus **brought** Him into the Court of Women **to do for Him according to the custom of the Law** previously mentioned (perhaps before they had offered these sacrifices?), God spoke to Simeon and told him that this Child, carried in the arms of Mary, was the One. This Child would grow up to redeem Israel and bring in the days of glory.

Simeon approached the Holy Family and **welcomed** Jesus into the crook of **his arms and blessed God**. (Did he request that he be allowed to hold the Child before taking Him into his arms? Either way, we can only imagine the surprise of His young Mother.)

The Elder breathed a prayer of relief and joy, calling God his own **Master** (Gr. *despotes*, used for the absolute ownership of a slave-owner) and himself God's own humble **slave** (Gr. *doulos*). His prayer begins with the word **now**, emphasizing that the longed-for days of the Messiah had arrived. God had fulfilled His promise, His **Word** to His servant: Simeon had indeed seen the designated Messiah, and God was now **dismissing** him **in peace**. (The present tense is used—**"Now You dismiss Your slave"**—indicating that the long-desired sight of the Child was itself God's dismissal of His weary and faithful servant.) In seeing the Child, Simeon's **eyes** had **seen** God's salvation, His long-anticipated victory. This salvation He had **prepared before the face of all** the **peoples** of the earth, before the whole watching world. This Messiah would be **a light** to the nations, providing a **revelation** for **the Gentiles** of God's blessed will. Moreover, He would be the true and lasting **glory** of God's covenant **people Israel**, bringing them the splendor promised by their prophets.

Though knowing that their Child was the designated Messiah, Jesus' **father and Mother were marveling at what was being**

spoken about Him, amazed that such things should come unbidden from the lips of a stranger.

Simeon, however, had yet other prophecies to utter. Pronouncing his blessing upon the parents of such a Child (for he **blessed them**, strengthening them to receive his further words), he turned to Mary with a special and darker word of prophecy.

All in Israel expected that the Messiah would be a light to the nations and the glory of Israel. What they did not expect was that He would be **appointed** by God **for the falling and rising of many in Israel**, that He would be **for a sign to be contradicted** and spoken against. All expected that the Messiah would be a figure of universal popularity and favor. Simeon reveals that Mary's Son would be a controversial figure as well, and that His mission would result in some in Israel **falling** from God's favor and others **rising**. All in the land would take sides, either for or against Him, with the result that their secret **questionings** would be **revealed**. They might not even know their own hearts. They might think themselves righteous and loyal to God while their hearts were cold. But the mercy that the Son of Mary would show to sinners would reveal the true state of their own hearts, and any secret disloyalties that lodged in the heart like an undetected cancer would be brought to light.

Thus her Son was not destined only for glory, but for misunderstanding as well, being called upon to tread the way of sorrows. This sorrow would touch her too, and would be like a great **sword** (Gr. *romphaia*, a broadsword) which would **go through** her **own soul** as well. This word would be fulfilled at the Cross, when the sorrows that darkened her life would once and for all pierce her through as she watched her beloved Son hang in pain before her eyes (John 19:25).

ॐ ॐ ॐ ॐ ॐ

36 And there was a prophetess, Anna the daughter of Phanuel, from the tribe of Asher. She was advanced in many days, having lived with a husband seven years from her virginity,

37 and she *was* a widow until eighty-four years,

> not leaving the Temple, worshipping night and
> day with fastings and supplications.
> 38 And at that very hour she came up and was
> thanking God, and speaking about Him to all
> those who were anticipating the redemption of
> Jerusalem.

Besides Simeon, there was one other who met the Holy Family that day—the **prophetess Anna, the daughter of Phanuel, from the tribe of Asher**. Like the prophets of old, her lineage is given (compare Amos 1:1; Micah 1:1; Nahum 1:1). She was **advanced in many days**, living with a husband for **seven years** until his death, and then as **a widow until** the age of **eighty-four years**, like Judith (Jud. 16:22–23). She did **not leave the Temple** grounds, but arrived there daily when the gates opened, leaving only when they finally closed at night, **worshipping night and day with fastings and supplications**. Since she lived close to God, God revealed to her also that the infant Messiah had come.

At that very hour and moment when the Holy Family was in the sacred courts, **she came up** to them and **was thanking God**, in solemn and grateful proclamation of God's goodness in sending His Messiah. And not to them only, but she continued **speaking about Him to all those** around them who like Simeon were **anticipating the redemption of Jerusalem**. Many in the Temple were keenly waiting for Messiah to come, and the old prophetess proclaimed to them that He had come indeed, and their rescue was at hand.

Simeon and Anna (feast day February 3) are not only historical figures, but have typical significance as well. They are types and embodiments of the spirit of Israel. Israel lived in anticipation that Messiah would come, and this keen desire finds embodiment in Simeon. Israel also was a prophetic people, and this vocation to prophethood finds embodiment in Anna. Through the testimony of Simeon and Anna, Christ finds His messianic office recognized and accepted by the humble of the land, by the true remnant of Israel for whom He came.

❧ EXCURSUS
ON THE SONGS OF PRAISE

These early chapters of Luke's Gospel are characterized by praise, foremost in which is a series of songs. An outburst of prophetic praise is a sign of the coming of the Kingdom, and so these early chapters that relate the angelic announcements to Zachariah and Blessed Mary, and the births of John and Jesus, are studded with such melodious outbursts.

Thus Mary cries out in praise in the timeless words of the *Magnificat* song in 1:46–55; thus Zachariah's tongue was first loosed in the words of the *Benedictus* song in 1:64, 67–79. At Christ's birth, the angels lifted up their bodiless voices in the words of the *Gloria in Excelsis* song in 2:14—a joyful hymn that was echoed in the praises of the shepherds to whom they appeared (2:20). When the aged Simeon saw the infant Christ, he too praised God in the Song of Simeon (2:29–32), expressing a joy shared by the aged prophetess Anna as well in her own anthems (2:38). The early chapters of Luke's Gospel provide the Church with a treasury of liturgical material for use in the services.

This note of triumphant praise and doxology as the hallmark of the Kingdom continues throughout St. Luke's Gospel, as Christ's works result in an outpouring of divine glorification. The paralytic whom Christ heals goes to his home glorifying God (5:25); all those who observe Christ raising a young man from the dead also glorify God for His power in Christ (7:16). The woman with a curved spine is healed and glorifies God for it (13:13), as does the leprous Samaritan healed by Christ (17:15). When the blind man near Jericho is healed by Christ, he too glorifies God, and all the people who see the miracle also praise God for it (18:43).

It was not only Christ's miracles which caused men to glorify God—His death did also. The centurion saw the way in which He died, and he also glorified God, declaring Jesus to be righteous and innocent (23:47).

The entire Gospel ends on this triumphant note of praise. For after the Ascension, the apostles returned with joy to Jerusalem and "were continually in the Temple, blessing God" (24:53). Praise forms the climax of the Gospel, its pinnacle and goal. Thus the Gospel of Luke is saturated with doxology, for such glorification of the Name of God is a sign that the Kingdom has truly come.

ॐ ॐ ॐ ॐ ॐ

39 And when they finished everything according to the Law of the Lord, they returned to Galilee, to their own city of Nazareth.
40 And the Child was growing and being strengthened, filled with wisdom, and the grace of God was upon Him.

St. Luke summarizes Christ's early childhood in a few words. When Joseph and Mary had **finished everything according to the Law of the Lord** (compare Luke's emphasis on their piety and zeal in performing the Law in vv. 22–24), **they returned to Galilee, to their own city of Nazareth**. In focusing on Nazareth as the place of His childhood, Luke prepares the scene for his next story, the journey from Nazareth to Jerusalem.

Luke's intention is not to give a complete overview of Christ's early life. In fact, he omits the story of the visit of the Magi (told in Matt. 2), and the fact that after the rites of cleansing in the Temple, they returned first to their new home in Bethlehem, only returning to Nazareth after first sojourning in Egypt (Matt. 2:13–23). For Luke, the only important geographical axis is that of Nazareth and Jerusalem (compare the annunciations of Gabriel in those cities in 1:8f and 1:26f), and he omits all other details. Nazareth is the place of humility, from which the humble Messiah comes (John 1:46); while Jerusalem is the covenanted city of God, to which the

Messiah goes (9:51; 13:33). St. Luke's story revolves around these two spiritual locations.

Jesus' childhood is summed up by saying that He continued **growing and being strengthened** by God, going from strength to strength, advancing in all the Father's will, **filled with** divine **wisdom**. Like His Forerunner, He continued to grow and become strong (1:80). But unlike John, He carried **the grace of God** in a remarkable way, preparing Him to fulfill His future messianic task.

§II.7. Jesus' Early Years; Passover Visit to the Temple

꒳ ꒳ ꒳ ꒳ ꒳

41 And His parents were going every year to Jerusalem for the feast of the Passover.

42 And when He became twelve years *of age*, they went up according to the custom of the feast,

43 and after finishing the days, when they returned, the child Jesus remained *behind* in Jerusalem. And His parents did not know it,

44 but supposed Him to be in the caravan, and went a day's journey. And they were seeking Him out among their relatives and acquaintances.

45 And when they did not find Him, they returned to Jerusalem, seeking Him out.

46 And it happened that after three days they found Him in the Temple, sitting in the middle of the teachers, both listening to them and questioning them.

47 And all who heard Him were beside themselves at His insight and His answers.

48 And when they saw Him, they were thunderstruck, and His Mother said to Him, "Child, why have You done thus to us? Behold, Your father and I *myself* have been seeking You painfully."

> 49 And He said to them, "Why were you seeking
>   Me? Did you not know that it was necessary
>   for Me to be in the things of My Father?"
> 50 And they *themselves* did not have insight into
>   the word which He spoke to them.
> 51 And He went down with them, and came to
>   Nazareth; and He was in submission to them.
>   And His Mother kept all *these* words in her
>   heart.
> 52 And Jesus was advancing in wisdom and age
>   and in favor with God and men.

A remarkable incident is related by St. Luke to show how God's grace rested upon Him. It was incumbent on every pious male Jew to appear before God in the Temple annually for **the feast of the Passover**, and Jesus' **parents were going every year to Jerusalem** to fulfill this joyful obligation. Jesus was soon to enter upon the age of manhood (at His thirteenth birthday), and in preparation for this, when **He became twelve years *of age***, He accompanied His parents when **they went up** to Jerusalem **according to the custom of the feast**.

Such a journey from Nazareth to Jerusalem was about ninety miles long and would have taken about three or four days to travel. There would have been many other pilgrims on the road as well, and all would travel in an atmosphere of festivity and joyful anticipation. Individual families would have traveled as part of a larger caravan, composed of members of their extended clan and close friends.

With the jubilant crowd, the Holy Family kept the Passover feast in Jerusalem (which was probably Jesus' first visit to the Temple since He had been brought to it as an infant). Pilgrims were only required to stay for two days, and **after finishing the days**, they began to **return** to their home in Nazareth as their caravan set off for home.

Often the women in the company traveled ahead of the men at a slower pace, with the men catching up with them at a prearranged campsite by the first nightfall. The group of those returning would be large, and when **Jesus remained *behind* in Jerusalem, His parents did not know it**, each one thinking that He was with the other, or perhaps with some others in the large **caravan**. It was only when they made camp at the end of the first **day's journey** (possibly at Shechem in Samaria, if they took the road directly northward) and **were seeking Him out among their relatives and acquaintances** that Mary and Joseph discovered that their Son was not with any of the caravan. With pounding hearts (experienced by any parent who has lost track of their child in a crowded place), **they returned to Jerusalem**.

This return journey could not begin until the next day (we may imagine how little sleep they both got that night), and they journeyed the entire day to cover the twenty miles or more that they had covered with carefree hearts the previous day. They arrived at Jerusalem after nightfall, and so could not begin to comb the city until the next morning—**three days** after they first left the Holy City with the returning caravan. (Once again, we may imagine that for this second night they slept little.)

By the day's end, **they found Him**—He was **in the Temple**, not in the Court of Women or of the Israelites, the normal place of prayer. Rather He was in one of the terraces alongside, taking active part in the Passover teaching offered by members of the Sanhedrin.

During the week after Passover, the members of the Sanhedrin of the Temple would teach in the terrace of the Temple. Those being taught would sit at the feet of the teachers, and would **question** them and give **answers** when counter-questioned in return. The young Jesus was there—and not sitting far back, but **sitting** boldly **in the middle of the teachers**, a keen and precocious pupil. The questions He asked and the answers He gave were so perceptive that **all who heard Him were beside themselves** with amazement **at His insight** into the Law **and His answers**. The word translated *beside themselves* is the Greek *existemi*, used in 2 Corinthians 5:13 to indicate a presumption of mental imbalance, and in Luke 8:56 to indicate astonishment—its more usual meaning. Evidently the replies of the young Jesus were startling in their depth of insight and beyond what anyone had seen.

When His parents **saw Him** there (possibly having combed through much of Jerusalem), they **were thunderstruck** (Gr. *ekplesso*; compare its use in Mark 7:37). Evidently, in the midst of this discussion of the things in the Law was the last place they expected to find Him. (Perhaps they had spent their time seeking Him among other children, or at the places where children might be expected to gather.) Distraught from worry (and lack of sleep), **His Mother said to Him, "Child, why have You done thus to us? Behold, Your father and I** *myself* **have been seeking You painfully."**

The question is a natural one. Jesus is addressed as **Child**—the Greek *teknon*—a more affectionate term than *pais*, the word translated "child" in 2:43. The word *teknon* is sometimes translated as "son" (compare its use in 15:31). But for all this affection, there is still a rebuke implied, as Mary asks her Son why He has treated His parents so badly. Why had He not let them know where He could be found before they all left Jerusalem? Because they did not know where He was, they had unwittingly left without Him, and now had been **seeking** Him **painfully**. (The word rendered *painfully* is the Gr. *odunaomai*—used in 16:24 to describe the torment of the rich man in the flames of Hades.)

The young Jesus does not answer disrespectfully, but He asks in return how it could be that they would not know where they could find Him. Where else could He be, but in the place where the Law of His Father was being taught? **Did** they **not know that it was necessary** for Him, as the designated Messiah, **to be in the things of** His **Father?**

The Greek is *en tois tou patros mou*, and is sometimes rendered "in the house of My Father," even though the word "house" is not present in the Greek. I suggest that the reference, however, is *not* to the house of the Father per se, but to the things of the Father in general. For, strictly speaking, Jesus was not found in the house of the Father—He was not found in the place of worship, in the Court of Women or the Court of the Israelites, but in the side terrace of the Temple. He was not engaged in *worship*, but in *instruction*, and His focus was on the Law of the Father. The young Jesus' point was that His parents ought to have known that He would be found where

His Father's Law was being taught and discussed, and should have sought Him there when they were leaving.

His reply, however, contains a hidden mystery, and His parents **did not have insight into the word which He spoke to them**. Jesus had said that He would of course be preoccupied in His Father's business, His Father's affairs. Up to this time, He had called Joseph His father, His *abba*, or papa. To say that He would of course be preoccupied in His papa's business and be found close to him sounded to Joseph and Mary like a contradiction. Wasn't Joseph His papa? And didn't Jesus' preoccupation with Joseph's business mean that He would stick close to Joseph? How could He explain His absence from Joseph by saying He was staying close to His father?

To Christians who have become liturgically accustomed to calling God "Father," Jesus' reply is not puzzling, but Joseph was not accustomed to the phrase "my Father" as designating the God of Israel. Joseph knew that Jesus was to be the Messiah, but he was not prepared for Jesus to refer to His God in such an intimate and familiar way.

As Jesus' manhood approaches, He begins to transfer His sense of belonging and of family loyalty from His earthly father to His heavenly One. This sudden transfer, coming hard on the heels of the trauma of almost losing Him, catches His parents off guard. St. Luke records this incident as a confirmation of Jesus' status as Messiah. Not only was His birth from a virgin prophesied by an angel, not only was He recognized in the Temple as the Messiah while yet an infant, but He also knew Himself to be in extraordinary familiarity with the God of Israel from early childhood. His claim to be Messiah, made after He had been baptized by John as an adult, was therefore no novel development, but was consistent with His entire life, even from before His birth.

Luke concludes his account with summarizing Jesus' return to Nazareth. Despite Jesus' transferal of ultimate family loyalty from Joseph to His heavenly Father, **He was in submission** to His parents throughout all that time. Identification with God as His true Father and consequent acceptance of God's mission did not involve a break with His earthly family.

St. Luke's mention of Jesus' submission to His earthly parents is not accidental, but is an image of Christ's humility in Israel. Though He was the divine Messiah, Jesus still submitted to His parents, and His messianic status did not mean that He despised their authority. In humility He bowed His neck to the domestic yoke in the home of Joseph and Mary. In the same way, though He was the divine Messiah, Jesus would still submit and bow His neck to the yoke of the Law as a devout Jew. In His later ministry as in His child-hood, His humility should not be misinterpreted as meaning that He was not the glorious Messiah, for that glory voluntarily clothed itself in humility. It was this mystery that His Mother pondered. As mentioned before (in 2:19), **His Mother kept all *these* words** and events **in her heart**, treasuring them and meditating on their significance. Meanwhile, Jesus continued **advancing in wisdom and age**, in His humanity learning more of God's Law, and growing ever taller and older. He advanced in **favor with God and men**. That is, **God** continued to prepare Him for His future ministry as Messiah, and His righteousness and insight into holy things was recognized by **men** also.

❧ III ☙

THE MINISTRY OF THE FORERUNNER
(3:1–22)

§III.1. The Forerunner Begins His Ministry

ॐ ॐ ॐ ॐ ॐ

3 1 Now in the fifteenth year of the governing-rule of Tiberius Caesar, when Pontius Pilate was governing Judea, and Herod was being tetrarch of Galilee, and his brother Philip was being tetrarch of the region of Ituraea and Trachonitis, and Lysanias was being tetrarch of Abilene,

2 in *the time* of the high-priesthood of Annas and Caiaphas, the Word of God came to John the son of Zachariah in the wilderness.

The story of Jesus' appearance on the world stage begins with the story of John the Baptizer, and so St. Luke prefaces his narrative about Jesus' ministry with the story of John. John's public manifestation to Israel took place **in the fifteenth year of the governing-rule of Tiberius Caesar**—that is, in about AD 26, if we calculate from the beginning of Tiberius's co-regency with Augustus. This detail in itself is enough to date John's rise, but St. Luke goes on to fill out the picture by listing those who were ruling locally at that time.

Tiberius Caesar had the **governing-rule** (Gr. *egemonia*) over the whole world, and this supreme rule was exercised locally by **Pontius Pilate**, who **was governing** (Gr. *egemoneuo*) **Judea** as prefect. **Herod** Antipas (son of Herod the Great, who slew the infants of Bethlehem, and of his wife Malthace) **was being tetrarch** (Gr. *tetraarcheo*) **of Galilee** in the north, while **his brother Philip** (son of Herod the Great and Cleopatra) **was being tetrarch of Ituraea and Trachonitis**, a region to the northeast of Galilee. **Lysanias was being tetrarch of Abilene**, a region to the north of Ituraea.

While these men were exercising secular power, **Annas** and his son-in-law **Caiaphas** were exercising spiritual power. Annas was elected to the **high-priesthood** in AD 6 (supposedly a lifetime office), but was deposed by the Romans in AD 15 and succeeded by his son Eleazar, who was in turn deposed after a couple of years and succeeded by Caiaphas. Though Caiaphas was officially the high priest, Annas remained the power behind the throne.

It was in the midst of such sovereigns, seated securely upon their thrones (see 1:52), that **the Word of God came to** humble **John the son of Zachariah in the wilderness,** far from the halls of power. The phrase **the Word of God came to John** has intentional echoes of the classic Old Testament formula for God raising up His prophets (see Jer. 1:2; Hos. 1:1). The voice of prophecy had been silent for hundreds of years, but God once again bursts upon the children of men with His Word of fire.

ॐ ॐ ॐ ॐ ॐ

3   And he came into all the surrounding-country of the Jordan, heralding a baptism of repentance for the forgiveness of sins;

4   as it is written in the book of the words of Isaiah the prophet, "A voice shouting in the wilderness, 'Prepare the way of the Lord, make straight His paths.

5   "'Every ravine will be filled up, and every mountain and hill will be humbled; and the crooked will be *made* straight, and the rough *paths made* into smooth ways,

6   "'and all flesh will see the salvation of God.'"

After John had received this Word, **he came into all the sur-rounding-country of the Jordan** (probably in the area north of the Dead Sea), **heralding a baptism of repentance for the forgiveness of sins**. Proclaiming that Jews should be baptized was very contro-versial indeed, for until then, only Gentiles were offered baptism, as a part of their conversion to Judaism. In those days, when a Gentile wanted to leave his sinful ways and become a Jew, he stated his desire to the local Jewish community, promising to keep all the Law. After being circumcised, he was baptized, immersing himself in water to wash away the stain of the Gentile world, just as Jews sometimes immersed themselves to wash away ceremonial uncleanness (com-pare Lev. 14:8). The converting Gentile was then considered a Jew.

This baptism was the model for John's baptism of his fellow-Jews. John heralded to all Israel that the Jews were as much in need of repentance as the Gentiles were. The messianic Kingdom was at hand, but the Jews were not ready to receive it. If Messiah came now and found Israel unprepared, He would come in judgment and wrath, not in reward and salvation. Let Israel repent! If any Jew responded to John's call for repentance, that person was to show that **repentance** by accepting **baptism**, trusting that when Messiah came in judgment, he would have **the forgiveness of sins** and be spared the wrath of God.

Many responded to John's uncompromising call, and there was a great national revival on the shores of the Jordan. Thus John's ministry helped prepare Israel for the coming messianic Kingdom, a work foretold by the prophets. Isaiah the prophet had predicted **"A voice shouting in the wilderness, 'Prepare the way of the Lord, make straight His paths'"** (Is. 40:3f). John was this voice, sounding again as the harbinger of the Kingdom.

Just as one would prepare the roads for the coming of a king by clearing debris and filling in potholes, so John by his preaching would **prepare the way** and road (Gr. *odos*) **of the Lord** Messiah. **Every ravine will be filled up, and every mountain and hill will be humbled** (Gr. *tapeinoo*; compare its use in 14:11 for the humbling of the proud). **The crooked will be *made* straight, and the rough paths *made* into smooth ways** and roads (Gr. *odos*). Just as such topographical revolutions would make an easy road for a visiting king, so John's spiritual revolution would give the messianic King speedy access into the midst of His people. And when He came, then **all flesh** would **see the salvation of God**. For the Messiah would not come just to bless Israel, but to illumine all the world (compare Simeon's words in 2:31–32).

(We note in passing how St. Luke and the other Evangelists apply the words of Isaiah about **the Lord** (Gr. *kurios*; Heb. *Yahweh*) to Jesus. Isaiah had spoken of the voice preparing the way for *Yahweh* to come; and St. Luke here applies it to the coming of *Jesus*, for in Jesus the Father is fully manifested. Jesus is Yahweh come in the flesh.)

§III.2. The Preaching of John the Forerunner

ॐ ॐ ॐ ॐ ॐ

7   He therefore was saying to the crowds who were going out to be baptized by him, "Offspring of vipers, who directed you to flee from the coming wrath?

8   "Therefore make fruits worthy of repentance, and do not begin to say within yourselves, 'We have Abraham *for our* father,' for I say to you that God is able from these stones to raise up children to Abraham.

9   "And the ax is already laid even at the root of the trees; every tree therefore that does not make good fruit is cut down and cast into the fire."

Luke focuses on the preaching of John, for although John was not the Messiah, but a prophet, John's words and prophetic teaching were important.

John's message to **the crowds** who came to him was blunt—to those who came to him in complacency of heart (such as the Pharisees; compare Matt. 3:7), John was not sparing. He denounced them as an **offspring of vipers**. With withering sarcasm, he demanded to know **who directed** them **to flee from the coming wrath**, for they were not truly repenting. Did they imagine that they were following *John's* direction by making such shallow repentance? Vipers might flee from the fire (such as in Acts 28:3), but they remained vipers all the same. Similarly, these hearers might make show of repenting, but their hearts still remained hard and unchanged. If they truly wanted to flee from the coming wrath, let them **make fruits worthy of repentance** and change their lives.

They must no more rely upon their Jewish nationality to save them. It was popularly believed that "all Israel had a share in the age to come," and it was too easy for John's hearers to rely upon being the chosen people as their ticket into the Kingdom. But it would not be so. They must **not** even **begin to say within** themselves, **"We have Abraham *for our* father,"** thinking that their biological descent from Abraham would avail them in the coming Judgment. They thought that because God had promised to bless the seed of Abraham (compare Gen. 12:3; 22:18), God was obliged to bless them, regardless of how they lived. It was not to be so. God would judge them for their sins, even if He had to **raise up children to Abraham from** the very **stones** that littered the riverbanks of Judea in such abundance. God would bless those stones before He would bless them in their sins, preferring the stones as the designated heirs of Abraham. There is probably here a play on words in the original Aramaic: God would take as Abraham's children and *sons* (Aram. *benayya*) the very *stones* at their feet (Aram. *abnayya*).

They must repent now, from their hearts. It was a matter of life-and-death urgency, for the **ax** of divine judgment was **already laid even at the root of the trees**. The chopping down of **every tree that** did **not make** the **good fruit** of repentance was about to begin. Like a woodsman who lays the ax at the place he is about to strike just before he swings his first blow, so God was preparing to strike. Those who did not amend their lives would be **cut down** by God and **cast into the fire** of the final judgment.

ॐ ॐ ॐ ॐ ॐ
10 And the crowds were questioning him, saying, "Therefore what shall we do?"

> 11 And answering he was saying to them, "Let the one who has two shirts impart to the one who does not have *one*; and let the one who has food do likewise."
>
> 12 And tax-collectors also came to be baptized, and they said to him, "Teacher, what shall we do?"
>
> 13 And he said to them, "Collect no more than what you have been directed."
>
> 14 And soldiers were questioning him, saying, "What shall we do, even we *ourselves*?" And he said to them, "Do not shake down anyone, or oppress anyone, and be satisfied with your ration-pay."

The people as a whole took the message to heart, and **were questioning him** (perhaps somewhat despairingly), **saying, "Therefore what shall we do?"** That is, how should they amend their lives to avoid the coming wrath? What did God want them to do?

Here was a typically Jewish question, and it concerned the nature of the Law. What did God require of the faithful Jew, and what was the essence of the Law? John the prophet answers: mercy and justice. Indeed, what did the Lord require of His people, but that they do justice and love kindness and walk humbly with their God (Mic. 6:8)? In everyday terms, it meant that **the one who has two shirts** must **impart** and share with **the one who does not have** even *one*, and **the one who has food** must **do likewise**, sharing his bread with the hungry beggar. In saying this, John is not giving a complete compendium covering every situation. He is revealing the heart of the Law and setting a paradigm for one's basic attitude. Up until that time, it was each man for himself. Now they must change and become their brothers' keepers.

Different groups came to him with different dilemmas. Some **tax-collectors also came to be baptized**, humbly asking their **teacher** what God required of them. Their work involved the gathering of custom and tolls, and they were especially hated as dishonest and corrupt, since many took the opportunity to line their pockets by collecting more than their due. John replied not that they should cease from their work of collecting taxes, but that unlike most tax-collectors, they must **collect no more than what** they had **been directed**.

Others came as well, such as the Jewish **soldiers** in the hire of Herod, whose jobs included policing and (some would say) oppression of their fellow-Jews in the name of Herod. They were in a difficult position also, as is hinted by the emphatic pronoun **we** *ourselves*. The sense is, "We who find ourselves in the position of Herod's men—is there any hope for us?" John replied that they too need not change their occupations, but must simply avoid abusing their power. Though many soldiers did so, they must **not shake down anyone**, demanding money or goods by threat of force. They must not **oppress anyone**, using their power to make unreasonable demands. They must **be satisfied with** their **ration-pay**, even though it was notoriously low, and not look for ways to seek what was not theirs.

In all this advice, John turns his hearers back to simple precepts of mercy and fairness, of compassion and justice. For the Pharisees, what God demanded was a complicated dance through a maze of rules and regulations. For John, God demanded a good and upright heart, a life of love and uprightness. If a man lived in that way, he would be saved in the day of final judgment.

> ꒰ ꒰ ꒰ ꒰ ꒰
>
> 15 Now while the people were expecting and all were questioning in their hearts about John, as to whether he *himself* might be the Christ,
> 16 John answered and said to everyone, "I *myself* baptize you with water, but the stronger One than I is coming, and I myself am not sufficient to loose the strap of His sandals; He *Himself* will baptize you in the Holy Spirit and fire.
> 17 "And His shovel is in His hand to clean out His threshing-floor and to gather the wheat into

> His barn; but He will burn up the chaff with
> unquenchable fire."

As John's popularity grew, **the people were expecting** the Messiah, and **all were questioning in their hearts about John, as to whether he *himself* might be** that Messiah. John had proclaimed that the Kingdom was at hand (see Matt. 3:2)—was he going to inaugurate the Kingdom himself? In such a state of messianic fever, **John answered** such concerns and put such speculations to rest. He **said** openly **to everyone** that he was not the Messiah. Indeed, the Messiah was a **stronger One than** John, so mighty that John was not fit to be compared to Him. It was commonly allowed that a Jewish slave might do all kinds of service for his master, but was not required **to loose the strap** of his master's **sandals**. That the master could do for himself! Yet the coming Messiah was so mighty that John was **not sufficient** to do even this menial work for Him. The coming Lord was so great that John was not fit even to be His slave.

This could be seen in the very baptism John administered. John's baptism was merely preparatory, but the Messiah's work would be its fulfillment. That is, John did not baptize to gather disciples for himself, but to make men ready for the coming Christ. And as earthly water differed from the fire of heaven (compare 1 Kin. 18:38 for an example of heaven's fire), so did John's work differ from Messiah's. John **baptized with water**, outwardly marking men as repentant; **the stronger One** would **baptize in the Holy Spirit and fire**, transforming men from within with the cleansing fire of the Spirit of God. (This prophecy is fulfilled in Christian baptism, for in it, through the laying on of hands/chrismation, men receive the fire of the Holy Spirit.)

Moreover, Messiah was almost at hand and His judgment about to begin. In those days, the farmer would clean out the threshed wheat on his threshing floor with a shovel. That is, the stalks of wheat, after they had been pounded or threshed, would lie on the threshing floor, the chaff and the grains of wheat lying together. To separate the chaff from the wheat, the farmer would take a shovel full of mixed grains and toss them into the air. The chaff was lighter, so the wind would carry it away, while the heavier grains of wheat would fall back to the floor, from where they could be gathered into the safety of the barn for storage.

The final judgment, as the final separation of the righteous from the unrighteous, is compared to this winnowing process. The **shovel** was even now **in** Messiah's **hand to clean out His threshing-floor**; the process of judgment was about to begin. There was no time to waste! The righteous who repented would be like the precious **wheat**, to be gathered **into** God's **barn**, safe for eternity. The unrighteous who refused to repent would find themselves like **the chaff**, for Messiah would **burn** them **up with** the **unquenchable fire** of Gehenna. Let John's hearers repent now, for the time was at hand!

ॐ ॐ ॐ ॐ ॐ

18 Therefore with many other exhortations also he preached *the good news* to the people.

19 But when Herod the tetrarch was reproved by him about Herodias, his brother's wife, and about all the evils which Herod had done,

20 he added this also to them all, that he locked up John in prison.

St. Luke concludes by assuring his reader that this was but some of John's preaching. He used **many other exhortations** and figures as well, as **he preached *the good news*** (Gr. *euaggelizomai*) **to the people**. John's work was thus the beginning of the Gospel (Gr. *euaggelion*) in that he proclaimed Christ to the people.

As part of John's uncompromising prophetic word, he had **reproved Herod the tetrarch** for marrying **Herodias, his brother's wife**, for this was clearly forbidden in the Law (Lev. 18:16). Herod was not only personally offended at such a rebuke, but also fearful that John's public denunciations might lead to a popular uprising. Therefore, **to all the evils which Herod had done**, the tetrarch threw this evil deed on the pile as well, **that he locked up John in prison**. Luke sees this as a revelation of the fate of the righteous in an unrighteous world, and therefore in some sense as John's

vindication. As a true prophet, John was receiving the same persecution that all the prophets before him had experienced. John's
experience foreshadows that of Jesus, who will also be persecuted
and killed.

§III.3. John Baptizes Jesus

> ॐ ॐ ॐ ॐ ॐ
> 21 Now it happened when all the people were
> baptized that Jesus also was baptized, and while
> He was praying, heaven was opened,
> 22 and the Holy Spirit descended upon Him in
> bodily appearance as a dove, and a voice came
> out of heaven, saying, "*It is* You *who* are My
> beloved Son, in You I am well-pleased."

Jesus' baptism is related by St. Luke as the climax of John's
ministry (even though John continued to baptize after Jesus' baptism; John 3:22–23). That is, John had already achieved widespread
popularity with **all the people** before Jesus came to him and **also
was baptized**. With his characteristic emphasis on the importance of
prayer, Luke notes that it was **while** Jesus **was praying** that **heaven
was opened** in the vision that designated Him as the Messiah. For
John proclaimed a baptism of repentance, and Jesus as the sinless
Son of God had nothing to repent of. Jesus was baptized, therefore,
because God willed to reveal Him as His Messiah in the vision that
followed. (From John 1:31–33 we learn that the recipient of the
vision and the revelation was John the Baptizer himself.)

The vision consisted of three things: an opening of the heavens,
the descent of the dove, and a divine Voice. That **heaven was opened**
(Gr. *anoigo*) echoes such passages as Isaiah 64:1 LXX, which speaks
of God opening (Gr. *anoigo*) the heaven in self-revelation, for Christ's
Baptism was such a divine revelation. God had opened the heavens
to speak again to the earth.

The opening of heaven allowed **the Holy Spirit** to **descend in
bodily appearance as a dove**. The phrase *in bodily appearance* is

the Greek *somatiko edei*, and it indicates not that the Spirit took the actual form of a dove, or that an actual bird settled upon Christ. Rather, it indicates that in the vision the Spirit had the *outward appearance* of a dove.

Why a dove? It is possible that this is a reference to the original creation, in which the Spirit of God hovered like a bird over the waters (Gen. 1:2). More probably a dove was chosen for the vision because the dove was an acknowledged image of purity and innocence (see Matt. 10:16), and its presence on Jesus singled Him out as the One who was innocent of sin.

At the same time as the Spirit rested upon Jesus, **a voice came out of heaven, saying, "*It is* You *who* are My beloved Son, in You I am well-pleased."** The Father spoke to Jesus (in the hearing of John, His Forerunner), saying that Jesus was the One (the pronoun **You** is emphatic in the Greek) who was His **beloved Son**, His Messiah. In Him the Father was **well-pleased**. That is, Jesus was the One who would do all the Father's will, and through whom He would bring in His Kingdom. Jesus' baptism was the fulfillment of John's ministry, and St. Luke relates it after describing all that John did, as its climax.

❧ IV ☙
CHRIST PREPARES FOR HIS MINISTRY
(3:23—4:13)

§IV.1. Christ's Genealogy

☙ ☙ ☙ ☙ ☙

23 And Jesus was Himself *at the* beginning about thirty years *of age*, being as was supposed the son of Joseph, the *son* of Eli,

24 the *son* of Matthat, the *son* of Levi, the *son* of Melchi, the *son* of Jannai, the *son* of Joseph,

25 the *son* of Mattathias, the *son* of Amos, the *son* of Nahum, the *son* of Hesli, the *son* of Naggai,

26 the *son* of Maath, the *son* of Mattathias, the *son* of Semein, the *son* of Josech, the *son* of Joda,

27 the *son* of Joanan, the *son* of Rhesa, the *son* of Zerubbabel, the *son* of Shealtiel, the *son* of Neri,

28 the *son* of Melchi, the *son* of Addi, the *son* of Cosam, the *son* of Elmadam, the *son* of Er,

29 the *son* of Joshua, the *son* of Eliezer, the *son* of Jorim, the *son* of Matthat, the *son* of Levi,

30 the *son* of Simeon, the *son* of Judah, the *son* of Joseph, the *son* of Jonam, the *son* of Eliakim,

31 the *son* of Melea, the *son* of Menna, the *son* of Mattatha, the *son* of Nathan, the *son* of David,

32 the *son* of Jesse, the *son* of Obed, the *son* of Boaz, the *son* of Salmon, the *son* of Nahshon,

33 the *son* of Amminadab, the *son* of Admin, the *son* of Ram, the *son* of Hezron, the *son* of Perez, the *son* of Judah,

> 34 the *son* of Jacob, the *son* of Isaac, the *son* of Abraham, the *son* of Terah, the *son* of Nahor,
> 35 the *son* of Serug, the *son* of Reu, the *son* of Peleg, the *son* of Heber, the *son* of Shelah,
> 36 the *son* of Cainan, the *son* of Arphaxad, the *son* of Shem, the *son* of Noah, the *son* of Lamech,
> 37 the *son* of Methuselah, the *son* of Enoch, the *son* of Jared, the *son* of Mahalaleel, the *son* of Cainan,
> 38 the *son* of Enosh, the *son* of Seth, the *son* of Adam, the *son* of God.

After relating the ministry of the Forerunner, St. Luke then tells how Christ began His own ministry. Before speaking of the words and deeds of Jesus, however, Luke gives His genealogy. In our own modern era, with its stress on the individual, such things as genealogies are often of marginal interest and are thought to have nothing to do with a person's identity. The ancient world had a more realistic and balanced view, and included one's pedigree as a contributing factor to one's personhood. They knew what we have often forgotten—that our own individual views and choices are often shaped by our culture and history.

The complete sources available to St. Luke in listing Christ's genealogy through Joseph are unknown. (We may take it as given that this is Christ's genealogy through Joseph and not, as some have suggested, through Mary: the list explicitly mentions Joseph and not Mary [v. 23]. Besides, if Luke's intention had been to give Christ's line through His Mother, why did he not simply say so and mention Mary by name?)

Though certainty is impossible, we may imagine that Luke received some of this information through the Mother of God herself. Also, some genealogical records were available in Jerusalem.

Concerning this list, certain points may be made.

Firstly, such genealogies as this make no attempt to be complete, nor to list every single descendant. The genitive (translated here as **son of**) does not necessarily mean that X was the immediate descendant or son of Y; X could equally well be the grandson or great-grandson of Y. There are gaps, therefore, in the complete list, and this makes a comparison of this list with the one in Matthew's Gospel difficult. The fact that this genealogy does not match exactly with the one in Matthew's Gospel is not problematic, since Luke and Matthew could simply be listing different individuals from the complete list.

Secondly, it is possible that this list records variations due to levirate marriage. According to the principle of levirate marriage in ancient Israel, if a man died without children, his brother would marry the widow and raise up a descendant for his deceased brother. The firstborn son of this marriage would be counted as the heir of the deceased man and would inherit his property (Deut. 25:5–6). Africanus (who died about AD 240) claimed to have received information from St. James's descendants regarding Christ's genealogy. (This is reported by Eusebius in his *History of the Church*, 1,7.) According to Africanus, Matthan (Matt. 1:15) had a son, Jacob, by a woman named Estha, and when Matthan died, his widow married Melchi (Luke 3:24), and had a son, Eli (3:23). This Eli married but died childless; his half-brother Jacob married Eli's widow, and by her had a child, Joseph. Thus this Joseph was the son both of Eli (legally) and Jacob (biologically). Africanus admits he cannot corroborate the story. (He also does not deal with the fact that this scenario involves the skipping of two generations between Melchi and Eli, namely Matthat and Levi, in 3:24.) But it is possible that levirate marriage was a factor in some of Joseph's ancestors.

Thirdly, note that St. Luke traces our Lord's ancestry back to **Adam, the *son* of God** (unlike Matthew, who only traces Christ's ancestry back to Abraham). This is because, whereas Matthew was writing with an eye toward the Jews and had as his main concern the portrayal of Jesus as the Jewish Messiah, Luke was writing for a Gentile audience and was concerned to portray Jesus as the Savior of the world. Thus Matthew sets Jesus in a thoroughly Jewish context, and Luke sets Him in a more universal one. That is why Luke traces Jesus back to Adam, the forefather of all men, and to God, who created Adam. By doing this, Luke emphasizes that Jesus came to be the Savior of all Adam's descendants. As Adam was **the *son***

of God by creation, so Jesus was the Son of God from all eternity, the Second Adam, the One sent by God to redeem all Adam's race.

Finally, Luke gives Jesus' genealogy through Joseph even though Joseph was not the biological father (this is indicated by Luke saying that Jesus was **as supposed, the son of Joseph**) because legal descent was always through the father. That is why Joseph's Davidic descent is stressed in 1:27. It is through Joseph's line that Jesus inherited the messianic throne of King David.

With a physician's eye for such physical things, Luke notes that *at the* **beginning** of Jesus' ministry, He was **about thirty years *of* age.** This round number (Luke is not concerned with months) is mentioned to show that Christ had come to mature manhood and was in full possession of His powers. (It was at thirty years of age that men were anciently thought mature enough to work in the Mosaic Tabernacle; Num. 4:23.) Jesus is thus introduced by Luke as stepping onto the stage of world history, ready to begin His work.

§IV.2. Christ's Temptation in the Wilderness

Luke narrates the temptation of Christ in the wilderness not just as a biographical fact, but also as a paradigm for Christians. The Holy Spirit descended upon Jesus as He stood praying after His baptism (3:21–22), even as the Holy Spirit descended upon the Christians at the time of their post-baptismal laying on of hands/chrismation (such as narrated in Acts 19:5–6). As Christ's experience of baptism and the Holy Spirit was followed by a time of temptation and testing by the devil, so it will be for Christ's disciples. After their baptismal initiation into the Church, they too must endure a time of conflict with the devil in the wilderness of the world. By showing how Christ vanquished the devil, St. Luke provides a model for how Christians can triumph over the devil in their own struggles with him.

୫ ୫ ୫ ୫ ୫

4 1 And Jesus, full of the Holy Spirit, returned from the Jordan and was led in the Spirit in the wilderness

> 2 for forty days, being tested by the devil. And He
>   did not eat anything in those days, and when they
>   were accomplished, He was hungry.
> 3 And the devil said to Him, "If you are the Son
>   of God, tell this stone to become bread."
> 4 And Jesus answered him, "It is written, 'Man
>   shall not live by bread alone.'"

After His Baptism, Jesus was **full of the Spirit**, and He **returned from the Jordan**, scene of His Baptism. He did not immediately begin His ministry, however, but was first **tested by the devil**. This was no overthrow of the will of God, though, but was allowed by Him. In the same way, the war on the Christians by the devil and the world does not mean that God has abandoned the Christians. Rather, God sovereignly uses the devil to fulfill His own purposes—in this case, the strengthening of Christ and His people. For just as the blade must be first tested before it is used in battle, so Christ is tested before He begins His battle against the forces of darkness.

So it is that Christ is **led in the Spirit in the wilderness for forty days**. The phrase *led in the Spirit* is significant (Gr. *egeto en to pneumati*), for it recalls Simeon coming "in the Spirit" (Gr. *en to pneumati*) into the Temple (2:27). As Simeon was led in a kind of ecstatic obedience into the Temple courts, so Christ also followed the lead of the Spirit throughout His time in the wilderness.

These were (we suggest) days of prayer and preparation for Christ, as He sought the will of His Father for His future ministry. As Moses communed with God on Mount Horeb for forty days (Deut. 9:9), so Christ communed with the Father throughout the time of His wilderness retreat. The devil sought in vain to disrupt this harmony, **testing** and tempting Christ all that time (the word translated *tested* is the Greek *peirazo*, which means both to test and to tempt).

At the end of this set period, when hunger was at its height, the devil attacked again, with special ferocity. Throughout the forty days, we may think that Satan's temptations were more diffused. Now Satan attacks with three precise temptations.

Why was this necessary for Christ? We suggest that because Christ took upon Himself the fullness of our human condition, it was necessary for Him to face demonic temptation in all its power in order to face in His own life the same temptations that we face in ours. Thus the apostolic writer says that Christ had to be made like His brothers in all things, and that it was because He Himself was tested that He is able to help us who are similarly tested (Heb. 2:17–18). Christ faced temptation for the same reason as He faced death—to triumph over it for our sakes.

In the first temptation, **the devil** appealed to Christ's sense of His own authority. **If** He was **the Son of God**, then He had authority over nature itself. The many stones that littered the ground of Judea looked very much like small loaves of bread (especially to one who was hungry). Let Christ use His authority to satisfy His own needs, and **tell this stone** at His feet **to become bread**. The temptation was to use His power for His own sake, and to let His appetites set the agenda for Him. It is a temptation we all endure as well—the temptation to be ruled by our passions and desires more than by God's will.

Christ responded by citing the divine Scripture (as He did in all the temptations), thereby setting an example for His disciples. The Scripture was given by God as a lamp in darkness to direct one's feet and show one the safe way to walk (Ps. 119:105). The devil might try to misdirect one's steps and lead one over the precipice, but what was written would show the right way.

It is significant too that all Christ's citations of Scripture during His temptations were from Deuteronomy. Israel was led in the wilderness for forty years, and tested (Gr. *peirazo*), to see whether or not they would keep God's commandments (Deut. 8:2 LXX); Deuteronomy was the scriptural testimony to that time of testing. Christ uses the Scripture given during that time of wilderness testing during His own time of trial. Lifting up the Word of God like a shield, **Jesus answered** the devil, **"It is written, 'Man shall not live by bread alone'"** (Deut. 8:3).

In the original context of this verse, God had fed the Israelites in the wilderness by daily rations of manna, to teach them to rely on Him and to show them that true life did not come from earthly food alone. The provisions of manna showed that true life came as one trusted God and referred everything to Him. In the same way, Jesus clung to the will of God and His commands as His sole reference point. He would not eat in obedience to His bodily hunger, but only as instructed by the Father. If the Father told Him to eat, then and only then would He eat. Bodily desires were subordinated to humble obedience to the Father.

꙳ ꙳ ꙳ ꙳ ꙳

5 And having led Him up, he showed Him all the kingdoms of the world in a moment of time.

6 And the devil said to Him, "To You I will give all this authority and its glory, for it has been delivered to me, and I give it to whomever I want.

7 "Therefore if You *Yourself* worship before me, it will all be Yours."

8 And Jesus answered and said to him, "It is written, 'You shall worship the Lord your God and serve Him only.'"

In the second temptation narrated by St. Luke, the devil **led** Jesus **up** to a high mountain, and **showed Him all the kingdoms of the world in a moment of time**. (This is probably the third and final temptation, which Luke records as the second one, thus inverting the original order which Matthew preserved in Matt. 4:1–11. It would seem that Luke wants to show the importance of Jerusalem as the place of final conflict, and so makes Christ's temptation there the final one.)

This second temptation began with the devil displaying **all the kingdoms of the world** to Christ, using his supernatural power to make them pass before Christ's gaze **in a moment of time**. The devil stated that it was to Christ that he would **give** them (the **You** is at the head of the sentence in the Greek, for greater emphasis), so that Jesus would stand as the ruler of all the world.

This was within Satan's power, he claimed, for **authority** over the nations with all the attendant **glory** had **been delivered** to him when Adam fell, and now Satan could **give it to whomever** he **wanted**. God had originally given the world to Adam and Eve to rule over as His representatives (Gen. 1:27–28), but when they fell into sin, that sovereignty was forfeited to the Tempter. Now it was the Evil One who was the god of this age and its ruler (2 Cor. 4:4), and the whole world lay in his authority (1 John 5:19). As it was then, he could give it to whom he would (and be the power behind the throne!).

Jesus could rule the whole earth. All He had to do was a simple act of obeisance, unseen by any mortal eyes. All He had to do was **worship before** the devil (Gr. *proskuneo*, to bow down in obeisance) and **it would all be** His. This is the timeless temptation to compromise one's allegiance to God for the sake of worldly gain. It is a temptation to compromise moral and spiritual integrity which comes time and time again to the children of men in their quest for success.

Once again Jesus lifts up the shield of the Scripture, and responds with a word from Deuteronomy 6:13: **"It is written, 'You shall worship the Lord your God and serve Him only.'"** The words rendered *worship* and *serve* are the Greek words *proskuneo* and *latreuo*. The verb *proskuneo* (as said above) means "to bow down," and in this context, to bow down in total submission. The verb *latreuo* means "to serve" in the sense of performing religious duties, especially liturgical ones; in these commentaries it is usually translated as "to worship" (compare its use in 2:37).

This saying in Deuteronomy 6:13 then means that ultimate homage and allegiance are given to God alone, and any other act of homage which threatens that is forbidden. We may not serve two opposing masters. (We may add that not all acts of homage do in fact threaten our allegiance to God. For example, a humble act of homage to one's king need not be idolatrous; compare such a bowing down in 2 Sam. 14:4.) The prostration the devil was suggesting, however, *was precisely meant as a detraction* from Christ's total loyalty to the Father, and this is why Christ refused it. In the same way, we too must take care that none of our earthly loyalties and allegiances conflict with the allegiance given to God.

ॐ ॐ ॐ ॐ ॐ

9   And he led Him into Jerusalem and stood Him
    upon the pinnacle of the Temple, and said to
    Him, "If you are the Son of God, cast Yourself
    down from here,

10 "for it is written, 'He will command His angels
    about you to guard you about,'

11 "and 'Upon their hands they will take you up,
    lest you strike your foot against a stone.'"

12 And Jesus answered and said to him, "It is said,
    'You shall not test-out the Lord your God.'"

In the third temptation, the devil **led** Christ **into Jerusalem**. (Thus the test reaches its climax in the Holy City.) With a presence invisible to mortal eyes, Satan **led** Jesus and **stood Him upon the pinnacle of the Temple**. This was probably the royal porch on the south side of the outer court. According to contemporary witnesses, such a height was high enough to cause giddiness if one looked down into the deep Kidron ravine below.

If Jesus was **the Son of God**, He could expect special protection from God. Let Jesus prove this, and thereby have the psychological security of knowing that He was invincible. Then He would not have to fear the future, but would know in advance that He was safe. Let Him **cast** Himself **down from here**, and have God miraculously catch Him, so that He would float serenely to the ground below. God would not mind! Had not God Himself **written** by the hand of the Psalmist that **He would command His angels** about the righteous man **to guard** him **about** (Ps. 91:11)? Such a result was doubly sure, for another Scripture said, **"Upon their hands they will take you up, lest you strike your foot against a stone"** (Ps. 91:12). If this was true of the righteous man in general, how much more would it be true of God's Messiah?

This was the temptation to find security against life's suffering *in advance*, and to be spared the uncertainty that comes from walking with God by faith. It was the perennial temptation to presume on God's care and to bend His will to ours. Such a presumption is especially common in religious folk—hence Satan's subtle (and lying) use of Scripture.

Christ does not argue with the devil about Scripture, nor point out how he is distorting its meaning. (This Scripture verse promises God's help to those who obediently follow Him, not to those who proudly presume on His care.) Rather than debating about the meaning of these verses, Christ simply responds with another Scripture, saying, **"It is said, 'You shall not test-out the Lord your God'"** (Deut. 6:16). (The word translated *test-out* is the Gr. *ekpeirazo*, a more intensive form of the verb *peirazo*, "to test.")

That is, one shall not "put God through His paces," as if it were His love that were on trial. Rather, one should trust that God will direct our steps as He knows best, and not presume on His unconditional protection. In obedience to this Scripture, Christ refuses to put God to the test by leaping from the Temple's pinnacle. By twisting the Scriptures, Satan had tried to beguile Christ into sinfully presuming upon God's care. But Christ refused to fall into the trap, taking His stand on the true meaning of the Scriptures.

By doing so, Christ calls us also to walk with God by faith, and to take whatever comes from His hand, confident that God's love knows what is best for us. We must not seek to bend God's will to our own (such as, for example, by "naming and claiming" what we want, and trying to use the Scripture as the means to accomplish our own will).

ॐ ॐ ॐ ॐ ॐ

13 And when the devil had accomplished every test, he departed from Him until an *appointed* time.

When the devil had accomplished every test, and exhausted every avenue he could think of, **he departed** from Jesus, and Jesus emerged triumphant from the arena of testing. But this was not the end of the Enemy's work. For Satan departed only **until an** *appointed* time and an opportune moment (Gr. *kairos*). For Luke, such a time came with the betrayal of Judas, when Christ was betrayed into the hands of His foes. Then Satan would test and sift the disciples like wheat (22:31); that would be the hour for Satan to exercise his dark authority (22:53). But for now, he had been decisively vanquished.

❦ V ❧

CHRIST'S MINISTRY IN GALILEE
(4:14—9:50)

§V.1. Christ Begins His Ministry

> ❧ ❧ ❧ ❧ ❧
> 14 And Jesus returned to Galilee in the power
> of the Spirit, and news about Him went out
> through all the surrounding-country.
> 15 And He was teaching in their synagogues, being
> glorified by all.

Luke then turns to Christ's ministry after He **returned to Galilee**. (In doing so, St. Luke omits our Lord's early ministry as narrated by St. John in John 1:35—4:42, and picks up the story where St. Mark began it in Mark 1:14—that is, after the arrest of John. It is possible that one reason for Christ's return to Galilee was that Galilee was safer for Him than Judea after John had been arrested.) Luke focuses on the power with which Jesus began His Galilean ministry. Though "full of the Spirit" from His baptism (4:1), after His time of testing He returned **in the power of the Spirit**—He emerged victorious from His temptations, full of divine power.

This divine power produced many miracles, and the **news about Him went out through all the surrounding-country**. It was not just at Capernaum (His new residence; compare Matt. 4:13; Luke 4:23), but in all the area around it that people were speaking of His triumphant homecoming to Galilee. He had done miracles in Judea (see John 2:23), and now He had returned. **He was teaching in their synagogues** (the local gathering place in each Jewish community) and healing the sick. His popularity was spreading, and He was **being glorified by all**.

§V.2. Christ Rejected at Nazareth

Luke tells the story of Christ's rejection at Nazareth in far more detail than does Matthew or Mark (Matt. 13:53–58; Mark 6:1–6a). For Luke, this rejection is important, and it foreshadows Christ's rejection by the majority of Israel. He came to His own (both locally and nationally), and His own did not receive Him (John 1:11). The rage of those of His hometown and their unsuccessful attempt to kill Him (4:29) foreshadowed the rage of those in Jerusalem and their successful attempt to kill Him (23:23). And just as the Lord intimated in this first exchange in Nazareth (4:26–27), God would respond by blessing the Gentiles rather than faithless Israel.

ॐ ॐ ॐ ॐ ॐ

16 And He came into Nazareth, where He had been nourished, and as He was accustomed *to do*, He entered into the synagogue on the Sabbath, and rose up to read.

17 And the scroll of the prophet Isaiah was given over to Him. And He unrolled the scroll, and found the place where it was written,

18 "The Spirit of the Lord is upon Me, because He anointed Me to preach *good news* to the poor. He has sent Me forth to herald freedom to the captives, and *recovery of* sight to the blind, to send forth into freedom those who are broken,

19 "to herald the acceptable year of the Lord."

20 And He rolled up the scroll and gave *it* back to the attendant, and sat down, and the eyes of all in the synagogue were staring at Him.

21 And He began to say to them, "Today this Scripture has been fulfilled in your ears."

22 And all were witnessing of Him, and marveling

> at the words of grace which were coming from
> His mouth, and they were saying, "Is not this
> *man* the son of Joseph?"

Luke then narrates the Lord's return to **Nazareth, where He had been nourished** and brought up as a child. It was in this very **synagogue** that Jesus had heard the Scriptures read throughout His youth; it was to this building that He was brought by Joseph and Mary and was taught, humanly speaking, to worship God. As such, it was filled with memories, and many of the faces present during that Sabbath service were ones Jesus had known for years.

As He was accustomed to do, Jesus **entered into** this **synagogue on the Sabbath** to attend the usual service. The service consisted of an introductory confession of faith and a series of prayers. This was followed by the heart of the service: the reading of the Law. Passages from the books of Moses were first read by several of the assembled men, and then translated from the Hebrew into a running Aramaic (or vernacular) paraphrase. Then came a lesson from the Prophets. This was followed by a prayer, and then one present might be asked to give a discourse based on what had been read. This task would often fall to distinguished visitors, if any were present (see Acts 13:15 for an example of this). On this day, Jesus was invited to read and to give the address.

He **rose up** from His seat **to read**. Having requested from the liturgical attendant **the scroll** containing the words of **the prophet Isaiah** (Gr. *biblion*, denoting not so much the biblical Book of Isaiah as the actual scroll itself), that **scroll was given over to Him. He** then **unrolled the scroll, and found the place where it was written, "The Spirit of the Lord is upon Me, because He anointed Me to preach *good news* to the poor"** (Is. 61:1–2). St. Luke dramatically relates our Lord's every move to convey to his readers the built-up drama of that day. Indeed, we can almost see Jesus carefully unrolling the large scroll and poring over it in silence until He finds the reading He wants; we can almost feel the tension and expectancy of the congregation as they watch Him unroll the scroll and wait for His words.

Christ chose for His reading (fixed lections for the Prophets were not then established) Isaiah's prophecy of the miracles of the Messiah. In this oracle, the prophet proclaimed that **the Spirit of the Lord** was **upon** him, and by this Spirit he had been **anointed to preach *good news* to the poor**. The word translated *anoint* is the Greek *chrio*, from which the title *Christos*, or "Christ," is derived; in the original Hebrew the word was *masah*, from which the title "Messiah" is derived.

Here then was a prophecy of the Messiah. He would come to **preach *good news*** (Gr. *euaggelizomai*, cognate with *euaggelion*, the "Gospel"), tidings which would lift the hearts of **the poor**. He had been **sent forth** as God's apostle (Gr. *apostello*) **to herald freedom to the captives** and *recovery of* sight to the blind; to herald to **those who are broken** and downtrodden that they themselves were **sent forth** (Gr. *apostello*) **into freedom**. In short, Messiah was sent **to herald** to all **the acceptable year of the Lord**—the long-anticipated time of Jubilee when the Lord God's favor was given to all. (Christ was evidently quoting rather freely as He translated the Hebrew into Aramaic, for the part about **sending forth into freedom those who are broken** is actually from Is. 58:6, so that Christ conflated the two passages in Isaiah.)

The reading from the scroll was a clear prophecy of the coming of the Messiah and the glorious work of liberation that He would do. It was a prophecy of the messianic Kingdom for which the hearers in the synagogue had been waiting all their lives.

Luke continues his dramatic buildup, saying that Christ **rolled up the scroll and gave *it* back to the attendant**, the *chazzan*, whose task it was to arrange for the services. He then sat down (the usual posture for delivering teaching in those days) and prepared to deliver His address. The tension must have been extreme, and Luke reports that **the eyes of all in the synagogue were staring at Him**, in fixed expectancy of what He was to say.

Christ **began** His address by declaring that **today this Scripture has been fulfilled in** their **ears**. That is, at the very moment they were hearing Christ's words, the Scriptural prophecy of the messianic era was coming true. From those astounding opening words, Christ went on to proclaim that the Kingdom of God was even then breaking in through Him and His work.

His message was electrifying in content and delivered with a power they had never experienced in a speaker before. **All were witnessing of Him**, telling each other how they had never before heard the like of it. They were **marveling at the words of grace which were coming from His mouth**. And it was this very thing that was troubling. For was **not this *man* the son of Joseph**, the very one they had known all their lives until this time, and the son of a mere carpenter? His family was not so very special. Who did He think He was, proclaiming that He was the One to bring in the Kingdom of God? This could only be done by the Messiah—did He dare to make such an audacious claim? Obviously He was not the Messiah, for the Messiah would come out of nowhere (compare John 7:27), and everyone knew that Jesus had come from Nazareth.

ॐ ॐ ॐ ॐ ॐ

23 And He said to them, "Doubtless you will quote this parable to Me, 'Physician, heal yourself!' Whatever we heard happened in Capernaum, do here also in Your hometown."

24 And He said, "Amen I say to you, no prophet is acceptable in his hometown.

25 "But I say to you in truth, there were many widows in Israel in the days of Elijah, when the heaven was shut up for three years and six months, when a great famine happened over all the land;

26 "and Elijah was sent to none of them, except to Zarephath of Sidon, to a widow woman.

27 "And there were many lepers in Israel in the *time* of Elisha the prophet, and none of them was cleansed, except Naaman the Syrian."

After the address, it was customary to have questions and discussion, and it was apparent from this discussion that those in the synagogue were turning against Him. They were skeptical of His message and had no faith that He was bringing God's Kingdom. They were all for demanding that Jesus prove Himself by doing miracles. Let Him do a miracle right now if He claimed such exalted status! They were an evil and adulterous generation and refused to believe without signs (Matt. 12:39).

Jesus knew their thoughts and faced their skepticism head on. **He said to them, "Doubtless you will quote this parable**, this popular proverb, **'Physician, heal yourself!'"** If a physician could really give health to others, he could give it to himself too. Since (as they had **heard happened**) He had done miracles in **Capernaum**, let Him work some in His **hometown** too and give them a taste of His miracle power!

This the Lord steadfastly refused to do. He was not surprised at their skepticism and their rejection. After all, He said, **no prophet is acceptable in his hometown**. Their rejection did not tarnish His divine authority, for He was only experiencing the rejection that all prophets experience. But **in truth** He must tell them that their rejection of Him meant that God would reject them.

They must not think such a thing impossible, as if God would never reject His people. For **there were many widows in Israel in the days of Elijah**, during the long drought and the famine that followed it (1 Kin. 17). All of these Israelite widows cried to God for help, but **Elijah was sent to none of them, except to Zarephath of Sidon**—to a foreigner, a humble **widow woman**. God withheld His blessing from His people because of their apostasy, giving it instead to a Gentile.

And this was not an isolated incident. For **there were many lepers in Israel in the *time* of Elisha the prophet** (2 Kin. 5), and all of them prayed to their God for healing. Nonetheless, **none of them was cleansed**. God bypassed all His covenant people and instead gave healing to the leprous **Naaman the Syrian**—another Gentile. In the same way, God would bypass them for their rejection of Jesus.

28 And all in the synagogue were filled with indignation as they heard these things;
29 and they rose up and cast Him out of the city,
and led Him to the brow of the hill on which
their city had been built, to down-cliff Him.
30 But He *Himself*, having gone through their
midst, went *away*.
31 And He went down into Capernaum, a city
of Galilee. And He was teaching them on the
Sabbaths;
32 and they were thunderstruck at His teaching,
for His word was with authority.

**All in the synagogue were filled with indignation as they
heard these things**. They were skeptical enough at Jesus' implied
claim to be the Messiah—but now to be themselves compared to
apostates and to be called worse than pagans! They were enraged at
this, and **they rose up and cast Him out of the city**. The shouting,
tumultuous mob hustled Him **to the brow of the hill on which
their city had been built** (for Nazareth was built on the slopes).
They were intending to **down-cliff Him** (Gr. *katakremnizo*), hurling
Him forty feet to His death on the valley floor below. But this was
not God's time, and **having gone through** the **midst** of the crowd
under the protecting hand of God, He **went *away***.

Leaving Nazareth, **He went down into Capernaum** again,
returning to His previous base of operation (compare the men of
Nazareth hearing reports of His work at Capernaum in v. 23). (Luke
says that Jesus **went down** into Capernaum, since Nazareth was
in the hills and Capernaum on the lakeside.) In Capernaum Jesus
continued **teaching them on the Sabbaths**, worshipping with them
in the synagogues, reading the Scriptures and giving instruction as
a prominent visitor. They **were thunderstruck at His teaching**, for
visiting teachers usually quoted some other authority (saying "Rabbi

so-and-so teaches thus regarding this passage"), but Jesus' **word was with authority**. He did not quote anyone else as His source, but sovereignly proclaimed what the passage meant.

§V.3. Christ's Work at Capernaum

§V.3.i. Teaching with Authority

ॐ   ॐ   ॐ   ॐ   ॐ

33 And there was a man in the synagogue having the spirit of an unclean demon, and he cried out with a great voice,

34 "Ah! What concern are we to You, Jesus the Nazarene? Have You come to destroy us? I know who You are—the Holy One of God!"

35 And Jesus rebuked him, saying, "Be muzzled and come out of him!" And when the demon had thrown him down in the midst, he came out from him without having injured him.

36 And astonishment came upon them all, and they were speaking with one another, saying, "What *is* this word? For with authority and power He commands the unclean spirits, and they come out!"

37 And the noise about Him was going out into every place of the surrounding-country.

As the counterpoint to Christ's rejection at Nazareth, Luke relates stories of Christ's success at Capernaum. (The men of Nazareth had heard rumors of this success; see v. 23.)

There was a man in the synagogue having the spirit of an unclean demon. (Luke uses the long phrase **the spirit of an unclean demon** for his Greek readers, who might not necessarily equate "having a spirit" with "having an evil spirit.") When the man saw Christ, the demon within him cried out in fear, **"Ah!"**—a long loud scream, we may imagine. For the demon recognized in the humble rabbi the messianic Judge, and thought that the final Judgment must be at hand and that Jesus had **come to destroy** him (as indeed He will on the Last Day). The demon-possessed man therefore **cried out with a great voice, "What concern are we to You?"** (that is, leave us alone!). In a futile attempt to use his knowledge of Jesus' identity as **the Holy One of God** to fend Him off (for knowledge of someone's name was thought to give power over that person), the demon cried out that he knew who He was.

The demon's protest was useless. **Jesus rebuked him, saying, "Be muzzled and come out of him!"** As a final act of violence, the demon **threw** the man **down in the midst** of the crowd as **he came out from him**. Christ's power to heal was proven to be supreme as the man arose from the floor **without** being **injured** by the demon at all.

As the man arose to new life, **astonishment came upon all** the crowd, and all at once **they were speaking with one another** in an excited babble of amazement. They were asking themselves, **"What *is* this word,"** this command to the demon, this new experience of liberation from evil? Normal Jewish exorcists worked by prayers and incantations, invoking other spirits and using magical texts, but Jesus cast out the demon with a mere word. He simply **commands the unclean spirits, and they come out!** They had never seen such **authority** and **power** before, and **the noise about Him**, the loud buzz of rumor (Gr. *exos*, used in Acts 2:2 to describe the noise of a mighty rushing wind), **was going out into every place of the surrounding-country.**

§V.3.ii. Healing

> ॐ ॐ ॐ ॐ ॐ
>
> 38 And He arose *and left* the synagogue, and entered into Simon's house. Now Simon's mother-in-law was distressed with a great fever; and they asked Him about her.
>
> 39 And standing over her, He rebuked the fever, and it left her; and she immediately arose and was serving them.

Christ was not only able to cast out demons with a word, but to heal also. After the synagogue service, **He arose** from there *and left* with Simon and His other friends and followers **and entered into Simon's house** for the usual post-synagogue Sabbath meal. The womenfolk present would have provided this hospitality for them, including **Simon's mother-in-law**, the lady of the house. She was not present with the others, however, for she was lying down, **distressed with a great fever**. (We note that Luke, as a physician, describes the condition not just as "a fever" as Mark 1:30 does, but as **a great fever**, a high one.) Simon and Andrew his brother asked Him about her, requesting that He heal her. Christ entered her room, and **standing over her, rebuked the fever**, as He had earlier that day rebuked the demon (v. 35), and **it left her**. She was healed so completely that **immediately she arose** from her bed and **was serving them** the meal, with the other womenfolk.

ॐ ॐ ॐ ॐ ॐ

40 And *while* the sun was setting, all who had any ailing with various diseases brought them to Him, and laying His hands *upon* each one of them, He was healing them.

41 And demons also were coming out from many, yelling and saying, "*It is* You *who* are the Son of God!" And rebuking them, He would not allow them to speak, because they knew Him to be the Christ.

42 And when day came, He departed and went into a wilderness place, and the crowds were seeking Him out, and came to Him, and were holding Him back from departing from them.

43 But He said to them, "It is necessary for Me to preach *good news* of the Kingdom of God to the other cities also, for I was sent for this *purpose.*"

44 And He was heralding in the synagogues of Judea.

News of what Christ had done in the synagogue and also in Simon's house had spread throughout the town, and *while* **the sun was setting** (that is, as soon as the Sabbath had ended), **all who had any ailing with various diseases brought them to Him**. And **laying His hands** *upon* **each one of them** (giving them each His individual attention), **He was healing them**.

This laying on of hands was not usual for healing within Judaism. But it was the practice to lay hands upon someone to impart a blessing (compare Mark 10:16), and Christ used this practice to impart healing as well.

His divine authority was confirmed by the **demons** He vanquished also, for they **were coming out from many, yelling** in vain protests of self-defense (compare v. 34) that He was **the Son of God**. Christ was insistent on rebuking such cries, however. He **would not allow** the demons **to speak, because they knew Him to be the Christ**.

Why did Jesus not want His identity as the Christ to become the focal point of His ministry? In that day, men conceived of the Christ (or Messiah) in political terms, as a military revolutionary who would overthrow the might of Rome and create an earthly kingdom. A movement centered on such a political understanding of messiahship would quickly get out of hand and bring reprisals from the Romans before its time. For this reason, Jesus refused to proclaim Himself as Christ to the masses. Until it was understood that His messianic Kingdom was not of this world, such a proclamation was too dangerous.

Early the next day, at dawn, Jesus **departed and went into a wilderness place** beyond the city limits to pray. Rather than seeking the approval of men, He sought the Face of God. But so great was His power that **the crowds were seeking Him out, and came to Him**. By their insistent entreaties, they strove to **hold Him back from departing from them**, wanting Him to remain in His new hometown of Capernaum. Thus Capernaum stands in stark opposition to Nazareth, which drove Him out.

Jesus refused to stay in Capernaum. Rather, **He said to them, "It was necessary** for Him **to preach** *good news* **of the Kingdom**

of God to the other cities also, for He **was sent for this** *purpose.*"
Jesus was intent only on fulfilling the will of the Father. Thus He
left Capernaum for a tour of the entire Roman province of **Judea**
(which included Galilee), and **was heralding** God's message **in the
synagogues.**

§V.4. The Call of Simon with James and John

From the parallel account in Mark 1:16f, it would seem that this
call of Simon with his partners occurred earlier than the rejection
at Nazareth narrated in 4:16–30. I suggest that Luke chose to relate
first the story of Christ's rejection at Nazareth (with the story of
contrasting acceptance in Capernaum), thereby deferring the story
of the call of Simon until this point for didactic reasons—for Luke
wanted to stress how the entire ministry of Jesus took place under the
shadow of rejection, in order to show more clearly the inevitability
of His final rejection by Israel at the Cross.

ॐ ॐ ॐ ॐ ॐ

5 1 Now it happened that while the crowd was
pressing upon Him and hearing the Word
of God, He was standing beside the lake of
Gennesaret;

2 and He saw two boats standing beside the lake,
but the fishermen had gotten out from them
and were washing the nets.

3 And He got into one of the boats, which was
Simon's, and asked him to put out a little from
the land. And He sat and was teaching the
crowds from the boat.

4 And when He had stopped speaking, He said
to Simon, "Put out into the deep and let down
your nets for a catch."

5 And Simon answered and said, "Master, we
toiled through the whole night and have taken

nothing. But at Your word, I will let down
the nets."

6   And when they had done this, they enclosed
a great multitude of fish, and their nets were
tearing,

7   and they gestured out to their partners in the
other boat for them to come to help them. And
they came and filled both the boats, so that they
began to sink.

8   But when Simon Peter saw it, he fell down at
Jesus' knees, saying, "Depart from me, for I am
a sinful man, O Lord!"

9   For astonishment had seized him and all those
with him at the catch of fish which they had
taken,

10 and likewise also James and John, sons of Zebedee, who were partners with Simon. And Jesus
said to Simon, "Do not be afraid; from now on
you will be catching men."

11 And having brought their boats to land, they
left everything and followed Him.

The story of the call of Simon is enlarged when seen within the
context of its parallels in Mark 1:16–20 and Matt. 4:18–22, as well
as in the context of our awareness of Christ's previous relationship
with Simon and his friends in John 1:35—2:11. From these sources
we learn that Jesus had spent much time with Simon, Andrew, James,
and John prior to the events of 5:1–11. They had become Jesus' disciples before (see John 1:35–42; 2:2), in the sense of spending time
with Him to learn from Him as their Teacher. They remained with
their families and worked to support them, but they had committed
themselves to following His teaching, even as Andrew had followed
John the Baptizer's teaching (John 1:35–36, 40).

Now it would seem that Christ was calling them to a longer
and more permanent discipleship, one that involved leaving their
livelihood permanently, and even leaving their families for a time to

follow Him in His journeys throughout Galilee and Judea. To this end, He found Simon and Andrew by the sea of Galilee. They had fished with the dragnet in the deep waters all night and had caught nothing (5:5). Now they were casting the smaller circle-net in the shallow waters near the shore, trying their luck with that (Mark 1:16). James and John were not far away, **washing** and restoring their **nets** after the night's work (Mark 1:19; Luke 5:2).

Christ was preaching to the gathering crowds and once again wanted their help, in particular, because **the crowd was pressing upon Him** and gathering in increasing numbers. Christ was **standing beside the lake**, and **He saw** His disciples' **two boats standing beside the lake** (Luke uses the same verbs and prepositions to describe both Christ and the boats). The answer was obvious: He could use one of the boats to sit in a little way out from the shore while He preached to the crowds.

By calling the disciples away from their fishing in this way, Christ was calling them to give up their livelihood and families to join Him in His work. Thus He challenged them to come after Him, and He would make them into fishers of men (Mark 1:17, 20). They were reluctant to follow such a radical challenge at that time. Perhaps they wondered how their families could be cared for financially if they followed His call to leave all and follow Him. But they were happy enough to lend Him the use of the boat for the morning.

So it was that **He got into one of the boats**, the one **which was Simon's, and asked him to put out a little from the land**. After Simon did so, Jesus **sat** (the normal posture for teaching), and all that morning **was teaching the crowds from the boat**, speaking the **Word** and message **of God** to them (v. 1).

After **He had stopped speaking**, and the crowds were dispersing, **He said to Simon, "Put out into the deep and let down your nets for a catch."** Perhaps Simon had protested that he couldn't leave his family to follow Jesus because of financial necessity—look, even last night's work was a complete waste! Surely Jesus could see that he couldn't leave his family like this! It was perhaps in response to this that Jesus told Simon to let down his nets for a catch.

This was, Simon felt sure, a fool's errand. Every fisherman knew that the best time for fishing in the deep was at night. If they hadn't caught anything then, they certainly wouldn't catch anything now! Simon protested to his **Master** that he had already **toiled** hard **through the whole night and taken** absolutely **nothing**. Why this wasted effort? They were tired, having fished all night and listened to Jesus' words all morning. Why not just give up and go to bed? Perhaps there was something in Jesus' look that made Simon trust His word. Anyway, **at** His **word**, he **let down the nets** one more time.

As soon as they **had done this, they enclosed a great multitude of fish**—so great that **their nets were tearing**, and to save them they needed help. **They gestured out** wildly **to their partners in the other boat** (perhaps pulled up on the beach?) **to come to help them** pull in the nets. **They came and filled** not just Simon's boat, but **both the boats**—so much so that **they *began* to sink**!

When Simon Peter saw it, **astonishment seized him**, and he knew he was cornered. (Luke uses the full apostolic name **Simon Peter** to show how this was Simon's final acceptance of his apostolic calling.) The poor fisherman still felt himself unequal to the task to which Jesus was calling him, and in desperation **he fell down at Jesus' knees** (the fish spilling over his ankles), **saying, "Depart from me, for I am a sinful man, O Lord!"** That is, he felt sure that Christ was looking for holy men, for heroes, for saints—not for him. When confronted with the divine majesty of Christ's miracle closing about him, Simon knew himself to be a man of unclean lips, one who dwelt in the midst of a people of unclean lips (compare Is. 6:5). He was no better than anyone else. Surely Jesus didn't want him! Let Him depart, leave him alone, and find someone more worthy!

Simon did not know that it was God's will to reveal the fishermen of the earth as most wise (see the troparion for Pentecost). Christ assured Simon that He would make him equal to his calling. Simon Peter should **not be afraid**—Christ had called him to become a fisher of men (Mark 1:17), and **from now on**, he would indeed **be catching men**.

So it was that **having brought their boats to land** (and distributed the money for the catch to their families?), Simon Peter and his companions **left everything and followed Him** (Mark 1:18, 20).

Though all of them followed Him, Luke's emphasis throughout has been on Simon, as the head of the apostolic band (compare Luke's emphasis on Simon in 22:31). Luke emphasizes Simon's call, and devotes more space to it than either Matthew or Mark did, because for Luke Simon is an image of discipleship. By seeing Simon's conversion, the inquirer may see the commitment required of all.

§V.5. Cleansing of a Leper

ॐ ॐ ॐ ॐ ॐ

12 And it happened that while He was in one of the cities, behold, a man full of leprosy! And having seen Jesus, he fell upon *his* face and besought Him, saying, "Lord, if You are willing, You can cleanse me."

13 And having stretched out His hand, He touched him, saying, "I am willing; be cleansed." And immediately the leprosy went away from him.

14 And He ordered him to tell no one, "But go away and show yourself to the priest, and offer for your cleansing, as Moses commanded, for a witness to them."

15 But the word about Him was going through *the region* even farther, and many crowds were gathering to hear *Him* and to be healed of their ailments.

16 But He would withdraw to the wilderness and pray.

St. Luke then narrates the story of how Christ cleansed a leper. Luke does not place this with any precision, though from the parallel in Matt. 8:1–4 we learn that it occurred after Christ descended from the mountain after a time of teaching. It also occurred **while Jesus was in one of the cities**—that is, the leper entered the city to find Jesus, so desperate was he to be healed. (Lepers were commanded in the Law to stay removed from people, lest they spread their contagion; Lev. 13:45–46.)

Luke gives this miracle story pride of place by relating it as the first miracle after Christ's initial entry into Capernaum and its area. The healing of leprosy was a demonstration of divine power. The term "leprosy" referred to any number of infectious skin diseases, but all of them meant disaster for the sufferer. A leper was driven from common society, doomed to a life of isolation and poverty, far from human warmth and family, cut off from the worship of Temple and synagogue. It was a kind of living death—and a fitting image for the sin that afflicts all the human race. No human being could heal such a scourge; when Naaman the Syrian was sent to Israel's king to be healed of his leprosy, the king cried out, "Am I God, that this man is asking me to cure a man of his leprosy?" (2 Kin. 5:7). Only God could cure the leper.

The afflicted man is described with medical precision as being **full of leprosy**. Having found Jesus (of whom he had heard so much), **he fell upon *his* face** before Him, making a full prostration as a kind of silent supplication. Rising no further than his knees, **he besought Him, saying** only, **"Lord, if You are willing, You can cleanse me."** The Lord **stretched out His hand** and **touched him**.

We must not miss the significance of this touch, for one did not touch lepers. If one did, one was made ceremonially unclean and risked physical contamination also. But the Lord's love and power were stronger than that living death.

As the Lord touched him, He did not pray a long prayer, but uttered just a few words: **"I am willing; be cleansed."** (In the Greek translation, this is but two words—*thelo, katharistheti*.) At this brief utterance, immediately the leprosy went away from him, and the man was cleansed. The Lord, however, did not want any more publicity, for already it was becoming difficult to enter the towns because of the crowds. He therefore **ordered him to tell no one** who had healed him. Rather, the former leper was ordered to **go away and show** himself **to the priest**, to be certified as clean, and then to **offer** a sacrifice **for** his **cleansing, as Moses commanded** in Leviticus 14:2f. This obedience to the Law was required not because Christ regarded Himself as under the Law, but simply **for a witness to** the Jews that the man had actually been healed.

The word about Jesus and His works could not be silenced, however, but **was going through *the region* even farther**. (From Mark 1:45 we learn that the man did not obey Christ's order to keep quiet about the miracle.) The result was that **many crowds were gathering to hear *Him* and to be healed of their ailments**.

When the bustle was at its worst, Christ would **withdraw to the wilderness**, to the places where He could be alone, **and pray**. Prayer is for Luke the hallmark of holiness, and so Christ is presented as a man of prayer. And if the Son of God needed to pray in solitude, how much more do we need to do so!

§V.6. Conflict with the Pharisees

St. Luke relates a series of stories showing Christ's continual conflict with the Pharisees, all of which constitute a gathering storm that will finally culminate in the Cross. The Pharisees were a lay brotherhood dedicated to the zealous keeping of the Law, as interpreted through the "tradition of the elders," or oral law interpretations current in their day. They were strict in keeping these minute regulations, and judgmental of others who were not as strict. Not surprisingly, they mostly rejected the call of John to repent of self-righteousness, and having rejected the Forerunner, they were set to reject Christ Himself also.

§V.6.i. Forgiving the Sins of the Paralytic

ॐ ॐ ॐ ॐ ॐ

17 And it happened on one of *those* days that He was teaching; and there were Pharisees and teachers of the Law sitting *there*, who had come from every village of Galilee and Judea and *from* Jerusalem; and the power of the Lord was in Him to cure.

18 And behold, men carrying upon a bed a man who was paralyzed! And they were seeking to bring him in and place him before Him.

19 And not finding how to bring him in because of the crowd, they went up on the roof and let him down through the tiles with his bed into the midst, before Jesus.

20 And seeing their faith He said, "Man, your sins are forgiven you."

21 And the scribes and the Pharisees began to question, saying, "Who is this one who speaks blasphemies? Who can forgive sins but God alone?"

22 But Jesus, having really-known their questionings, answered and said to them, "Why are you questioning in your hearts?

23 "Which is easier: to say, 'Your sins have been forgiven you,' or to say, 'Rise and walk'?

24 "But that you may know that the Son of Man has authority on the earth to forgive sins"—He said to the one who was paralyzed—"I say to you, rise, and take up your bed, and go to your house."

25 And immediately he arose before them, and took up that on which he was lying, and went away to his house, glorifying God.

26 And everyone was seized with alarm and *began* glorifying God; and they were filled with fear, saying, "We have seen baffling *things* today!"

The first conflict story involves Christ's claim to have authority from God to forgive sins. **On one of *those* days**, Jesus **was teaching** in a house (probably Simon's), and **there were Pharisees and teachers of the Law sitting *there*** also, listening to His instruction (to judge it). Luke stresses that this was a representative group, whose attitudes typified those of the Pharisees and scribes generally, since they **had come from every village of Galilee and Judea and *from* Jerusalem**. Not only were they present, but **the power of the Lord** God which **was in** Jesus **to cure** was also present that day, making a conflict all but inevitable. (No doubt many others had been healed earlier that morning.)

Into this room, **behold**! (the word is used by Luke to indicate how unexpected this was), **men** came **carrying upon a bed a man who was paralyzed**. **They were seeking** to bring their paralyzed friend into Jesus' presence and **place him before Him** to be healed. The great crowd surrounding the house made this impossible—a single man could scarcely squeeze through such a multitude, let alone four men carrying another on a pallet or light mattress.

These refused to give up. They **went up on the roof** (the roofs of those houses were flat and accessible by exterior steps), removed the tiles, and **let him down with his bed** or stretcher **into the midst** of the crowd, setting him **before Jesus**.

Seeing their faith, Jesus said to the afflicted one, **"Man, your sins are forgiven you."** The term **man** is a title of courtesy and formality, corresponding to our modern title "sir" (like "woman," used in John 2:4; 19:26, which corresponds to our modern title "madam"). That is, Jesus treated the poor abased man with dignity, even though he was a sinner and in need of forgiveness.

And the man did need forgiveness. The insight of those days was that healing for the body is bound up with forgiveness for the soul, since a man is a compound of both. It may not be the case in every instance that a specific sickness is caused by a specific sin. But in general, sickness afflicts humanity because humanity is sinful and fallen, and to be fully whole, human beings need both forgiveness and healing. With His divine insight, Christ knew that this man particularly needed forgiveness, and so He brought him pardon as the preparation for physical healing.

The scribes and the Pharisees, however, were aghast at the authority claimed in this utterance. For Christ was claiming to have the authority to pronounce that, on the Day of Judgment, God would not require an accounting of this sin, but would then deem it forgiven. Who was Jesus, a man on earth, to speak for God in heaven, and thus usurp an authority which was God's alone? **Who is this one**, this carpenter, **who speaks blasphemies?**

Jesus had sure knowledge of their secret reasonings and doubts.

He **really-knew** (Gr. *epiginosko*, a stronger verb than *ginosko*, "to know") their inner questionings, and He answered them, **"Why are you questioning in your hearts?"** Why did they doubt Him and reject His authority so quickly? For **which is easier: to say** the words **'Your sins have been forgiven,'** or to say the words, **'Rise and walk'?** They had to admit that both were equally impossible for mere men on earth. Such men could not forgive sins—but neither could they heal a paralytic by saying a few words. But let them **know that the Son of Man had authority on the earth to forgive sins**!

Here Jesus said **to the one who was paralyzed, "I say to you, rise, and take up your bed, and go to your house."** In response, the paralytic **immediately arose before them all**, and obediently **took up that on which he was lying, and went away to his house**, all the while **glorifying God** with loud shouts. The crowd as a whole joined him in these shouts, as they *began* **glorifying God. Everyone** present (even the Pharisees) was **seized with alarm** at such a naked display of divine power. They were **filled with fear** at such a spectacle and confessed they had **seen baffling** *things* **today**.

The word translated *baffling* is the Greek *paradoxos*, from which the English word "paradox" is derived. It means "contrary to opinion or expectation." It seemed impossible to everyone that men on earth could share God's heavenly authority in such a palpable fashion. How indeed could a man forgive sins and presume to act in God's place? And yet here it was so. The Incarnation thus proves itself baffling to fallen religious wisdom, leaving the philosophical orators as "voiceless as fish" (from the Akathist hymn).

§V.6.ii. Call of Levi and Fellowship with Tax-collectors

ॐ ॐ ॐ ॐ ॐ

27 And after these things He went out, and beheld a tax-collector named Levi sitting at the tax-table, and He said to him, "Follow Me."

28 And he left everything behind, and arose and followed Him.

29 And Levi gave a great reception for Him in his

> house; and there was a big crowd of tax-collectors and others who were reclining with them.
> 30 And the Pharisees and their scribes were grumbling against His disciples, saying, "Why do you eat and drink with tax-collectors and sinners?"
> 31 And Jesus answered and said to them, "Those who are healthy have no need of a physician, but those who are sick.
> 32 "I have not come to call the righteous, but sinners to repentance."

The story of the call of the **tax-collector named Levi** is told with a minimum of detail. Levi (called Matthew in Matt. 9:9) had doubtless heard of Jesus before that day. But Levi was a tax-collector, one who sat at his **tax-table** as a customs officer, collecting toll taxes from merchants traveling over roads or bridges. As such, he was shunned by respectable people and detested for the corruption which was proverbial in tax-collectors. He probably assumed that the wonder-working rabbi would want little to do with him.

It was all the more shocking when Christ **beheld** him and came over to speak with him. The word rendered *beheld* is the Greek *theaomai*, which means "to fix one's gaze upon something." Christ did not simply notice Levi in passing; He stared at him, reading his secret heart—and his secret desire to break free from his old life. Coming up to his tax-table, **He said to him, "Follow Me."** Hearing this call to be forgiven and to follow the famous rabbi into the adventure of a new life, Levi **left everything behind, and arose and followed Him**. When he left his tax-table that day, he also left behind all his past life, and began a new life as Christ's disciple.

So great was Levi's joy in being accepted just as he was and being given this new chance that he **gave a great reception** for Jesus **in his house**. Levi invited the only people he knew and who would come to his house—that is, **tax-collectors and other** immoral people. There was thus **a big crowd** of them in his house who **were reclining** at table **with** Levi and Jesus (such feasts were taken while reclining on couches, in the Roman manner).

To eat with someone and accept their hospitality in that day meant to accept *them*. The respectable people like **the Pharisees and their scribes** would never accept such sinners. They were scandalized that Jesus would eat with such riffraff—and made no secret of it. At some point (perhaps the next day after the feast), they **were grumbling against** Jesus' **disciples, saying, "Why do you eat and drink with tax-collectors and sinners?"** If the disciples claimed to be pious and to teach God's Law, how could they lower themselves to be friends with such people? (In using the word *grumble*— Gr. *gogguzo*—Luke evokes echoes of Israel's grumbling at God in the wilderness; Num. 14:27 LXX.)

Although they addressed Jesus' disciples and not Jesus Himself, the Lord answered them. In His compassion and desire to reclaim the Pharisees too, He did not rebuke their judgmentalism. Rather, He strove to help them see the situation from a new perspective, saying, **"Those who are healthy have no need of a physician, but those who are sick."** Granted, the tax-collectors and sinners were spiritually sick—that was exactly why Jesus went to them! The physician obviously goes to the homes of **the sick** and surrounds himself with their sickness—that is his job. The physician does not confine himself to visiting the **healthy**, for such **have no need** of his visits. In the same way, Christ **did not come to call the righteous** and confine Himself to visiting them. He came to call and visit **sinners**—only thus could He call them **to repentance**.

§V.6.iii. Conflict over Fasting

> ৩৯ ৩৯ ৩৯ ৩৯ ৩৯
>
> 33 And they said to Him, "The disciples of John
>   often fast and make supplications; the *disciples*
>   of the Pharisees also *do* likewise, but Yours eat
>   and drink."
> 34 And Jesus said to them, "Can you make the sons
>   of the bridal-chamber fast while the bridegroom
>   is with them?
> 35 "But *the* days also will come; and when the

> bridegroom is taken away from them, then they
> will fast in those days."

The respectable people there had another complaint as well: **"The disciples of John** the Baptizer **often fast and make supplications**, interceding for Israel; and those who follow the examples of **the Pharisees also *do* likewise, but Your** disciples **eat and drink."** (From Matt. 9:14, we learn that some who followed John's teaching had joined this crowd of perplexed piety and wanted an explanation.) The joining together of **the disciples of John** with **the *disciples* of the Pharisees** is significant. From such passages as 7:30 and Matthew 3:7, we conclude that these two groups did not have much in common. Their agreement about anything—such as the necessity of weekly fasting—made our Lord's apparent disregard for it all the more puzzling.

The pious in Israel indeed fasted twice a week, on Mondays and Thursdays. On those days, they ate nothing until evening. It seems that Levi's feast took place on one of those days, so that Jesus and His disciples were breaking one of the Jewish "canons." This was, to them, clearly wrong—all religious people kept such customs; how could Jesus so easily overthrow such conventions of piety? To these people who stumbled at Jesus' feasting, true piety was inflexible piety—what mattered was the rules.

Jesus did not rule out fasting. But He did not fast inflexibly. Rather, He subordinated conformity to rules and canons to responsiveness to human need and God-given opportunity. God was calling Him to bring Levi and his friends into the Kingdom, and that meant taking this opportunity and receiving their hospitality, even if it was a fast day.

Even they could see how fasting must give way before something more important—such as a wedding. In those days, the wedding feast would go on for seven days. Even though it might be a Monday or a Thursday, they obviously could not **make the sons of the bridal-chamber** (the technical term for the wedding guests) **fast while the bridegroom was with them**. Such fasting would have been a great insult to the bride and groom. While the joyful wedding feast went on, fasting was suspended for the wedding guests. So it was with the joyful matter of recovering sinners—fasting was suspended for that day.

The Lord then continues with a grim irony not understood at that time—and only later understood in light of the Cross. They must not worry—His disciples would fast soon enough! **The days** of mourning **will also come**, the time when the wedding party will be over and **the bridegroom is taken away from them. They will fast** enough **in those days**! In terms of the parable, this meant, "One cannot fast until the party ends." But in light of the Cross, it also meant, "The time of lightheartedness will end with My death—then will come the time for fasting."

> ৠ ৠ ৠ ৠ ৠ
>
> 36 And He was also telling them a parable: "No one splits a patch from a new garment *and* puts it on an old garment; otherwise both the new *garment* will split, and the patch from the new will not match the old.
> 37 "And no one puts new wine into old skins; otherwise the new wine will tear the skins, and it will be spilled, and the skins will be destroyed.
> 38 "But new wine must be put into fresh skins.
> 39 "And no one, after drinking old *wine,* wants new *wine*; for he says, 'The old is good.'"

As usual, the Lord clinched His teaching by **also telling them a parable**, a visual image. **No one splits a patch from a new garment** *and* **puts it on an old garment**. That was stupid for two reasons: it both **split** and ruined **the new *garment*** from which the patch was torn off, and furthermore, that **patch from the new** garment **will not match the old** one onto which it is sewn. That is, when the patched garment was washed the next time, the new patch would shrink and tear away from the old already shrunk garment, leaving a worse hole. Thus there would be two ruined garments. In the same way, the new Kingdom requires new ways of piety and a new flexibility. One cannot inherit the Kingdom while clinging to old inflexible ways.

It is the same with new wine. **No one puts new wine into old skins**. The old wineskins are tough and leathery, with no stretchable "give" to them. If one puts freshly fermented **new wine** into them, the wine will expand too much for the skins and will burst and **tear the skins**. The wine **will be spilled** and lost, **and the skins will be destroyed** too. **New wine must be put into fresh** and stretchable **skins** to avoid this catastrophe. Once again, one cannot combine the new with the old.

Christ concludes with a wry comment about the difficulty of accepting such flexibility and change: **no one, after drinking old *wine*, wants new *wine*; for he says, 'The old is good** enough.'" That is, such a one thinks the old wine goes down smoothly enough. He is complacent and reluctant to leave what he knows. No new vintage for him! In the same way, the Pharisees were like rigid old men who will miss out on the new wine and the inebriating joy of the Kingdom. Just try to change their mind!

§V.6.iv. Conflict over the Sabbath

ॐ ॐ ॐ ॐ ॐ

6 1 Now it happened that on a Sabbath He was passing through grain fields, and His disciples were picking and eating the heads, rubbing them in *their* hands.

2 But some of the Pharisees said, "Why do you do what is not permitted on the Sabbaths?"

3 And Jesus answering them said, "Have you not read this, what David did when he was hungry, he and the ones with him,

4 "how he entered the House of God, and took and ate the Bread of the Presentation, which is not permitted to be eaten except by the priests alone, and gave it to those with him?"

> 5   And He was saying to them, "The Son of Man
>   is Lord of the Sabbath."

Having related conflict with the Pharisees over the matter of His
authority to forgive sins (5:21), His eating with sinners (5:30), and
His occasional disregard for fasting rules (5:33), Luke now relates
two stories of conflict with them over the Sabbath.

The Sabbath was pivotal to Jewish piety, and the Pharisees
followed a series of complex regulations regarding what was and
was not allowed on that day. The Law simply forbade work on the
Sabbath (Ex. 20:8–11), but the Pharisees had elaborately detailed
rules regarding what constituted work, and it was these secondary
elaborations of the Law that Christ broke.

Thus **it happened that on a Sabbath** Jesus and His disciples
were **passing through grain fields, and His disciples were picking and eating the heads** of grain as they walked, **rubbing them
in *their* hands** to remove the chaff. The casual eating of grain by
travelers in this way was allowed by the Law (Deut. 23:25). But to
the Pharisees, the disciples were **doing what was not permitted on
the Sabbaths**—by picking the heads, the disciples were harvesting;
by rubbing them in their hands, they were threshing; by blowing
the chaff away, they were winnowing. That is, they were doing no
less than three kinds of work on the Sabbath and thereby provoking
God's anger.

When the Pharisees challenged the disciples, the Lord stepped
in to defend them. **Answering them**, Jesus said, **"Have you not
read this, what David did when he was hungry, he and the ones
with him, how he entered the House of God, and took and ate
the Bread of the Presentation, which is not permitted to be
eaten except by the priests alone**? Not only did David eat what
was technically forbidden by the Law (Lev. 24:9), he also **gave it to
those with him**!"

Christ was referring to the story in 1 Samuel 21, when David
was fleeing from Saul. Hungry and in need, David had no choice
but to eat the only bread available, the Bread of the Presentation,
the twelve loaves of the Showbread which were set out in the Holy

Place every day. This proved that cultic details of the Law (such as work restrictions on the Sabbath) were to give way before human need. Meeting human need was at the heart of the Law, and by the Pharisees' fixation on inflexible rules, they showed that they had no understanding of what the Law was really about—including the Sabbath.

In the course of His reply to them, Christ **was saying to them, "The Son of Man is Lord of** that **Sabbath."** The Pharisees were blind to the true purpose of the Sabbath and how to keep it. But they were blind also to something greater: the authority of Christ. As the Messiah and Lord of men, He was **Lord of the Sabbath** as well, and had the authority to pronounce what was or was not allowed on it.

This was a breathtaking claim, for only God was Lord of the Sabbath, since He was the One who gave it to Israel. In claiming to be the Sabbath's Lord, Jesus was again claiming divine authority.

§V.6.v. Conflict over Healing in the Synagogue on the Sabbath

ॐ ॐ ॐ ॐ ॐ

6   And it happened on another Sabbath that He entered into the synagogue and was teaching; and there was a man there whose right hand was withered.

7   And the scribes and the Pharisees were keeping *watch* on Him, if He healed on the Sabbath, that they might find *reason* to accuse Him.

8   But He knew their questionings, and He said to the man having the withered hand, "Rise and stand in the midst!" And he rose and stood in the midst.

9   And Jesus said to them, "I ask you, is it permitted on the Sabbath to do good, or to do bad, to save a life, or to destroy *it*?"

10 And after looking around on them all, He said

> to him, "Stretch out your hand!" And he did
> *it*, and his hand was restored.
> 11 But they themselves were filled with folly and
> talked together with one another *about* what
> they might do to Jesus.

Luke presents one final conflict with the Pharisees, another battle over the Sabbath. He presents this as the culmination of the conflict, for after this conflict Jesus' foes gathered together to plan how to destroy Him (v. 11).

This conflict **happened on another Sabbath**. Jesus **entered into the synagogue** (probably in the town of Capernaum) **and was teaching. There was a man there whose right hand was withered**, paralyzed and useless. (Luke, with the eye of a physician, notes that it was the man's **right** hand, the one most needed for any work.) This man, it would seem, was well-known to all the locals, perhaps because he had made known his desire to be healed by Jesus. The man's mere presence in the synagogue was a standing invitation to Jesus to heal, and **the scribes and the Pharisees were keeping** *watch* **on Him** to see **if He healed on the Sabbath, that they might find** *reason* **to accuse Him**. Knowing Jesus' rejection of their Pharisaical regulations, they thought such a healing likely. Jesus Himself **knew their** internal **questionings** and their malevolent thoughts, and He was not cowed by them.

Doubtless all in the synagogue that morning had their eyes keenly fixed on Jesus, waiting breathlessly to see what He would do. They did not have to wait long. Jesus **said to the man having the withered hand, "Rise and stand in the midst!"** Obediently, the man **rose and stood in the midst**, coming forward to the front of the synagogue where the Lord was. The battle lines were drawn. The man stood beside Jesus, finding himself also the target of the bitter stares of the Pharisees. The Pharisees remained in their haughty and inflexible pride, taking their stand (as they thought) on God's Law.

Ignoring the stares of His adversaries, Jesus asked the crowd a question: **"Is it permitted on the Sabbath to do good, or to do bad, to save a life, or to destroy *it*?"** Let the assembled synagogue give a ruling on this legal question, and say which of the two courses of action now available to Him on this Sabbath was the best way to honor the day—by doing a good deed, saving life and restoring health, or by evildoing, leaving a man in his suffering. The question was not whether or not the afflicted man should wait. The question was, the man having made his request, what was the Sabbath-honoring way to proceed?

No reply is given: the crowd either agreed with the Pharisees or lacked the courage to voice their disagreement with them. The Lord **looked around on them all**, doubtless grieved at their hardhearted refusal to stand with their afflicted townsman in his hour of need. Turning from the crowd, **He said to** the man, **"Stretch out your hand!"** And the man **did *it*, and his hand was restored**.

The crowd's reaction is likewise not recorded by Luke. But the response of **the scribes and the Pharisees** is recorded (for that is the intended antecedent subject of v. 11). They were **filled with folly and talked together with one another** from that day on, trying to find **what they might do to Jesus**.

The word translated *folly* is the Greek *anoia*; it is used in 2 Timothy 3:9, where it is also translated "foolishness." The thought is that of the godless who are filled with senseless and foolish fury. As the Scripture said, "A man's folly brings his way to ruin, and his heart rages against the Lord" (Prov. 19:3). In the same way, Christ's adversaries were beside themselves with senseless wrath, their folly manifesting itself in their plots against the Lord.

§V. 7. Choice of the Twelve and the Sermon to All the Disciples

ॐ ॐ ॐ ॐ ॐ

12 And it happened in these days that He went out to the mountain to pray, and He spent the night in prayer to God.

13 And when day came, He called His disciples to Him and chose twelve from them, whom He also named apostles:

> 14 Simon, whom He also named Peter, and
> Andrew his brother; and James and John; and
> Philip and Bartholomew;
> 15 and Matthew and Thomas; James *the son
> of* Alphaeus, and Simon who was called *the*
> Zealot;
> 16 Judas *the son of* James, and Judas Iscariot, who
> became a traitor.

In these early **days**, Jesus escaped from the teeming crowds that followed Him and **went out to the mountain to pray, and spent the night in prayer to God**. Jesus often slipped away from the multitudes to pray (5:16), but here He spends the entire night in prayer to God, presumably for guidance about His next move in choosing the Twelve. Which men were to be chosen to be the Twelve was crucial, and that was why Christ **spent the** whole **night in prayer** before making His choice.

After His all-night vigil, **when** the next **day came**, Jesus **called His disciples to Him** to join Him on the mountain. We do not know how large a crowd this was, but we are reminded of the nucleus of 120 who remained with Peter and the others after the Ascension (Acts 1:15). Out of such a crowd of committed disciples, Christ **chose twelve**. The number **twelve** is significant. Just as the people of Israel had its genesis in the twelve patriarchs, so Christ's new and messianic Israel would find its source in these twelve men. In choosing twelve to be His official representatives and ambassadors, Christ was laying the foundation for Israel's total renovation and renewal. His followers were not to be just another movement within Israel. Rather, they were to constitute the leaven that would change all of Israel completely. The old Israel, based on race and lineage, must die, to be reborn as an Israel of the Spirit. That the apostles were twelve in number is a promise of that future rebirth.

He **also named them apostles**. The concept of *apostle* is rooted in the Jewish concept of the ambassador (Heb. *shaliach*, or "sent one"). It was to these men especially that Christ would commit His teaching and later give His authority as rulers of His Church.

In stressing that Christ **went out to the mountain to pray** (and not to just any wilderness place, as in 5:16), Luke perhaps intends to draw a parallel to Moses. Moses ascended Mount Sinai for communion with God and then called Aaron to join him as his colleague (Ex. 19:20–24); Christ now ascends the mountain and then chooses twelve to join Him in His work.

Luke then gives the list of the Twelve, drawn it would seem from an already existing list, since he refers to Levi (mentioned in 5:27f) as **Matthew**, the name he was later known by in the Church.

First comes **Simon**, since he was leader of the apostolic band, with the comment that Jesus **also named** him **Peter**. He is paired with **Andrew his brother**, perhaps for ease of remembering (in Mark's list, Andrew comes after Peter, James, and John; Mark 3:16–18). Next come the other brothers **James and John**, the sons of Zebedee, mentioned in 5:10 as partners with Simon. Together with Simon Peter, the Zebedee brothers formed a kind of inner circle among the Twelve (compare 8:51; 9:28).

Philip and Bartholomew come next. Philip was an early follower of Christ (see John 1:43); Bartholomew was also known as Nathanael in John's Gospel. (The synoptic Gospels mention Bartholomew but not Nathanael, while John's Gospel mentions Nathanael but not Bartholomew. Nathanael was Philip's friend and also an early disciple [John 1:45]; he was also present at the resurrection appearances of Christ to His apostles [John 21:2]. It would seem therefore that this one man was known by both names.)

Next come **Matthew and Thomas**, then **James *the* son *of* Alphaeus**. This last is in Luke's list paired with **Simon who was called *the* Zealot**. The term "zealot" means "fervent one" (as in English), but came to be the technical term for a Jewish party of men who advocated the violent and revolutionary overthrow of Roman power in Palestine. It would seem that Simon was from this party (though perhaps the name "Zealot" came to be widely used for the group after this time). In joining Jesus' movement, Simon was repudiating one of the main principles of his former revolutionary comrades.

Last comes the pair of **Judas *the son of* James** and **Judas Iscariot**.

(Perhaps they are paired in this list because of the coincidence of their names.) Judas the son of James answers to Thaddaeus in Mark's list (Mark 3:18). It is possible that Judas was his actual name, but that Thaddaeus (from the Greek Theudas?) was the preferred nickname. Judas Iscariot comes last, since he was the one **who became a traitor**. At present, his treachery was not a part of him, and he was numbered with the others as one of the Twelve. The presence of a future traitor among the Twelve is a lesson to all, challenging us to persevere in our faith until the end. Betrayal and apostasy always remain dreadful possibilities; for this reason we are bidden to pray every Liturgy that we may remain faithful and not give to Christ the kiss that Judas did.

ॐ ॐ ॐ ॐ ॐ

17 And He came down with them and stood on a level place; and *there was* a great crowd of His disciples, and a great multitude of people from all Judea and Jerusalem and the seacoast of Tyre and Sidon,

18 who had come to hear Him and to be cured of their diseases; and those who were troubled with unclean spirits were being healed.

19 And all the crowd was seeking to touch Him, for power was coming out from Him and curing everyone.

After this, Christ **came down with** the Twelve, perhaps after remaining with them for a few hours while those not chosen to be among the Twelve went away. Regardless of the time spent on the mountain with the Twelve, Christ descended from the height and **stood on a level place** on the hillside, where He could address **a great crowd of His disciples**. (In Matt. 5:1f, this descent is not mentioned, for Matthew is concerned to stress the mountainous locale of the sermon that follows, perhaps to show how Christ's teaching parallels the words God gave on Mount Sinai. The teaching was indeed given from a mountain or hill, though on the lower slopes.)

The crowd of followers that awaited Jesus' descent was a large one. They had followed Him when He withdrew to the sea as well (Mark 3:7–8), and they came **from all** the province of **Judea**, including **Jerusalem**. (We note in passing Luke's special interest in the Holy City.) They also came **from the seacoast of Tyre and Sidon**, the pagan area to the north. That is, they converged on Him from throughout Israel and beyond, **to hear Him and to be cured of their diseases**, a great throng of hungry hearts and sick bodies. Not only the sick, but also worse yet, **those who were troubled with unclean spirits**. These also **were being healed** after Christ descended with the apostles to teach and heal, proclaiming the Kingdom by word and deed. Indeed, **all** that **crowd was seeking to touch Him, for** divine **power was coming out from Him and curing everyone**. Luke gives us a picture of God's Kingdom being manifested among men—a picture and prophecy of the future work of the apostolic Church.

༃ ༃ ༃ ༃ ༃

20 And He lifted up His eyes to His disciples, and was saying, "Blessed *are you who are* poor, for yours is the Kingdom of God.

21 "Blessed *are you who* are hungry now, for you will be fed *to the full*. Blessed *are you who* weep now, for you will laugh.

22 "Blessed are you when men hate you, and separate you *from themselves*, and reproach you, and cast out your name as evil, because of the Son of Man.

23 "Rejoice in that day, and leap, for behold! Your reward is great in heaven, for their fathers were doing the same things to the prophets.

24 "But woe to you *who are* rich, for you are receiving *in full* your comfort!

25 "Woe to you *who are* filled now, for you will hunger! Woe, you who laugh now, for you will mourn and weep!

> **26** "Woe, when all men speak well of you!—for
> their fathers were doing the same things to the
> false-prophets.

Luke now gives an example of the teaching Jesus gave to His disciples, and how He challenged them to live differently from those in the world. He begins by saying that Jesus **lifted up** (Gr. *epairo*) **His eyes to His disciples**. This is significant, and means more than that Jesus looked at the great crowd of His followers before He began speaking to them (which would in any case be assumed). The feeling is one of Jesus lifting up His eyes to them in beneficence, as a prelude to blessing. The feel is the same as that of the priestly blessing in Numbers 6:22–26 LXX, where the Lord is asked to lift up (Gr. *epairo*) His face upon His people and give them peace.

The Lord's teaching begins with a series of benedictions and curses, as He turns the world with its values upside down (vv. 20–26). The Lord's disciples were drawn mostly from the **poor**, from the rabble that the rich, pious, and important Pharisees thought accursed (John 7:49). They were scorned and despised by the world, considered to be deluded and destined for God's wrath as impious Lawbreakers. (Indeed, there were many tax-collectors and sinners among them.) The Lord, however, pronounces them **blessed**, fortunate, to be envied by all the world. (The word rendered *blessed* is the Gr. *makarios*, used in the Greek Septuagint to translate the Heb. *asre*, "happy," such as in Ps. 1:1; in classical Greek, the word is used to denote the happiness of the gods.)

Those who are **poor** are pronounced **blessed**. They may be destitute, forced to rely on God for everything, but theirs is **the Kingdom of God**, and one day they will rejoice in its limitless riches and splendor. The image in the Psalter of the oppressed and righteous poor man who belongs to God (e.g. Ps. 34:6; 72:2) finds fulfillment in them. That is, they are blessed not *because* they are poor and financially needy, but *despite* their poverty and *because their poverty causes them to rely on God and put their hope in Jesus*. They have little to lose in the world, and so all the more willingly give up all they have to follow the Lord.

Those who are **hungry now** are also **blessed**. Throughout their long and hard lives, they have longed for God to vindicate them and give them justice. One day He will, and in the age to come they will be **fed *to the full***. The word rendered *fed to the full* is the Greek *chortazo*, meaning "to eat until stuffed full, to gorge." (It is used of the birds gorging on the flesh of the godless slain in Rev. 19:21.) One day God will vindicate them, and they will feast in His Kingdom.

Those who **weep now** are pronounced **blessed** and fortunate, though everyone thinks them otherwise. They may weep over their destitution and suffering, but a time will come when all their tears will be wiped away, and they will **laugh** with joy in the age to come. God has promised that the oppressed righteous man will one day laugh in triumph at his foes (Ps. 52:6), and the disciples of Jesus will experience that vindication.

Jesus pronounces a final and climactic benediction on His disciples. When **men hate** them and **separate** them from common society; when they **reproach** them and insult them to their faces as heretics; when they **cast out** their very **name** as if it were **evil**, slandering them to all, and all **because** they dare to confess their allegiance to **the Son of Man**—then they are truly **blessed**.

The time was fast approaching when His disciples would be thus ostracized and even banned from the synagogues (John 9:22; Matt. 10:17). Their neighbors might consider this to be the ultimate calamity, but Jesus says it will be the crowning blessing of all. Indeed, they should **rejoice in that day, and leap** up for joy. For **behold** and see what the world would never expect: the **reward** waiting for them **in heaven** is **great** and worth any such suffering. The **fathers** of those who persecute them **were doing the same things to the prophets** of old. Those prophets persevered and received their eternal reward, and all now count them blessed. Let Jesus' disciples also persevere as the descendants of the prophets, and receive the prophet's reward.

Jesus came as the divine plumb line for Israel, to reveal what was in the hearts of men, be it humility or pride. The humble poor who came to Him would rise, but the proud who resisted His call would fall (2:34). Thus, He came not only to bring blessing on those who came to God, but woe and judgment on those who refused. As

Jesus' followers were to be thought fortunate, so those who rejected Him were truly to be pitied—alas for them!

Thus, Jesus pronounces God's woes upon the rich and self-satisfied who spurn His message. (Once again, the judgment comes not simply from being wealthy, but from letting one's wealth deter one from entering the Kingdom of God; compare 18:24–25.) God's Word always comes as such a double-edged sword—even the Law not only brings blessings upon the obedient but curses as well upon the apostate and disobedient (see Deut. 28).

In the Greek, the woes Christ pronounces come in increasing terseness and power: in the first two woes, He says, "woe to you"; in the third He uses the shorter "woe, you who"; and in the final woe, simply "woe, when." The increased grammatical terseness of the woes expresses a crescendo of doom. The main target of these woes is those who despise and reject Christ's followers—including, most notably, the Pharisees (compare John 7:49).

As the first benediction is pronounced upon those who are poor, so the first **woe** is pronounced upon those *who are* **rich**. (All of the woes are the mirror images of the preceding blessings.) These rich spurn the poor and scoff at Jesus' message. The **comfort** due to them they are already now **receiving *in full***. (The word translated *receive in full* is the Gr. *apecho*, used for official receipt of goods; compare its use in Phil. 4:18.) Like Lazarus in the torments of Hades, there will be no more comfort or joy for them (16:25).

A **woe** is pronounced upon those *who are* **filled now**, who have stuffed themselves to satiety in this age. Though smug in self-righteousness, they **will hunger** in the age to come, for there they will experience the want of God's blessing and Presence in their spiritual destitution.

With increasing terseness, Christ pronounces God's **woe** on those **who laugh now**. That is, those who now deride the pious poor as hopeless and deluded idealists, who laugh the righteous man to scorn (see Ps. 22:7), in the age to come **will weep** over the ruin to which they themselves have come.

Finally, **woe**, Christ says, **when all men speak well of you.** When the world exalts you among men, and the powers of the age applaud you, then know that your time of catastrophe awaits at the Judgment, for what is exalted among fallen men is an abomination before God (16:15). The **fathers** of old **were doing the same things to the false-prophets**, showering them with acclaim (1 Kin. 22; Jer. 28). As the disciples of Jesus are in spiritual succession to the prophets, so these worldlings are in succession to the false-prophets. Rejection of Christ and His disciples may preserve one's popularity in this age, but it will bring the wrath of God in the end.

ॐ   ॐ   ॐ   ॐ   ॐ

27 "But I say to you who hear, love your enemies, do good to those who hate you;

28 "bless those who curse you, pray for those who assail you.

29 "To the one who strikes you on the cheek, present him with the other also; and from the one who takes your garment, do not withhold also your shirt.

30 "To everyone who asks of you, give; and from the one who takes your things, do not ask for *them* back.

31 "And just as you want men to do to you, do likewise to them.

Our Lord continues to turn the world upside down in a series of precepts (vv. 27–38). His disciples, if they have ears to **hear** Him, should hearken to His revolutionary words. The customary way among men is measured by justice—to meet kindness with kindness and hostility with retaliation. One loves one's friend, but if that friend turns and becomes one's enemy, one responds in kind. Christ overturns such logic, and says that His disciples must measure their hearts' deeds not by justice, but by grace. No act of insult or hostility must allow them to turn from their determination to do good to all men. Love must be without limit, without boundaries—like the love of God. The teaching of this whole section is given in conscious opposition to the teaching customarily received from the Pharisees (see Matt. 5:20–22, 43–44 as examples of this conscious opposition).

Thus Jesus' disciples must **love** their **enemies** and not, as one might expect, look for ways to retaliate and do them harm when the opportunity arises. Instead they must **do good to those who hate** them when opportunities for doing such deeds of kindness arise. When their neighbor **curses** them and invokes God's wrath upon them, they must not retaliate with curses of their own. Instead they must respond by invoking God's benediction, **blessing** them. When their neighbor **assails** them and persecutes them, they must respond by **praying** for them.

If their neighbor **strikes** them **on the cheek** as an insult (for such acts were intended as public insults, not as acts of assault), His disciples must not strike back. Instead, they must **present** the agitated party with **the other** cheek **also**, as an expression of total non-retaliation. It is the same with theft as with insult. If their neighbor **takes** the outer **garment** from them, the disciples must **not withhold also** their inner **shirt**. The follower of Jesus is to exhibit an unshakable inner peace; he must be so far from retaliation that he heaps up gifts on the aggressor.

This love must be universal. **To everyone who asks** alms, they must **give**, and **from the one who takes** their **things** surreptitiously, they must **not ask for *them* back** once they discover the theft.

In all of these startling images and precepts, Christ is appealing to the heart, intending to jolt His hearers into an inner revolutionary transformation. He is not legislating, not laying down laws to be embodied in civil legal codes. That is, He is not suggesting that laws against theft be repealed, or that armies and police forces be disbanded for the sake of nonresistance. He is presenting a series of stunning examples of refusal to retaliate, of someone who with a kind of divine perversity does the opposite of what is expected. These examples are not necessarily meant to be followed literally. (In His own case, when struck on the cheek, He challenged the aggressor to justify the blow in order to lead him to repentance; see John 18:22–23.) Rather, they are offered to the disciple to inspire him to transcend the vicious circle of blow and counterblow, and to walk in the higher plane of undiscriminating love. They are aids to lift the disciple above the demands of mere justice.

The principle of mutuality is common to all these examples as their foundation. That is, **just as you want men to do to you**, so you should **do likewise to them**. It is this principle which should govern the behavior of His disciples and be applied by them in every situation.

ॐ ॐ ॐ ॐ ॐ

32 "And if you love those who love you, what grace is that to you? For even sinners love those who love them.

33 "And if you do good to those who do good to you, what grace is that to you? Even sinners do the same.

34 "And if you lend *money* to those from whom you hope to receive, what grace is that to you? Even sinners lend *money* to sinners, that they may receive back an equal *amount*.

35 "But love your enemies, and do good, and lend *money*, expecting nothing, and your reward will be great; and you will be sons of the Highest, for He is kind to the ungrateful and evil.

36 "Be compassionate, just as your Father is compassionate.

37 "And do not judge and you will never be judged; and do not sentence *as guilty*, and you will never be sentenced *as guilty*; release and you will be released.

38 "Give and it will be given to you; good measure, pressed, shaken, overflowing, they will give into your bosom. For by the measure that you measure it will be measured in return to you."

St. Luke continues with this second section of the Lord's sermon to His disciples. Having given them a series of extraordinary exhortations, He strives to persuade them to live on this higher plane. They hope, as good Jews, to receive a blessing from God as the reward for their piety. Surely they can see that following His precepts is the only way to do that?

By loving their enemies (v. 27), they are loving those who will almost certainly repay their kindness with hatred and take advantage of their love. The temptation is to limit love to their friends. But **if** they **love** only **those who love** them**, what grace** (Gr. *charis*) **is that** to them; how can they hope to win God's favor through that? **For even sinners love those who love them**, and obviously lawless sinners can expect no reward from God. (Luke has changed the original "tax-collectors," preserved by Matthew in Matt. 5:46, to the more general word "sinners" for the sake of his Gentile audience, who might not catch the Jewish reference to tax-collectors as notorious sinners.)

And **if** they **do good** deeds and are kind **to those who do good to** them, **what grace is that to** them? For **even sinners do the same** and cannot hope to be rewarded by God for it. (It seems as if Luke has again changed Matthew's specific greeting of a friend in peace, preserved in Matt. 5:47, to the more general "do good," changing also Matthew's Jewish reference to godless "Gentiles" to the more general reference to "sinners.")

The Lord has a third example. **If** they **lend** *money* (Gr. *danizo*) **to those from whom** they **hope to receive**, what is the merit in that? That is, they extend a loan to someone hoping not only to recover the money (that goes without saying), but also to **receive back an equal amount** of good will the next time *they* need a favor. As the modern proverb goes, "I'll scratch your back and you scratch mine." **Even sinners** do that; how can Jesus' disciples think it praiseworthy in the eyes of God? Jesus' followers must lend money when it is needed, even if the borrower will never respond with gratitude in the future.

In all these examples, therefore, the Lord shows that for an act to win God's grace and favor, it must go beyond the simple self-serving of doing good to friends. It must involve doing good to those who are *not* your friends. These examples (vv. 32–34) show that one must **love** one's **enemies**, and **do good** to them, and **lend** *money* to them, all the while **expecting nothing** in return from them. The beneficence must not be motivated by hope of gain, but simply by the love of God. Only then will one receive a **great** and bountiful **reward** for one's piety. Then they **will be sons of the Highest**, as God gives them the blessing reserved for His own children.

This blessing of God upon His sons, then, presupposes that they act like their heavenly Father. **He is kind to the ungrateful and evil**, and Jesus' disciples must be kind to the ungrateful and evil too if they would receive the Father's reward. They must **be compassionate, just as** their **Father is compassionate**, and show love even to their evil enemies.

When their enemies insult and wrong them (for the context is still that of dealing with one's enemies, vv. 27, 35), one must **not judge** them. That is, one must not condemn or denounce one's foe with a censorious spirit. One must not **sentence** him *as guilty*, "writing him off" and looking to retaliate or take revenge. Instead, one must **release** and pardon, for only so will the disciple himself **be released** and pardoned by God.

It is important to see that in forbidding the disciple to **judge** (Gr. *krino*), Christ is not calling for the suspension of the moral faculty. Christ is not saying that the disciple may not pronounce his enemies' actions to be morally wrong—for how can one pardon a man if one does not recognize that there is something to pardon? Rather, Christ is forbidding His disciple to usurp the role of God and assign amounts of blame, as if the disciple could see into the secret heart to weigh motivation. The disciple's task is not to give up on his adversary as a lost cause, but to continue to love and seek the person's final repentance and eternal good.

The disciple must give mercy and love to all, even to the one who has hurt him. If you will **give**, Jesus says, then **it will be given to you** in return by God. God will respond, giving a **good measure** of His blessing. The image used is of a measuring jar filled with grain. The grain is **pressed** down so that the measure will hold all the more, and **shaken** together, so that it fills every corner. Even more grain is added to it, so that it comes **overflowing** when God **gives** it **into your bosom** (Gr. *kolpos*, used here to describe the garment over one's chest, folded so as to create a pocket). For God will use **the measure that you measure** in His dealings with you. If you use a small measure, stingily doling out tiny bits of mercy, then God will give similarly small bits of mercy in return. But if you openly give large and generous amounts of mercy, then God will likewise return such generosity and mercy to you.

ॐ ॐ ॐ ॐ ॐ

39 And He also spoke a parable to them: "Is a blind *man* able to guide a blind *man*? Will they not both fall into a pit?

40 "A disciple is not above the teacher, but everyone, *when* prepared, will be as his teacher.

41 "And why do you see the chip that is in your brother's eye, but do not consider the log that is in your own eye?

42 "Or how are you able to say to your brother, 'Brother, let me cast out the chip that is in your eye!' when you yourself do not see the log that is in your eye? Hypocrite! First cast out the log from your eye, and then you will see *clearly* to cast out the chip that is in your brother's eye.

43 "For there is no fine tree which makes decayed fruit; nor again, a decayed tree which makes fine fruit.

44 "For each tree is known by its own fruit. For they do not pick figs from thorns, nor do they gather grapes from a *briar* bush.

45 "The good man from the good treasure of his heart brings forth what is good; and the evil man from the evil *treasure* brings forth what is evil; for his mouth speaks from the abundance of his heart.

In the third and final section of this sermon, Christ presents a series of parables concerning the nature of true discipleship

(vv. 39–49). First comes a parable or image about the necessity of the disciple clinging to the right teacher. These images underscore how controversial Christ was and how His teaching presented men with a choice of fundamentally different approaches. For the Pharisees were always close at hand to contradict Jesus and His approach to the Law (see for example 6:2, 7). This sermon (and all of Christ's teaching) is given against the background of this constant barrage of contradiction.

So the disciple must settle it in his mind to follow Christ and not listen to the criticisms of the Pharisees. They are spiritually blind to what God truly commanded in His Law. And **is a blind *man* able to guide** another **blind *man*?** The thought is preposterous! Surely they **will both fall into a pit** and come to disaster. Any **disciple is not above the teacher**. The aim and method of discipleship in that day was for the disciple to memorize and internalize all the views of the rabbinical teacher to whom he attached himself and to make all the views of his teacher his own. Thus **everyone, *when* prepared** and fully trained, **would be as his teacher**—neither better nor worse. If the Pharisaical teacher is blind to truth, then the pupil trained by him cannot help but be similarly blind himself.

Hence the necessity of choosing the right teacher. In coming to Christ, His disciples must utterly shut their ears to the teaching and approach of the Pharisees. They must choose either Christ or the Pharisees and not try to combine them both. One cannot combine the new with the old any more than one can safely put new wine in old wineskins (5:37–38).

Christ offers another parable: that of two men, one with a small chip of wood in his eye and the other with an entire log in his eye, sticking out of his head for all the world to see. It is meant to be an impossible and humorous image, and not an actual life situation. The Pharisees (the unnamed rival teachers throughout this passage) can **see** clearly enough (they claim) **the chip in** their **brother's eye**, but they fail to **consider the log that is in** their **own eye**. They are keen to teach, all right—keen to say helpfully to their neighbor, **"Brother, let me cast out the chip that is in your eye!"** when they themselves do **not see the log that is in** their own **eye**, protruding for all the world to see. In casting the Pharisees as the fool of the parable and holding them up to ridicule, Christ reveals their folly in order that His hearers may see for themselves how blind the Pharisees truly are.

The Pharisee is truly a **hypocrite** in his failure to attend to his own faults before dealing with the perceived faults of others. If the Pharisee truly wants to help men, let him **first cast out the log from** his own **eye**. That is, let him cast away the Pharisaical regulations that blind him to truth. **Then** he **will see** *clearly* **to cast out** any **chip that** might be **in** his **brother's eye**!

Christ offers another parable to help His hearers understand the necessity of clinging to Christ's teaching alone—that of the two trees. A good tree, one that is healthy, can make good fruit. The tree beside it which is decayed and rotten (Gr. *sapros*), eaten by disease and insects, cannot possibly produce good fruit, but must of necessity make fruit as diseased as the tree. **No fine tree** can **make decayed fruit; nor again** can **a decayed tree make fine fruit**. In coming to Christ, men are assured of receiving the good fruit of truth, whereas if they come to the Pharisees they can only receive the rotten fruit of blind legalism.

Each then must choose where he will go to find truth—to Christ or the Pharisees. Men do **not pick figs from thorns**. How stupid to go to a **thorn** bush and hope to find **figs** there! (Once again Christ ridicules His opponents by using this preposterous image.) Or how foolish to try to **gather grapes from a** *briar* **bush**! Better to try the grapevine. In the same way it is fatuous for any to go to the Pharisees in the hope of gathering sound interpretations of the Law or lessons for life.

For the Pharisees have only **evil** *treasure*, a load of false interpretations and erroneous insights. How can they bring **what is good** from it? The image is of two men storing up loads of different things: one stores up good treasure in his house, items of worth and value. The other stores up garbage and worthless junk. If one has collected only junk, one has only junk to give.

The place where every man stores his treasure and values is the human heart. It is in the heart that one keeps the good treasure of truth and wisdom or the evil treasure of censoriousness and error.

And what is in the heart will overflow through the mouth, **for** the **mouth speaks from the abundance of** the **heart**, from whatever fills it. In the heart of the Pharisees lie only sin and smallness of mind—how can anything else flow from their mouths? Who can expect good teaching from such a source?

> ॐ ॐ ॐ ॐ ॐ
>
> 46 "And why do you call Me 'Lord, Lord' and do not do what I say?
>
> 47 "Everyone who comes to Me, and hears My words, and does them, I will show you whom he is like:
>
> 48 "he is like a man building a house, who dug and went deep and laid a foundation upon the rock, and when a flood happened, the river broke against that house and was not strong enough to shake it, because it had been built well.
>
> 49 "But the one who has heard and has not done is like a man who built a house upon the earth without a foundation; and the river broke against it and immediately it fell in, and the wreck of that house was great."

The Lord concludes with a final parable, encouraging His disciples not just to come to Him as the source of truth, but also to carry out His words in their daily lives. For what could be more useless than to address Him with a great show of deference as **Lord, Lord**, and then to go away and **not do what** He **said**?

Once again a choice of two ways is presented, and the examples of two men are held up for consideration. One **man** was **building a house**, and he **dug and went deep** into the earth and **laid a foundation** for his house **upon the rock.** It was hard work, but it proved to be indispensable. For **a flood happened, and the river** or torrent from it **broke against that house**, but was **not strong enough to shake it, because it had been built well.** Another man built his house, but this one **built upon the** bare **earth, without a foundation**. The same flood came to his house as to his wiser neighbor's (as life's floods will come to all), and when **the river broke against it**, the house **immediately fell in, and the wreck of that house was great**.

The one who built well was like **everyone who comes** to Jesus and not only **hears** His **words**, but also **does them**. The fool who built without a foundation was like every one of those listening to Jesus then and **hearing** His words with joy, but **not doing** them. The final Judgment will come, just as the flood in the parable came. The time for ensuring that one survives that tempest is *now*. Now is the time for obedience. When the flood of judgment comes at the end, it will be too late.

§V.8. Healing the Centurion's Slave

ॐ ॐ ॐ ॐ ॐ

7 1 When He had finished all His words in the hearing of the people, He entered into Capernaum.

2 And a certain centurion's slave who was *held in* honor by him was sick and about to die.

3 And when he heard about Jesus, he sent elders of the Jews asking Him to come and *bring* his slave to salvation.

4 And when they had come to Jesus, they urged Him diligently, saying, "He is worthy for you to grant this;

5 "for he loves our nation, and *it was* he who built the synagogue for us."

6 Now Jesus was going with them; and when He was already not far from the house, the centurion sent friends, saying to Him, "Lord, do not harass *Yourself further*, for I am not sufficient that You should enter under my roof;

7 "therefore I did not even consider myself worthy to come to You, but say the word, and my servant will be healed.

8 "For I *myself* also am a man placed under authority, having soldiers under me; and I say to this one, 'Go!' and he goes; and to another, 'Come!' and he comes; and to my slave, 'Do this!' and he does *it*."

9 Now when Jesus heard these things, He marveled at him, and having turned to the crowd following Him, said, "I say to you, not in Israel have I found such great faith!"

10 And when those who had been sent returned to the house, they found the slave in health.

After the choosing of the Twelve and the teaching that followed it, **when He had finished all His words in the hearing** of the assembled crowd, He continued down the slope of the hill and **entered into Capernaum**. In that town, there was **a certain centurion**. (Capernaum was part of a major trade route, so that Roman soldiers may well have been there even before their general presence in Galilee in AD 44.) This man's **slave was sick and about to die**. This was no ordinary slave, but one who was *held in* honor by the centurion as a valuable asset to him, and for whose sake the centurion was prepared to go to extraordinary lengths. Though the slave was too sick to be moved, the soldier was not content to let nature take its course. **When he heard about Jesus** returning to town, **he sent elders of the Jews asking Him to come and *bring* his slave to salvation** and healing (Gr. *diasozo*, to bring through to safety).

The houses of Gentiles were unclean for Jews, and no pious Jew would enter into one lest he be defiled. The soldier had asked his Jewish friends to bring Jesus a request to heal the servant, and, in his distraction, perhaps phrased this request in the vaguest of ways—"ask Jesus of Nazareth to help us!"

The Jewish elders of the local synagogue found Jesus as He was entering the town and brought their friend's request. Such a request on behalf of one of the Gentiles was unusual, to say the least, and so **they urged** Jesus **diligently**, bringing many arguments to persuade Him to help one of the *goyim*, saying, **"He is worthy for you to grant this** extraordinary favor, **for he loves our nation, and** *it was* **he who built the** local **synagogue for us."**

Jesus readily agreed to the request and was going with them to the pagan's home. **When He was already not far from the house, the centurion** could see that Jesus, contrary to his intention, was going to enter right into his house, in defiance of Jewish rules regarding ceremonial purity. As one who had learned to respect Judaism with its customary restrictions, and feeling a great sense of his own unworthiness, the horrified soldier **sent** some of his **friends** to prevent Christ's further progress. Taking yet another message from the pious pagan, they were **saying to Him, "Lord, do not harass** *Yourself further"* and cause Yourself any further trouble. The Gentile knew that he was **not sufficient** (Gr. *ikanos*, "fit, adequate") that a Jew like Jesus **should enter under** his **roof**. He would not ask Christ to contract ritual defilement for his sake.

Indeed, he **did not even consider** himself spiritually **worthy** (Gr. *axioo*) **to come** to the wonder-working Prophet himself, but sent his friends the Jewish elders as a more worthy substitute. That was the reason he did not come himself—not because he could not be bothered, but on the contrary, because he felt himself unworthy of Christ's Presence. He knew that Jesus had such power from God that He need only **say the word**, **and** his **servant would be healed**.

For as a soldier, the centurion knew all about authority. He himself **also was a man placed under authority**—one who had complete control of his forces. He need only **say to this one, "Go!"** and he would **go**. He could know this for a certainty, and did not need to see the subordinate carry out his order to know that it would be fulfilled. That is how true authority works: it can accomplish things at a distance. The centurion recognized that Jesus had authority from God, and that therefore Jesus too could accomplish things at a distance. He did not need to trouble Himself to actually come to the centurion's house to heal; He need only **say the word**, and the distant healing would be accomplished.

Here was extraordinary faith, and **when Jesus heard these things** from the centurion's friends, **He marveled at him**. He **turned to the crowd** of Jewish elders and onlookers **following Him**, exclaiming, **"Not** even **in Israel have I found such great faith!"** Here was a wonder—and a sign of future wonders to come. For this Gentile's faith was a sign that other Gentiles could yet come to put their trust in the Jewish Messiah (Matt. 8:11–12). To the hopeful friends of the unseen and humble Gentile, Christ said that they could return to find their request granted. And so it turned out—**when** they **returned to the house, they found the slave in health**.

It was not just that the slave was brought safely through so that he would slowly recover. Rather, here was an instantaneous and complete healing. (Luke the physician uses the more medical term *ugiaino*, "to be in health," whereas Matthew in Matt. 8:13 uses the more general term, and says that he was "cured," Gr. *iaomai*.)

§V.9. Raising the Widow's Son

> ཨ྅ ཨ྅ ཨ྅ ཨ྅ ཨ྅
>
> 11 And it happened on the next *day* that He went to a city called Nain; and His disciples were going with Him, *along* with a large crowd.
>
> 12 Now as He drew near to the gate of the city, behold! one who had died, an only-begotten son of his mother, was being carried out; and she was a widow; and a large crowd from the city was with her.
>
> 13 And when the Lord saw her, He had heartfelt *love* for her and said to her, "Do not weep."
>
> 14 And He came up and touched the bier; and the bearers stood *still*. And He said, "Young *man*, I say to you, arise!"
>
> 15 And the dead man sat up and began to speak. And He gave him to his mother.
>
> 16 And fear took them all, and they were glorifying God, saying, "A great prophet has arisen

> among us!" and "God has visited His people!"
> 17 And this word about Him went out all over
> Judea and in all the surrounding-country.

On the next *day* after the healing of the centurion's servant, Jesus **went to a city called Nain**, a town six miles southeast of Nazareth. **His disciples were going with Him, *along* with a large crowd**, and as **He drew near to the gate of the city**, this multitude collided with another multitude. Luke signals the dramatic surprise of the collision with the word **behold!** For here were two crowds, one crowd entering through the city gates, jubilant and exulting, with Life at its center, and the other crowd exiting through those gates, mournful and wailing, with death at its center.

Luke sketches the reasons for their sorrow with a few deft strokes: **One who had died** was being **carried out** on a bier; he was **the only-begotten son of his mother**, and this woman **was a widow**. That is, the boy was the woman's only source of support, and his death left her alone and desolate in the world. In her desperation and grief, the Lord **had heartfelt *love* for her**.

The word rendered *had heartfelt love* is the Greek *splagxnizomai*, cognate with the noun *splagxna*, or "innards." These innards or bowels (so translated in the Authorized Version) were the metaphorical seat of emotion, and the verb used here signifies a love that wells up from the inmost depths. Here was no superficial sorrow, but a compassion that overflowed from a depth of emotion. As Christ approached that crowd, He **said to her, "Do not weep,"** for He was about to sweep away the cause of her grief.

It would seem that the Lord's cry to the distraught woman was given from a distance, when the two crowds were still closing in on one another. (The bereaved woman would have been leading the funeral procession, as Christ was leading His own followers.) It was not until **He came up and touched the bier** that **the bearers** of it **stood *still*.** Looking down at the youth, **He said, "Young *man*, I say to you, arise!"** In raising the dead youth, Christ did not pray long or labor to raise the child, as Elisha did when he raised a lad from death (2 Kin. 4:29–35). Rather, He uttered a single, simple

153

command (a mere four words in the Greek) as One who had complete and sovereign authority over life and death. And **the dead man sat up**, and was so completely recovered that he **began to speak**. Christ helped him off the bier and **gave him** into the arms of **his** tearful **mother**.

The effect on the crowd of mourners was stunning—**fear took them all**, and **they were glorifying God** for this mighty miracle. They cried out, "**A great prophet has arisen among us!**" recognizing in Jesus the same power of God that was manifested in the prophets of old. Truly **God** had **visited His people** through the mighty prophet from Nazareth! **This word** and news **about Him went out all over Judea, and in all the surrounding-country**—that is, through the length of Palestine.

§V.10. Commendation of John

18 And the disciples of John declared to him about all these things.

19 And calling to *him* a certain two of his disciples, John sent *them* to the Lord, saying, "Is *it* You *who are* the Coming One, or do we expect another?"

20 And when the men had come to Him, they said, "John the Baptizer has sent us to You, saying, 'Is *it* You *who are* the Coming One, or do we expect another?'"

21 In that hour, He healed many of diseases and scourges and evil spirits; and He granted *that* many blind *people* might see.

22 And He answered and said to them, "Go and declare to John what you have seen and heard: blind *people* see again, lame *people* walk, lepers are cleansed, and deaf *people* hear, dead *people* are raised, poor *people* have good news *brought to them*.

> 23 "And blessed is the one who does not stumble
> over Me."

After such remarkable works, **the disciples of John declared to him about all these** miracles and of Jesus' spreading popularity. John was by this time languishing in prison (having been imprisoned just before Jesus returned to Galilee, in 4:14). The effects of the dark confinement of his dungeon cell began to tell upon such a free spirit of the wilderness as John was, and he began to entertain doubts that Jesus was truly the Messiah.

For John (like others) had expected the Messiah to be a figure of judgment, cleaning out the threshing-floor of Israel, gathering the righteous into God's Kingdom and burning up the unrighteous with the unquenchable fire of divine wrath (3:17). As one who was himself suffering acutely from the persecution of the unrighteous Herod, John was impatient for Jesus to act like the Messiah. The Messiah's work (John thought) was to strike against the sinners and to rescue the oppressed. When would Jesus start? John was languishing in prison, while Jesus was feasting with sinners! In perplexity of heart, John **called to *him* a certain two of his** trusted **disciples** and **sent *them* to the Lord** with this question from John: **"Is *it* You *who are* the Coming One**—the Messiah—**or do we expect another?"** It was not so much a genuine question as an anguished challenge from a suffering man, a call for Jesus to begin His work of messianic judgment, if He was in fact the Messiah.

John's disciples came to Jesus amid the teeming crowds. They waited and saw all the miracles that He did, how He **healed many of diseases and scourges** (that is, debilitating conditions; compare the use of the word *scourge* in Mark 5:29), delivered them from **evil spirits**, and even **granted *that* many blind *people* might see**. At length they gained access to Him and delivered their message.

Jesus did not disdain them for the question, nor offer any word of rebuke to His Forerunner. Neither did He seek to persuade them or to argue. He simply told them to **go and declare to John** the things they **had seen and heard**. They need not believe Jesus' claims, only the evidence of their own senses. All around them, blind *people* could **see again**, **lame** *people* could **walk**, **lepers** were **cleansed**, **deaf** *people* could **hear**, the **dead** were **raised** to new life. And—as the climax—the humble **poor have good news *brought to them***. Hope had arrived for the hopeless at last.

The Lord's words to John were drawn from the prophecies of Isaiah, 35:5 and 61:1. That is, Jesus was fulfilling the work the prophets said the Messiah would do. Christ thus did not respond to John's challenge with self-assertions of His authority, but let His works speak for Him. By hearkening to the testimony of His miracles—long predicted by the prophets—anyone could know the truth about Him.

Christ concluded His message to John with a benediction: **Blessed is the one who does not stumble over Me**. That is, God will bless any who accept Jesus as He is and do not stumble over Him, rejecting Him because He does not fit their preconceptions about what a Messiah should be. This blessing is proffered to John as well. Thus Christ concludes with a hidden challenge of His own. John had challenged Jesus to strike in judgment at sinners; Jesus challenges him in return to open his mind to a wider concept of what Messiah was called to do in this age.

ॐ ॐ ॐ ॐ ॐ

24 And after the messengers of John had gone away, He began to say to the crowds about John, "What did you go out into the wilderness to behold? A reed being shaken by the wind?

25 "But what did you go out to see? A man clothed in soft apparel? Behold, those in glorious apparel and living in indulgence are in the *kings'* palaces!

26 "But what did you go out to see? A prophet? Yes, I say to you, and more than a prophet!

27 "This is the one about whom it is written, 'Behold, I send My messenger before Your face, who will prepare Your way before You.'

> 28 "I say to you, among those born of women,
> there is no one greater than John; yet the least
> in the Kingdom of God is greater than he."
> 29 And when all the people and the tax-collectors
> heard, they justified God, having been baptized
> *with* the baptism of John.
> 30 But the Pharisees and the lawyers nullified
> God's intention for themselves, not having been
> baptized by him.

After the messengers of John had gone away, Jesus spoke to the crowds about John. Those crowds had all thought John to be a true prophet and had themselves been baptized with his baptism. Did John's question to Jesus mean that John had fallen away, beaten down by his imprisonment? Herod was no friend of Jesus—was John starting to side with him? What would Jesus say about their former hero? Would He denounce him for his seeming lack of support?

In response, Christ has nothing but praise for John, and He steps forward as John's defender and champion. Some may want to turn against John now that he is in prison and suggest that Herod has worn him down, that John is vacillating, giving in to Herod like any one of Herod's flattering courtiers. Christ dares any such to speak. That is not the John they all know. **What did** they **go out into the wilderness to behold** at the beginning? Did they go there to gawk at a reed being shaken by the wind (such as were common in the wilderness)? They could see early on that John was no insubstantial reed, one easily swayed by the winds of popularity and opinion. He was a man of principle, moved by no tempest or threat.

Again Christ fires out a rhetorical question, insisting that His hearers recognize John's worth. **"But what did you go out to see? A man clothed in soft apparel?"** Did they troop out to the desert to admire a courtier, all dressed up in **glorious apparel** of gold and silk? Then they went to the wrong place, for those in such finery, those used to **living in indulgence**, were to be found **in the *kings'* palaces**, not in deserts. They could see early on that John was no dandified yes-man, one easily cowed by suffering and deprivation. He was a true ascetic, able to speak the truth, whatever the cost. John was not yielding to Herod, and his question to Jesus did not mean that he had gone over to Herod or sold out his principles.

A third time Christ insists on the crowd giving a verdict about John. **But what did** they **go out** in the desert **to see? A prophet**, as they once thought? Yes, Jesus affirmed, John was indeed a true prophet. And **more than a prophet!** For John was **the one about whom it was written** in the prophets, **"Behold, I send My messenger before Your face, who will prepare Your way before You"** (Mal. 3:1). That is, John was himself the Forerunner, the harbinger of the Kingdom.

That Kingdom was now at hand. Here then was John's commendation and glory—that the Kingdom he had announced was indeed at hand. Christ assured everyone: **Among those born of women** (that is, of all men everywhere) **there is no one greater than John**. He was the greatest of all in the Law and Prophets. But the time of the Law and the Prophets was coming to an end, as John had said, and the Kingdom of God was coming, with all its majesty. And so great was that **Kingdom of God** that the **least** of its members would be **greater than** John.

When all the people and the tax-collectors heard this, they were convinced, and **they justified God**. They acknowledged God's justice, accepting and vindicating God's work in Jesus. They were able to see Jesus not as a rival to John, but as the fulfillment of all John had done and as John's true successor.

However, **the Pharisees and the lawyers** (that is, those skilled in the Jewish Law and its interpretation) did not accept Jesus—any more than they accepted John. The **tax-collectors** and other sinners accepted John, and so more easily swung over and accepted Jesus too. The Pharisees and their kind had **not been baptized by him** and were not impressed by Jesus' generous commendation. They did not accept that God was working in Jesus, and thus they **nullified** and thwarted **God's intention for themselves**. God had meant to save them through Christ, but their rejection of Jesus made this impossible.

ॐ ॐ ॐ ॐ ॐ

31 "To what therefore will I liken the men of this generation, and what are they like?

32 "They are like children sitting in the marketplace who call to one another; and they say, 'We played *the flute* for you, and you did not dance! We bewailed, and you did not weep!'

33 "For John the Baptizer has come eating no bread and drinking no wine; and you say, 'He has a demon!'

34 "The Son of Man has come eating and drinking; and you say, 'Behold, a man *who is* a glutton and a wine-drinker! A friend of tax-collectors and sinners!'

35 "But wisdom is justified by all her children."

As the Pharisees scoffed at Christ for His commendation of John, Jesus had some words for them too. They claimed to be great **men**, but they were like squabbling children—little **children sitting in the marketplace** or public square, as children did. Everyone had seen children playing at their games. One group of children wanted to "play wedding," and they pretended to **play *the flute*** (as flutes were played at weddings). The other group of children refused to go along with that game, and the first group were full of complaints that they **did not dance**. Then the first group changed their mind, wanting to "play funeral" instead, and **bewailed** in a pretended funeral lament. Their playmates opposite refused to join them in that game either, and so the first group again complained that they **did not weep**. The first group of children wanted the second to do exactly whatever they wanted and were full of childish whining when they could not get their way.

The Pharisees were just like them, the Lord said. There was evidently no pleasing them. **For John the Baptizer had come eating no bread and drinking no wine**. He was a true ascetic of the desert and ate only locusts and wild honey (Mark 1:6). The Pharisees wanted John to dance to their tune of feasting, to dance to their flute-playing, but John would not. They denounced him, crying out, **"He has a demon!"** His asceticism proves he is mad!

You would think they would like Jesus then—for **the Son of Man came eating and drinking** (as John did not). But they denounced Him too, crying out, **"Behold, a man *who* is a glutton and a wine-drinker! A friend** and companion **of** notorious **tax-collectors and sinners!"** With childish perversity, they denounced John because he did not eat or drink, and Jesus because He did.

Nonetheless, **wisdom is justified by all her children.** All who are truly wise acknowledge wisdom when they see it, and recognize the divine wisdom in both John and Jesus. Children always recognize their mother, and so do the wise of this age recognize the authenticity of Christ and His Forerunner.

§V.11. Forgiving a Sinful Woman

ॐ ॐ ॐ ॐ ॐ

36 Now one of the Pharisees was asking Him to eat with him. And He entered into the Pharisee's house and reclined.

37 And behold! A woman who was a sinner in the city, when she really-knew that He was reclining in the Pharisee's house, brought an alabaster *flask* of perfume,

38 and standing behind *Him* at His feet, weeping, she began to shower His feet with tears, and was wiping them with the hair of her head, and *fervently* kissing His feet, and anointing *them* with the perfume.

39 Now when the Pharisee who had called Him saw this, he said in himself, "If this *man* were a prophet, He would know who and of what sort this woman is who is touching Him, that she is a sinner."

40 And Jesus answered and said to him, "Simon, I

> have something to say to you." And he says, "Say
> *it*, Teacher."
> 41 "A certain moneylender had two debtors: one
> owing five hundred denarii, and the other, fifty.
> 42 "*When they* did not have *resources* from themselves
> to repay *him*, he graciously *forgave* them both.
> Which of them therefore will love him more?"
> 43 Simon answered and said, "I take *it* the one whom
> he graciously *forgave* the more." And He said to
> him, "You have judged correctly."

Luke then relates a story to illustrate the compassion of Christ for sinners. It took place at the occasion when **one of the Pharisees was asking Him to eat with him**. Though the time and place of this meal is not given, it is possible that this was at the meal held after attending the synagogue on a Sabbath. Whatever the precise time, Jesus accepted the invitation. He **entered into the Pharisee's house and reclined** at table with him and the assembled guests. Such meals were taken lying on couches, with the guests facing a low table, leaning on their left arms, leaving their right arms free to feed themselves, their unshod feet extending away from the table.

Why had this Pharisee invited Him? He was no great admirer of Jesus, for we learn from verses 44–46 that he omitted the customary marks of respect that such a distinguished guest should receive. We can never know all his motives, but it seems that he invited Jesus to his home to see this controversial figure for himself. Many had said He was a prophet, though He ignored the rules of the Pharisees, and this Pharisee wanted to put Him to the test. It seems that he omitted the customary marks of welcome to show his Pharisaical colleagues that he was as yet at least neutral toward their hated foe.

The meal was interrupted by an unwelcome and unexpected visitor. (Luke uses the word **behold!** to indicate how unexpected this visitor was.) **A woman who was a sinner in the city**—that is, a notoriously immoral woman, probably a prostitute—made her appearance. She had heard Jesus' message of forgiveness at some earlier time, and the Lord's invitation for the weary to come to

Him to find rest struck a chord in her heavy-laden soul (see Matt.
11:28–30). In response to His proclamation to the crowds, she had
believed and rejoiced in the promise that God would accept sinners
into His Kingdom, and she was determined to find Him to thank
Him herself.

She heard that He was to be in the home of a certain Pharisee,
and she confirmed this fact from others (Gr. *epiginosko*, **really-
know**). Barging past the astonished guests (for it was scandalous
for such a woman to enter the house of a Pharisee), she **brought an
alabaster *flask* of perfume** with her, probably intending to anoint
the Lord's head with it, after the customary manner of anointing.

She found Him reclining at the table, His feet extending towards
her, and she broke down. She perhaps intended to speak with Him
and thank Him, and then anoint His head with some of the perfume, but the emotions of gratitude overwhelmed her, leaving her
speechless. All she could do was **stand behind *Him* at His feet,
weeping** helplessly. Unable to control herself, she knelt down and
began to shower His feet with tears. The assembled guests, we may
imagine, were silent and aghast. As the tears flooded Jesus' feet, she
felt she should wipe them away, and for this purpose, she removed
her veil and **wiped** His feet **with the hair of her head**. The guests
were even more aghast. A respectable woman never unveiled her
hair in this public way, and for this woman to do this and even to
use her hair as a towel for Jesus was unbelievably scandalous. Their
shock would not have been lessened when she began *fervently* **kissing His feet** (Gr. *kataphileo*, a stronger verb than *phileo*, "to kiss")
and **anointing *them* with the perfume**. In her love for Jesus, the
woman was oblivious to the stares of hostility aimed at her from all
others in the room.

As for the Lord's host, **when** he **saw this, he said in himself,
"If this *man* were a prophet** as many claimed, **He would know
who** this woman was that was **touching Him** and more especially
of what sort she was, **that she is a sinner."** A righteous rabbi would
never permit himself to be touched by a prostitute like this, and if
Jesus were a prophet, He would know that she was a prostitute and
would send her packing. Obviously Jesus was not a prophet after

all! We can imagine the Pharisee refusing to look at the woman, disgusting sight that she was.

Jesus, however, did not think her a disgusting sight, and in His compassion strove to reveal this to His host. As a teacher, He prepared to give a teaching and proposed a question in a typical rabbinic manner. He introduced His lesson by calling His host by name, **Simon,** saying He had **something to say**, some teaching to deliver. Though Simon internally rejected Jesus' authority, politeness demanded he accept the lesson and bid Him **say it**. (In His use of Simon's name, we note how Christ strives to save the Pharisees as well and lead them to repentance.)

The Lord proposed the following scenario: **A certain money-lender had two debtors: one owing five hundred denarii** (about a year and a half's wages for the working man) **and the other** owing **fifty**, a mere month and a half's wages. When he discovered that *they* **did not have** *resources* **from themselves to repay** *him***, he** graciously *forgave* **them both.** Christ then posed the question, requiring the Pharisee's legal ruling: **"Which of them therefore will love him more** and thank him the most heartily?"

Simon answered airily, with little thought, **"I take** *it* and assume **the one whom he graciously** *forgave* **the more."** That was obvious. What kind of a question was that? The Lord agreed with Simon's verdict and commended him for his ruling: **"You have judged correctly."**

꒰Ꙩ꒱ ꒰Ꙩ꒱ ꒰Ꙩ꒱ ꒰Ꙩ꒱ ꒰Ꙩ꒱

44 **And turning toward the woman, He said to Simon, "Do you see this woman? I entered into your house; you did not give Me water for My feet, but she** *herself* **has showered My feet with tears, and wiped** *them* **with her hair.**

45 **"You did not give Me a kiss; but she** *herself*, **since** *the time* **I entered, has not stopped** *fervently* **kissing My feet.**

46 **"You did not anoint My head with oil, but she** *herself* **anointed My feet with perfume.**

163

> 47 "Therefore, I say to you, her sins, which are many, have been forgiven, for she loved much; but the one who is forgiven little loves little."
> 48 And He said to her, "Your sins have been forgiven."
> 49 And the ones reclining with Him began to say within themselves, "Who is this who even forgives sins?"
> 50 He said to the woman, "Your faith has saved you; go in peace."

Up until now, Simon doubtless felt that his guest had made a poor showing: He had proven by letting the sinner touch Him that He was no prophet, and had posed an obvious and pointless question. Then Christ lowered the boom. He **turned toward the woman** and instructed Simon to **see this woman** as well. (Up to that time, we may think he had studiously refused to look at her.) *She* was the lesson Simon must learn.

For let him consider this: When Christ **entered into** Simon's **house**, he **did not give** Jesus **water for** His **feet**, or wash them as was usual, but **she *herself*** (the pronouns to describe the woman are all emphatic in the Greek) gave them a nobler washing and **showered** His **feet with tears**. Simon **did not give** Jesus a single **kiss,** the customary greeting due a distinguished rabbi, but **since *the time*** He **entered** (hyperbolically speaking), she did **not stop *fervently* kissing** His **feet**. Simon **did not anoint** Jesus' **head with oil** as He entered, but **she *herself* anointed His feet with perfume**. In every way, she exceeded Simon in the love she showed Jesus.

What did this shocking display of love mean? Simon had answered himself: that she had been **forgiven**, for Simon had himself ruled that one who is forgiven much **loves much**. The Lord was not ignorant of the fact that she was a sinner, as Simon supposed. He knew she had **many** sins. But **her sins had been forgiven** by God as she accepted Christ's Word. This forgiveness was evidenced by her great display of love.

There was another lesson also, which the Lord gently adds: **the**

one who is forgiven little loves little. Simon had shown little love to Jesus, and this meant that he had little forgiveness from God. Let Simon hear this also, and learn to love!

Up until now, the Lord had not said a word to the woman weeping over His feet. Now He turned to speak to her and set His seal to what she had grasped in hope: **"Your sins have been forgiven."** Some present might have thought He would disabuse her of the illusion that God had forgiven her, but Christ confirmed her in the gift. What He had promised in a prior proclamation He now gave her for all to see.

This further scandalized the Pharisee's other dinner guests, and they **began to say within themselves, "Who is this who even forgives sins?"** For who can presume to pronounce the verdict only God can give at the Last Judgment? But Christ would have the woman ignore them and trust in Him. He assured her that her **faith** had **saved** her, and He bade her **go in peace**.

§V.12. Touring Cities

ॐ ॐ ॐ ॐ ॐ

8 1   And it happened afterwards that He was going through every city and village, heralding and bringing good news of the Kingdom of God, and the Twelve *were* with Him,

2   and also certain women who had been cured of evil spirits and ailments: Mary who was called Magdalene, from whom seven demons had gone out,

3   and Joanna the wife of Chuza, Herod's manager, and Susanna, and many others who were serving them from their possessions.

Luke now adds that Christ's ministry was not confined to Galilee (though all of the previous stories were centered there). Rather, **He was going through every city and village** in the land, **heralding**

God's proclamation, **bringing good news** (Gr. *euaggelizo*) that **the Kingdom of God** was at hand. By saying that **the Twelve *were* with Him**, Luke presents us with an image of the Church, for here was Christ surrounded by His apostles, bringing the Gospel to all the world.

St. Luke adds that **certain women who had been cured of evil spirits** and other physical **ailments** were also with Him. These pious women followed Him in the company of His disciples and **were serving them from their possessions**. That is, they put their own financial resources at the disposal of Jesus and His apostles, enabling them all to eat as they traveled from place to place.

Three women are singled out, partly because they featured prominently in the later Christian communities, and also because Luke wants to establish these witnesses of Christ's death and Resurrection as long-time disciples, able to verify all that Christ did and said in His ministry (compare 23:49, 55; 24:1f).

First was **Mary**, called **Magdalene** because she came from the (perhaps notorious) city of Magdala (so-named from its prominent tower, *migdal* in Hebrew), about three miles from Tiberias, on the west side of the Sea of Galilee. She is further described as one **from whom seven demons had gone out**, for Christ had set her free from many demonic afflictions of mind and body. **Seven** here is a symbolic number, indicating the severity of Mary's plight. (We note in passing that there is no suggestion that she is to be identified with the sinful woman mentioned in 7:36f.)

Also mentioned is **Joanna, the wife of Chuza, Herod's manager**. The word rendered *manager* is the Greek *epitropos*, which also means "foreman, steward, guardian." Chuza was a highly placed official at Herod's court and is perhaps to be identified with the royal official mentioned in John 4:46–54. Whatever Chuza's identity, Joanna would have been a source for the Christians of information concerning what went on at Herod's court.

Finally **Susanna** is mentioned, whose name means "lily." Though she is part of the company of women who witnessed the death and Resurrection of Christ (23:49, 55; 24:1f), nothing more is known of her.

§V.13. Parables of the Kingdom

ॐ ॐ ॐ ॐ ॐ

4   And when a large crowd was coming together, and those from every city were coming to Him, He spoke by means of a parable:

5   "The sower went out to sow his seed; and as he sowed, some fell beside the way and was trampled on, and the birds of heaven ate it up.

6   "And others fell on the rock, and having come up, it withered, because it had no moisture.

7   "And others fell in the midst of the thorns, and the thorns came up with it and choked it out.

8   "And others fell into the good earth, and having come up, made fruit a hundredfold." As He said these things, He was calling out, "He who has ears to hear, let him hear!"

9   And His disciples were asking Him what this parable might be.

10 And He said, "To you it has been given to know the mysteries of the Kingdom of God, but to the rest, *it is* in parables, that seeing they may not see, and hearing they may not have insight.

11 "Now the parable is this: The seed is the Word of God.

12 "And those beside the way are those who have heard; then the devil comes and takes the Word from their heart, lest they believe and be saved.

13 "And those on the rock are those who, when they hear, welcome the Word with joy; and these do not have a root; they believe for a time, and in time of testing fall away.

14 "And the ones fallen into the thorns, these are those who have heard, and as they go on, they are choked out with worries and riches and pleasures of life, and do not bring fruit to maturity.

> 15 "And the ones in the good earth, they are *those* who have heard the Word in a good and upright heart, and hold it fast, and bear fruit with perseverance.

When a large crowd was coming together in those days, **He spoke by means of a parable**. The word *parable* is the Greek *parabole*, and literally means something "thrown beside" something else, set down for comparison. The literary form was very diverse, including not only involved allegories (such as the one that follows) but also proverbs, fables, and enigmatic sayings. By using such images, Jesus was able to reach into the hearts of common men like those coming to hear Him.

The parable of the sower had to do with the nature of the Kingdom of God. It was not as many expected—they thought that the Kingdom would come cataclysmically and in political form, and that when Messiah came, He would rally an army of angels and men and sweep the sinners out of the land, exalting Israel to a place of supremacy in the world. It would thus come to all Jews equally, regardless of the state of their heart, regardless of their response to God.

The parable of the sower reveals that such is not the nature of the Kingdom. That Kingdom would not come cataclysmically and equally to all in Israel; all would not be saved and enjoy the Kingdom simply because they were Jews. Rather, their experience of the Kingdom would depend on the state of their individual hearts. If they had hard and faithless hearts, the coming Kingdom would not profit them. It was only the true of heart who would experience the blessedness of the Kingdom of God.

Christ elaborates this basic message by pointing to the different types of soil. All had seen a **sower** as he **went out to sow his seed**, and how the seed fared as it fell onto different locations. The sower walked the footpaths through the fields and threw his seed far and wide. Most landed on the intended fields, though some seed inevitably landed in less hospitable locations. It was the same with Christ as He sowed **the Word of God**, the Gospel message that men should repent and accept His teaching—His message fell into all kinds of hearts.

In the parable, **some** seed **fell beside the way and was trampled on, and the birds of heaven ate it up**. In the same way, some **heard** Jesus' Word, but **the devil comes** (through the lies of Jesus' adversaries) and **takes the Word from their heart, lest they believe** what Jesus says **and be saved** in the age to come.

Other seed **fell on the rock** beside the footpath, which was covered over by a thin layer of soil. This seed, **having come up, withered, because it had no moisture**, no real root system. In the same way, some who **hear** Jesus **welcome the Word with joy**, but because they **do not have a root** or any sense of depth or interiority, though **they believe for a time, in time of testing** and trial they **fall away**. They prove themselves to be shallow enthusiasts, unable to endure persecution.

Other seed **fell in the midst of the thorns, and the thorns came up with it and choked it out**, for the thorns consumed all the goodness from the soil, leaving none for the precious seed. In the same way there were some who **heard** the Word, but **as they go on** through life **they are choked out with worries and riches and pleasures of life**. The pursuit of wealth and all the pleasure it can bring consumes all their energies, and they **do not bring fruit to maturity** in their lives, but ultimately also prove to be fruitless.

Some, however, do benefit from the Word of the Kingdom that Jesus proclaims. For some seed **fell into the good earth, and made fruit a hundredfold**, bearing an abundant crop. In the same way there are those who have **heard the Word**, receiving **it in a good and upright heart**, and they **hold it fast** within themselves, guarding it and refusing to let earth's trials and temptations take it from them. These **bear fruit with perseverance**, living as true disciples until the end. In them and in them alone will the Kingdom of God come and bear fruit.

Not all Jesus' hearers were immediately prepared to accept such a revolutionary notion of the coming Kingdom, and so when Christ finished His parable, He urged them to open their minds, **calling** out in a loud voice, **"He who has ears to hear, let him hear!"**

Indeed, though His disciples had open minds, they still could not immediately grasp His meaning, and so they **were asking Him** (at an opportune moment) **what this parable might be**. In explaining its meaning to them, He assured them that it had been **given** them **to know the mysteries of the Kingdom of God**. They were the initiated to whom such meanings were plainly spoken. **But to the rest** of the crowd, He spoke **in parables** only. For to them, Christ's teaching came as both illumination and judgment, depending on the state of their hearts. If they had open hearts and open minds, they would be able to grasp His meaning and be illumined. But if they refused to open their minds, the inner meaning would remain closed. In this way the prophetic judgment of Is. 6:9 would be fulfilled, and in **seeing** Him the crowd would **not see**, and **hearing** His words, they would **not have insight**. His words would result only in judgment. For God worked in Jesus not only to reward and call the humble, but also to judge and condemn the proud.

ॐ ॐ ॐ ॐ ॐ

16 "No one after kindling a lamp covers it with a vessel, or puts *it* under a bed, but puts *it* on a lampstand, that those coming in may see the light.

17 "For there is nothing hidden that will not become manifest, nor *anything* secret that will never be known and come to light.

18 "Therefore watch out how you hear; for whoever has, to him will *more* be given; and whoever does not have, even what he seems to have will be taken from him."

Luke adds another parable of Jesus, that of the lamp. Every evening, in every Jewish home would take place the ritual of lamp-lighting. The ancients had a horror of the dark, so a lamp would be brought into a room and lit, whereupon all pious Jews would recite a blessing, thanking God for the light. And **no one after kindling** this **lamp covers it with a vessel** or a container, nor would they

put *it* under a bed, where its light could not be seen. Obviously they would **put *it* on a lampstand, that those coming in** the room **may see the light.**

In the same way, Christ gives His teaching in order to illumine His hearers and give them spiritual light. They must not listen to His Word and then do nothing about it. That would be as senseless as lighting a lamp and then hiding its light. For just as the light of a lamp reached all in the house, so Christ's light would eventually illumine all their deeds, as they would be judged on the Last Day. There was **nothing hidden** that would **not become manifest** to all, **nor *anything* secret** that would never **come to the light**. Rather, all their deeds would one day **be known**—and judged. Therefore they must **watch out how** they **hear** and let Christ's words sink into their hearts.

For judgment will surely come, confirming each one in his spiritual wealth or poverty. The spiritually wealthy one, the one who **has**, the one who hears Christ's words and does them, to this one **will *more* be given** by God. In this age such a one knows the blessing of God, and in the age to come he will know greater blessing still. But to the spiritually impoverished, the one who **does not have**, the one who hears Christ's words and does *not* do them, to this one **even what he seems to have will be taken from him**. He seems to be blessed (being rich, well-fed, full of laughter, well-spoken of by all; compare 6:24–26), but all this will be taken away on the Last Day, and he will find himself truly desolate and impoverished in the age to come.

§V.14. Jesus' True Family

ॐ ॐ ॐ ॐ ॐ

19 And His mother and brothers came to Him, and they were not able to meet with Him because of the crowd.

20 And it was declared to Him, "Your mother and Your brothers have been standing outside, wanting to see You."

> 21 But He answered and said to them, "My mother
> and My brothers are those who hear the Word
> of God and do it."

Immediately after these parables, Luke relates a story about Jesus' true family. This juxtaposition reinforces the message that the ones who watch out how they hear (v. 18) and who take care to do the Word of God they hear (v. 21) are Jesus' true kin.

In the story, Jesus' **mother and brothers came to Him**, but **were not able to meet with Him because of the crowd**. It is implied that this was no simple family visit, but a concerted effort to hinder Him in His work, and that it is for this reason that Christ refuses to give them an audience.

We may ask in passing what the holy Theotokos was doing in this hostile delegation. Certainly Jesus' own brothers did not believe in Him (John 7:5), but it is impossible to think that Mary shared this incomprehension. Luke had already made clear that she was blessed precisely because she *did* believe (1:45). But Mary was a powerless widow with no other children, and was brought along by the others as a sort of "bargaining chip." Christ's unbelieving kinsmen hoped that her presence would add persuasiveness to their demands; and as a widow woman, Mary had little to say about it.

Someone received their message, and it was **declared** loudly **to Him, "Your mother and Your brothers have been standing outside, wanting to see You."** Here was a public challenge, a call to Him to acknowledge as primary the claims of kin and family, and to submit to the family's authority.

Christ met the challenge boldly, answering that He was now no longer under such authority, but only under the authority of His heavenly Father. Family did indeed have claims on His loyalty—but those wanting Him to break off His work were not such family, and He owed no loyalty to them. Rather, His true family, His true **mother and brothers**, were **those who hear the Word of God** which He was proclaiming **and do it**. It was to His disciples that He would give His loyalty, for they were His true kin.

§V.15. Christ's Authority over All

§V.15.i. His Authority over Nature's Violence

ॐ ॐ ॐ ॐ ॐ

22 Now it happened on one of those days that He and His disciples got into a boat, and He said to them, "Let us go over to the other side of the lake." And they put out.

23 But as they were sailing He fell asleep, and a storm of wind came down upon the lake, and they were filling up *with water* and were in danger.

24 And they came to Him and roused Him, saying, "Master, Master, we are perishing!" And being roused, He rebuked the wind and the surging of the waves, and they stopped, and a calm happened.

25 And He said to them, "Where *is* your faith?" And they were afraid and marveled, saying to one another, "Who then is this, that He commands even the winds and the water, and they obey Him?"

Luke next relates a series of stories showing Christ's authority, demonstrating His power over the violence of nature, over demons, over chronic sickness, and even over death.

In the first story, it is related that Christ and His disciples **got into a boat** on the shores of the lake of Galilee, and Jesus said to them, **"Let us go over to the other side of the lake."** Christ was exhausted from His labors, and **as they were sailing He fell asleep**, despite the fact that a storm was brewing.

Such storms swept down quite suddenly upon the Sea of Galilee, and this is what happened as they were crossing to the eastern side of the lake. **A storm of wind came down upon the lake,** churning up the waves so that the boat was **filling up *with water*,** swamping them, and they **were in danger** of drowning. Such was Christ's exhaustion that He slept soundly through it all.

The disciples were experienced fishermen, well-acquainted with perils on the water, and they knew that (humanly speaking) they were in mortal danger from the sea. They **came** to Jesus where He lay asleep in the stern (Mark 4:38) and **roused** Him, shouting, **"Master, Master, we are perishing!"**

Being **roused** and fully awake, **He rebuked the wind and the surging of the waves.** The turbulence **stopped, and a calm happened**. As suddenly as the storm came, it disappeared, instantly obedient to the words of Jesus, who rebuked the violence of untamable nature as He rebuked the violence of the demons (4:35).

Having dealt with the storm on the waters, He turned next to the internal storm that rocked the hearts of His disciples. He had a word of rebuke for them also as He demanded, **"Where *is* your faith?"** Did they really think that God would let His Messiah perish with His followers in the sea? Doubtless they had no immediate answer, but after a while (perhaps after Christ returned to His interrupted sleep), they asked themselves in whispers, **"Who then is this, that He commands even the winds and the water, and they obey Him?"** Only God could tame the teeming, restless sea (compare Job 38:8–11), and yet here Jesus had rebuked its raging violence almost casually, stilling its fury with a single utterance. They knew in their hearts that He was God's Chosen One, but were nonetheless stunned by such a naked display of power.

§V.15.ii. His Authority over Demons

26 And they sailed down to the region of the Gerasenes, which is opposite Galilee.

27 And when He had come out upon the land, a certain man from the city *who* had demons met Him, and for a considerable time he was not clothed in a garment, and was not remaining in a house, but among the tombs.

28 And seeing Jesus, he cried out and fell before Him, and said in a great voice, "What am I to You, Jesus, Son of the Most High God? I beseech You, do not torture me!"

29 For He had been ordering the unclean spirit to come out from the man. For it had seized him many times; and he was bound with chains and fetters and guarded, and he would tear the bonds and be driven by the demon into the wilderness *places*.

30 And Jesus asked him, "What is your name?" And he said, "Legion," for many demons had entered into him.

31 And they were urging Him not to command them to depart into the abyss.

32 Now there was a considerable herd of pigs feeding on the mountain; and they urged Him to allow them to enter into those. And He allowed them.

33 And the demons came out from the man and entered into the pigs; and the herd rushed down the slope into the lake and were drowned.

34 And when those feeding *the pigs* saw what had happened, they fled and reported *it* in the city and in the country.

35 And they went out to see what had happened; and they came to Jesus, and found the man from whom the demons had gone out sitting at the feet of Jesus, clothed and sound-minded, and they were afraid.

36 And those who had seen *it* reported to them how the man who was demon-possessed had been saved.

37 And all the multitude of the country of the Gerasenes and the surrounding-country asked Him to depart from them, for they were distressed with great fear; and He got into a boat and returned.

> 38 But the man from whom the demons had gone
> out was beseeching Him to be with Him, but He
> dismissed him, saying,
> 39 "Return to your house and describe what God
> has done for you." And he went away, heralding
> throughout the whole city what Jesus had done
> for him.

When they reached the other side and had **sailed down to the region of the Gerasenes**, He **came out upon the land**. This region was near to the town that is modern Kersa. It was then a predominantly Gentile area, and Christ hoped to get some rest from His exhausting labors in Israel.

It was not to be. As soon as they came to land, **a certain man from the** nearby **city** *who* **had demons met Him**. He had evidently seen Jesus and His disciples approach the shore, and the demons within the poor wretch recognized their final Judge. The man was something of a local sensation—**for a considerable time he was not clothed in a garment**, but ran about naked. Also, for some time he was **not remaining in a house** or living with any shreds of stability. Instead, he wandered **among the tombs** outside the city, far from the comfort of human society. His family and loved ones had tried to restrain him, but to no avail. For the demonic mania **seized him many times**, and though his friends had **bound** him **with chains** on his wrists **and fetters** on his feet to restrain him and **guarded** him, **he would tear the bonds** to pieces in his frenzy and **be driven by the demon into the wilderness** *places* outside of the town.

In his misery, the man **cried out** to Jesus **and fell before Him**, asking for help in wordless supplication. In compassion, Christ began ordering the unclean spirits to come out from the man. The spirits ruling the man, however, were not minded to submit. They shouted **in a great voice, "What am I to You, Jesus, Son of the Most High God? I beseech You, do not torture me!"** That is, the demons recognized Jesus as the final Judge and thought that the final Judgment was at hand. They thought to fend off the Lord, demanding that He not meddle with them (and their unfortunate prey).

In response, Christ demanded, **"What is your name?"** for knowledge of a name gave authority over the one named. The demons could not resist, and confessed their name was **Legion, for many demons had entered into him**. A Roman legion consisted of six thousand soldiers, and by taking this name, the demons indicated that a tremendous invasion of the man had taken place.

The demons knew that the end of their sovereignty over the man was at hand and feared that Christ would send them **into the abyss**, the place of punishment for evil spirits. **They were urging Him not to command** this, but to **allow them to enter into** the **considerable herd of pigs** that was **feeding on the mountain** nearby. This way they would be spared the punishment they dreaded. The Lord granted this request, for if He were to force them out violently against their will, the cost to the demoniac would have been very great. Later on, when the Lord forcibly expelled a single demon from a boy, that demon convulsed the boy so badly that he nearly died (9:42; Mark 9:26). Perhaps it was out of compassion for the man having such a multitude of demons that He allowed the demons to leave quietly.

The demons, however, did not have power even over the pigs (as our church exorcisms remind them: Second Exorcism of Baptism). When **the demons entered into the pigs**, **the herd** panicked and **rushed down the slope into the lake and were drowned. Those feeding** *the pigs* **saw what had happened**, for the slope was perhaps a mere forty yards from the shore. Climbing down the bank, they saw their herd floating dead in the water. **They fled and reported** *it* **in the city and in the country**, publishing the news as far as they could. When people came to see for themselves, **they found** the former lunatic calmly **sitting at the feet of Jesus, clothed** (perhaps in one of the disciples' extra garments) **and sound-minded** for the first time in years, and they heard from the swineherds how the man **had been saved** by Jesus. **They were afraid**, fearful of such power, and **they asked** Jesus **to depart from them**.

In that crowd of trembling foreigners, there was one who did not want Jesus to depart: the man who had been saved from his life of demonic misery. As Jesus **got into a boat** to return to the Jewish side of the lake, the man was continually **beseeching Him** that he might **be with Him** as one of His disciples. The Lord, however, knew that his place was with his loved ones, and **He dismissed him**, sending him home. But He sent him away with a mission. He must **describe** for all his family and friends **what God**, the God of Israel, **had done** for him. Significantly, the man returned home and was **heralding throughout the whole city what Jesus had done for him**. By this, St. Luke means his reader to understand how Jesus exercises all the power and authority of God on earth.

§V.15.iii. His Authority over Sickness and Death

꣗ ꣗ ꣗ ꣗ ꣗

40 And as Jesus returned, the crowd welcomed Him, for they had all been expecting Him.

41 And behold! there came a man named Jairus, and he was a ruler of the synagogue; and he fell at Jesus' feet, and was urging Him to come into his house;

42 for he had an only-begotten daughter, about twelve years old, and she was dying. But as He went, the crowds were choking His *way*.

43 And a woman who had a flow of blood for twelve years, and could not be healed by anyone,

44 came up behind Him and touched the fringe of His garment; and immediately her flow stopped.

45 And Jesus said, "Who *is* the one who touched Me?" And while they were all denying it, Peter said, "Master, the crowds are hemming *You* in and crushing about You."

46 But Jesus said, "Someone touched Me, for I *Myself* know that power has gone out from Me."

47 And when the woman saw that she had not escaped notice, she came trembling and fell down before Him, and declared before all the

> people the reason she had touched Him, and
> how she had been immediately cured.
> 48 And He said to her, "Daughter, your faith has
> saved you; go in peace."

As soon **as Jesus returned** from the region of the Gerasenes, **the crowd welcomed Him, for they had all been expecting Him**, hoping to see some more miracles. As He was teaching and healing, an unexpected event occurred (marked by Luke with his customary **behold!**): **there came a man named Jairus** forcing his way through the crowd to Jesus. He was **a ruler of the synagogue** (that is, one who shared the task of taking care of the building itself and arranging for the conduct of the services), and he **fell at Jesus' feet** with an urgent plea.

He **was urging** Jesus to leave the crowd and **to come into his house** to attend to his **only-begotten daughter**, who was **about twelve years old**, for **she was dying**. Indeed, it had taken him so long to get through the crowd that by now she must be dead (compare Matt. 9:18). In response to his anguished request, the Lord began the slow trek through town to the man's house. The way there was laboriously slow because **the crowds were choking His *way*** (Gr. *sumpnigo*, the same word used in 8:14 for the thorns choking out the seed).

As the Lord waded His way through the crushing crowd, there was in that throng **a woman who had a flow of blood for twelve years**. She had an internal hemorrhage, and this made her ritually unclean. It also made ritually unclean anyone she touched, and thus barred her from all meaningful social contact, as well as from the worship of the synagogue and the Temple. She could not enter a crowd (like this one) without spreading the contagion, and so could not come to Jesus (who was also surrounded by a crowd). In her desperation, she entered the crowd nonetheless and **came up behind** Jesus. She could not tell Him what her problem was without revealing that she had been spreading her ceremonial uncleanness to Him and to everyone else. But she thought that if she just **touched the fringe of His garment**, that would be enough to heal her, and she could escape healed and unnoticed, since everyone in that crowd was touching and jostling Him. Sure enough, when she did this, **immediately her** internal **flow stopped** and she was healed.

She was not, however, to escape unnoticed as she planned. Immediately after she had touched the fringe or tassel of Jesus' garment (probably the tassels pious Jews wore on the corners of their robes in conformity with Num. 15:39), Jesus stopped dead in His tracks and said, **"Who *is* the one who touched Me?"** (We may imagine the effect of this apparently inane question and delay upon the father of the dying girl, for whom every moment was precious.) All were denying that they had touched Him in particular, and Peter (perhaps somewhat embarrassed by such a strange question) quietly said to his Lord, **"Master, the crowds are hemming *You* in and crushing about You."** In other words, who *isn't* touching You?

Jesus, however, was referring to a particular touch, for He knew **that power had gone out** from Him in response to the will of the Father and touch of faith. **When the woman saw that she had not escaped notice, she came trembling and fell down before Him, and declared before all the people the reason she had touched Him.** Such a public confession took courage, for she had committed an outrage in spreading her ritual contagion to all there. Would the Lord rebuke her as the prophet Elisha rebuked Gehazi when he tried to deceive him (2 Kin. 5:25–27)? No wonder the poor woman **came trembling**! The Lord, however, dealt with her with His customary compassion and confirmed the healing she had received. Addressing her tenderly as **daughter**, He simply said, **"Your faith has saved you; go in peace."** His power was stronger than any contagion or any sickness, however longstanding; all her affliction gave way before His sovereign authority.

ॐ   ॐ   ॐ   ॐ   ॐ

49 While He was still speaking, someone comes from *the house* of the synagogue-ruler saying, "Your daughter is dead; do not harass the Teacher any longer."

50 But when Jesus heard, He answered him, "Do not

> be afraid; only have faith, and she will be saved."
>
> 51 And when He had come into the house, He did not allow anyone to enter with Him, except Peter and John and James and the child's father and mother.
>
> 52 Now they were all weeping and lamenting for her; but He said, "Do not weep, for she is not dead, but is sleeping."
>
> 53 And they were laughing at Him, knowing that she was dead.
>
> 54 But seizing her by the hand, He called, saying, "Child, arise!"
>
> 55 And her spirit returned, and she rose immediately; and He directed that *something* be given her to eat.
>
> 56 And her parents were beside themselves; but He ordered them to tell no one what had happened.

Through this delay, the father of the dying girl was (we may imagine) wringing his hands. Now his worst fears were realized, and **while** Jesus **was still speaking, someone comes from** his house **saying, "Your daughter is dead; do not harass the Teacher any longer."** (Luke uses the historic present, so that we can almost see the sad messenger approaching.) They were too late. There was nothing left but to return to the house of death and bury the young girl, who was just approaching marriageable age, and to begin the rites of mourning. The girl was his only-begotten child, and all his joy died with her.

As the man's world dissolved around him, Jesus interrupted and said, **"Do not be afraid; only have faith, and she will be saved."** Faith in Jesus had saved the woman with the hemorrhage, and faith could save this girl as well. When the Lord at length **had come into the house**, He **did not allow anyone to enter** into the dead girl's room **with Him, except Peter and John and James**, as well as, of course, **the child's father and mother**. (We note in passing how Luke groups **Peter and John** together, unlike Mark, who in Mark

5:37 groups Peter with James. Luke knows that Peter and John were friends; compare Luke 22:8; Acts 3:1; 8:14. Luke does this again in 9:28, where he narrates Christ's Transfiguration.)

The whole house was in tumult, with professional mourners engaged in their mournful flute-playing and wailing, and **all were weeping and lamenting for her** as the funeral rites were beginning. Christ informed them that their sad services were not required, for **she was not dead**, but was merely **sleeping**. It seemed to them to be a poor joke, for in their proud contempt they discounted that the Prophet from Nazareth could know something they did not, and they had seen her die with their own eyes. They **were laughing at Him**, confident He was wrong.

The Savior was not wrong, for when Christ is present, death indeed becomes but a sleep, as the dead rise again. **Seizing her** strongly **by the hand**, Jesus **called** out to her, as to someone in a far land (Gr. *phoneo*, a word that often contains nuances of high volume; compare its use in 23:46), **saying, "Child, arise!"** In response, **her spirit returned** to her body and **she rose immediately**, standing up with her full energy. This was not a groggy and gradual awakening, but an instantaneous return to healthful vigor: she was not only alive, but hungry. Doubtless she asked for food, and when her parents asked Christ what they should do, **He directed that *something* be given her to eat**, as she was requesting. Her parents were beside themselves with amazement and joy, but the Lord **ordered them to tell no one what had happened**. Already the crowds were thronging Him. Such news as this could only make it more difficult for Him to move about.

§V.16. The Mission of the Twelve

ॐ ॐ ॐ ॐ ॐ

9 1   And He called the Twelve together and gave them power and authority over all the demons, and to heal diseases.

2   And He sent them out to herald the Kingdom of God and to cure.

3   And He said to them, "Take nothing for the way, neither a staff, nor a bag, nor bread, nor money, and do not have two shirts.

4   "And whatever house you enter, remain there, and go out from there.

5   "And as many as do not welcome you, as you go out from that city, shake off the dust from your feet as a witness against them."

6   And going out, they were going through the villages, *bringing* good news and healing everywhere.

The Lord then **called the Twelve together and gave them power and authority over all the demons, and to heal diseases**. As sharers in His mission, they were now to become sharers in His authority as well, able to do the same works as He. Instead of simply accompanying Him on His journeys (8:1), they were now to be **sent out** themselves to **herald the Kingdom of God and to cure** diseases. The Twelve were to perform miraculous works of healing as confirmation of their message that the Kingdom of God was at hand. Thus, there would be as little excuse before God to reject their Word as there was to reject His.

They were to go forth immediately, as they were, with no added preparations, relying entirely upon whatever welcome and hospitality they would receive. Thus they were to **take nothing for the way**, or the road. They were not to fetch **a staff** if they did not have it in their hand, nor a beggar's **bag** to collect money while on the road, nor a supply of **bread** for several days' journey, nor **money** to buy the bread (literally, "silver," used here as a general term for money). Nor were they to **have two shirts**, the extra one being used for camping outdoors. They were to rely entirely upon God and the welcome that He would provide through sympathetic listeners.

They were to enter a town and find lodging with whoever offered them hospitality, however humble. **Whatever house** they first **entered** in this way, they were to **remain there**, and not strive to find better and more prestigious accommodations. When the time came to leave that town and travel to the next one, they were to **go out from there**, leaving their original lodging. They were thus to avoid local rivalries and local politics, and remain focused on their work.

As many cities as did **not welcome** them and refused to give them accommodation and a hearing, they were to leave immediately, refusing to stay and argue. They were to treat those cities as devout Jews treated Gentile towns: just as a Jew would wipe the dust from his feet as he crossed the border and reentered the Holy Land, so the apostles were to **shake off the dust from** their **feet** when they went forth from that town, **as a witness against them**. On the Last Day, God would judge that town for its rejection of the apostolic message. In obedience to their Lord, the Twelve went forth and **were going through the villages, *bringing* good news**, preaching the Gospel (Gr. *euaggelizo*), **and healing everywhere**. Their miracles provided proof that they were speaking for God, and there would be no excuse not to heed them.

---

7 Now Herod the tetrarch heard of all that was happening; and he was perplexed, because it was said by some that John had risen from the dead,

8 and by some that Elijah had appeared, and by others, that some prophet of the old *prophets* had risen.

9 And Herod said, "John I myself beheaded; who then is this about whom I hear such things?" And he was seeking to see Him.

Their mission and the work of Jesus were so successful that even **Herod the tetrarch** (that is, one who had authority over a fourth part of the land) **heard of all that was happening**. With his guilty conscience, **he was perplexed** and at a loss to explain this new revival within his territory. Previously John the Baptizer had proclaimed that the Kingdom of God was at hand, and Herod had John imprisoned and later executed. Now this same message of the Kingdom was spreading even further, and with accompanying miracles. Herod (son of the infamous Herod the Great) evidently did not know much of Jesus, and was unaware that John and Jesus were contemporaries. Herod did not hear of Jesus until after John's death, and he assumed that Jesus was **John** after **he had risen from the dead**. Certainly that was the consensus of many in his court. How else could this new Prophet be doing such miracles?

There were other estimations of Jesus too. **Some** said that **Elijah had appeared**, whose literal return was expected from the prophecy of Malachi 4:5–6. **Others** were of the opinion that **some prophet of the old _prophets_ had risen** (such as Jeremiah), and that the reported miracles were the result of this resurrection. Herod was tormented by the question—and by the persistence of this religious fervor in his territory. **John** he himself **beheaded**, and he knew that John was dead. So **who then** was **this about whom** he was **hearing such things?** Could it really be John returned—as his guilty conscience feared? So it was that **he was seeking to see** Jesus, to discover for himself if his fears were true.

§V.17. Bread in Bethsaida

ॐ ॐ ॐ ॐ ॐ

10 And when the apostles returned, they described to Him what they had done. And taking them along with Him, He withdrew by Himself to a city called Bethsaida.
11 But the crowds knew _this_ and followed Him, and welcoming them, He was speaking to them about the Kingdom of God and curing those who had need of healing.
12 And the day began to decline, and the Twelve came and said to Him, "Dismiss the crowd, that they may go into the surrounding villages

and farms and get lodging and find provisions;
for here we are in a wilderness place."

13 But He said to them, "You *yourselves* give them
something to eat!" And they said, "There are
not with us more than five breads and two fish,
unless we *ourselves* go and buy food for all these
people."

14 (For there were about five thousand men.) And
He said to His disciples, "Have them recline in
groups of about fifty each."

15 And they did so and had them all recline.

16 And having taken the five breads and the two
fish, and having looked up to heaven, He
blessed them and broke *them*, and was giving
them to the disciples to set before the crowd.

17 And they all ate, *even* to the full, and the broken
pieces left over by them were picked up, twelve
baskets *of them*.

After Jesus' apostles **returned** from their mission tour, **they
described to Him what they had done.** After their exciting and
exhausting work, they badly needed to rest, and so **taking them
along with Him,** Jesus **withdrew by Himself to a city called
Bethsaida.** This was Bethsaida-Julias, on the northeastern side of
Lake Galilee, so named to distinguish it from the other Bethsaida
on the western side of the lake. This eastern Bethsaida was near a
deserted place where they could take a much-needed rest, away from
the crowds of Galilee.

It was not to be. The crowds knew where He had gone and
followed Him to His destination, running together from all places
(Mark 6:33). (It was not a long trek: from Capernaum, the trip was
only about four miles.) When Christ and the Twelve disembarked
from their boat, they were met by yet another multitude.

Christ did not spurn them, or put His own needs before theirs.
Instead, **welcoming them, He was speaking to them** at length
about the Kingdom of God and curing those many **who had**

need of healing. They were downcast and lost, and were drawn to Jesus because in Him they could find healing and life. The Lord spent the day caring for them. **The day began to decline**, and a crisis began to loom. Here were **about five thousand men**, not counting the women and children, making a vast multitude of perhaps some fifteen thousand people. They had nothing to eat, and since they were **in a wilderness place**, far from homes, farms, and shops where they could buy food, many might faint away. Some of the Twelve came up to Him to tell Him of the coming crisis, opining that He should **dismiss the crowd** now, **that they may go into the surrounding villages and farms and get lodging and find provisions**. Indeed, they would have to scatter far and wide, for one town could not feed such a large crowd!

Christ countered that the disciples themselves (the Greek pronoun is emphatic) should **give** the people **something to eat**. It was, of course, an invitation for them to trust in His messianic power. God fed Israel of old in the wilderness, and could do so again through His Messiah.

The apostles, however, were not on that wavelength, but still looked only to their own human resources. After a quick tally, they reported that **there were not** with them **more than five breads**, or barley loaves, **and two fish**, small pickled fish eaten as a side dish. This was all they had—unless He was suggesting that they themselves somehow were to **go and buy food for all these people**! They mentioned this last option only to discount it as ludicrous—that couldn't be what He meant, for such a purchase was far beyond their resources.

Ignoring their failure of faith, Christ moved to meet the needs of the multitude. He directed them to **have** the crowd **recline in groups of about fifty each**. They were to recline as for a feast and await their meal, arranging themselves as if reclining at separate tables. The disciples **did so and had them all recline**—though they doubtless wondered where the food was to come from.

The Lord **took the five breads and the two fish**, the meager resources of man, and prepared to multiply them by His divine power. Christ **looked up to heaven**, to His Father, the source of all, for here was no ordinary blessing, but the miraculous power of God. (Normally one recited the customary blessing over food looking down at the food.) He **blessed** the loaves and fishes, chanting the usual Jewish blessing, **and broke *them***, and began **giving *them* to the disciples to set before the crowd**. He continued to break loaf after loaf, fish after fish, until there was a supernatural abundance. Indeed, **they all ate, *even* to the full.** The word rendered *to the full* is the Greek verb *chortazo*, translated in Rev. 19:21 as "to gorge." Not only was there enough for all, but **the broken *pieces* left over by them** were enough to fill **twelve baskets**, the little wicker carrying baskets that pious Jews customarily wore as part of the daily traveling attire.

The lesson was plain: As God provides food to all flesh, opening His hand to satisfy the desire of every living thing (Ps. 136:25; 145:16), so through Christ He feeds those who trust in Him, for Christ is the true power of God.

§V.18.   Peter Confesses Jesus to Be Christ; First Passion Prediction

ॐ ॐ ॐ ॐ ॐ

18 And it happened that while He was praying alone, the disciples were with Him, and He asked them, saying, "Who do the crowds say that I am?"

19 And they answered and said, "John the Baptizer, and others, Elijah; but others, that some prophet of the old *prophets* has risen."

20 And He said to them, "But who do you *yourselves* say that I am?" And Peter answered and said, "The Christ of God."

In the Markan material, this confession of Jesus as the Messiah does not follow immediately after Jesus' multiplication of the loaves, but is narrated after a whole series of other events (Mark 6:45—8:26). It is the same in Matthew's Gospel—the Petrine confession of

Jesus as Messiah does not follow immediately after the multiplication of the loaves in Matthew 14:13–21, but is also narrated after a series of other events (Matt. 14:22—16:12). Though it is possible that Luke omits this material simply to allow space on his scroll to narrate other events (such space was limited), it seems likely that there is a special reason why St. Luke chooses to narrate the story of Peter's confession here, immediately after the story of the loaves.

I suggest that Luke narrates it here to show its close link with what precedes it, and to show Christ's connection with His gathered Church. The story of the loaves had a eucharistic resonance for the Church, since it uses classic eucharistic vocabulary. Christ's taking of the bread, His blessing and breaking and giving it to His apostles foreshadows the Last Supper (22:19), as well as His post-Resurrection fellowship when He would make Himself known to His disciples through the breaking of the bread (24:30, 35). The apostolic Church, which celebrated the Eucharist weekly, could not but read their own eucharistic experience back into Christ's multiplication of the loaves. By narrating the Church's confession of Jesus as Messiah immediately after this, St. Luke shows that the Christ of Israel manifests His Presence now through the worship of the Church.

The story begins **while** Jesus **was praying alone**. This detail is not present in Mark's or Matthew's account, and Luke mentions it to stress that Peter's confession was the fruit of Christ's prayer. Christ was praying that the Father would reveal His true significance to His disciples, and His prayer was answered. After His prayer, **He asked them, saying, "Who do the crowds say that I am?"** The disciples were delighted to relate the foolish guesses of the masses. Perhaps with a laugh, they responded that many felt He was **John the Baptizer**, risen from the dead, and others opined that He was **Elijah** returned from heaven, and **others** still **some prophet of the old *prophets***, also **risen** again with supernatural power. Amidst such lighthearted ridicule of these views, Jesus casts His own challenge to them, chilling their easy pride. That's what mere men think, but what about them? Do they know who He is? With perhaps keen glance, He asks them, **"But who do you *yourselves* say that I am?"**

Peter was ready for the challenge, for he had been taught by the Father (Matt. 16:17), and he answered steadily, **"The Christ of God."** For us today, such a confession seems self-evident, but that is because Peter's confession has already shaped our understanding. In that day, the Christ was thought to be a military figure—one who would appear on clouds of glory to destroy God's enemies and rout the hated Roman armies. For people to see that the peaceful and homeless Nazarene was not simply the one *designated to be* the Messiah in the future but was *even now* that Messiah involved the overturning of all traditional thought regarding the nature of the Messiah and the Kingdom.

ॐ ॐ ॐ ॐ ॐ

21 But He warned them and ordered *them* to tell this to no one,

22 saying, "It is necessary for the Son of Man to suffer many *things*, and be rejected by the elders and chief-priests and scribes, and be killed, and on the third day to be raised."

23 And He was saying to all, "If anyone wants to come after Me, let him deny himself, and take up his cross daily, and follow Me.

24 "For whoever wants to save his life will lose it, but whoever loses his life because of Me, this one will save it.

25 "For what is a man profited if he gains the whole world, and loses or forfeits himself?

26 "For whoever is *thoroughly*-ashamed of Me and My words, of this one will the Son of Man be *thoroughly*-ashamed when He comes in His glory, and the *glory* of the Father and of the holy angels.

27 "But I say to you truly, there are some of those standing here who will never taste death until they see the Kingdom of God."

Such a revelation of Jesus as Messiah, however, was not for everyone, for most could not yet come to terms with its implications. To confess that the Messiah had arrived was to summon Israel to arms, to military combat. Indeed, Christ had barely avoided being caught up in such a call to arms (John 6:15). He therefore **warned them and ordered *them* to tell this to no one**. Indeed, the disciples also had yet to learn the true nature of messiahship, and that it was **necessary for the Son of Man to suffer many *things,* and be rejected by the elders and chief-priests and scribes, and be killed**. They, like others, had thought of the Messiah only in terms of victory and glory. Now they must learn that being Messiah also involved pain, betrayal, defeat, and death. Only after this was He to **be raised**.

The apostles' reactions to this new teaching are not recorded, and Luke shifts the focus to Christ's generalized teaching **to all** His disciples. At the next opportunity, Christ warned all who **wanted to come after** Him and follow Him as His disciples that they too must be prepared for pain, defeat, and death. The potential disciple must **deny himself**, renouncing his deepest desires for survival and worldly success, and **take up his cross daily**, and in this way **follow** Him.

The image of taking up a cross was a stunning and a horrifying one. They had all seen the poor wretches Rome condemned to death taking up their crosses and struggling with them to the place of execution. A man taking up his cross was a man on his way out of the world. Jesus says it is the same for whoever would follow Him: that one must be prepared to sacrifice all the world for the Kingdom. And this is not a single and isolated effort, but a daily experience of world-renunciation.

Here is the paradox: If one clings to safety and comfort, refusing to follow Jesus because the cost is too high, if one **wants to save his life** and preserve all his worldly happiness, that one will **lose it**. It is the one who **loses his life** because of Jesus who will ultimately **save it**.

Discipleship is hard. But it is the only sensible path. **For what is a man profited if he gains** even **the whole world** by his refusal to follow the hated Nazarene and in the end **loses or forfeits himself?** In this short parabolic saying, the Lord asks His hearers to evaluate

191

this bargain: If a man is offered even the whole world in exchange for being killed, how sensible is that? One would keep one's life, even if it meant forgoing wealth, comfort, and fame. In the same way, to preserve one's reputation and wealth in this age by siding against Christ is senseless, for it means that one will lose his soul in the age to come.

For that age to come will represent true justice. If one is ***thoroughly*-ashamed** of Jesus and His **words** in this age, then Jesus will in return be ***thoroughly*-ashamed** of **this one** when He **comes in His glory, and the *glory* of the Father and the holy angels** in the age to come. Here it is easy to give in to cowardice and to renounce the humble Nazarene, defenseless and inglorious as He seems. But the Nazarene will one day be powerful and glorious, and able to judge all who renounce Him. Let His disciples be strong in this age and hold to their allegiance, no matter what the suffering, no matter what the cost.

That day of glory seemed far off. But a foretaste of it was soon to come, as a confirmation that Christ's true glory would one day be revealed. Indeed, there were **some of those standing** there even now who would **never taste death until they saw the Kingdom of God**. Some of His listeners would know for themselves the truth of His words.

§V.19. The Transfiguration

Christ's prediction in verse 27 about some of His hearers not tasting death until they had seen the Kingdom of God finds its fulfillment in the Transfiguration. (The account of the Transfiguration immediately follows this prediction in all three Synoptic Gospels.) Those who heard Christ's words about discipleship wondered if they would live to see the Kingdom, and Christ was assuring them that some present actually would see it with their own eyes. The reference was of course to Peter, John, and James, who would behold Christ in His Kingdom glory within the next days.

ॐ ॐ ॐ ॐ ॐ

28 And about eight days after these words, it happened that He took along Peter and John and James, and went up to the mountain to pray.

The chronology of the Transfiguration in Luke has occasioned comment. Both Matthew and Mark say that it occurred six days after Christ spoke His prediction (Matt. 17:1; Mark 9:2), while Luke affirms that it took place **about eight days** later. What are we to make of this?

Perhaps a key to understanding Luke's calculation lies in remembering that the Transfiguration took place at night (note the apostles' sleepiness in v. 32), and probably after midnight. Christ was in the habit of praying long into the night (see Mark 6:46–48, where Christ prayed until the fourth watch of the night, i.e. until 3:00 A.M.), and on this occasion, **He took along Peter and John and James** with Him when He **went up to the mountain to pray**. The amount of time that elapsed between Christ's prediction and the Transfiguration depends on how one counts the days between them. Matthew and Mark count only the intervening days, while Luke counts the day of the prediction as one day and the post-evening time of the Transfiguration as another day.

Thus, if Christ uttered His prediction (say) on Monday afternoon and the event happened early the following Monday morning (say 2:00 A.M.), then the perceived contradiction is removed. Matthew and Mark would count Monday to Tuesday as one day and the event as happening late Sunday night for a total of six days, while Luke counts each Monday to be one day and the event as happening early Monday for a total of eight days.

Whatever the chronology, Christ took His inner circle with Him for His time of prayer. Luke alone mentions Christ's prayer at this time, and by this he seems to suggest that Christ's Transfiguration before Peter, John, and James was the fruit of His prayer, even as were His original choice of the Twelve (6:12) and the confession of Peter (9:18). The mountain is not named, though Mount Tabor, rising 1300 feet above sea level between Nazareth and the Sea of Galilee, is the traditional site.

ॐ　ॐ　ॐ　ॐ　ॐ

29 And it happened that while He was praying, the appearance of His face became different, and His apparel became white and flashing.

30 And behold! two men were speaking with Him, who were Moses and Elijah,

31 who, appearing in glory, were speaking of His exodus which He was about to fulfill at Jerusalem.

32 Now Peter and those with him had been burdened with sleep; but when they became fully alert, they saw His glory and the two men standing with Him.

33 And it happened as these were separating from Him, Peter said to Jesus, "Master, it is good for us to be here; and let us make three tents: one for You, and one for Moses, and one for Elijah"—not knowing what he was saying.

34 And while he was saying these things, a cloud occurred and was overshadowing them; and they were afraid as they entered into the cloud.

35 And a Voice occurred from out of the cloud, saying, "This is My Son, My Chosen One; hear Him!"

36 And when the Voice had occurred, Jesus was found alone. And they were silent, and declared to no one in those days anything of what they had seen.

It was **while He was praying** into the night that **the appearance of His face became different, and** even **His apparel became white and flashing**. (The word translated here *flashing* is the Gr. *exastrapto*, used to describe the blinding flashing of lightning.) More surprising (Luke uses his characteristic **behold!** to show how unexpected it was), **two men** appeared out of nowhere and were **speaking with Him—Moses and Elijah, appearing in** heavenly **glory, speaking** with Christ **of His exodus which He was about to fulfill at Jerusalem**. That is, they were speaking of Christ's departure (Gr. *exodos*) from this world through His Cross, Resurrection, and Ascension. (It was perhaps the sound of their conversation that awoke the sleepy apostles.) Although **burdened with sleep** at that hour, they soon **became fully alert** and **saw** their Master's **glory**.

It is important for us to remember how important such a revelation was. The Jews all expected the Messiah to be a figure of heavenly glory and radiant splendor. Those who suspected that Jesus was the designated Messiah were doubtless puzzled by His ordinary appearance. Should not the Messiah shine with heavenly glory and be attended by saints and angels? Jesus appeared to all men in the dress of a simple field preacher, a humble carpenter, and this was a stumbling block.

This stumbling block was removed before the eyes of the watching apostles that night as they beheld His true and proper glory. As He walked among men, that glory was veiled. Now, for the apostles' sakes, the veil was temporarily removed, and they could see their Lord as He truly was.

Peter (as usual) speaks first and **says to Jesus, "Master, it is good for us to be here."** He offered to **make three tents**—one each for Jesus, **for Moses,** and **for Elijah**. He remembered how God's glory appeared to this same Moses through the Tent of Meeting (Ex. 33:9), and he sought to somehow preserve this manifested glory. Perhaps after these tents were made, Jesus could return here, with Moses and Elijah also, each to their appointed tent! It was an inane suggestion, and Luke acknowledges that Peter, fresh from sleep, did **not know what he was saying**.

Christ did not have time to reply to Peter's novel suggestion, for **while** Peter **was saying these things, a cloud occurred** and began **overshadowing them**. This was the Cloud of the Divine Presence, such as overshadowed the Tabernacle and Temple of old (Ex. 40:35;

1 Kin. 8:10), and not surprisingly, **they were afraid as they entered into the cloud**. Then **a Voice occurred from out of the cloud**—the very Voice that created the world out of nothing (Gen. 1:3)—the voice of the transcendent Father. As He spoke in a vision to John the Baptizer (3:22), so He spoke to the apostles, saying, **"This is My Son, My Chosen One; hear Him!"** No sooner had the Voice spoken than **Jesus was found alone**. When they all walked down the mountain the following morning, **they were silent** about the vision and **declared to no one in those days anything of what they had seen**. Once again, such a revelation of Jesus as Messiah would not have been understood by the masses, but would have been seen as a summons to military mobilization.

What did it all mean? Why did Moses and Elijah appear to Jesus, and not some other ancient prophet? What did their sudden departure mean? To men steeped in the Old Testament, the answers were plain. Moses was the great Lawgiver, and Elijah was the greatest of the prophets. Together they embodied the Law and the Prophets, the whole Old Testament dispensation. As they spoke with Jesus of His own *exodos*, His death and Resurrection, it was a living illustration of how all the Scriptures point to Him and His Cross, of how the Christ must suffer and only then enter into His glory (see 24:26).

Jesus was not, as some might have supposed, simply one more prophet in a line of many prophets. He was not subordinate to Moses or the Law. Rather, Moses and the Prophets were subordinate to *Him* and witnessed to Him. All Israel's sacred history was merely a preparation for His Gospel ministry. Peter, in suggesting that three tents be erected, failed to appreciate this, for he thought that Jesus was no more than one among two other equals. He did not see that Moses and Elijah were simply a preparation for Jesus, destined to fade when He arrived. And fade they did, leaving Jesus alone. That is, the Old Testament was to give place to the New Testament, the Law and the Prophets giving place to Christ. As the Voice of the Father said, all were to **hear Him** and to focus on Jesus alone. The Old Testament dispensation was drawing to its close.

§V.20. Descent from the Mountain and Healing the Demoniac Child; Second Passion Prediction

ॐ ॐ ॐ ॐ ॐ

37 And it happened on the next day that when they had come down from the mountain, a large crowd met Him.

38 And behold! a man from the crowd shouted, saying, "Teacher, I beseech You to look upon my son, for he is my only-begotten,

39 "and behold, a spirit takes him, and he suddenly cries out, and it convulses him with foaming, and as it breaks him, it leaves him *only* with difficulty.

40 "And I besought Your disciples that they might cast it out, and they were not able."

41 And Jesus answered and said, "O faithless and perverse generation! How long will I be with you, and bear with you? Bring your son here."

42 And while he was still coming to *Him*, the demon tore him and convulsed him. But Jesus rebuked the unclean spirit, and cured the child, and gave him back to his father.

43 And they were all thunderstruck at the greatness of God. But while everyone was marveling at all that He was doing, He said to His disciples,

44 "Let these words sink into your ears; for the Son of Man is about to be delivered into the hands of men."

45 But they did not understand this word, and it was hidden from them that they might not discern it; and they were afraid to ask Him about this word.

Since the vision of the Transfiguration took place at night, it was **the next day** when they **came down from the mountain**. Immediately upon Jesus' return to His disciples, **a large crowd met Him**. Once again, the unexpected happened (signaled by the exclamation **behold!**)—the Lord's disciples had failed to cast out a demon when requested to do so.

It began with **a man from the crowd**, who **shouted** at Jesus as he saw Him approaching His disciples, crying for attention and addressing Jesus deferentially as **Teacher**. The man was distraught, and his explanation was to the point: he had an **only-begotten son** who was grievously afflicted by a demon. Whenever the **spirit takes him**, the boy **suddenly cries out** in distress as the demon **convulses him**, causing **foaming** at the mouth. It **breaks** the child (that is, it throws him on the ground), and **leaves him** *only* **with difficulty**. He **besought** Christ's disciples about the boy, asking **that they might cast it out**—and **they were not able**. Now the man was beside himself with desperation. If even Jesus and His men could not help his child, what was he to do?

Jesus was not fazed. The problem was not insufficient power, but their insufficient faith. The man was part of a **faithless and perverse generation**. With wearied resignation, Jesus asks **how long** He was to **be with** them and **bear with** them. (A poignant question, given the nearness of His exodus from the earth; compare v. 31.) Like a physician certain of His cure, He tells the man to **bring** his **son here** to Him.

Though the man had little faith in Jesus' power, the demon had no such reservations. **While** the boy **was still coming to** Jesus, **the demon** within the boy **tore him** again, dashing him to the ground, and **convulsed him**, as it had many times before. The spirit's panic-stricken display of power was to no avail, however, and Jesus quickly and easily cast it out. The people in the surrounding crowd were **all thunderstruck at the greatness** and majesty **of God** manifested in Jesus' work, no doubt breaking into shouts and cheers.

Christ's popularity continued unabated, and **everyone was marveling** in those days **at all that He was doing**. But the Lord did not want His apostles to be misled by such cheers, and He said to them privately, **"Let these words sink into your ears; for the Son of Man is about to be delivered into the hands of men."** They should not think their Master's current popularity would last forever, but must be forewarned that it would not be so, and take that warning to heart. Though He was popular now, all too soon He would be **delivered into the hands of men**, betrayed, rejected, scorned, and hated.

The disciples **did not understand this word** and remained ignorant of how it could be so. He had spoken before of how He would be rejected and killed (9:22), and this was the second time in a week or so that He had spoken in such parables. What could it mean? For us it is obvious that Christ was speaking no parable when He spoke of His being rejected and killed, but it was not obvious to the apostles. They knew Him to be the Messiah, and the Messiah was to live forever (John 12:34), and to go from victory to victory as a conquering hero. What could this talk about His defeat and death mean? Though uncomprehending, **they were afraid to ask Him about this word**. Instead, they kept it inside them, hoping that the frightening image had some other meaning (see also 18:31ff and comments).

§V.21. The Disciples Quarrel over First Place

༄ ༄ ༄ ༄ ༄

46 And a questioning entered among them as to which of them might be the greatest.

47 But Jesus, knowing the question in their heart, took hold of a child and stood him beside Himself,

48 and said to them, "Whoever welcomes this child in My Name welcomes Me; and whoever welcomes Me welcomes Him who sent Me; for he who is littlest among you all, this one is great."

So little did the apostles understand their Lord's words about Him being rejected in this age that they were filled with thoughts of the earthly glory that would come to them with the Kingdom of God. Accordingly, **a questioning**, a debate, **entered among them as to which of them might be the greatest**. That is, when this Kingdom came with all its (as they supposed) earthly glory, which of them would occupy positions of prominence in it?

The Lord, it seems, had not heard the details of their debate, but nonetheless, He **knew the question in their** secret **heart** and the false understanding of greatness that prompted it. Each of the apostles thought himself great and wanted a chief position in the Kingdom. But true greatness is not based on self-promotion, as they supposed.

With great sensitivity, Christ did not rebuke them for their selfish ambition. Instead, He **took hold of a child** (possibly one of Peter's children or relatives?) **and stood him beside Himself** in the midst of them all, where they all could see him, thereby identifying the child with Himself. The lesson, He said, was this: **"Whoever welcomes this child in My Name welcomes Me; and whoever welcomes Me welcomes Him who sent Me."** That is, even though the one sent by Jesus has little or no status in the world (as children had no status in those days; see Gal. 4:1), yet he is to be welcomed as the Lord Jesus Himself would be welcomed, and even as the Father who sent Him. Those whom Christ sends in His Name stand at the end of a holy chain of authority leading back to God Himself. The apostles must not despise one whom they consider to have no status. Worldly status counts for nothing; what counts is humility.

Therefore **he who is littlest among** them **all**—the one who humbles himself to do the work of a servant, content with no more status than a child has—**this one** is truly **great**. Greatness in the Kingdom will be the reward of humility and having a servant's heart in this age. The apostles' striving for the first place shows that they are not yet worthy of it.

ॐ ॐ ॐ ॐ ॐ

49 And John answered and said, "Master, we saw someone casting out demons in Your Name; and we were forbidding him because he is not following with us."

> **50** But Jesus said to him, "Do not forbid *him*; for
> he who is not against you is for you."

In response to such a rebuke, John tries to deflect Christ's attention to what he considers to be the failings of others outside the
ranks of the apostles—in this case, **someone** who was **casting out
demons in** Jesus' **Name**, even though **he was not following with**
them and was not a baptized disciple of Jesus. John considered this
unauthorized use of Jesus' Name unacceptable. The Twelve had
received such authority to exorcise (9:1), but not this man. The verb
tense used is the imperfect (**were forbidding**), indicating that the
apostles' exchange with the man had been lengthy and heated, and
perhaps not too successful. By calling this to Jesus' attention, John
hopes that Jesus will step in and officially forbid such exorcisms—and
commend the apostles for their zeal.

The Lord, however, is not distressed by the exorcist's behavior.
Instead He tells John **not** to **forbid** *him* to use His Name for exorcism as he has been doing. People were then being drawn into two
polarized camps regarding Jesus, and **whoever** was **not against**
them was therefore **for** them. The exorcist had not sided with Jesus'
foes, and the apostles must welcome whatever testimony to Jesus
the exorcist could give by his actions. The man was serving Christ's
cause in his own way. In giving this direction, Christ also delivers
another gentle rebuke to the disciples' jealous pride of place and
their ambition.

ཚ VI ཚ

JOURNEYING TO JERUSALEM
(9:51—19:27)

St. Luke includes here another distinct section of his Gospel, with most of its material not found in Mark. This present section, 9:51—19:27, is about Christ's journey to Jerusalem, and this final geographical goal is repeatedly mentioned throughout the section (13:32–33; 17:11; 18:31). However, Luke does not mean to suggest one single and uninterrupted journey from Galilee to Jerusalem (that final journey to the Holy City would take place only later). He records a whole series of more or less disconnected stories, which took place at different locations. For example, in 10:38–42 Luke narrates the story of Christ's visit to the home of Mary and Martha in Bethany, near Jerusalem (see John 12:1–2), and then later in 17:11–19 relates the story of Christ passing between Galilee and Samaria. It is obvious therefore that during this time Christ visited Jerusalem in the south more than once.

The sense in which all of this material can be thought of as a journey to Jerusalem is that from this time on, Christ was resolute in His intention to face the final conflict He knew was awaiting Him there. After Peter confessed that Jesus was the Christ (9:18–20), He began to prepare His apostles for His death, repeatedly predicting it (9:22, 44; 17:25; 18:31–33). After that historic confession and His Transfiguration, the rest of His ministry took place beneath the shadow of the Cross.

§VI.1. Christ's Patience and Samaritan Hostility

> ཚ ཚ ཚ ཚ ཚ
>
> 51 And it happened when the days of His taking-up were being fulfilled that He established His face to go to Jerusalem;

52 And He sent messengers before His face. And they went and entered a village of the Samaritans to prepare for Him.

53 And they did not welcome Him, because His face was going to Jerusalem.

54 And when His disciples James and John saw it, they said, "Lord, do You want us to command that fire come down from heaven and consume them?"

55 But He turned and rebuked them.

56 And they went to another village.

This final part of Christ's ministry, when He was preparing His apostles for His death, is described as when **the days of His taking-up were being fulfilled**. That is, the days when He would be betrayed, killed, raised, and taken to heaven were slowly drawing near as the conflict between Him and His foes became ever fiercer, with repeated attempts on His life (see John 7:1; 8:59; 10:31). (We note the importance of the Ascension for Luke, for he summarizes all the final events of Christ's life as His **taking-up**, or Ascension. Luke is the only one of the Gospel writers to narrate the Ascension—which he does twice, in Luke 24:51 and Acts 1:9.)

It was during this time in His ministry that He **established His face** (a Hebraism for "resolutely intended"; see 2 Chr. 20:3; Dan. 11:17) **to go to Jerusalem**. That is, He made Jerusalem the focus and final goal of His work and was intent on ministering there, whatever the danger.

As a preparation for one such visit to Jerusalem (possibly the one recorded in John 7:10f, though certainty is impossible), **He sent messengers before His face**. These were men sent on ahead (possibly selected from among the Twelve) **to prepare for Him**, securing adequate lodging and supplies in the village in which He was to stay. Such advance preparations were necessary because of the large entourage following Jesus. The Samaritan village to which His messengers came, however, **did not welcome Him**. They refused to give them the requested food and lodging, **because His face**

was going to Jerusalem. The Samaritans hated Jerusalem as a rival site to their own holy mountain of Gerizim (John 4:20) and as the capital of the Jews. Because Jesus was traveling as a pilgrim to that city, they refused to help Him in any way.

When the messengers returned with this news, the rest were indignant. Jesus had always refused to share the Jewish prejudice against the Samaritans (see John 4:1f), and this was how they repaid Him! James and John (nicknamed "sons of thunder," possibly because of their inclination to such outbursts) thought of how the prophet Elijah called down fire from heaven to destroy his foes (2 Kin. 1:9–12), and they were convinced that here was a situation that warranted similar treatment. They asked the Lord if He **wanted** them to **command that fire come down from heaven and consume them**, evidently just waiting for the word.

The Lord would have none of it. **He turned** round on them **and rebuked them** for such a thought. Here was the time to turn the other cheek (6:29). Leaving the Samaritan village that rejected them to the mercy and judgment of God, **they went to another village** to try to find lodging there.

In the original text of Luke, it would seem that the words of the rebuke are not mentioned. That led some to fill in what they felt was a lack. In some manuscripts, verses 55–56 add Jesus' rebuke: "You do not know what kind of spirit you are of; for the Son of Man did not come to destroy men's lives, but to save them." That is, the disciples did not recognize what kind of attitude was to characterize them and how far they were from it. Like their Master, they were to seek men's salvation, not their destruction. Though these words are not original to Luke's Gospel, they seem to be an authentic saying of Jesus.

℞ EXCURSUS
ON THE CITY OF JERUSALEM

The city of Jerusalem and its Temple have special significance in Luke's Gospel. His Gospel begins and ends in the Temple (1:5f; 24:52), and it is in the Temple, as the locus of revelation, that Jesus is first recognized as the Christ (2:22f). Luke inverts the order of the last two temptations of Christ (the three temptations almost certainly ended with Satan's offer of the world to Jesus if only He would worship him, for Christ responds to this temptation by telling Satan to "begone"; Matt. 4:10), so that in Luke's Gospel the temptations culminate at the Temple. Luke alone reports Jesus' saying that all true prophets must meet their end in Jerusalem (13:33). Though Matthew relates Christ's resurrection appearances as centering in Galilee (Matt. 28:7–16; compare Mark 16:7), Luke focuses on His appearances in Jerusalem (Luke 24:13f). Luke alone relates Christ's word that the Gospel must be heralded to all nations "beginning from Jerusalem" in order to fulfill the Scriptures (24:47).

For Luke, Jerusalem with its Temple is the heart of the Jewish world, the center and image of God's revelation to Israel. For Christ to fulfill God's Word to Israel, it was necessary for His work to culminate in the Holy City.

This is seen in Luke's Acts of the Apostles as well, the basic outline of which is given in Acts 1:8: The Church witnesses to all nations by the power of the Spirit, beginning at Jerusalem and spreading out into all Judea and into Samaria and even to the ends of the earth. This work begins in Jerusalem, focusing on the Temple there (2:46; 3:1), and ends in Rome, the center of the Gentile world. The Gospel's progress from Jerusalem to Rome is a sign that the Gospel was truly universal. It fulfilled God's promises to Israel (beginning in Jerusalem), but was meant for all the world.

§VI.2. Christ's Claims on His Disciples

ॐ ॐ ॐ ॐ ॐ

57 And as they were going on the way, someone said to Him, "I will follow You wherever You go."
58 And Jesus said to him, "The foxes have dens, and

the birds of the heaven have dwellings, but the Son of Man does not have *a place* to lay *His* head."

59 And He said to another, "Follow Me." But he said, "Allow me first to go and bury my father."

60 But He said to him, "Leave the dead to bury their own dead; but as for you, go and declare the Kingdom of God."

61 And another also said, "I will follow You, Lord; but first allow me to take my leave of those at home."

62 But Jesus said to him, "No one who puts his hand to the plow and looks to the things behind is useful for the Kingdom of God."

Luke then relates three brief sayings about the nature of discipleship. The first two occurred earlier in Christ's ministry (compare Matt. 8:18f), but Luke places them here together with the third saying to show that Christ's resolution to go to the Cross must be matched by the resolution of His disciples to follow Him no matter what the cost.

The first saying is occasioned by **someone** who approaches Him as He and His disciples are **going on the way**, in the midst of a journey someplace. This person (a scribe, as we learn from Matt. 8:19) offers loyalty, promising to **follow** Jesus **wherever** He will **go**, to whatever destination. Christ challenges him to count the cost, asking him if he is willing to follow Christ in His homelessness. For Christ is unique in His humility: even the wild animals, untended by man, have their homes—**the foxes** have their **dens, the birds of the heaven** have their **dwellings** and nests—**but the Son of Man does not have *a place* to lay *His* head**. Unlike even the humblest animals, He is to wander from place to place, dependent on the kindness and hospitality of men. Is the potential disciple willing to embrace this hardship?

Luke relates a second saying. **To another**, Christ said, **"Follow Me,"** urging him to accompany Him in His journeys from town to town. From Matthew 8:21, we see that the man was already a disciple, so that the Lord's request is not unreasonable. The man is willing to follow Him, but not right away. He has family obligations he feels he must discharge **first**, including caring for his aged father. After his father dies and he has **buried** his **father**, then (and only then) will he obey Christ's summons. (It is apparent that the man's father had not yet died, for burials took place shortly after death, and the man would not be speaking to Christ during this time.)

Christ's reply is uncompromising. The disciple whom the Lord called must **leave the dead to bury their own dead**. The dead belong to the dead! Let them carry out such duties. The one whom Christ has called is like one alive from the dead (John 5:25), and such a one no longer belongs to this age. Christ's call thus takes precedence over all earthly duties, freeing the one called to **go and declare the Kingdom of God**.

The third saying also illustrates how obedience to Christ's call comes before all other earthly duties—even the sacred duties of family. Another one who is summoned says that he will **follow** Jesus. But he asks leave to **first** go and **take** his **leave of those at home**. For those who knew the Scriptures, this reminded them of Elijah's call of Elisha. Elisha asked to be allowed to kiss his parents farewell before following Elijah, and Elijah permitted it (1 Kin. 19:19–20).

Christ does not directly forbid this to His potential disciple, but He warns him of the danger of divided loyalty, saying, **"No one who puts his hand to the plow and looks to the things behind is useful** or fit **for the Kingdom of God."** One who is plowing a straight furrow dares not look at what he has already plowed, for this would be fatal to plowing a straight furrow in front of him. In the same way, the potential disciple is urged not to look longingly to **the things behind**, to the joys of his past life, for this would be fatal to true discipleship. Christ would have him eagerly leap into his new life, so excited that he scarcely cares for his old one. His family would understand if the boy went off, engaged in the service of a great king, with no opportunity to say goodbye. They would rejoice for his good fortune. This is the opportunity Christ is in fact offering him. If he has trouble tearing himself away from his old life, it is because he cannot grasp what Christ is calling him to.

§VI.3. The Mission of the Seventy

ॐ ॐ ॐ ॐ ॐ

10 1   Now after these things, the Lord commissioned
seventy others and sent them two by two before
His face to every city and place where He Himself was about to come.

After these things (meaning the events reported in the previous
chapters, comprising the bulk of Christ's outreach to Galilee), the
Lord determined to spread His message in the towns between Galilee
and Jerusalem, such as in the Transjordan area east of the Jordan
River. Time was running out (it was perhaps the late summer of the
year, prior to the spring when the Lord would be crucified), and it
was urgent that more hear the Lord's Word. Moses had gathered
seventy elders to help him in his task (Num. 11:16–17), and Christ
commissioned seventy men as well to help take His proclamation
of the Kingdom to Israel. He **sent them two by two**, so that they
could sustain and encourage one another in their work. (Sending
them out by twos also gave them the quality of authentic witnesses,
for it took two witnesses to verify facts; Deut. 19:15.)

They were sent **before His face to every city and place where
He Himself was about to come**. This does not mean that Christ
intended to come on a kind of follow-up visit to every place they
visited. This would make their work redundant, and anyway would
be logistically impossible in a short time. Rather it means that they
were to function as an advance force, preparing the ground before
Him so that His journeying to Jerusalem could be smooth and safe.
Their mission was a limited one, lasting perhaps a month or so.

ॐ ॐ ॐ ॐ ॐ

2   And He was saying to them, "The harvest
is plentiful indeed, but the workers are few;
therefore beseech the Lord of the harvest to
send out workers into His harvest.

3   "Go; behold, I send you as lambs in the midst of wolves.

4   "Do not carry a purse, nor a bag, nor sandals, and greet no one along the way.

5   "And into whatever house you enter, first say, 'Peace to this house!'

6   "And if a son of peace is there, your peace will rest upon him; otherwise it will turn back to you.

7   "And remain in the same house, eating and drinking what they have; for the worker *is* worthy of his reward. Do not move from house to house.

8   "And into whatever city you enter, and they welcome you, eat what is set before you;

9   "and heal those in it who are ailing, and say to them, 'The Kingdom of God has come near to you!'

10 "But into whatever city you enter and they do not welcome you, go out into its streets and say,

11 "'Even the dust of your city which clings to our feet, we wipe off against you; yet know this, that the Kingdom of God has come near!'

12 "I say to you, it will be more tolerable in that day for Sodom than for that city.

The counsel Christ gives the Seventy is much the same as He gave to the Twelve when He sent them out on their limited mission sometime earlier (9:1f). The task of harvesting men and bringing them to discipleship (John 4:35–38) might seem to be daunting, for **the harvest** was **plentiful indeed** and **the workers** like them but **few**. There were many who needed to hear the Word, and the Lord's disciples had many enemies. But God was **the Lord of the harvest** and was sovereign over Israel. Just as the lord or owner of a harvest could hire and send out more workers to reap his crop if he needed them, so God could **send out** more **workers into His** own **harvest**. With such a task before them (a task not exhausted by the work of the Seventy), they must **beseech** God to **send out** more **workers** for the age-long missionary enterprise.

When Christ told them to **go** out for their work, He left them with no illusions about the hostility they would face. Indeed, He was **sending** them out **as lambs in the midst of wolves**, into mortal danger. They must therefore beware and rely entirely upon the help of God.

And they must travel lightly and quickly. They must **not carry** in their hands any extra provisions—not **a purse** containing money to buy provisions, nor **a bag** for begging, **nor sandals** in case the ones they wore broke. Instead, they must depend on God to provide them with whatever they needed. Further, they must **greet no one along the way**, for such greetings were long and involved, and their work required urgency (compare a similar urgency in 2 Kin. 4:29). Such defiance of etiquette was unusual and highlighted the importance of their mission.

When they **entered** a **house**, they were **first** to **say, "Peace to this house!"** This was the usual greeting, but here it is vested with a special significance, for **if a son of peace** was **there** (that is, a man with a peaceful and true heart, destined to receive God's peace in the age to come), then God's **peace would rest upon him** and would bless him as Christ's messenger stayed with him. **Otherwise**, if the man refused hospitality, the blessing of peace would **turn back** to the messenger who offered it, and the household would have no blessing. In speaking of this greeting, Christ is not speaking of mere formalities, but of offering the householder salvation. For the Seventy were there *as representatives of Christ*, and were bringing His peace to men. For the householder to accept their greeting (that is, to accept them into his home and offer hospitality) was for him to accept Christ.

In **whatever house** the disciples were welcomed, they were to **remain in** that **same house**. They were **not** to **move from house to house**, seeking better lodgings. Also they were **to eat and drink what they had** to hand, **whatever** was **set before** them, and not be concerned about whether it was ritually unclean (as some places in the Gentile-dominated Transjordan might be). This food was their

reward, and they should gratefully accept it, even as **the worker** cheerfully accepted his wages.

The disciples must do this in **whatever city** they **entered** and found a **welcome**. They must accept the proffered hospitality as God's provision for them, and **heal those** in that city **who were ailing, and say to them, "The Kingdom of God has come near to you!"** Their miracles of healing proved that the power of the Kingdom was in their midst. But if the city did **not welcome** them, and refused them any hospitality because of their name as Christ's disciples, they were to **go out into its streets** (where they could be seen by all) and enact a parable of judgment and denunciation. They were to treat that city as pious Jews treated pagan lands upon reentering the Holy Land, proclaiming, **"Even the dust of your city which clings to our feet, we wipe off** as a witness **against you; yet know this, that the Kingdom of God has** indeed **come near!"** On the Last Day, the inhabitants of such towns can never say that they had no chance to save themselves. On **that day, it will be more tolerable for** notorious **Sodom than for that city**, and the doom faced by the inhabitants of Sodom (Gen. 19) will pale in comparison to the punishment the inhabitants of that city will endure.

ॐ ॐ ॐ ॐ ॐ

13 "Woe to you, Chorazin! Woe to you, Bethsaida! For if the *works of* power had been done in Tyre and Sidon which happened in you, they would have repented long ago, sitting in sackcloth and ashes.

14 "But it will be more tolerable for Tyre and Sidon in the judgment than for you.

15 "And you, Capernaum! Will you be exalted to heaven? You will be brought down to Hades!

16 "The one who hears you hears Me, and the one who rejects you rejects Me; and he who rejects Me rejects the One who sent Me."

The Lord's main work in Galilee had been completed, and most of its towns had heard His message. Some of those towns had on the whole rejected Christ, and Christ laments over them—hoping that the towns the Seventy will preach in will be more receptive. Thus Christ pronounces **woe** to the town of **Chorazin** (modern Kerazeh, two miles northeast of Capernaum), as well as **woe** to **Bethsaida**. Alas for these cities, for divine judgment awaits them on the Last Day. Along with Capernaum, many of those cities had seen Jesus do those same **works of power**, so they had no excuse for not accepting His message. Indeed, if those same miracles **had been done in Tyre and Sidon** (proverbial for their pride; Is. 23; Ezek. 28), even those hardhearted cities **would have repented long ago**, even to the point of **sitting in sackcloth and ashes**, in utter self-abasement.

These cities of Galilee managed to prove themselves even more hardhearted, and so **it will be more tolerable for Tyre and Sidon in the** final **judgment** than for them. With withering scorn the Lord turns on His own **Capernaum**, the city which He had previously made His base of operations. Did they think they would **be exalted to heaven** just because He made His residence there? They would **be brought down to Hades**, the land of the dead! The ancient king of Babylon thought in his pride that he would be exalted to heaven, and he was brought down to Hades and laid waste (Is. 14:13–15, 23). It would be the same with Capernaum and its impenitent inhabitants on the Last Day.

The disciples must speak their message fearlessly, confident that they were speaking for God and that God would vindicate their word in the end. The one willing to **hear** them also **heard** the Lord Jesus who sent them, and the one who **rejected** them also **rejected** Jesus—and God also, for God **sent** Jesus with this message. They must not let hostility silence them, for they came with all the authority of the Most High.

ॐ ॐ ॐ ॐ ॐ

17 And the Seventy returned with joy, saying, "Lord, even the demons submit to us in Your Name!"

> 18 And He said to them, "I was observing Satan fall from heaven like lightning.
>
> 19 "Behold, I have given you authority to walk upon serpents and scorpions, and over all the power of the Enemy, and nothing will ever hurt you.
>
> 20 "But do not rejoice in this, that the spirits submit to you, but rejoice that your names are written in heaven."

As said above, the mission of the Seventy was not to last long (perhaps a month or so), for Luke narrates their return immediately after narrating their sending. They returned with joy (to a pre-arranged place, at a prearranged time) and reported to Christ that **even the demons submit to** them **in** His **Name**. The exuberance with which they report this makes one think that these exorcisms went beyond their initial mandate of merely healing the sick (10:9). People in the towns had brought their demon-possessed to them to be cured, and the Seventy found that their exorcisms had worked. They returned to Christ half-giddy with excitement over their unexpected authority.

The Lord rejoices with them, saying, **"I was observing Satan fall from heaven like lightning."** The imperfect tense used here (**I was observing**) suggests that Christ was referring to His continual receiving of reports of their success. The success of their exorcisms meant that Satan's reign was coming to an end, and was a pledge that soon he would **fall from heaven like lightning**, cast down from his preeminence, a defeated foe (John 12:31). They might indeed rejoice, for the Lord had **given** them **authority to walk upon serpents and scorpions**, to tread down all harmful and evil forces, **all the power of the Enemy**. The authority to preach in His Name carried with it authority over the demons, and that was why their exorcisms had worked. God would protect them; **nothing** would **ever hurt** them in their battle against the Evil One.

The Seventy must beware, however, for their excitement over their authority could lead to pride and presumption. The focus of their rejoicing must not lie in their own power, and **that the**

spirits submit to them. Rather, their focus must be on God and the salvation He bestows, and **that** their **names were written** by God **in heaven**. In the heavenly register of His favorites (the divine equivalent to the register of favorites that kings kept; compare Esther 6:1–3), God would count them as His friends. Let *this* be the source of their rejoicing! To rejoice over one's power could lead to pride; this joy leads to humility and gratitude.

ॐ ॐ ॐ ॐ ॐ

21 At that very hour He exulted in the Holy Spirit, and said, "I praise You, O Father, Lord of heaven and earth, that You hid these things from the wise and insightful and revealed them to babes. Yes, Father, for thus it was well-pleasing before You.

22 "All things have been delivered to Me by My Father, and no one knows who the Son is but the Father, and who the Father is but the Son, and anyone to whom the Son intends to reveal *Him*."

At that very hour (that is, in the days when He had been rejected by His own towns of Capernaum, Chorazin, and Bethsaida; 10:13–15), Christ nonetheless exploded in praise to God. Many times His prayers were private, as He slipped away to the wilderness to pray (5:16). Here, however, He openly **exulted in the Holy Spirit**, bursting forth with prophetic ecstasy (compare Simeon's ecstatic entrance into the Temple "in the Spirit" in 2:27). The word rendered *exulted* is the Greek *agalliao*, used of the Mother of God in 1:47 for her own ecstatic praise to God. Christ was not discouraged that so many had rejected Him. Rather, He rejoiced in the plan of God, confessing His wisdom (the verb translated **praise** is the Gr. *exomologeo*, often translated "confess").

This was the plan of God, the sovereign **Lord of heaven and earth**—that the truth about Christ be **hid from the wise and insightful**, from the self-important and sophisticated, and **revealed** only **to babes**, to those with humble and trusting hearts. Thus the proud would stumble over Him, and the truth would elude them, for truth is discovered by the heart, not the head. But the humble and tired may find truth and salvation, be they ever so slow and uneducated. That indeed was **well-pleasing before** God, and was how He planned that salvation be open to any and all who would seek it in humility.

Thus **all things** were **delivered** to Christ **by** His **Father**, so that Christ could offer salvation to any of the weary and burdened who came to Him (Matt. 11:27–28; John 17:2). As the saving Messiah, Jesus was exalted over all, and **no one knew who** He was **but** the **Father**. Those of Capernaum might *claim* to know Him and reject Him for His humble origins (Mark 6:3), but they did not truly know who He was—only the Father truly knew Him. In the same way, the Jews who rejected Jesus might claim to know the Father, but only **the Son** truly knew **the Father—and anyone to whom the Son intended to reveal** *Him*. For as the true Messiah, Jesus could give knowledge of God to His disciples.

ॐ゜ ॐ゜ ॐ゜ ॐ゜ ॐ゜

23 **And turning to the disciples, He said privately, "Blessed** *are* **the eyes which see what you see,**
24 **"for I say to you that many prophets and kings wished to see what you** *yourselves* **see, and did not see** *them*, **and to hear what you hear, and did not hear** *them*."

The prayer in verse 21 the Lord uttered publicly, but when He was alone with the disciples, He **said privately** to them how privileged they were. They had a revelation of the Father which was the culmination of all Israel's sacred history. They were **blessed**, for **many** of the most exalted in Israel's history, even the **prophets and kings**, longed for the days of the Messiah and fervently **wished to see what** the disciples were now **seeing** and **hearing**. To the disciples was given a privilege not given even to the prophets and kings—that of living in the days of the Kingdom and of experiencing its salvation. The cities of Capernaum were blind and deaf to the glory—but the disciples' eyes and ears, opened by humility, could receive it.

§ VI.4. The Lawyer's Question and the Parable of the Good Samaritan

> ॐ ॐ ॐ ॐ ॐ
>
> 25 And behold! a certain lawyer rose up and tested Him out, saying, "Teacher, what shall I do to inherit eternal life?"
>
> 26 And He said to him, "What is written in the Law? How do you read *it*?"
>
> 27 And he answered and said, "You shall love the Lord your God with your whole heart, and with your whole soul, and with your whole strength, and with your whole mind; and your neighbor as yourself."
>
> 28 And He said to him, "You have answered correctly; do this and you will live."

Next St. Luke introduces **a certain lawyer** (that is, an expert in the Jewish Law) who **rose up** in the crowd from where he had been sitting, listening to Jesus' teaching. He wanted **to test Him out** (Gr. *ekpeirazo*, a stronger verb than *peirazo*, "to test") and see whether or not Jesus measured up to his own legal standards of Pharisaic righteousness. So it is that he challenges Jesus (though politely, calling Him **Teacher**) and puts to Him the question, **"What shall I do to inherit eternal life?"** The verb *do* is in the aorist tense, indicating a once-for-all action. The lawyer is asking Christ what one *mitzvah* or commandment he can accomplish, what exploit he can do that will assure him of eternal life in the age to come.

Christ returned him to the Law in which supposedly he was an expert, asking, **"What is written in the Law? How do you read *it*?"** What was the essence of man's obligations according to the Law? The man answered with a citation of Deuteronomy 6:5 and Leviticus 19:18, saying, **"You shall love the Lord your God with your whole heart, and with your whole soul, and with your whole strength, and with your whole mind; and your neighbor as yourself."** Christ agreed with the lawyer's summary, and confirmed that his interpretation of the Scriptures was right. The man had **answered correctly**—love to God and man was what God demanded; if he would **do this** (the verb *do* is here in the present tense, indicating a life of such love), then he would **live**.

୬ଡ଼ ୬ଡ଼ ୬ଡ଼ ୬ଡ଼ ୬ଡ଼

29 But wishing to justify himself, he said to Jesus, "And who is my neighbor?"

30 Jesus replied, "A certain man was going down from Jerusalem to Jericho; and he fell among thieves, and they stripped him and inflicted blows, and went away leaving *him* half dead.

31 "Now by chance a certain priest was going down on that way, and when he saw him, he passed by on the other side.

32 "And likewise also a Levite, when he came to the place and saw *him*, passed by on the other side.

33 "But a certain Samaritan who was journeying came upon him, and when he saw him, had heartfelt *love*,

34 "and came to him and bandaged up his wounds, pouring on oil and wine, and he mounted him on his own beast, and brought him to an inn, and cared for him.

35 "And on the next day he took out two denarii and gave them to the innkeeper and said, 'Care for him, and whatever more you spend, when I return, I *myself* will render you.'

The lawyer apparently felt that he had not put Christ through much of a test. After all, Jesus had answered his question with a question, and then simply approved of his answer. Moreover, he felt somewhat convicted in his own heart, perhaps because he himself had trouble loving those who irritated him. The Law (in Lev. 19:18) called for love of **neighbor** (Gr. *plesios*, literally, "one beside a

person"—but **who** in fact *was* this **neighbor**? Were the hated
Gentiles his neighbors? Was the grasping tax-collector who cheated
him his neighbor? The lawyer was intent upon limiting the scope
of persons he was required to love (plus he felt a bit foolish having
answered his own question in v. 27), and so he refused to sit down.
Instead, and **wishing to justify himself**, he asked again, **"And** just
who is my neighbor?"

The Lord took up this second question and **replied** with a parable. **A certain man was going down from Jerusalem to Jericho**.
During this seventeen-mile journey, the road descended some 3300
feet, which meant there were plenty of places for thieves to hide on
either side of the steep incline. It was, in fact, a stretch of road famous
for its danger from thieves. And sure enough, this man **fell among
thieves**, who **stripped him** of his clothes (clothes were expensive
and a source of wealth) and **inflicted blows** on him. Having beaten
him to a pulp, they **went away leaving *him* half dead**.

The man's predicament was dire—but help was at hand. For
by chance a certain priest was going down that way. (Here was
good luck, for the road was usually deserted.) He was fresh from
serving at the holy Temple, and he would surely help the man. But
(to the surprise of those listening to the parable), when the priest
saw him, he passed by on the other side of the road, careful not
to touch him (perhaps thinking he was already dead and fearing
ritual defilement, or perhaps he simply refused to become involved).
Likewise also a Levite was on that road. **When he came to the
place and saw *him***, he also refused to help the man and **passed
by on the other side**.

The man's time was running out, for if help did not come soon,
he would die by the roadside, without medical attention. Then **a
certain Samaritan who was journeying came upon him**. (His
Samaritan identity is stressed, with the word "Samaritan" coming at
the beginning of the sentence in the Greek.) All listening to Christ's
parable felt that this was the limit of the poor man's misfortunes.
The Samaritans all hated the Jews—especially Jews coming from
Jerusalem (compare 9:53). All expected the Samaritan to kick the
man now that he was down and try to rob him further. But instead,

when the Samaritan **saw him**, he **had heartfelt *love*** for him (Gr. *splagxnizomai*, to have compassion from one's inner heart). Whereas the righteous priest and the Levite had refused to get near him, the hated Samaritan **came to him**, rushing up to the fallen unfortunate, and **bandaged up his wounds, pouring on oil and wine** as first aid. He then **mounted him on his own beast**, so that he walked while the injured man rode. He **brought him to an inn and cared for him**, nursing him through the long night.

Even then his care did not cease. He could stay with him no longer, but he refused to abandon him. Instead, **on the next day**, he **took out two denarii** (that is, two days' wages for a laborer) **and gave them to the innkeeper, and said, "Care for him**, nursing him slowly back to health, **and whatever more you spend, when I return, I *myself* will render you** all that is owed." Here was true generosity. The usual cost for a day's stay at such an inn was one-twelfth of a denarius, so that the man gave the innkeeper enough money for the injured man to stay there over three weeks. Moreover, the Samaritan was willing to write a blank check to help a total stranger. And this was all the more amazing, for Samaritans might have been expected to refuse help to a Jew.

---

           ৩৯ ৩৯ ৩৯ ৩৯ ৩৯

36 "Which of these three seems to you to have become a neighbor to the man who fell among the thieves?"

37 And he said, "The one who did mercy towards him." And Jesus said to him, "Go, and you *yourself* do likewise."

The parable had evidently overcome the lawyer. At the end of that tale of astonishing love (which by its greatness showed the lawyer how small and limited his own heart's love was), Christ asks the lawyer for another legal interpretation. **"Which of these three seems to you to have become a neighbor to the man who fell among the thieves?"** The question was carefully crafted—the lawyer asked Christ who his neighbor *was*, and Christ replied by showing him *how to be* a neighbor—thereby saying that one's neighbor was anyone in need, regardless of race or religion.

The lawyer got the point, but had trouble answering. The correct answer was, "The Samaritan was the neighbor." But the lawyer, like all Jews, hated the Samaritans for their race and their religion, and he could not bring himself to say the word "Samaritan." All he could gasp out was, **"The one who did mercy towards him."** That was enough for the Lord. He replied, **"Go, and you *yourself*** (the pronoun is emphatic in the Greek) **do likewise."** The lawyer had thought to overcome Jesus, but found himself overcome by the Lord's wisdom. The parable had pierced him to the heart, leaving him with a clear direction for his life.

§VI.5. Martha and Mary

ॐ ॐ ॐ ॐ ॐ

38 Now as they were going, He entered into a certain village; and a woman named Martha welcomed Him in.

39 And she had a sister called Mary, who also sat beside the Lord's feet, hearing His word.

40 But Martha was distracted with much service, and she stood by Him, and said, "Lord, is it not a concern to You that my sister has left me alone to serve? Then tell her to help me!"

41 But the Lord answered and said to her, "Martha, Martha, you are worried and in an uproar about many things;

42 "but one thing is needful, for Mary has chosen the good part, which will not be taken from her."

Luke next tells the story of how Jesus **entered a certain village**, where **a woman named Martha welcomed Him in**. The village was Bethany, near Jerusalem (John 11:1), and the event happened during one of Christ's several journeys to Jerusalem in the months preceding His death. Luke omits the name of the village in order to save Jerusalem as the culmination of Christ's work (see 9:31).

Martha **had a sister called Mary**. Though it was the role of women in those days to attend to the meal preparation and to leave the men to their own discussions, Mary **also sat beside the Lord's feet, hearing His word**, along with the rest of His (male) disciples. Many rabbis would not have permitted such a thing (some said that the Torah was better burnt than taught to a woman), but Jesus had no such reservations about having women disciples learn along with the men. In the time before the meal was served, Mary sat with the men, drinking in her Lord's discourse in humble submission.

Martha (evidently the older of the two sisters and the head of the household; it is possible that she was a widow) was therefore left to do all the meal preparation and serving by herself, and she **was distracted with much service**. She seems to have been a woman with an eye for detail—perhaps too much of an eye for detail! We can imagine her annoyance rising with every passing minute, and her stealing impatient glances at her sister Mary (who remained oblivious to them, having all her attention focused on Christ). At last Martha could stand it no longer. Bypassing her (as she thought) irresponsible and selfish sister, she appealed directly to Jesus Himself. She came up to Him and **stood by Him**, right in His face, towering over her seated sister, and demanded that He order Mary to do her duty.

She addressed Him respectfully as **Lord**, but could not conceal her exasperation at His apparent thoughtlessness. She asked with some feeling, **"Is it not a concern to You that my sister has left me alone to serve?"** The word translated *left* is the Greek *kataleipo*, sometimes rendered "to abandon"; Martha felt that Mary was clearly derelict in her duty. Surely He could see that Mary was being selfishly thoughtless. **"Then tell her to help me!"**

The Lord refused to turn against Mary, who was motivated by devotion. He answered the older sister tenderly, as **"Martha, Martha,"** but He had a gentle rebuke for her. Poor Martha, she was always **worried and in an uproar about many things**. (The word rendered *in an uproar* is the Gr. *thorubazo*, cognate with the word used in Acts 17:5 for Jews setting a city in an uproar over the apostles' preaching and in Mark 5:39 for a house crowded out with wailing mourners.) Martha meant well with her detailed hospitality, but the good she had chosen was the enemy of the best she might have chosen. Martha had let herself get caught up in the multitude of works that she thought were essential, and could not see that but **one thing was needful** and essential—devotion to Jesus. Mary had chosen the good part, and had focused on what was truly essential, and this would **not be taken from her**. She could stay where she was. (In defending Mary's choice, Christ thereby invites Martha to join her—or at least to sit more lightly on the importance of her work of serving.)

By including this story of the attitudes of Mary and Martha, Luke throws light on the nature of Christian discipleship. Martha (though a beloved disciple of Jesus, and His close friend) was here an image of Judaism, with its single-minded focus on works of merit. They thought that salvation came by performing many *mitzvoth*, many commandments, and were distracted by their much serving. Mary was an image of the Christian disciple, the one who finds salvation by humbly receiving the Lord's Word. The Jews might resent the disciples of Jesus for their laxity about the Law, even as Martha resented Mary that afternoon. But the disciples had chosen the good part, that which leads to salvation, and that would not be taken from them.

§VI.6. Teaching on Prayer

ॐ ॐ ॐ ॐ ॐ

11 1   **And it happened that while He was praying in a certain place, after He had stopped, one of His disciples said to Him, "Lord, teach us to pray just as John also taught his disciples."**

2   **And He said to them, "Whenever you pray, say, 'Father, let Your Name be sanctified. Let Your Kingdom come.**

3   **"'Give us each day our bread for the following *day*.**

> 4   "'And forgive us our sins, for we *ourselves* also
>   forgive everyone who is indebted to us. And
>   lead us not into testing.'"

In antiquity, prayers were usually said aloud, with upraised hands. **In a certain place**, Jesus **was praying**, and when His disciples heard that **He had stopped**, they took the opportunity to make a request. **John** the Baptizer had **taught his disciples** to pray (possibly giving them a model prayer, as a paradigm), and **one of** Jesus' **disciples** wanted Him to do the same. The disciple was perhaps impressed with the depth of Christ's communion with the Father and longed for this himself.

Christ responds by giving them a model prayer, known by the Church as "the Our Father," or "the Lord's Prayer." It was not a prayer meant for all men generally, but only for His disciples. **Whenever** they prayed, they were to **say** the following prayer, which would set the tone for all their prayers.

The form in which Luke gives this prayer is different from that found in Matthew 6:9–13 (though some manuscripts of Luke's Gospel have altered the original Lukan form so as to harmonize the prayer with that of Matthew's Gospel). Luke has abbreviated the prayer in translating it from its original Hebrew liturgical setting, and gives only the gist of it. (He does the same in other parts of his Gospel, such as in translating the original Jewish phrase, "the abomination of desolation standing in the holy place," to the more Gentile-friendly phrase, "Jerusalem surrounded by armies"; compare Matt. 24:15 with Luke 21:20.)

The prayer begins with the invocation of the transcendent God of heaven as **Father**—almost certainly *Abba* in the original Aramaic. Thus the God invoked is not distant from the disciple, but close and familiar, his "papa." Jesus hereby shares His sonship with His disciples—He calls God His *Abba* (being the eternal Son by nature), and they are to call God their *Abba* too (being God's sons by adoption and grace).

The first petition is not for human needs, but is concerned with God's honor. Of first and foremost concern to Jesus is that God's

Name be sanctified in the earth. God's Name is not simply His verbal label, but His manifested power. In Psalm 54:1 and 20:1, God's Name is the open manifestation of His strength ("Save me, O God, by Your Name . . . May the Name of the God of Jacob protect you"), and for God's Name to be **sanctified** or hallowed is for men to acknowledge God as holy when they see His power. (Compare Is. 29:23 and Ezek. 36:23 for this understanding of sanctifying God's Name.) Presently the world does not honor God, and His judgments are "on high, out of their sight" (Ps. 10:5). Christ would have us pray that men see God's judgments and honor Him as God.

The second petition is linked with the first, for it prays that God's **Kingdom** may **come**. Ultimately this will be fulfilled at the Second Coming, when the kingdom of the world becomes the Kingdom of the Lord God and of His Christ (Rev. 11:15), and it is to this final consummation that we are to look. To be sure, the Kingdom of God comes in the earth through the Church, existing throughout this age in hidden form (see 17:21), but this petition looks to its fulfillment, to the day when, after the powers of the heavens are shaken, the Kingdom will finally draw near (21:26–31).

It is only after these two petitions regarding God's Name and His Kingdom have been prayed that the disciples are then instructed to pray for their own needs. The third petition therefore asks that God **give us each day our bread for the following** *day*. By **bread**, all of our physical needs are meant. In our present affluent society, we must be reminded of what those needs actually are, for we are tempted to think that we "need" much more than we actually do. As St. Paul teaches, "If we have nourishment and shelter, with these we will be satisfied" (1 Tim. 6:8).

The phrase translated *for the following day* is the Greek word *epiousios*, which is notoriously hard to translate, since it scarcely exists in extant ancient literature outside this context. Some (such as Origen in the third century) have suggested that it means "necessary for existence"—i.e. the bread we need. Some suggest that it is related to the word *epiousa* as found in Acts 16:11, where it is translated "the following day," and that is the meaning adopted here. Christ therefore tells us to pray each day for the needs of the morrow, taking our life one day at a time.

The fourth petition is for God to **forgive us our sins**. Each day, we sin against God, and it is these daily sins for which we ask remission. Christ assumes that His disciples are repenting of these sins (in a daily examination of conscience), and part of this repentant heart involves being tenderhearted to **everyone who is indebted to us**. Thus, Christ assumes that His disciples have **forgiven** those who have sinned against them, tearing up the spiritual IOUs from others which they have accumulated throughout the day. God's daily forgiveness is only offered on this basis, and to refuse to forgive one's brother is to place oneself outside the reach of God's forgiveness.

The final petition is that God **lead us not into testing**. The word rendered *testing* is the Greek word *peirasmos*, sometimes rendered "trial," or "temptation." This is not a petition to be spared the experience of being tempted to sin—this is scarcely possible in this age. Christ was tempted in all things (Heb. 2:18; 4:15), and it is unlikely that God will spare us something which He refused to spare His own Son. Rather, by **testing** the Lord here means the experience of succumbing to Satanic attack (thus this petition could be expanded to include our "deliverance from the Evil One"; Matt. 6:13). It was this testing that Christ told His disciples in the Garden of Gethsemane that they should pray to avoid (22:40), since Satan was going to sift them like wheat (22:31). This final petition is a cry that, through God's mercy, we will emerge victorious from any attack and hold firm to our faith.

༄ ༄ ༄ ༄ ༄

5 And He said to them, "Who among you will have a friend, and will go to him at midnight, and say to him, 'Friend, lend me three breads,

6 "'for a friend of mine has arrived from a journey, and I do not have *anything* to set before him';

7 "and that one from inside will answer and say, 'Do not cause me toil; already the door has been shut, and my children are with me in the bed;

> I am not able to arise to give you *anything*?
>
> 8 "I say to you, even though he will not arise to
> give him *something* because he is his friend, yet
> because of his impudence he will arise to give
> him as much as he needs.
>
> 9 "And I say to you, ask, and it will be given to
> you; seek, and you will find; knock, and it will
> be opened to you.
>
> 10 "For everyone who asks, receives; and he who
> seeks, finds; and to him who knocks, it will be
> opened.

Having given His disciples a model prayer to pray, Christ then gives them the incentive to pray boldly. He does this by telling a parable. In the parable, Christ pictures a man in distress: Close to midnight, he answers his door to find that a **friend** of his **has arrived from a journey**. (People often traveled at night then, to avoid traveling during the heat of the day.) Much to his distress, he finds himself unable to satisfy the sacred demands of hospitality and feed his newly arrived friend, for he has no food in the house. In that culture, it was imperative to set some food before a guest, and so he **goes** to his neighbor **at midnight** (addressing him deferentially as **friend**—as well he might at that time of the day!) and asks him to **lend** him **three breads**, three loaves, that he might **set** them **before** his guest.

Christ asks the question, "What will the neighbor do?" Does anyone among them really think **that one from inside** would answer, **"Do not cause me toil; already the door has been shut, and my children are with me in the bed; I am not able to arise to give you *anything*"**? (The house pictured is a one-room dwelling, where all the family slept together on a straw mat, and where getting up to open the door would awaken the whole house.) Obviously not! For **even though** the sleepy neighbor **will not arise to give him** *something* **because he is his friend, yet because of** the distressed neighbor's **impudence** in hammering on his door at that hour, **he will arise to give him** something—and not just a bit, but **as much**

as he needs. The bonds of friendship might not be enough to secure the request, but the shameless hammering at the door will.

The lesson is clear: If a neighbor will respond to boldness by giving what is requested, how much more will God do so? Thus, the disciples should be bold. Christ Himself tells them they should **ask** God for what they need, for it **will be given** to them; they should **seek** in prayer for what they need, for they **will find** it provided; they should boldly **knock** on the door of heaven with the same boldness as the man knocked on his neighbor's door, for the door **will be opened** to them, and God will provide them with **as much as** they **need**. This is not a hit-and-miss thing. It is the way God will respond to **everyone** who asks. (We note that Christ is talking about the experience *of His disciples*, not the invariable experience of everyone who has ever prayed.)

ॐ ॐ ॐ ॐ ॐ

11 "And what father *is there* among you, if his son will ask for a fish, instead of a fish will give him a serpent?

12 "Or even *if* he will ask for an egg, will give him a scorpion?

13 "If you *yourselves,* therefore, being evil, know how to give good gifts to your children, how much more will the Father from heaven give the Holy Spirit to those who ask Him?"

These assurances are backed up with another comparison to human generosity and willingness to give. **What father** was there **among** those listening who would, **if his son** would **ask for a fish** for a meal, **instead of a fish give him a serpent?** Or even if the boy would **ask for an egg**, who would **give him a scorpion?** Obviously no one! No father, even the most selfish, would meet his son's request for something good by giving him something dangerous. Fathers might be sinners, **evil**, men who drank iniquity like water (Job 15:16), and yet even *they* knew **how to give good gifts to** their **children**. They were willing to give good gifts of food to their hungry children—**how much more will the Father from** His throne in **heaven give** good gifts **to those who ask Him** on earth? And not just good things such as they ask for in prayer, but even **the Holy Spirit**, the sum and crown of all His gifts.

(It is possible that this reference to the Spirit is Lukan, and that Jesus originally spoke of God giving "good things"—compare Matt. 7:11—for Luke wants to stress the role of the Spirit in the life of the Church. This interpretive translation therefore is meant to teach us how the Church's access to God in prayer finds its highest fulfillment in the prayer for the Holy Spirit in baptism; compare Acts 8:15; 19:5–6.)

§VI.7. More Conflict with the Pharisees and Their Generation

§VI.7.i. Can Satan Cast Out Satan?

> ॐ ॐ ॐ ॐ ॐ
>
> 14 And He was casting out a demon, and it was mute; and it happened that when the demon had gone out, the mute *man* spoke; and the crowds marveled.
>
> 15 But some from them said, "By Beelzebul, the ruler of the demons, He casts out the demons."
>
> 16 And others, to test *Him*, were seeking from Him a sign from heaven.
>
> 17 But He knew their thoughts and said to them, "Every kingdom divided up against itself is desolated, and a house *divided* against itself falls.
>
> 18 "And if Satan also is divided up against himself, how will his kingdom stand? For you say that by Beelzebul I cast out the demons.
>
> 19 "And if I *Myself* by Beelzebul cast out the demons, by whom do your sons cast *them* out? Therefore they will be your judges.
>
> 20 "But if by the Finger of God I *Myself* cast out

> the demons, then the Kingdom of God has
> reached you.
>
> 21 "When the strong *one*, fully-armed, guards his
> own court, his possessions are in peace;
>
> 22 "but when a stronger *one* than he comes upon
> him and conquers him, he takes away from him
> his panoply on which he had trusted, and gives
> away his spoils.
>
> 23 "He who is not with Me is against Me; and he
> who does not gather with Me, scatters.

In his compendium of Christ's teaching, St. Luke turns next to Christ's conflict with the Pharisees and some of the teaching it occasioned. Luke first narrates the time when Christ **was casting out a demon** that caused the man it was in to be **mute** (and blind as well; compare Matt. 12:22). After **the demon had gone out, the mute** *man* **spoke,** and this created such a stir that the crowds marveled. Indeed, some even began to wonder if Jesus might not be the Messiah, the Son of David (Matt. 12:23). **Some** people from the crowd, scribes come from Jerusalem (Mark 3:22), tried to counter such a view, arguing that it was **by Beelzebul, the ruler of the demons**, that **He casts out the demons**. The name **Beelzebul** was derived from the Hebrew *baal zebul*, "Lord of the House," or temple, and was originally a title for the pagan god Baal. It had been transformed into the derisive title *Baal Zebub*, "Lord of the flies," in 2 Kings 1:2, and was used at the time of Jesus as a title for Satan. Jesus' detractors in the crowd were suggesting that it was only because Jesus was in collusion with the devil that He was able to perform such spectacular exorcisms. **Others** in the crowd thought the debate could be solved by **a sign from heaven**, such as an audible voice, God speaking and telling them all that Jesus possessed divine authority.

The Lord responded by showing them what their accusation that He was in collusion with the devil meant—it meant there was a civil war in Satan's realm, with Jesus forming a kind of rebel force against His "master" Satan. This was impossible, for everyone knows that

every kingdom divided up against itself is desolated and cannot stand, and that even a house or family cannot survive internal strife, but will **fall**. Their accusation that it was **by Beelzebul** that He **cast out the demons** meant therefore that Satan's **kingdom** could not **stand**, and that Satan could no longer oppress men. This was clearly untrue, for Satan (alas) was as active as ever. Obviously Satan was not being menaced *from within*, but attacked *from without*.

Besides, everyone knew that exorcism, by its very nature, was an assault on Satan's realm, and that exorcisms therefore could only be effective with God's help. Otherwise, **by whom** did their **sons cast out** the demons, if not by God's help? Jesus was referring to Jewish exorcists, men who cast out demons with long prayers and by invocations of God's Name. Therefore, **they** would be the **judges** in this controversy, and the examples they provided would prove that Jesus' exorcisms were done with God's power.

Indeed, Jesus' exorcisms, done not with long prayers and invocations, but with a simple word of command, were manifestations of **the Finger of God**, God's power on the earth (see Ex. 8:19 for the term), and they meant that **the Kingdom of God has reached** them.

To make things clearer still, Jesus told a parable about a home invasion. **When** a **strong *one*, fully-armed, guards his own court,** his own palace, **his possessions** are **in peace** and safe from plunder. A would-be robber cannot just walk in and rob him at will. If he tries, the strong one will resist the robber and cut him down. It is only when **a stronger *one* than he comes upon him** violently **and conquers him**, and **takes away from him his panoply** of armor **on which he had trusted,** that this stronger one can rob him and **give away** his panoply as **spoils**. It is the same with Satan. Satan is strong and capable of keeping his demon-possessed prey captive and secure. Jesus is only able to liberate the demon-possessed and perform exorcisms because He first assaulted Satan and conquered him.

In this matter, no neutrality was possible. One must side *with* Jesus (considering Him a performer of exorcisms by divine power) or *against* Him (considering Him a demonic deceiver). **He who was not with** Jesus was **against** Him, and if one did not **gather**

with Him, becoming His disciple, then one was thereby **scattering**. The issue of by whom He cast out demons made the matter of loyalty acute.

ॐ ॐ ॐ ॐ ॐ

24 "When the unclean spirit goes out from the man, it goes through waterless places seeking rest, and not finding *it*, it says, 'I will return to my house from which I came out.'

25 "And when it comes, it finds *it* swept and adorned.

26 "Then it goes and takes along seven other spirits more evil than itself, and they enter in and dwell there, and the last *state* of that man becomes worse than the first."

The people hearing Jesus and experiencing His exorcisms and healings were, in fact, at a crossroads. If they refused to side with Jesus after experiencing such things, they were like a man who experienced an exorcism, only to relapse into a worse fate, a more severe demonic possession. Better the poor wretch had never been exorcised in the first place than to come to this! It was the same with those who heard Jesus—better they should never have experienced His power than to experience it, turn against Him as a demonic deceiver, and finally benefit nothing. They had seen His power—let them not turn against Him!

§VI.7.ii. Keeping the Word

ॐ ॐ ॐ ॐ ॐ

27 And it happened while He said these things, a certain woman from the crowd lifted up *her* voice and said to Him, "Blessed *is* the womb that bore You, and the breasts which You sucked!"

> **28 But He said, "Rather, blessed *are* those who hear the Word of God and keep it."**

It was while Christ was warning the people not to reject Him as a deceiver that **a certain woman from the crowd lifted up *her* voice**, pronouncing a blessing on Him—and this brought forth yet another warning. The woman's blessing was typically oriental in style, pronouncing a blessing upon His mother: **"Blessed *is* the womb that bore You, and the breasts which You sucked!"** That is, the woman praised Christ, acknowledging Him as a true prophet, saying that the mother of such a son must have been especially blessed. Jesus, however, saw a danger hidden in the well-intentioned but thoughtless cry of praise. (He was always quick to rebuke such thoughtless praise; see Mark 10:17–18.) The assumption behind the blessing was that blessedness came as a result of biology, and that His mother was blessed simply because she gave birth to Him.

Christ took care to correct such a notion, for it was this very notion of "blessedness through biology" which was leading Israel astray. More precisely, Israel thought they would be blessed because of their biological relation to Abraham and the patriarchs. They were biologically descended from Abraham and were of the "holy race," and therefore God must bless them. They felt they would be blessed by God because they could say, "We have Abraham for our father" (compare 3:8), and their rejection of Jesus' message could not detract from that.

Jesus knew this to be wrong, and so He said that **rather** (Gr. *menoun*; used as a corrective; compare such a use in Rom. 9:20) it was only **those who hear the Word of God** which He was preaching and who **keep it** who would be finally **blessed**. Let those who saw His works and heard His words acknowledge them as of God, if they would be blessed!

(We note that this passage does *not* suggest that the Mother of God is not blessed. As a matter of fact, Luke is emphatic that she *did* hear the Word of God and keep it; see 1:45, 48; 2:19, 51. The passage does not focus on Mary as a person, but on the source of blessedness, be it for Mary or for anyone else.)

§VI.7.iii. A Wicked Generation Seeks for a Sign

ॐ ॐ ॐ ॐ ॐ

29 And as the crowds were increasing, He began to say, "This generation is an evil generation; it seeks for a sign, and a sign will not be given to it, but *only* the sign of Jonah.

30 "For just as Jonah became a sign to the Ninevites, thus will the Son of Man also be to this generation.

31 "The Queen of the South will be raised with the men of this generation at the judgment and will condemn them, because she came from the ends of the earth to hear the wisdom of Solomon, and behold! *one* greater than Solomon *is* here.

32 "The men of Nineveh will stand up with this generation at the judgment and will condemn it, because they repented at the heralding of Jonah; and behold! *one* greater than Jonah *is* here."

As **the crowds** around Him were **increasing**, so too was the controversy about who He was. Some had asked that He produce a Voice from heaven, identifying Him as a true prophet and not a deceiver (v. 16). It seems that this desire was shared by many.

This desire for **a sign** Christ denounced as evidence that His hearers were part of **an evil generation**, one with hearts not true and open to God. If their hearts had been open and true, they would have discerned before now that Jesus was truly of God. Their insistence on hearing a Voice from God testifying to Jesus, in face of so many other of His miracles, meant that their hearts were hard. They were unworthy of hearing God's Voice, and therefore **a sign** would **not be given** to them. **The sign of Jonah** would come—Christ's Resurrection from the dead, when He appeared only to His disciples

(Acts 10:41), coming from the tomb as Jonah came from the belly of the fish and appeared to **the Ninevites**—but this was not a sign for the people. They were demanding a public spectacle, and this was explicitly refused.

They had proven themselves unworthy of hearing any more from God, since they had not responded to what they had already received. This made them worse than the pagans. The pagan **Queen of the South had come from the ends of the earth** (1 Kin. 10). Assuming that she came from southwestern Arabia, she made a journey of twelve hundred miles, all **to hear the** far-famed **wisdom of Solomon**. Christ was far **greater than Solomon**, and He was right in their midst, yet the men of that generation failed to appreciate His greatness. The Queen of Sheba therefore will **be raised** by God along with **the men** of that faithless **generation at the** final **judgment,** and she **will condemn them** by her previous devotion to truth and her recognition of the greatness of Solomon. That is, her recognition of Solomon's greatness will provide the yardstick against which the faithlessness of Christ's generation will be judged and condemned.

The men of Nineveh too were pagans, and yet **they repented** of their sins and hardness of heart when they heard **the heralding of Jonah** (Jon. 3). Thus they **will stand up** in the final resurrection **at the judgment** along with that **generation** and **will condemn it**. Their example of repentance will show up the sinful impenitence of Jesus' audience for what it is, for the men of Nineveh repented when they heard Jonah's preaching, but that generation refused to repent even when they heard the preaching of Jesus, who was far **greater than Jonah**.

Thus Jesus warned the great crowds who gathered around Him of their danger and challenged them to repent.

VI.7.iv. Seeing the Light

ॐ ॐ ॐ ॐ ॐ

33 "No one, after lighting a lamp, puts *it* in a hidden *place*, nor under the measure, but on the lampstand, that those who enter may see the light.

34 "The lamp of the body is your eye; when your eye is simple, your whole body also is *full of* light, but when it is evil, your body also is *full of* darkness.

35 "Watch out, therefore, that the light in you may not be darkness!

36 "If therefore your whole body *is full of* light, with no dark part in it, it will be wholly *full of* light, as when the lamp illumines you with its rays."

Luke then relates the Lord's parable of the lamp. It was the custom of those days to light a lamp every evening (with the accompanying blessing), putting it where it could give light to everyone in the room. It is inconceivable, the Lord says, that **after lighting** that **lamp**, one would **put *it* in a hidden *place*** (such as under a bed), or put it **under** a **measure** or container. That would defeat the whole purpose of lighting the lamp. Obviously one would put it **on the lampstand, that those who enter** the room **may see the light**.

Christ, as the Lamp of God, shines with divine light, illumining all men by His divine teaching. They need no other signs. Jesus' words are enough for illumination.

That presupposes a right attitude. Those with right hearts will benefit from the Lord's teaching; but those with wrong attitudes will not benefit at all. This is compared to the human **eye**, which functions as **the lamp** or light-giver for **the body**. When the **eye is simple** and healthy (Gr. *aplous*, "sincere"), it can conduct the light of any lamp to the rest of the body, and then **the whole body** will be *full of* **light**. But if one's eye is **evil** or diseased, it cannot transmit that light, even though the light might be shining, and then the body instead will be *full of* **darkness**. What is crucial for illumination is the state of the eye, and what is crucial for being illumined by Christ's teaching is the attitude of the hearers. The light of Christ shines clearly enough—the question is whether or not one's heart is able to receive it.

If they were able to receive it, then they would know light indeed. Just as a healthy eye makes one's **whole body *full of* light, with**

no dark part in it, so also for the true-hearted hearer of Christ's teaching. The whole life of the disciple will be **wholly *full of* light**, knowing the full light of God's favor. **When the lamp illumines with its rays**, it banishes all the darkness of night, and when one's heart is full of the teaching of Christ, then all spiritual darkness is banished, too. Christ's hearers therefore should **watch out** and receive His teaching with humility. Otherwise, if they reject Him as a deceiver, **the light in** them will be extinguished and will be replaced by **darkness**.

VI.7.v. The Pharisees and Uncleanness

> ॐ ॐ ॐ ॐ ॐ
>
> 37 Now when He had spoken, a Pharisee asks Him to eat *breakfast* with him, and He went in and reclined.
> 38 And when the Pharisee saw *it*, he marveled that He was not first baptized before the breakfast.
> 39 But the Lord said to him, "Now you Pharisees cleanse the outside of the cup and the plate, but your inside is full of robbery and evil.
> 40 "Senseless *ones*! Did not He who made the outside make the inside also?
> 41 "But give alms *for* inner things, and behold! everything is clean for you.

After one of His conflicts with the crowd, **a Pharisee asks Him to eat *breakfast* with him**. The word rendered *eat breakfast* is the Greek *aristao*, cognate with the noun *ariston*. This term designated the first meal of the day (compare its use in John 21:12), as contrasted with *deipnon*, the main meal taken in the evening. Christ was as willing to eat with the Pharisees as with notorious sinners, desiring to lead all to salvation, and so **He went in and reclined** at table with him. The Pharisee's motives for inviting Jesus are not stated; perhaps he simply wanted to see the famous rabbi up close and decide for himself what he thought of Him.

237

Most Pharisees and those claiming such piety always **first baptized** their hands (that is, ceremonially washed their hands; the Greek is *baptizo*) before eating a meal, but Christ had no use for such practices. (It needs to be stressed that this washing was for ritual purity only and had nothing to do with hygiene.) Since Christ was reputed to be a prophet, His Pharisaical host **marveled** at such an omission, no doubt commenting on it at table and asking why this was.

In response to this public challenge and question, Christ began an extended criticism of the whole spirit of the Pharisaical movement. His response was not so much a personal criticism of His host as it was a teaching lesson. The breakfast was not simply a social occasion—as a famous teacher, Christ was expected to give teaching. His host did not have to wait long for Jesus to oblige.

First Jesus targets the externalism of the Pharisees. They concerned themselves only about outward compliance with a series of rules, leaving the inner motivation behind such compliance out of the picture. They were keen to **cleanse the outside of the cup and the plate** (compare such ritual cleansings in Mark 7:4). Outwardly they were punctilious enough and oh so pious—but inwardly their hearts were **full of robbery and evil**, teeming with greed and envy. Pharisaism thus promoted a stunning contrast between the inward and the outward. This was **senseless**—for **did not** God **who made the outside make the inside also?** God cares for inner purity as much as for outer purity. He commands both pure motives and pure deeds.

What then should they do? They should concentrate on charity, and then, just like that, **behold! everything** would **be clean** for them, and they would not have to worry about such things as ritual purity. If they would **give alms** (Gr. *eleemosune*) and focus upon mercy and compassion to the poor, the **inner things** of their hearts would be taken care of, and they would not have to worry about rituals of hand-washing. Alms and true cleansing go together. (This was probably apparent from a play on words in the original Aramaic of the saying, for the Aramaic word for "to cleanse" is *dakki*, while the Aramaic word for "to give alms" is *zakki*.)

§VI.7.vi. Woe to the Pharisees and Lawyers

> ஃ ஃ ஃ ஃ ஃ
>
> 42 "But woe to you, Pharisees! For you tithe mint
> and rue and every herb, and bypass justice and
> the love of God; but these are the things it was
> necessary to do and not disregard those *others.*
> 43 "Woe to you, Pharisees! For you love the first-
> seats in the synagogues and the greetings in the
> marketplaces.
> 44 "Woe to you! For you are like unseen tombs,
> and men who walk over them do not know it."

The Lord then continues with a denunciation of the Pharisaical movement, that His host might not fall into its errors. Christ laments their fate if they do not repent, pronouncing **woe** upon them with ever-increasing thunder (the **woe to you, Pharisees** in verses 42 and 43 gives place to a briefer **woe to you** in verse 44, as if the divine patience with them draws ever shorter).

He first denounces them for their lack of spiritual proportion. The Law commanded that men tithe their crops to God, giving ten percent of whatever their farms and gardens produced to the priests and Levites (Deut. 14:22). The Pharisees were so scrupulous in fulfilling this commandment that they even **tithed** such small garden herbs as **mint and rue**, though not ordered to do so by the Law itself. At the same time, they would **bypass justice and the love of God**, treating their neighbor with unjust contempt and not loving God as they should. Thus they overlooked the very heart of the Law, while pretending to keep it with zeal and precision. The contrast between the minute observance of small details (even when not so commanded) and the wholesale neglect of the important things is, once again, stunning. They need **not disregard** such things as tithing, but **it was necessary** to attend to justice and the love of God as the most important.

Next He denounces them for their ostentatious pride. They **love the first-seats in the synagogues**, the places of honor up at the front, facing the people, where all the people could admire their preeminence. They love receiving **greetings in the marketplaces**, delighting as the people stand up and bow as they pass by, addressing them respectfully as "Rabbi." They insist on such public honors and are vexed if they are not forthcoming, for they consider themselves better than the common man.

Finally the Lord denounces them as being **like unseen tombs**, unmarked graves, which **men walk over** and **do not know** that they are doing so. The Lord here refers to the Jewish practice of marking graves with whitewash to identify them as graves. Even casual contact with a grave brought ritual impurity, and so great care was taken to let people know where the graves were, lest anyone walk over one. The Pharisees were like such unmarked tombs. Coming into contact with them and their teaching brought spiritual defilement to men who were not even aware that they were being defiled.

ॐ   ॐ   ॐ   ॐ   ॐ

45 And one of the lawyers says to Him in reply, "Teacher, in saying these *things*, You abuse us also."

46 But He said, "Woe to you lawyers, also! For you load men with loads hard to bear, while you yourselves will not touch the loads with one of your fingers.

47 "Woe to you! For you build the tombs of the prophets, and your fathers killed them.

48 "Therefore, you are witnesses and *give* consent to the works of your fathers, because they *themselves* killed them, and you *yourselves* build *their tombs*.

In the midst of this teaching, **one of the lawyers** present spoke up and protested. (By **lawyer** is meant one of the experts on the Jewish Law; they were famous for their minute legal distinctions and their burdensome legal rulings about what was and was not allowed.) The man piped up, saying, **"Teacher, in saying these *things*, You**

abuse us also." Though he addresses Jesus respectfully as **Teacher**, he feels that the criticism of the Pharisees condemns him and his approach to the Law as well, and he calls on Jesus to except him from His blanket condemnation of the Pharisees.

Jesus does nothing of the kind. Instead, He continues relentlessly, adding, **"Woe to you lawyers, also!"** They are as bad as the Pharisees and must share their condemnation. For they **load men** down **with loads hard to bear** by making rulings all but impossible to carry out. By piling requirement on requirement, they make the common man scarcely able to move without breaking some law; he is left gasping and helpless, like a beast of burden weighed down under a staggering load. The lawyers, however, are not inclined to use their ingenuity to help the poor man to find some way out; they will **not touch the loads** at all to lessen the burden, even **with one of** their **fingers**. All of the lawyers' skills are used to multiply laws and to increase the burden, never to decrease it.

Woe to them! They are one with their fathers and ancestors, the ones who misunderstood the will of God in ancient days and **killed the prophets**. What is the proof of this? That they **build the tombs of** those **prophets**! With savage irony, our Lord uses the fact that the lawyers build and adorn the tombs of the prophets as proof that they are like their fathers who killed them. It is as if the lawyers are working hand-in-glove with their ancestors and finishing the job they started. **They** *themselves*, their ancestors, **killed the prophets**, while the lawyers, their descendants, **build** *their tombs*. It is as if they are complicit in the murder of the prophets—"You kill them and I'll bury them!"

༄ ༄ ༄ ༄ ༄

49 "For this *reason* also the Wisdom of God said, 'I will send to them prophets and apostles, and *some* of them they will kill and persecute,'

50 "that the blood of all the prophets, poured out since the foundation of the world, may be required of this generation,

51 "from the blood of Abel to the blood of

> Zechariah, who perished between the altar and
> the House. Yes, I tell you, it will be required of
> this generation!
> 52 "Woe to you, lawyers! For you have taken
> away the key of knowledge; you did not enter
> yourselves, and those who were entering you
> forbade *entrance*."

The Lord then pronounces sentence upon the religious establishment of His day. As One who knows the inner **Wisdom** and Counsel **of God**, Jesus declares that He will **send to them prophets and apostles**, His own Christian messengers, for them to **kill and persecute** as well. This is all that is required for the Judgment of God to catch up with them all. Once the persecution of His followers in the decades to come has been accomplished, their measure of iniquity will be full (see Gen. 15:16 for the concept of the judgment of God waiting until the time is ripe), and judgment would fall in full measure.

Indeed, such judgment has been storing up for a long time, and when it finally comes, God will **require** of that **generation** the **blood of all the prophets poured out since the foundation of the world**. God has not fully avenged the blood of the righteous which has been unjustly shed—but He will. Indeed, all the unjust blood spilled throughout their entire Old Testament history will be required of them. From the murder of **Abel** (Gen. 4:8, the first murder mentioned in the Scriptures) to that of **Zechariah, who perished between the altar and the House** of God (the last murder committed by Jewish authorities mentioned in the Scriptures, in 2 Chr. 24:20–21), all those injustices will be charged to those who reject Christ and His apostles. (The reference is to the destruction of Israel by the Romans in AD 70.) The hardhearted will be judged at last.

The case of the **lawyers**, like Israel's in general, is hopeless. For they have **taken away the key of knowledge**, stealing from the people the possibility of knowing God through the Scriptures, leaving only a mass of impossible requirements. Not only do they **not**

enter the Kingdom themselves by learning and obeying what the Law truly demands, they corrupt others as well. **Those who were entering** and who might have profited by the Law, they **forbade** *entrance* into the Kingdom through their insistent misinterpretations.

ॐ ॐ ॐ ॐ ॐ

53 And when He went out from there, the scribes and the Pharisees began to have a terrible grudge and to *watch* what came from His mouth about many *matters*,

54 lying in wait for Him to catch Him in something from His mouth.

After such a sweeping condemnation of the whole Pharisaical approach to God and His Law, **the scribes and the Pharisees began to have a terrible grudge** against Jesus. They were now His implacable foes, and this denunciation hardened the opposition that had been present in many all along. They began to *watch* **what came from His mouth about many** *matters*, trying to see if there was something they could use against Him. Like hunters, they were **lying in wait for Him, to catch** and ensnare Him **in something from His mouth**. With brooding malevolence, they scrutinized His every word.

§VI.7.vii. Beware of the Leaven of the Pharisees

ॐ ॐ ॐ ॐ ॐ

12 1 Meanwhile, after myriads of the crowd had gathered together so that they were trampling on one another, He began saying to His disciples first, "Beware of the leaven of the Pharisees, which is hypocrisy.

2 "But there is nothing covered up that will not be revealed, and hidden that will not be known.

3 "So whatever you have said in the dark will be

---

heard in the light, and what you have spoken into the ear in the storerooms will be heralded upon the housetops.

4 "And I say to you, My friends, do not be afraid of those who kill the body, and after these *things* have no more that they *can* do.

5 "But I will show you of whom to be afraid: Be afraid of the One who, after He has killed, has authority to cast into Gehenna; yes, I tell you, be afraid of this One!

6 "Are not five sparrows sold for two assaria? And not one of them is forgotten before God.

7 "But even the very hairs of your head are all numbered. Do not be afraid; you are more valuable *than* many sparrows.

8 "And I say to you, every one who confesses Me before men, the Son of Man will confess him also before the angels of God;

9 "but he who denies Me before men will be *completely* denied before the angels of God.

10 "And every one who will say a word against the Son of Man, it will be forgiven him; but he who blasphemes against the Holy Spirit will not be forgiven.

11 "And when they bring you in before the synagogues and the rulers and the authorities, do not worry about how or what you should speak in your defense, or what you should say,

12 "for the Holy Spirit will teach you in that same hour what it is necessary to say."

As the Lord's popularity increased to the point that **myriads** (or ten thousands) **of the crowd had gathered together** so that they **were trampling on one another**, He warned His disciples **first** (that is, privately) not to let such popularity go to their heads. That is, He warned them to **beware of the leaven of the Pharisees, which is**

hypocrisy. Such a vice is called **leaven** or yeast because just a little bit of it can influence the whole—let a bit of hypocrisy remain in the heart, and it will soon corrupt one's whole spiritual life. The Pharisees were denounced as hypocrites because they claimed to be pious, while inwardly they cared nothing for what God really wanted. Their demands for a sign proved them to be part of a corrupt generation (11:16; Mark 8:11–15).

The disciples must remember that on the Last Day, all their secrets will be revealed and all acts of hypocrisy shown for what they are. On that Day, **nothing** that has been **covered up** will **not be revealed**, nothing **hidden** will **not be known**. **Whatever** secret denials are **said in the dark** will then be **heard in the light**, and secrets **spoken into the ear in the** inner **storerooms** will be as openly known as if they had been **heralded upon the housetops**. Let the disciples, then, be fearless; let them not play the hypocrite for fear of the Pharisees' persecution. Let their proclamation of the truth be as open in this age as all secrets will be in the age to come.

The Lord encourages His followers by calling them His **friends**, and He urges them **not** to **be afraid** of persecution. As His friends, let them be loyal to Him. Let them not fear **those who kill the body** and after such punishments **have no more that they *can* do**. Christ will **show** them whom to fear the most—let them **be afraid of** God, **the One who, after He has killed, has authority to cast into** the eternal **Gehenna** of fire. The punishment men can inflict is limited and temporary, while the punishment God will inflict is eternal and lasting. **Yes**, indeed, let the wise man be afraid of offending *Him* by his apostasy, since he must choose whom to offend, either God or the Pharisees.

They need not fear their foes, however, for God will care for those He loves. God cares for the humblest of creatures, even the **sparrows** and small birds. Are not **five** of them sold **for two assaria**? (An *assarion* was one-sixteenth of a *denarius*, which was a day's wage for a working man, so that such birds—sold as food for the very poor—cost next to nothing. Indeed, in Matt. 10:29 the price is given as two sparrows for one *assarion*, so that our present passage reflects the bargains of the marketplace—when one spends two *assaria*, an extra sparrow is thrown in for free!) Nonetheless, **not** a single **one of them** is **forgotten before God**, but all are under His care. The disciples are **more valuable *than* many sparrows**, and if God cares for the birds, how much more will He care for the disciples?

They should **not be afraid**; God treasures them as valuable to Him—even down to the last hair. The **very hairs of** their **head** are **all numbered**, lest God should lose track of one precious hair. The disciples can boldly confess Christ, no matter what the opposition from the Jewish authorities.

Christ will reward them abundantly for doing so. He assures them that **everyone who confesses** Him **before** the sneering and hostile faces of **men**, He, the victorious **Son of Man**, will confess at the final judgment before the radiant and cheering angels of God. Certainly that final court will be a more glorious tribunal, surpassing the courts of the synagogues as **angels** surpass **men**. Let them not fear to confess Christ, whatever the cost! For he who would **deny** (*arneomai*) Christ **before men** in this age, fearing human disfavor and persecution, will find himself *completely* **denied** (*aparneomai*, a more intensive form of the verb) **before** those **angels** on the Last Day.

The Pharisees accused Christ of being in league with Satan and of performing His miracles, not by the power of God's Holy Spirit, but by the power of Beelzebul (11:15). Thus they were not just **saying a word against** Jesus Himself and insulting Him. Such a sin could **be forgiven**. But the Pharisees, in attributing Christ's exorcisms to the devil, were thereby **blaspheming against the Holy Spirit**, and this sin would **not be forgiven**, no matter what their prayers and good deeds. Only repentance of this sin and faith in Jesus as Messiah could cleanse it away. As long as they rejected Christ as a deceiver, they could have no forgiveness from God.

Persecution from these Jewish authorities will surely follow. They will **bring** the disciples **before the synagogues** to be tried in the local courts and flogged (Matt. 10:17); they will drag them before **rulers and authorities** of the nations (Matt. 10:18). The disciples need **not worry about how** they should find a lawyer, **or what** they **should speak in** their **defense, or what** they **should say** about Jesus. They are God's own prophets (compare 11:49) and will be filled with the Spirit when the time comes (see for example Acts 4:8). **The Holy Spirit** will **teach** them **in that same hour** of need **what it is necessary to say**. Let them avoid fear-filled hypocrisy and confess Christ with boldness.

§VI.8. "Divide Up the Inheritance": Teaching on Wealth and the Kingdom

§VI.8.i. Refusal of Request

ॐ ॐ ॐ ॐ ॐ

13 And a certain *one* from the crowd said to Him, "Teacher, tell my brother to divide up the inheritance with me."

14 But He said to him, "Man, who appointed Me a judge or divider over you?"

15 And He said to them, "See *to it* and guard against all greediness, for though one has an abundance, his life is not from his possessions."

As our Lord was speaking privately with His disciples, **a certain one** came to Him **from the crowd** with a formal request. Rabbis were often asked to function as arbiters in domestic disputes, so that their superior knowledge of the Law (and their casuistry) could find a way out of domestic legal dilemmas. The man from the crowd came to Jesus, addressing Him respectfully as **Teacher** (or Rabbi), and presenting to Him just such a domestic legal disagreement. It would seem that the man's elder brother had inherited the family property and was reluctant to divide up the ancestral inheritance by giving his younger brother a piece of it. It seems that the elder brother wanted the family to live together to preserve the property intact, while the younger brother here refused to live with him but still wanted the share of the property to which he felt he was morally entitled. It was with this dilemma that he came to Jesus, asking Him to **tell** his **brother to divide up the** family **inheritance with** him.

Christ replies with formality. **Man** is here not a rude reply (compare the use of "Woman" in addressing His Mother in such a context as John 19:26), but corresponds with our modern English "sir." This formality is meant to distance Christ from the man and his request. For the man was not seeking salvation, but was motivated by greediness, which he had allowed to cloud his relationship with his brother. Moreover, he was not truly open to hearing wisdom from Christ, but was simply trying to use Him to achieve his own ends. The Lord knew that God had not sent Him into the world to iron out such petty quarrels, nor **appointed** Him such a **judge or divider over** such disputes. He had sent Him to teach salvation to the humble.

And so, in fulfilling His true task, Christ not only refuses to be drawn into the man's family quarrel, but He also warns him to **see *to it*** that he **guard against all greediness**. The man evidently thought that if he could inherit some of the family wealth, he would be contented and happy, but Christ knew that true **life** does **not** come **from** a man's **possessions**, even if **one has an abundance** of them. If the man would be truly contented, let him cast such greed from his heart. What matters is being rich towards God.

§VI.8.ii. Parable of the Rich Fool

> ॐ ॐ ॐ ॐ ॐ
>
> 16 And He told them a parable, saying, "The field of a certain rich *man* bore bountifully.
> 17 "And he was questioning within himself, saying, 'What will I do, since I do not have a place to store my crops?'
> 18 "And he said, 'This I will do: I will bring down my barns and build larger ones, and there I will store all my grain and my goods.
> 19 "'And I will say to my soul, "Soul, you have many goods laid up for many years! Rest, eat, drink, be glad!"'
> 20 "But God said to him, 'Senseless *one*! This night your soul is demanded of you; and what

> you have prepared, to whom will it be *given*?'
> 21 "Thus *is* the one who treasures up for himself
> and is not rich toward God."

To teach this more effectively, Christ went on to **tell them a parable** about **a certain rich *man*** whose **field bore bountifully,** so that he too had a dilemma: Where would he **store** all those **crops**? After **questioning within himself**, he finally hit upon a solution. With a definitive **this I will do**, he announced that he could **bring down** his **barns and build larger ones**! It was **there** that he would **store all** his **grain** and his **goods**, his seed for sowing and his harvested crops. Then he could sit back and **say to** his **soul, "Soul, you have many goods laid up for many years!** You've got it made! **Rest, eat, drink, be glad!"** (The man's soliloquy with his soul is meant to sound somewhat comic and ridiculous.)

In the eyes of the world, the man was indeed wise, and had managed his money wisely. But in the eyes of God, the man was **senseless** and a fool. For the man had spent all his energies taking care of himself, obsessing about money, with never a thought for the poor. He considered that *he* was the final owner of all his wealth ("*my* crops, *my* barns, *my* grain, *my* goods," even "*my* soul"), and did not see that all was lent to Him as a trust from God, for the use of which he was accountable to Him. He had planned for **many years** to come, not realizing that he might not have many years. Indeed, God said, **this** very **night** his **soul** was **demanded** of him, and he was to leave all his wealth behind. All the plans that he had **prepared** would now profit him nothing, and **to whom** would his wealth now **be *given*?** Certainly not to him! The man's true problem was not that he had too many possessions and no place to store them; his true problem was that death was imminent and he remained in spiritual poverty.

Christ draws the conclusion for the younger brother who was so obsessed with getting his share of the family wealth. **Thus** is the way of **the one who treasures up for himself and is not rich toward God**. That is, such a one is senseless, thinking that money can make him happy, all the while ignoring his responsibilities before God to help the poor. For God called the man not to *acquire* wealth, but to *give it away* (v. 33).

§VI.8.iii. "Do Not Be Worried"

🙞 🙞 🙞 🙞 🙞

22 And He said to His disciples, "For this *reason* I say to you, do not worry about *your* life, as to what you will eat; nor about *your* body, as to with what you will clothe yourself.

23 "For life is more than food, and the body than clothing.

24 "Consider the ravens, for they neither sow nor harvest; and they have no storeroom or barn; and God feeds them; how much more valuable you are than the birds!

25 "And which of you by worrying is able to add a cubit to his *allotted* age?

26 "If therefore you are not able *to do such* a small thing, why do you worry about the rest?

27 "Consider the lilies, how they grow; they neither toil nor spin, but I say to you, Solomon in all his glory did not clothe himself like one of these.

28 "If God thus clothes the grass in the field, which today is and tomorrow is cast into an oven, how much more *will He clothe* you, O you of little faith!

29 "And do not seek what you will eat, and what you will drink, and do not be upset.

30 "For these things all the nations of the world seek after; but your Father knows that you need these things.

31 "But seek His Kingdom, and these things will be added to you.

32 "Do not be afraid, little flock, for your Father

is well-pleased to give you the Kingdom.

33 "Sell your possessions and give alms; make yourselves purses which do not *grow* old, an inexhaustible treasure in heaven, where thief does not draw near, nor moth destroy.

34 "For where your treasure is, there will your heart be also."

After this, the Lord spoke more generally **to His disciples** about wealth. His parable had revealed how foolish it is to hoard one's riches. The rich fool in the parable was consumed with anxiety over such material things, but they must **not worry about** their **life** and the concerns of the **body**, such as **what** they **will eat**, or **with what** they **will clothe** themselves. They must be concerned for loftier priorities than **food** and **clothing**, priorities such as doing the will of God. That is what **life** and **the body** are really about.

They needn't worry, for God will take care of their needs, leaving them free to seek higher things. Do they doubt this? Then let them **consider the ravens** (Gr. *korax*, denoting ravens, crows, and other such birds). **They neither sow nor harvest**. Unlike the rich man in the parable, **they have no storeroom or barn** at all. But when they cry to God with their raucous voices (Ps. 147:9), **God feeds them**. **How much more valuable** are the disciples **than the birds!**

Or let them **consider the lilies**, the scarlet poppies and purple anemones that flower by their feet, and **how they grow**. **They neither toil nor spin**, but they grow beautifully all the same, because God provides for them, so that even **Solomon in all his** fabled **glory** of scarlet and purple robes **did not clothe himself** as beautifully as **one of these**. **If God thus clothes the** mere **grass in the field, which** is so ephemeral and short-lived that **today** it **is and tomorrow** it **is cast into** a baking **oven** to be used as fuel, how much more will He clothe the disciples? Of what **little faith** they are!

It is plain, then, that there is no need for them to worry about the basic needs of life. Worse than being unnecessary, such worry is futile and accomplishes nothing anyway. **Which** of them can change his situation simply **by worrying** about it? Is that one **able**, for example, **to add** so much as a single **cubit**, a single measure, **to his *allotted* age?** God made everyone's days to consist of a certain number of such handbreadths (Ps. 39:5)—can anyone present show how to increase the number simply by worrying? **If therefore** they are **not able *to do such* a small thing** as to add a single measure to their lifespan, **why** do they **worry about the rest?** Let them acknowledge their powerlessness and leave it all with God.

God can be trusted to take care of them. They need **not seek what** they **will eat, and what** they **will drink**, nor **be upset** and all in a turmoil over it. The word rendered *be upset* is the Greek *mete-orizomai*, literally, "to be raised up." The thought here is of being up in the air, anxious, unable to rest. The word is used in Psalm 131:1 for the proud and restless soul. The Lord would have His disciples at peace, trusting in God, quiet as a weaned child resting against its mother (Ps. 131:2).

All the nations of the world, the Gentiles who do not know the God of Israel, **seek after** such material things with anxiety—and Christ's disciples ought to be better than those Gentiles. Their **Father knows that** they **need these things**. Let them leave it with Him. Their concern must be to **seek His Kingdom**, to make it their abiding focus to do what He commands. If they will do this, then **these things** they need, their food and clothing, will **be added** to them as well.

They need **not be afraid**. Though they are small and helpless, they are God's **little flock**, and their Shepherd will care for them. Indeed, the **Father** is **well-pleased to give** them **the Kingdom** they are seeking. That is, this free bestowal is His established decision, His settled intention. In light of this joy, they can **sell** their **possessions** and use them to **give alms** to the poor. This will **make** for them fat **purses** in the age to come, purses that will **not *grow* old** and be destroyed, losing their contents. It will be an **inexhaustible treasure in heaven**—far better than anything they could store in large barns (compare v. 18). For there no **thief** can **draw near** to plunder their gold, nor will any **moth destroy** their fine garments (the usual sources of wealth in those days).

If they will trust in God and leave it to Him to care for them and reward their earthly generosity, all will be well. They want to have their hearts with God in heaven—so let them give away their wealth and store up treasure there with Him. It is an invariable principle that **where** one's **treasure** is, **there** will one's **heart be also**. If they would escape the earthbound life, let them seek the Kingdom and not earthly riches.

§VI.8.iv. The Coming Kingdom

> ॐ ॐ ॐ ॐ ॐ
>
> 35 "Let your loins be girded and your lamps burning.
> 36 "And you be like men anticipating their lord when he returns from the wedding *feasts*, that when he comes and knocks, they may immediately open to him.
> 37 "Blessed *are* those slaves whom the lord will find keeping alert when he comes! Amen I say to you, he will gird himself and have them recline and will come alongside and serve them.
> 38 "Whether he comes in the second, or even in the third watch, and finds *them* thus, blessed are those *slaves*!
> 39 "But know this, that if the house-master had known at what hour the thief was coming, he would not have let his house be broken into.
> 40 "You *yourselves* also be prepared; for the Son of Man is coming at an hour that you do not think *He will*."

The Lord's reference to God giving them the Kingdom (v. 32) leads to teaching about waiting for the final Kingdom of God, which Christ will bring with Him at His Second Coming. Since the Father has chosen to give Christ's disciples the Kingdom, they must live in constant readiness for it, for only so can they receive the proffered gift.

To show the need for readiness, Christ tells a parable: His

disciples must be like slaves waiting to greet their master upon his return after a somewhat lengthy absence. The picture is of slaves **anticipating their lord when he returns from** days at **the wedding** *feasts* (the plural, **weddings feasts,** is used, indicating a celebration lasting several days). The master has not told them when he will return, and the slaves must keep the house in readiness for his return at all times—even if the return be in the middle of the night.

Thus, they must **let** their **loins be girded** and their **lamps** be kept **burning**. In those days, men wore long, loose, sweeping garments, and in order to do any work, they had to first gird their robes about their waists to permit freedom of movement. The waiting slaves must live with their flowing clothes tied about their waists so that they can spring into action for their master at a moment's notice. They must also keep their lamps full of oil and burning, so that they can see to respond instantly should their master return in the middle of the night. Only by living in such readiness will they be prepared to welcome him properly and **open to him when he comes** home and **knocks** at the door to secure entrance. The master will give no advance notice—he might return in **the second or even in the third watch** (that is, 9:00 P.M. to midnight, or even from midnight to 3:00 A.M.)

If **the lord** comes home suddenly to **find** them **keeping alert** and able to welcome him, **blessed** will be **those slaves!** What a reward their master will have for them! Indeed, the master will exalt them above their former status as slaves and treat them like his equals, even like honored guests. (So extraordinary was this behavior and so uncharacteristic of earthly masters regarding their slaves, the Lord prefaces His words about the slaves' reward with His customary, **"Amen I say to you,"** assuring His disciples that His words are true.) For acts such as **girding** oneself (compare John 13:4), **having** one **recline** at table, and **coming alongside** one to **serve** him food were the acts of slaves, not of masters. A man would do this with his equals and his honored guests, but never with his slaves. Christ is hereby teaching His disciples that in the age to come, they will be exalted beyond anything they can imagine.

But the consummation of the Kingdom (at the Second Coming)

will come suddenly, and with no prior warning. The disciples therefore must live in constant readiness and righteousness throughout this long age. Let them **know** and be sure of that! It is the same with a **house-master** who was surprised when a burglar broke into his house, digging through the clay wall. If the householder **had known at what hour** that **thief was coming, he** would have waited for him and **would not have let his house be broken into**. But the thief was hardly likely to give him advance notice of his plans! The householder must therefore be vigilant at all times. In the same way, Christ will not give advance warning of His Second Coming, so that His disciples **also** must **be prepared** for His return at *all* times. Christ will return at such **an hour** as men **do not think *He will*.**

ॐ ॐ ॐ ॐ ॐ

41 And Peter said, "Lord, are you saying this parable to us, or to everyone also?"

42 And the Lord said, "Who then is the faithful *and* prudent steward whom the lord will appoint over his servants, to give *them* their rations at the *appointed* time?

43 "Blessed *is* that slave whom his lord finds thus doing when he comes!

44 "Truly I say to you, he will appoint him over all his possessions.

45 "But if that slave says in his heart, 'My lord delays in coming,' and begins to strike the servants and the servant-girls, and to eat and drink and get drunk;

46 "the lord of that slave will come on a day which he does not expect, and in an hour he does not know, and will cut him in two, and put *him to have* his part with the faithless.

47 "And that slave who knew his lord's will and did not prepare or do according to his will will be beaten *with* many *blows*,

48 "but the one who did not know, and did *things*

> worthy of blows, will be beaten *with* few. And
> from everyone to whom much was given, much
> will be sought from him; and to whom much was
> committed, of him they will ask all the more.

Christ's words about people not being ready for His Coming sounded a bit ominous to Peter. On hearing that the Kingdom could possibly bring judgment to those who were unprepared, Peter asks a question. Is Jesus **saying this parable** to them, to the Twelve, **or to everyone also**? Surely Christ must be directing His warnings at the outsiders, and not at His disciples. For how could His disciples ever suffer when the Kingdom came? Surely these ominous warnings were not meant for them!

In reply, Christ expands on His parable about the waiting slaves, showing that His previous warnings were meant for all, including the Twelve. Does Peter want to know who is the one who will inherit the staggering blessings of the Kingdom (those blessings mentioned in v. 37)? Then let Peter tell Him **who then is the faithful *and* prudent steward**. That faithful and prudent one is the one who will be **blessed**! Being an outward disciple of Jesus is not enough to assure blessing in the age to come; one must be faithful and prudent, and be **found doing** one's set tasks when Christ **comes** back. This is the one whom Christ **will appoint over all** His **possessions**, rewarding him richly in the age to come.

So the disciple must persevere in his righteousness and not presume that he will inherit the Kingdom regardless of his works. **If** the **slave** in the parable, the steward of the household, **says in his heart, "My lord delays in coming** back," and **begins to** abuse his fellow-servants, if he begins to **strike** his subordinates, cuffing the other **servants and servant-girls**, if he begins to **eat and drink** whatever and how much he likes as if it all belonged to him, and even to **get drunk**—why then, there will be no blessing. Indeed, **the lord of that slave will come on a day which he does not expect** and exact the severest penalty. He will even **cut him in two**, as one would do to a criminal, so that the faithless servant will *have* **his part with the faithless**.

The apostles therefore should not presume that their privileged position brings them any immunity from judgment. Just the opposite! For **from everyone to whom much was given, much will be sought from him; and to whom much was committed, of him they will ask all the more**. Everyone will be responsible for living according to the spiritual light he has received—and the apostles have received much spiritual light. God will be just. If one **knows** God's **will**, having responded to the Gospel with open eyes, and yet still does **not prepare** for the Second Coming by living in righteousness, then that one will **be beaten *with* many *blows*** in the age to come. That is, such a one will be punished severely at the Judgment. But if another one **does not know** the Gospel and yet does those very same things which were **worthy of blows** in the first, that one will only be **beaten *with* few** blows (that is, will receive a lighter punishment at the Judgment), for this second one is also responsible only for living according to the more limited light he has received. To be blessed, one must be faithful!

---

୬୬ ୬୬ ୬୬ ୬୬ ୬୬

49 "I have come to cast fire upon the earth; and how I wish it were already kindled!

50 "But I have a baptism to be baptized with, and how distressed I am until it is finished!

51 "Do you think that I came to give peace on the earth? No, I tell you, but rather division.

52 "For from now on, five in one house will be divided up: three against two, and two against three.

53 "They will be divided up, father against son, and son against father; mother against the daughter, and daughter against the mother, mother-in-law against her daughter-in-law, and daughter-in-law against the mother-in-law."

Christ longs for the Kingdom to come and to cleanse men with the fire of the Spirit. This work He refers to as **casting fire upon the earth**. The Spirit with which He will baptize His followers is compared to the divine fire (3:16), and this fire indeed fell upon the earth on the Day of Pentecost (Acts 2:3). Christ wishes it **were already kindled**, and that already His disciples were being transformed. But this will have to wait, for He **has a baptism to be baptized with**, and the transformation of men by the Spirit's power cannot come until after that (see John 7:39). This **baptism** is His suffering on the Cross, when He will be drowned in sorrow, and all God's waves will roll over Him (Ps. 42:7). How **distressed** He is until He can **finish** this work of the Father!

This suffering of His is inevitable, given the fallen and sinful hearts of men. Peter (and others with him) may imagine that the coming Kingdom will bring only blessing to Israel, but it is not so. Though some in Israel have true and open hearts (like the Twelve), others are implacable opponents of God's will. Thus Christ **came** not simply to **give peace on the earth**. **No**, He solemnly assures them, He came to bring **division** and dissension, as His truth divides the humble from the proud, those open to God from those opposed to Him.

Such division will strike even such formidable unities as the family, which normally nothing can divide. Even **one** small **house** consisting of no more than **five** people will find itself **divided up** by the truth He brings. **Father** and **son** usually stand together in unbreakable solidarity, but even this unity will find itself sundered by the Gospel, as Jesus' claims take precedence even over the sacred and primordial claims of family loyalty. Some in the family will accept Christ, and others reject Him, so that even such a small family will teem with dissension. Not only will **father** range himself **against** his own **son**, but **mother** will strive **against daughter**, and **mother-in-law against daughter-in-law**. The hostility will be mutual (not only will the father be against the son, but the son against the father) and utterly divisive (it will not be a case of four being against one, but rather the family being equally divided, with **three against two**). And this division will not be a passing phase, but a permanent state, existing **from now on**. The Gospel sword of truth (compare Matt. 10:34) is soon to strike deep into the heart of the world, judging its thoughts and intentions (Heb. 4:12).

ॐ ॐ ॐ ॐ ॐ

54 And He was also saying to the crowds, "When you see a cloud rising over the west, immediately you say, 'A rainstorm is coming,' and thus it happens.

55 "And when a south-*wind* is blowing, you say, 'It will be hot,' and it happens.

56 "Hypocrites! You know *how* to prove the face of the earth and the heaven, but how *is it that* you do not know *how to* prove the *appointed* time?

57 "And why do you not even judge for yourselves *what is* righteous?

58 "For as you are going away with your opponent to a ruler, make an effort on the way to be released from him, lest he drag you before the judge, and the judge deliver you to the bailiff, and the bailiff cast you into prison.

59 "I say to you, you will never come out from there until you have rendered even the last lepton."

Luke continues with Christ's public teaching **to the crowds**, continuing the theme of Israel's faithlessness. How blind they are! Christ reproaches them for being **hypocrites**. For **when** they **see a cloud rising over the west, immediately** and with ease they **say**, **"A rainstorm is coming"** (bringing rain from the Mediterranean), and they are exactly right. **When** they feel a **south-*wind* blowing** (bringing heat from the desert), they all **say** to each other, **"It will be hot,"** and again they are correct. They can **prove** and discern such great things as **the face of the earth and the heaven** (with its heavenly cloud and its earthly wind), but do **not know *how to* prove** and discern **the *appointed* time** (Gr. *kairos*), though it is right under their noses. The future they can read well enough—how is it that they cannot read the present? Can they **not even judge** for themselves *what is* **righteous** and true? Can they not see for themselves that He is bringing the truth and know how to respond in faithfulness?

Time is running out for them. It is like a man **going away with** his **opponent to a ruler**, to have their dispute tried in court. If that man were smart, he would **make an effort** while **on the way** to be reconciled to his foe and to **be released from** the accusation his foe was going to bring against him. If that man squandered the opportunity and did not reconcile himself to his opponent, soon it would be too late. He would be **dragged before the judge** and condemned, **the judge** would **deliver** him **to the bailiff** in charge of the debtor's prison, and **the bailiff** would **cast** him **into the prison**. There justice would be done, and, Christ assures the crowds, the wretch would **never come out from there until** he had somehow **rendered even the last lepton**, paid every last bit of the debt. (A *lepton* was one one-hundred-twenty-eighth of a *denarius*, the smallest Greek coin.) That is, there would be no mercy.

It is the same for that faithless generation. They had best repent, accept Christ's Word, and be reconciled with God. For otherwise, they will feel God's wrath and endure His judgment in all its merciless rigor.

§VI.9. "Worse Galileans?": Teaching on Repentance

§VI.9.i. Report on Galileans

> 𝕏 𝕏 𝕏 𝕏 𝕏
>
> **13** 1 Now at the same time there were some present who declared to Him about the Galileans, whose blood Pilate had mixed with their sacrifices.
>
> 2 And He answered and said to them, "Do you think that these Galileans were sinners above all *other* Galileans, because they suffered these *things*?
>
> 3 "No, I tell you, but unless you repent, you will all likewise perish.
>
> 4 "Or those eighteen upon whom the tower in

> Siloam fell and killed them, do you think that
> they were debtors above all the *other* men
> dwelling in Jerusalem?
> 5 "No, I tell you, but unless you repent, you will
> all likewise perish."

While Christ was speaking about judgment (12:59), some
brought news of men who they felt sure had been judged and condemned by God. These were some **Galileans whose blood Pilate
had mixed with their sacrifices**. Galileans in general were famous
for their hot-headed impulsiveness, and Pilate was famous for his
brutality. It often proved a potent combination. It would seem
that several of these men from Galilee (possibly Zealots) had been
offering sacrifices in Jerusalem, and while there were encouraging
their fellow-Jews to rebel in some way against Rome. In retaliation, Pilate had them arrested and slain, so that they were killed at
about the same time as their sacrificial animals were being offered.
Thus their **blood** and the blood of **their sacrifices** were in that way
mixed. Some who observed this felt that God had abandoned these
Galileans, and that they must have somehow done some great sin
to deserve being so abandoned.

Jesus feels that such self-righteousness is entirely misplaced—
especially coming from that generation, which is rejecting Him.
He responds by demanding whether His hearers really think those
Galileans were sinners above all *other* Galileans simply **because
they suffered** like that. Do His hearers really believe that they themselves are more pleasing to God than those poor Galilean wretches?
No, Christ insists, they are just as bad. In fact, if they do not **repent**,
they will **all likewise perish**. God is about to judge that generation
for their sins (11:50), bringing the Romans to obliterate the Jewish
state in AD 70.

It was the same with **those eighteen upon whom the tower of
Siloam fell and killed them**. Siloam was the name of a reservoir in
Jerusalem, and the tower may have been part of a building program
to improve its aqueduct water supply. It would seem that during its
construction, the tower fell upon some of the workers, killing them.

Many felt that such a terrible misfortune was evidence of some sin, and that they were more righteous than those who were killed. Those who were killed must have been great **debtors**, men who owed God a great debt of sin, and that was why judgment struck them. Christ repudiates this suggestion too. The ***other* men dwelling in Jerusalem** are no better than those who were killed (compare 13:34). In fact, if there is no repentance, they all will **likewise perish**. God's judgment hangs over them like a dangling sword. Let them repent now if they would escape His wrath!

§VI.9.ii. Parable of the Fig Tree

ॐ ॐ ॐ ॐ ॐ

6 And He was telling this parable: "A certain *man* had a fig tree planted in his vineyard; and he came seeking fruit on it, and did not find *any*.

7 "And he said to the vineyard-keeper, 'Behold, for three years I have come seeking fruit on this fig tree and not finding *any*. Cut it down! Why does it even waste the ground?'

8 "And he answered and said to him, 'Lord, let it *alone* for this year also, until I dig around it and cast in manure;

9 "'and if it indeed bears fruit in the coming *year*, *good*, but if not, cut it down.'"

In order to make clear the urgent necessity for repentance, Christ began **telling this parable**. It was about **a certain *man*** who **had a fig tree planted in his vineyard**. Not unnaturally, **he came seeking fruit on it**, and year after year, he **did not find *any***. In exasperation he said to his vineyard-keeper that **for three years** he had labored over this fig tree in vain. He had had enough. **"Cut it down!"** he instructed his gardener, **"Why does it even waste the ground** it was on?" He could use the space there to plant something that *would* bear fruit.

The vineyard-keeper, however, persuaded him to give the fig tree one more chance. He besought the owner and **lord** of the vineyard to **let it *alone* for this year**. Let him **dig around it and cast in manure** to fertilize it. **If it indeed** would **bear fruit in the coming year—good**! **But if not**, then he would gladly **cut it down**.

The parable was a blood-chilling one for those who understood it. The **three years** was about the time of John and Jesus' ministries combined, and during this time God, the **Lord** of the Vineyard, had come **seeking** for the spiritual **fruit** of repentance and faith in Israel, and was **not finding *any***. Israel as a whole was rejecting Jesus, as it had rejected John. God would not strike in judgment yet, but give Israel another chance. During this last **year** of Christ's ministry, He would labor to teach them, giving them one last chance to repent and **bear fruit**. But **if** they did **not**, they were **wasting the ground** in Palestine and taking up space there for no reason. God would **cut** them **down**, using the sword of the Romans, and bring them to national extinction.

§VI.10. Healing a Crippled Woman on the Sabbath

ॐ ॐ ॐ ॐ ॐ

10 And He was teaching in one of the synagogues on the Sabbaths.

11 And behold! a woman having a spirit of illness *for* eighteen years; and she was bent over, and was not able to unbend *herself* at all.

12 And when Jesus saw her, He called out and said to her, "Woman, you are loosed from your ailment."

13 And He laid His hands upon her, and immediately she was made straight again, and was glorifying God.

14 And the synagogue-ruler, indignant because Jesus had healed on the Sabbath, was saying to the crowd, "There are six days in which it is necessary to work; therefore come on them and be healed, and not on the Sabbath day."

15 But the Lord answered him and said, "Hypocrites! Does not each of you on the Sabbath
loose his ox or his donkey from the manger
and lead it away to *let* it drink?

16 "And this one, being a daughter of Abraham,
whom Satan has bound, behold, for eighteen
years, was it not necessary *for her* to be loosed
from this bond on the Sabbath day?"

17 And as He was saying this, His opponents
were being put to shame; and all the crowd
was rejoicing over all the glorious things being
done by Him.

St. Luke then relates a story of how Christ healed in **one of the synagogues** on one of **the Sabbaths**, and thereby excited the wrath of the synagogue-ruler. This was a perfect example of Israel refusing to repent and bear spiritual fruit (vv. 5, 9) and of why God's judgment would one day come.

It was as He was **teaching** in the synagogue that He saw **a woman having a spirit of illness**, a curvature of the spine that was the work of the devil. She had suffered this affliction *for* **eighteen years**, being **bent over** so far that she could not **unbend** *herself* to stand erect and pray (the proper posture for prayer was standing erect), nor look her neighbor directly in the eye. It was a degrading affliction, and one that she had probably suffered from her whole adult life. It seems as if her appearance in the synagogue was unexpected (Luke prefaces it with a **behold!**), and it is possible that she was warned by some not to come and present herself to Jesus for healing on the Sabbath. If that is so, her presence there would have indeed caused a bit of a stir.

As expected, Jesus did not shrink from healing her, even on the Sabbath. As soon as **Jesus saw her, He called out to her** in the crowd, saying, **"Woman** (or "Madam," as modern English would have it), **you are loosed from your ailment."** This was her invitation to come forward through the crowd, and when she reached the Lord, **He laid His hands upon her, and immediately she**

was made straight again, and began **glorifying God** for the healing.

The **synagogue-ruler**, however, did not glorify God for the healing. Rather, he was **indignant because Jesus had healed on the Sabbath**, which for him constituted work and a violation of the Law. He could not see the glory of God, only sin and rule-breaking. Furious as he was, he did not have the courage to rebuke Jesus publicly, and so rounded on the woman herself and the watching crowd. He rebuked her under the pretense of teaching the crowd how to honor the Sabbath, exhorting them and saying, **"There are six days in which it is necessary to work; therefore come on them and be healed, and not on the Sabbath day."** The woman (still standing up before them all) began to feel ashamed, as if she had done a great sin in presenting herself to be healed.

The Lord, however, was not slow to come to her defense, denouncing those who agreed with the synagogue-ruler as so many **hypocrites**. For **each of** them **on the Sabbath** would **loose his ox or his donkey** from its bond and tether **and lead it away to** *let* it **drink**. They would loose their animals from their bonds and relieve the suffering of thirst. How much more should **this one** (did our Lord point to the woman as He said this?), being no animal but a **daughter of Abraham** and heir of his covenant, **be loosed from** her **bond**?

Satan had bound her in this affliction, **behold** (think of it!) **for eighteen years**. Wasn't that enough time to suffer? They had compassion on animals; how could they not have compassion on this woman? How could they let her suffer another day? And what better way to honor the Sabbath than by setting this captive free? Thus it was **necessary** to loose her from Satan's bond as soon as possible. (Those who suggest that the woman should have waited one more day to be healed thus miss the point. Eighteen years was long enough to wait. Besides, Christ was in the synagogue then, and would move on. For the woman, it was now or never.)

As He spoke in the woman's defense, **His opponents were being put to shame**, having nothing to say in reply. Moreover, **all the crowd was rejoicing** over this and **over all the glorious things**

being done by Him. The woman could walk out of the synagogue erect, dignified, and joyful, amid the cheers of the crowd.

§VI.11. Parables of the Kingdom

> ॐ ॐ ॐ ॐ ॐ
>
> 18 Therefore He was saying, "What is the King-
> dom of God like, and to what will I liken it?
> 19 "It is like a mustard seed, which a man took
> and cast into his own garden; and it grew and
> became a tree; and the birds of the heaven
> nested in its branches."
> 20 And again He said, "To what will I liken the
> Kingdom of God?
> 21 "It is like leaven, which a woman took and hid
> in three pecks of meal, until the whole *batch*
> was leavened."

Because some of the people were rejoicing over Christ's victory over the Pharisaical synagogue-ruler (v. 17), **therefore** Christ strove to take advantage of their openness and to teach them about the Kingdom of God. As mentioned above (in the commentary of 8:4ff), many people thought the Kingdom would come as a single, cataclysmic event in which the sinners were slain and the righteous rewarded. These two parables correct such a notion.

In the first parable, Christ **likens** and compares the nature of **the Kingdom of God** to **a mustard seed**. The mustard seed was proverbially small, yet when a man **cast** it **into his own garden, it grew and became a tree**, one so large that **the birds of the heaven nested in its branches**. The image is drawn from such Old Testament passages as Ezekiel 17:23, which speaks of the Kingdom of God growing taller than all the other kingdoms of men, like a tree tall enough to provide shelter for the birds.

This image, with its contrast between the small beginnings and the great completion, is presented again in the second parable, that of the leaven. This parable tells of a woman who took a little **leaven** or yeast and put it into a batch of **meal, three pecks'** worth (Gr. *sata*, corresponding to about 7 quarts, and making enough bread to feed 160 people). The tiny bit of leaven was enough to **leaven** the **whole** *batch*.

In both of these parables, the contrast is between tiny beginnings and universal diffusion at the end. The ministry of Jesus seemed to many to be small and insignificant. He had no outward glory, no mighty army, no political connections—just a small group of twelve ordinary men, attended by a large rabble of sick and needy. Was this the Kingdom of God that would one day topple Rome from its throne and fill the universe with the glory of God? But small beginnings can lead to great things—as the examples of the mustard seed and the bit of leaven reveal.

§VI.12. "Few Being Saved?": Teaching on the Narrow Door

22 And He was proceeding through cities and villages, teaching and making *His* way to Jerusalem.

23 And someone said to Him, "Lord, *are* there *just* a few who are being saved?" And He said to them,

24 "Strive *in contest* to enter by the narrow door, for many, I tell you, will seek to enter in and will not be strong enough.

25 "After the house-master has arisen and shut *fast* the door, and you begin to stand outside and knock at the door, saying, 'Lord, open to us!' then He will answer and say to you, 'I do not know where you are from.'

26 "Then you will begin to say, 'We ate and drank before Your *presence,* and You taught in our streets!'

27 "and he will speak, saying to you, 'I do not know where you are from; withdraw from me, all workers of unrighteousness!'

28 "There will be crying and gnashing of teeth there

> when you will see Abraham and Isaac and Jacob
> and all the prophets in the Kingdom of God, but
> you *yourselves* cast outside.
> 29 "And they will come from east and west, and from
> north and south, and will recline in the Kingdom
> of God.
> 30 "And behold, *some* are last who will be first, and
> *some* are first who will be last."

As the Lord was **proceeding through cities and villages** on His way **to Jerusalem**, one of His disciples asked Him the question, **"Are there *just* a few who are being saved?"** The question was not asked out of idle theological curiosity, but out of genuine perplexity. For it was a proverb in Judaism that "all Israel has a share in the age to come," and yet Jesus and His message were meeting with more and more opposition. Did this mean that the proverb was wrong? Were just a few out of Israel being saved?

As usual, Christ refuses to answer the man's question directly, and instead answers the question he should have asked, namely, "What must *I* do to be saved?" To that question, the Lord says that he must **strive *in contest* to enter by the narrow door**. The word rendered *strive in contest* is the Greek *agonizomai*, cognate with the word *agon*, which means "contest, wrestling match, race." The words savor of the athletic arena and show what great effort is required of those who would be saved. They must struggle like that to **enter by the narrow door**, as if squeezing through a narrow space. **Many will seek to enter in and will not be strong enough** to do so; they will give up the struggle, unable to squeeze through.

Why this struggle? What makes the door into eternal life so narrow and so difficult to squeeze through? The comforts of life and the love of popularity. If one became a disciple of Jesus, one would certainly be persecuted (compare Mark 4:17) and would lose one's reputation. **Many** were unwilling to pay such a price and were **not strong enough** to endure such persecution. They will find themselves unable to enter through the door, encumbered and bulky as they are with their big respectable reputations.

So let him who would be saved **strive *in contest*** now, casting away concern with reputation and popularity. Let him enroll as Jesus' disciple now, whatever the cost. For later it will be too late. They will find the Lord to be like a **house-master** holding a banquet who **has arisen and shut *fast* the door** to his house after all the invited guests have come. No others will be admitted after the banquet has begun, whatever their pleading.

On the Day of Judgment, they will **stand outside** the eternal Banquet **and knock at the door, saying, "Lord, open to us!"** But He will not open to them. Instead, He **will answer** from within, **"I do not know where you are from,"** treating them like absolute strangers. On that terrible day they will begin to protest their exclusion, saying, **"We ate and drank before Your *presence*, and You taught in our streets!"** Jesus *must* remember them. They shared table fellowship with Him and listened to His teaching. But their pleading will be in vain, for such merely external connections with Christ are not enough; what is needed is true discipleship. The Lord will be immovable in His determination to exclude them and will insist that He **does not know where** they **are from**. He will insist that they **withdraw from** Him, along with **all** other **workers of unrighteousness**.

Their grief at being eternally shut out will be terrible, for they **will see Abraham and Isaac and Jacob and all the prophets** sitting down to feast **in the Kingdom of God**, while they themselves are **cast outside**, unable to join these ancient Jewish worthies in their feasting. Indeed, even Gentiles will come to take the places they thought they would occupy at that table, **coming from east and west and from north and south**. These heathen will stream in from the four corners of the earth to find a place in the Kingdom. There will be room for the Gentiles, but not for Jews like them! The seeming unfairness of it all will cause **crying and gnashing of teeth** in helpless rage.

For the Kingdom of God will overturn all the standards they think they can depend on. *Some* **who are last** now will finally **be first** (as the despised Gentile finds a place at the head table), and *some* **who are first** now (such as the popular Pharisees) will finally

be last (as they find themselves excluded from the Kingdom).

§VI.13. Herod's Threat and Jerusalem

༃ ༃ ༃ ༃ ༃

31 In the same hour, some Pharisees came to *Him*, saying to Him, "Depart and go from here, for Herod wishes to kill You."

32 And He said to them, "Go and tell that fox, 'Behold, I cast out demons and perform cures today and tomorrow, and the third *day* I will be finished.'

33 "But it is necessary for Me to go on today and tomorrow and the next *day*, for it is not possible for a prophet to perish outside of Jerusalem.

34 "O Jerusalem, Jerusalem, that kills the prophets and stones those sent to her! How often I wished to gather together your children, the way a hen *gathers together* her brood under her wings, and you did not wish *it*!

35 "Behold, your House is left to you! And I say to you, you will never see Me until *it* comes when you say, 'Blessed *is* He who comes in the Name of the Lord!'"

Not all the **Pharisees** were opposed to Jesus, and some of them **came to *Him***, warning Him, **"Depart and go from here, for Herod wishes to kill You."** Herod had arrested John the Baptizer and had him killed, and these Pharisees had some information that he was closing in on Jesus too. Jesus should therefore flee from the place where He was and save Himself.

They advise that Jesus **go** (Gr. *poreuomai*) from there, and Jesus replies that they should **go** (*poreuomai*) themselves. Let them go back to Herod, that low and cunning **fox**, with this message from Him: **"Behold, I cast out demons and perform cures today and**

tomorrow, and the third *day* I will be finished." It was a message of courage—and of some insolence! To call someone "a fox" was quite provocative, for the fox was portrayed as somewhat ignoble. And Jesus was saying that He refused to run or alter His timetable. He would continue to **cast out demons and perform cures** as God commanded, working **today and tomorrow**. It was only after that, on **the third *day***, that He would **be finished**—and would die in Jerusalem. (The reference to **the third *day*** is the normal Jewish way of saying simply "soon.") Jesus refused to be driven off prematurely before He had finished all that God had for Him to do.

He was told to **go** from there (Gr. *poreuomai*), and indeed it was **necessary** for Him to **go on** (Gr. *poreuomai*) **today and tomorrow and the next *day***. He would not cut short His work out of fear of being killed. With biting irony, He declares Himself invincible and immune from being killed, so long as He stays out of Jerusalem. It is not **possible for a** genuine **prophet to perish outside of Jerusalem**! It was Jerusalem that had the privileged role of killing the prophets, a privilege they would share with no other city. He was safe in Herod's territory, since He was far from that murderous town.

Christ then turns from biting irony to heartfelt grief over the Holy City. He addresses the city tenderly, calling out, **"O Jerusalem, Jerusalem!"** This is the city that **kills the prophets and stones those sent to her** by God to call her to repentance. Why does she have to be like that? **How often**, in His previous visits there, did He **wish to gather together** her **children** and citizens, **the way a hen *gathers together*** her beloved **brood under her** protective **wings**! Christ often **wished** to gather them safely into the Kingdom, but they **did not wish** to be so gathered. The city continued in its hard-hearted impenitence, resisting all God's overtures of love.

There is nothing for it. **Behold**, let them face this shocking fate: their **House**, the Temple, is **left** to them. God is abandoning His Temple, leaving them without the divine protection they boast of and rely on. They can be sure of this too—they will **never see** Jesus in blessing until they cry, **"Blessed *is* He who comes in the Name of the Lord!"** Unless they acknowledge Him as Messiah (as they do at His triumphal entry; 19:38), there will be no blessing for the city.

§VI.14. Dinner with the Pharisees

§VI.14.i. Healing on the Sabbath

> ॐ ॐ ॐ ॐ ॐ
>
> **14** 1 And it happened when He went into a house of one of the rulers of the Pharisees on the Sabbath to eat bread, that they were observing Him.
>
> 2 And behold! a certain man was suffering from dropsy in front of Him.
>
> 3 And Jesus answered and spoke to the lawyers and Pharisees, saying, "Is it permitted to heal on the Sabbath or not?"
>
> 4 But they were quiet. And He took hold of him, and cured him and dismissed *him*.
>
> 5 And He said to them, "Which one of you will have a son or an ox fall into a well, and will not immediately draw him up on a Sabbath day?"
>
> 6 And they were not able to answer back to these *things*.

Luke then relates a series of teachings Christ gives when dining with one of the Pharisees. We have seen from verse 31 that not all the Pharisees were implacably opposed to Him. This **Pharisee** was **one of the rulers**. The term **ruler** here possibly means that the man was one of the ruling Sanhedrin, which met in Jerusalem (compare such a use of the term in 18:18; 23:13). After the synagogue service **on the Sabbath**, this man invited Jesus to come to his house **to eat bread**, sharing the midday meal after the service. Many prominent people were at this meal, including **lawyers** (that is, experts in the Jewish Law) and other **Pharisees**. These last were apparently more suspicious of Jesus than their host, and **they were observing Him** throughout the meal.

The word rendered *observing* is the Greek *paratereo*, used in 20:20 of the scribes who were watching Christ like a hawk, scrutinizing His every move to find some weakness. At this meal, the attention of the lawyers was drawn to one man there, a man who **was**

suffering from dropsy, a disease that makes the cavities of the body swell up with fluid. (He seems to have come for the express purpose of being healed, for after being healed, he was dismissed.) The plight of such a man was obvious to all, and the man's being right **in front of** Christ constituted a kind of silent invitation to Jesus to heal him. These lawyers and Pharisees were watching Christ to see if He would. It was still the Sabbath, and everyone there knew the Pharisees thought such a healing would be a breach of the Sabbath day and therefore a sin. Would Jesus defy the convictions of His host by healing the man or not?

Since there were so many lawyers present, **Jesus answered** their unspoken question and put to them a legal question about the Law. Was it **permitted to heal on the Sabbath or not?** They all thought it was not, but **were quiet**, silently sullen in their convictions and afraid to oppose Him. Christ therefore **took hold** of the sufferer (probably laying His hands upon him), **and cured him and dismissed *him***, allowing him to go home.

Then came the legal lesson. Obviously such a healing was permitted by God, and was not in true violation of His Law. If they would think for a minute about their own practices, they would see this. **Which one** of them **will have a son**—or even a mere **ox**—**fall into a well and will not immediately draw him up** out of it, even if it were **on a Sabbath day?** And such a task took a lot of effort, with much time and strain. Yet one would do it anyway, even if it were just to help an animal. If one were permitted to alleviate such suffering on the Sabbath, even at the cost of such strenuous exertion, how much more was Christ permitted to alleviate worse suffering with a mere word, by simply taking hold of a man! Not surprisingly, the experts **were not able to answer back to these *things*** and remained silent.

§VI.14.ii. Places of Honor at the Table

ॐ ॐ ॐ ॐ ॐ

7 And He was speaking a parable to those who were called when He fixed *His attention* on how

they had been choosing the first-places, saying to them,

8 "When you are called by someone to a wedding *feast*, do not recline in the first-place, lest someone more honored *than* you may have been called by him,

9 "and he who called you and him will come and say to you, 'Give place to this *man*!' and you will begin with shame to take the last place.

10 "But when you are called, go and recline in the last place, that when the one who has called you comes, he will say to you, 'Friend, go up higher!'; then it will be glory to you before *the presence of* all who recline at the table with you.

11 "For everyone who exalts himself will be humbled, and he who humbles himself will be exalted."

The Lord, as a celebrated teacher, was expected to give some sort of teaching and speak edifying words throughout the course of the meal. He did not disappoint them. He had **fixed** *His attention on how* the other guests **had been choosing the first-places** at the table. In those days, one did not just sit anywhere at the table, but had one's place assigned according to one's social importance. The selection of the best seats therefore constituted a claim to superior importance—and in the case of the Pharisees, probably a claim to superior holiness.

Jesus therefore told **a parable**, a story with a hidden meaning and application. The parable came in the form of social advice. **When you were called by someone to** some big and public occasion, such as **a wedding** *feast*, the Lord said, you should **not recline in the first-place** of the table. Important guests often arrived late for such feasts, and if **someone more honored** *than* you had **been called** and invited, that person would dislodge you. Your host would **come** over to where you were and publicly **say to you, "Give place to this** *man*!" You would be openly disgraced, and would **begin with**

shame to take the last place. What should you do then? **When you are called, go** and humbly **recline in the last place**. That way, when the host **comes** to you, **he will say to you, "Friend, go up higher!"** He will honor you openly as his friend, his familiar equal, and **it will be glory to you** before all the others present.

This was a parable, not social advice. Christ was not telling people how to manipulate their way into getting public honor. Rather, He was revealing the results of pride and of humility. When the dinner guest **exalted** himself, choosing the best seat, he **was humbled**, but when he **humbled himself**, choosing the last place, he was **exalted**. Thus it will be **for everyone**. In the Kingdom of heaven, God will exalt the humble, bestowing salvation, but He will humble the proud, excluding them from His favor.

§VI.14.iii. Inviting the Poor

12 And He was also saying to the one who had called Him, "When you make a breakfast or a supper, do not call your friends or your brothers or your relatives or rich neighbors, lest they also call you in return, and repayment come to you.

13 "But when you make a reception, call the poor, the crippled, the lame, the blind,

14 "and you will be blessed, since they do not have *anything* to repay you; for it will be repaid to you at the resurrection of the righteous."

Christ did not end His teaching there. **He was also saying** to His host a further lesson, showing him how to use his wealth to eternal advantage. The meal they were enjoying had doubtless cost a lot (a ruler from the Sanhedrin would have been a man of some substance), and Christ was always quick to point out the dangers of wealth.

So it is that He bids His host remember the poor. At this feast, doubtless only important people had been officially invited. That was not wrong, but there was a better way. When the ruler **made a breakfast or a supper** (that is, either the first meal of the day, such as this one, or the main evening meal), he should not just invite the usual crowd, his **friends**, **brothers**, **relatives**, or his **rich neighbors**. He should take care to also **call the poor, the crippled, the lame,** and **the blind**. For if he called his social equals and betters, they would also call him to their banquets **in return, and** so **repayment** would **come** to him on earth.

If the host wanted to be really **blessed** in the Kingdom of God, let him invite the social riffraff and feed the poor, for these **do not have *anything* to repay** him. They could not invite him to luxurious banquets to return the favor. And because justice comes ultimately to all, and since these could not repay him for his kindness, God would repay him. The host who gave to the poor would be **repaid** by God **at the resurrection of the righteous**. As the Law said, "He who is kind to the poor lends to Yahweh, and He will repay him for his deed" (Prov. 19:17).

§VI.14.iv. Parable of the Refused Banquet

ॐ ॐ ॐ ॐ ॐ

15 And when one of those who were reclining with Him heard this, he said to Him, "Blessed *is he* who will eat bread in the Kingdom of God!"

16 But He said to him, "A certain man was making a great supper, and he called many;

17 "and at the hour of the supper, he sent his slave to say to those who had been called, 'Come, for all is now prepared!'

18 "But they all began with one *accord* to ask to be excused. The first said to him, 'I have bought a field, and I am compelled to go out to see it; I ask you, have me excused.'

19 "And another one said, 'I have bought five yoke of oxen, and I am going to try them out; I ask you, have me excused.'

> 20 "And another one said, 'I have married a wife, and for that *reason* I am not able to come.'
>
> 21 "And the slave arrived and declared these *things* to his lord. Then the house-master became angry and said to his slave, 'Go out quickly into the streets and lanes of the city and bring in here the poor and crippled and blind and lame.'
>
> 22 "And the slave said, 'Lord, what you commanded has been done, and still there are places.'
>
> 23 "And the lord said to the slave, 'Go out to the ways and the hedges and compel *them* to come in, that my house may be filled.
>
> 24 "'For I tell you, none of those men who were called will taste of my supper.'"

Upon hearing of eternal rewards for the faithful (v. 14), **one of those who were reclining** at the table **with Him**, perhaps having drunk too well, lifted up his voice in a self-congratulatory cry of joy, pronouncing a blessing upon those faithful Jews who would **eat bread** like this **in the Kingdom of God**. He was happy to be included among those who were sharing the feast with Jesus and His host and was certain he was to be one of the **blessed** and the saved in the age to come.

This is just the sort of spiritual complacency that is dangerous. St. Paul was later to write, "Let the one who thinks he stands watch out lest he fall" (1 Cor. 10:12), but this man, confident in his Jewish respectability, was sure he would be blessed at the end and saw no need for inner vigilance. After all, he was a Jew (probably a Pharisee too)—how could God fail to be impressed?

So it was that our Lord told a parable to all those present, warning of such spiritual complacency. It was true that Israel was the Chosen People and had been called by God to inherit the Kingdom. But being called was not enough. Each one also had to respond personally to that call with humble faithfulness. If they responded with haughty pride (rejecting God's present call which Jesus was proclaiming), they would not inherit the promised salvation.

It was like **a certain man** who **was making a great supper**. He **called** and invited **many** to his feast, telling them of the future date. Then, in conformity to the custom of those days, when the actual **hour of the supper** had come, **he sent his slave** to those who had been invited, telling them the time of the long-heralded feast had arrived. The slave bade them all **come**, for **all** was **now prepared**.

Though they had been invited, incredibly **they all began with one *accord* to ask to be excused**. And the excuses they offered were so flimsy as to constitute a studied insult to the one who had invited them. **The first** man to whom the slave messenger came said, **"I have bought a field, and I am compelled to go out to see it; I ask you, have me excused."** This made no sense. Who would look at a field only *after* he had bought it, paying money for it sight unseen?

The second man to whom the slave came had a similarly invalid excuse, and he offered it in an even more abrupt way, not even claiming (as the first man did) that he was **compelled** by circumstances. This second man suggested that he had **bought five yoke of oxen** (a big purchase; one or two yoke of oxen were enough for the common man's needs) and was **going to try them out**. He also asked to be **excused**. Once again, this made no sense. Who would buy five yoke of oxen before first seeing if they were healthy and suitable?

The third man to whom the messenger came was the worst of all. He did not even ask to be excused (as the first two men did). Rather, he simply said, **"I have married a wife, and for that *reason* I am not able to come."** This was absurd. Newly contracted marriage was a reason to be excused from the dangerous labors of an impending military battle (Deut. 20:7), but not from the joys of a feast! All three of these excuses were in reality outrageous slights against the master of the feast—and this in an age when such insults were deadly serious.

When **the slave arrived** back home **and declared these *things* to his lord**, the lord was suitably **angry**. He was determined that the ingrates who had first been invited and who had treated his generosity with such contempt be thoroughly disowned and excluded from his bounty. Now they could *not* come! Instead, the slave was bidden to **go out quickly into the streets and lanes of the city**

and to **bring in** to the festal hall **the poor and crippled and blind and lame**. Those poor who had never expected to be treated to such munificence were now to be honored with the invitation.

The slave reported that what his **lord commanded** had in fact **been done**, and yet **still there** were unfilled **places** at the feast. The lord of the feast was insistent that, even so, those originally invited were to remain excluded. If there were places left, then the slaves were ordered to **go out to the ways and the hedges** of the city, searching around the hedges and walls of estates where the indigent poor lurked. Let the slaves **compel** such as they found **to come in** to the feast, assuring the incredulous people they found there that the offer of a free feast from a stranger was true. Let the slaves not take no for a answer, but do everything to persuade them to freely come. Let them do anything to bring these strangers in, **that** the lord's **house may be filled**.

The Lord Jesus turned to those present at the feast, assuring them of the deadly truth (the **I tell you** is in the plural, indicating that Jesus was speaking to His audience, not in the singular, as if the lord were still addressing his slave). The deadly truth was this: **none of those men who were called will taste of** the **supper**.

This was chilling indeed. The **man** who **made** the **great supper** was obviously an image of God, who was preparing the great feast for all creation in the age to come. The **many** who were first **called** were the pious people of Israel, those who were the designated heirs of the Kingdom of God. They had long been promised this final triumphal feast through their prophets, and now, through Jesus and His apostles, they were given word that **the hour** for the Kingdom had at last arrived. Israel should hearken to Jesus and His messengers and **come** with faith.

Incredibly, the pious ones in Israel (such as the Pharisees) rejected the long-expected invitation when it finally came. Like boorish people who insulted the generosity of their benefactor by refusing to come to his feast, the self-satisfied ones in Israel all alike rejected Jesus' word. Jesus was announcing the imminent arrival of the Kingdom, yet these refused to come to the feast.

What would God do? Like the man in the parable whose

generosity had been insulted and spurned, God would respond by offering the Kingdom to others. If the Pharisees would not come with faith, then others would! Indeed, the riffraff of the land (imaged by the wretched **poor**, the **crippled**, **blind** and **lame**), the tax-collectors and prostitutes, would enter into the very Kingdom the Pharisees had refused (Matt. 21:32). More than this, God would call even those far off (imaged by those lurking about **the ways** and **the hedges**), the distant Gentiles, to come. His **House** would **be filled**—but not by any of those originally invited.

The chilling truth was that by their refusal of Jesus' message, the self-satisfied Pharisees had forfeited their ancient covenanted right to the Kingdom of God—God was determined that **none of those men** would ever **taste of** His saving **supper**. Thus being called or invited to the supper was not enough, nor was being a respectable Jew sufficient to secure a place in the age to come. The response of faith was also required. It was possible to be a Jewish heir to the promised Kingdom and yet still fail to secure a place there.

§VI.15. The Cost of Discipleship

> ৡৢ ৡৢ ৡৢ ৡৢ ৡৢ
>
> 25 Now great crowds were going with Him; and He turned and said to them,
> 26 "If anyone comes to Me, and does not hate his own father and mother and wife and children and brothers and sisters, and in addition, even his own life, he is not able to be My disciple.
> 27 "Whoever does not bear his own cross and come after Me is not able to be My disciple.

Luke then relates Christ's words to the **great crowds** about the cost of discipleship, placing them within the broader context of His journeying toward Jerusalem. Christ had Jerusalem as His focus and goal, and it was in Jerusalem that He would die. Were the crowds that thronged Him willing to pay the same price as the cost of their obedience to God?

So it was that during one of these journeys, **He turned**, stopping His journey long enough to teach and challenge them. **If anyone** would **come** to Him and enlist as His disciple, that person must **hate his own father and mother and wife and children and brothers and sisters**. By *hate* Christ means "reject" (compare such a usage in Mal. 1:3). He is not counseling the emotion of hatred. Rather He means that one must reject even the deepest and most sacred bonds of family and kinship if these threaten the disciple's prior loyalty to Him. The disciple must love Christ and choose obedience to Him over every other impulse—even the impulse of self-preservation. For the disciple must hate **even his own life** and choose martyrdom over apostasy.

This ruthless loyalty to Christ is imaged by one **bearing his own cross**. Christ's hearers had seen men bear their own crosses. When the Romans condemned to death a criminal whom they wanted to make an example of, they would scourge the criminal, laying his back open to the bone with spiked whips. The poor wretch would then be made to carry the horizontal crossbeam on his shoulders to the place of execution. He would there be nailed to the crossbeam, which was then hoisted up and affixed to a vertical beam. After they had nailed his feet, the criminal would be left to die. A man who was bearing his cross was a man on his way to die.

It is this grisly image which Christ uses as the image of discipleship. If anyone is not willing to die to the world's claims on his loyalty, and even to suffer actual martyrdom for Christ, that man is **not able to be** His **disciple**. Discipleship is by definition total.

⁂ ⁂ ⁂ ⁂ ⁂

28 "For who among you when he wants to build a tower, does not first sit and count the cost, *to see* if he has *enough* for completion?

29 "Otherwise, when he has laid his foundation and is not able to finish *it* up, all who observe *it* will begin to mock him,

30 "saying, 'This man began to build and was not able to finish up!'

> 31 "Or what king, when he goes to encounter
> another king in war, will not first sit and decide
> whether he is able with ten thousand to meet the
> one coming against him with twenty thousand?
> 32 "Or else, while he is still far off, he sends an
> embassy and asks *terms* of peace.
> 33 "Thus, therefore, no one of you who does not
> take leave of all his own possessions is able to
> be My disciple.

The effect of such teaching on the crowds could be imagined. They thought Jesus was bringing in a Kingdom in which all good Jews would triumph as rulers, and were horrified that such a cost might be demanded of them. The Lord does nothing to lessen their discomfort or to set the standard any lower. Rather, He tells two parables, urging them to consider in advance whether they are equal to such a challenge.

They must count the cost before enlisting as His disciple. They knew all about calculating things in advance and the folly of hasty action. For **who among** them, if he **wanted to build a tower**, did **not first sit** down **and count the cost,** *to see* if he had *enough* **for completion?** (Watchtowers were often built in vineyards to guard against thieves in harvest time.) The prudent farmer did not build without first calculating if he had sufficient funds to do the whole job. For if he did, he might simply **lay** his **foundation** and run out of money, and find that he was **not able finish** *it* **up**. Then all who passed by his lands would **observe** the foundation standing empty and **begin to mock him** for his stupidity. He would be known far and wide as the **man** who **began to build and was not able to finish up**. Calculation must precede action.

This was even more true in war. Suppose there was a **king** who went to **encounter another king in war**. When that first king learned that his opponent was **coming against him with** an army of **twenty thousand**, he would surely **first sit** down and **decide whether** or not **he was able** with his smaller army of **ten thousand** to effectively **meet** him. If his smaller army had a strategic advantage that would ensure victory, he would indeed go out to battle. But if not, while that second king **was still far off**, the first king would **send an embassy** to **ask *terms* of peace**. Advance calculation was a matter of life and death!

It was to be the same with anyone wanting to be His disciple. That one must first sit down and count the cost. Was such a one willing to **take leave of all his own possessions**? Was he willing to sacrifice all his worldly comfort, wealth, and reputation? Was he willing to sit lightly on all the attractions the world could offer and renounce all other loyalties but loyalty to Him? If not, that one was not **able to be** His **disciple**.

ॐ ॐ ॐ ॐ ॐ

34 "Therefore, salt is good; but if even the salt has become foolish, with what will it be seasoned?
35 "It is useful neither for soil nor for manure; they cast it outside. He who has ears to hear, let him hear!"

Discipleship to Jesus was good, but if one turned back, that one did not get partial marks for trying. It was the same as salt. **Salt was good**, but if that **salt became** insipid, with what could one **season** it? The formerly good salt was now useless. It was **useful neither for soil nor for manure**; men simply **cast it outside** as garbage.

The salt referred to here was that which was obtained from the Dead Sea. Evaporation produced a mixture of salt and carnallite, and some would take the carnallite for use as salt. This salt would therefore be a salt which had become insipid and had lost its saltiness. True salt was very valuable. Among other things, it was used **for soil**, as a fertilizer, and was also added to **manure**, to slow the process of fermentation until the dung was ready to be used. But insipid salt was useless even for these humble uses. Men **cast it outside**, knowing it was now good for nothing—an image of the lost being thrown outside the Kingdom into the outer darkness (Matt. 8:12). Insipid salt is therefore an image for disciples who have **become foolish** and fallen away from their commitment to Jesus.

This is the explanation of Jesus' saying that **salt has become foolish**. The verb in Greek is *moraino*, and all its other uses in the New
Testament refer to foolishness, not to insipidity of taste (see Rom.
1:22; 1 Cor. 1:20). But how can salt become foolish? It would seem
that Luke reproduces a play on words from the original Aramaic. In
Hebrew (and in Aramaic also no doubt), the root *tpl* has a double
meaning. The word *tapel* means "insipid things" (compare Job 6:6),
while the word *tiplah* means "folly" (compare Job 1:22). Just as salt
that loses its savor is useless and to be rejected, so the disciple who
becomes foolish in his apostasy is also useless. Luke chooses the
second meaning of the Semitic word to make plain the application
of the parable to potential disciples.

§VI.16. Eating with Sinners

§VI.16.i. Parable of the Lost Sheep

> ॐ॰ ॐ॰ ॐ॰ ॐ॰ ॐ॰
>
> **15** 1 Now all the tax-collectors and the sinners were
> drawing near to Him to hear Him.
> 2 And both the Pharisees and the scribes were
> grumbling on, saying, "This *man* welcomes
> sinners and co-eats with them."

St. Luke next relates a series of parables Christ told about the
nature of God's love. Like many of His parables, it was occasioned
by some misunderstanding. In this case it was occasioned by Christ's
loving acceptance of sinners, which the Pharisees mistook for a failure
to condemn sin. When Christ was teaching, **all the tax-collectors**
and other notoriously immoral **sinners were drawing near to hear
Him**. It would seem that after His teaching (perhaps given in a
synagogue), when the time came for Him and His disciples to have
their meal together, He would **welcome** those **sinners and co-eat
with them**. That is, Christ did not just "eat" with them (Gr. *esthio*)

but **co-ate** with them (*sunesthio*), accepting them as His co-equals and His friends. It was because of this that **the Pharisees and the scribes were** openly **grumbling on** (*diagogguzo*, a more intense form of *gogguzo*, "to grumble"). If He were truly a holy man who did the will of God (as He claimed), He would have nothing to do with those sinners. He would certainly not rejoice with them over a meal.

It was to answer this attitude that Christ told the following parables.

ॐ ॐ ॐ ॐ ॐ

3 And He told them this parable, saying,

4 "What man among you, having a hundred sheep and having lost one of them, does not leave behind the ninety-nine in the wilderness and go after the one which is lost, until he finds it?

5 "And having found *it*, he puts *it* on his shoulders, rejoicing.

6 "And when he comes to his house, he calls together his friends and his neighbors, saying to them, 'Co-rejoice with me, for I have found my sheep which was lost!'

7 "I tell you that in this way there will be *more* joy in heaven over one sinner who repents than over ninety-nine righteous *persons* who have no need of repentance.

In His first parable, Christ spoke of a shepherd who, **having a hundred sheep** in his flock, **lost one of them. What man among you**, Christ asked, if he were that shepherd, wouldn't **leave behind the ninety-nine**, even if it meant leaving them **in the** dangerous **wilderness, and go after the one** that was **lost**, searching all over **until he found it? And having found *it***, he would **put *it* on his shoulders** to carry it home, **rejoicing** all the way. Then, when he arrived home, he would **call together his friends and his neighbors** for a great party, **saying, "Co-rejoice with me, for I have found my sheep which was lost!"**

In that same way, Christ said, **there will be *more* joy in heaven over one sinner who repents than over ninety-nine righteous *persons* who have no need of repentance.** If heaven rejoices like the happy shepherd, and holds high festival over one sinner return-ing to the way of righteousness, surely Jesus should also feast and celebrate with sinners who were coming to hear Him and to begin their return to God.

§VI.16.ii. Parable of the Lost Coin

> ॐ ॐ ॐ ॐ ॐ
>
> 8   "Or what woman, having ten drachmas, if she loses one drachma, does not kindle a lamp and sweep the house and seek carefully until she finds *it*?
>
> 9   "And having found *it*, she calls together her friends and neighbors, saying, 'Co-rejoice with me, for I have found the drachma which I had lost!'
>
> 10 "In this way I tell you, there is joy before the presence of the angels of God over one sinner who repents."

Christ reinforced His point with another parable. It was not only working men (such as shepherds) who could understand the need for such joyful partying, but women too. For **what woman, having ten drachmas, if she lost one** of them, would not do the same? Indeed, she would **kindle a lamp** to search through all the dark places of her home (such peasant houses had no windows to let in light), **sweep the house** thoroughly, and **seek carefully**, turning the place upside down **until she found *it***. Then, **having found *it***, she too would **call together her friends and neighbors** for a party, saying, **"Co-rejoice with me, for I have found the drachma which I had lost!"**

The *drachma* was a silver Greek coin, in value about the same as a *denarius*, a day's wage for the common laborer. (The *drachma* does not seem to have been in circulation in Palestine at that time; it seems that Luke has translated the original name of the lost coin into a term more familiar to his Gentile readers.) The woman valued the coin not just for its monetary worth, but probably also because it formed part of her dowry. The return of the lost coin to the other nine was a cause for all to come together to celebrate. And **in this** same **way**, Christ assured His hearers, there is **joy** in heaven **before the presence of the angels of God over one sinner who repents**. God rejoices with His angels in heaven when the search for the sinful person results in his return to righteousness. Obviously Jesus and His disciples should rejoice and feast with that sinner on earth!

§VI.16.iii. Parable of the Lost Son

ॐ ॐ ॐ ॐ ॐ

11 And He said, "A certain man had two sons;

12 "and the younger of them said to his father, 'Father, give me the part of the wealth that falls to me.' And he apportioned his life's *possessions* between them.

13 "And after not many days, the younger son gathered everything together and left home for a far region, and there he scattered out his wealth in dissolute living.

14 "Now when he had spent everything, a mighty famine happened throughout that region, and he began to be in need.

15 "And he went and clung to one of the citizens of that region, and he sent him into his fields to feed pigs.

16 "And he was desiring to fill his belly with the pods which the pigs were eating, and no one was giving *anything* to him.

287

The Lord had one more parable to tell, one that would go like an arrow into the heart of the Pharisees and challenge them to change their attitude and accept the returning sinners. This parable involved **a certain man** who **had two sons. The younger of them** (who was probably about seventeen years old, for eighteen to twenty was the normal age for men to marry) **said to his father, "Father, give me the part of the wealth that falls to me."** In response, the father **apportioned his life's *possessions* between them.**

The younger boy was anxious to escape from the (as he thought) boring security of his father's house, and so **after not many days,** he **gathered everything** he had **together** into cash **and left home for a far region,** traveling far from the watchful eye of his father. There he did things he never could have done at home, indulging in **dissolute living,** feasting, getting drunk, and using prostitutes. Such living was costly, and he **scattered out his wealth** in short order. The Greek verb translated *scatter out* is *diaskorpizo*, an intensive form of *skorpizo*, "to scatter"; the boy threw his money around everywhere, as a farmer scattered his seed (compare such a use in Matt. 25:24). The folly of such living was soon apparent, for **when he had spent everything, a mighty famine happened throughout that region,** and the boy **began to be in need.** Not only was there now no money for feasting and for prostitutes, there was no money for basic food!

There was nothing for it. The Jewish boy **went and clung to one of the** Gentile **citizens of that region,** imploring his mercy and asking for a job. There were not many jobs available to him, and the Gentile farmer **sent** the boy **into his fields to feed pigs.** For a Jew, there was not much lower to go.

Nonetheless, the boy did have still lower to go. Even with such a job, he could not feed himself properly, and he was so hungry that he **was desiring to fill his belly** and stuff himself **with the pods which the pigs were eating.** Despite his misery and his begging others for food, **no one was giving *anything* to him.** He could not gather alms, and no one would feed him. The boy had left the watchful care of his father only to find himself utterly wretched and in danger of starvation.

ॐ ॐ ॐ ॐ ॐ

17 "But when he came to himself, he said, 'How many of my father's paid *servants* have bread left over, but I *myself* am perishing here with famine!

18 "'I will arise and go to my father and will say to him, "Father, I have sinned against heaven and before you;

19 "'"'I am no longer worthy to be called your son; make me as one of your paid *servants*."'

At last a turning point came. The boy **came to himself**, waking up to his situation like a man awaking from sleep. Just as the sinners feasting with Christ that day had repented and were beginning to turn their lives around, so the boy in the parable also decided to change his life. Here he was, working for this heartless Gentile and **perishing with famine** when he could be working for his father at home. For **how many** of his **father's paid** *servants* ate enough to live and even **had bread left over**! Here was the only sensible thing to do: He would **arise and go to** his **father**, throwing himself on his mercy. He would say, **"Father, I have sinned against heaven** itself, justly provoking God's punishment, **and** also **before you. I am no longer worthy to be called your son**. I do not ask for you to take me back. But please **make me as one of your paid** *servants*; give me a job so that I may eat and live." His father might reject him and refuse to give him a job. He might still be angry from the reports of the boy's dissolute living that he had heard and might drive him away. But it was the boy's only chance.

ॐ ॐ ॐ ॐ ॐ

20 "And he arose and came to his own father. But while he was still a far distance off, his father saw him, and was *filled with* heartfelt love, and ran and fell on his neck, and *fervently* kissed him.

> 21 "And the son said to him, 'Father, I have sinned against heaven and before you; I am no longer worthy to be called your son.'
>
> 22 "But the father said to his slaves, 'Quickly bring out the first robe and clothe him, and give a ring for his hand and sandals for his feet;
>
> 23 "'And bring the fattened calf, slaughter *it*, and let us eat and be glad!
>
> 24 "'For this my son was dead, and he lives again; he was lost, and has been found.' And they began to be glad.

Armed with this plan, the boy **arose and came to his own father**, walking the many miles he had once cheerfully put between himself and the security of home. **While he was still a far distance off,** however, **his father saw him,** perhaps recognizing his walk. (It is possible that the father had been staring down that road often, hoping against hope for his son's return.) Instantly he **was *filled with* heartfelt love** (Gr. *splagxnizomai*), his innards (Gr. *splagxna*) stirred at the sight of his beloved boy. He **ran** to the boy as he slowly trudged home (an astonishing show of love—adult men did not run in that culture) **and fell on his neck**, weak and overwhelmed with joy, and ***fervently* kissed him** over and over again (the Greek verb here translated *fervently kissed* is *kataphileo*, more intensive than *phileo*, "to kiss").

The son began to recite his prearranged speech, but could only get as far as **"I am no longer worthy to be called your son."** In his joy, the father interrupted him, so that the boy did not get a chance to say the line, "Make me as one of your paid servants" (compare v. 19). The father directed one of his household servants (who had followed the father when he saw him run from the house) to **quickly** make preparations to receive the lad back as he was before he left. There was no time to lose, and nothing to discuss, no apologies to make, no explanations to give. The servant was to **bring out the first robe** (the best one in the house) **and clothe** the boy, so that he could again have the dignity he once had, and cast aside the filthy rags of his former misery. The slave was to **give a ring for his hand** (no mere piece of jewelry, but the sign of authority within the home) and **sandals for his feet**. This last was the sign of freedom (for slaves went unshod), and that he was home (for the master of the house wore shoes at home, while guests removed their footwear at the door). From head to toe, the boy was to be restored to his happy former state. More than that, the servant was to **bring the fattened calf**, the one reserved for special occasions of festivity, and **slaughter *it*** for the homecoming feast. It was time for all to **eat and be glad**, **for this my son** (said the father, beaming upon him) **was dead, and he lives again. He was lost** to them and now **has been found**. Quite fittingly, **they began to be glad** and to celebrate with feasting.

ॐ ॐ ॐ ॐ ॐ

25 "Now his older son was in the field, and when he came and drew near the house, he heard music and dancing.

26 "And he called to *himself* one of the servants and was inquiring what these things might be.

27 "And he said to him, 'Your brother is here, and your father has slaughtered the fattened calf, because he has received him back in healthy *condition.*'

28 "But he was angry, and did not want to go in; and his father came out and was urging him.

29 "But he answered and said to his father, 'Behold, for so many years I have been serving *as slave* to you, and I have never ignored your commandment, and you have never given me a goat, that I might be glad with my friends;

30 "'But when this your son came, who has eaten up your life's *possessions* with prostitutes, you slaughtered for him the fattened calf!'

Into this happy ending, the Lord brought the **older** brother, a discordant note in that joyful chorus. He was working dutifully **in the field** and at the day's end, **when he came and drew near the house, he heard music and dancing** with its clapping. At first he was happy to hear such festivity, though puzzled as to what had caused it. **He called to *himself* one of the servants and** began **inquiring** what the unplanned party was for. The servant replied, **"Your brother is here, and your father has slaughtered the fattened calf, because he has received him back in healthy *condition*,"** safe and sound.

The elder brother could hardly believe his ears. That his kid brother, after ruining his parents' good name by his far-famed immoral escapades and breaking their hearts, had the audacity to return home! And, on top of that, his father had not only taken him back, but had even thrown this gala party for him! It was too much to bear. He **was angry, and did not want to go in** the house to join the festivity. One can almost see him outside the house, pacing and fuming.

As the older boy refused to come in, **his father came out** to him and began **urging him** to join them. In this we see again the astonishing love of the father, for that culture demanded that the son obediently come in to the father, not that the father should humbly go out to the son. Even so, the older son would have none of it. **"Behold,"** he responded hotly (we can nearly hear the raw resentment in the lad's voice), **"for so many years I have been serving *as slave* to you** (Gr. *douleuo*, cognate with *doulos*, slave; the boy had been a hardworking and dutiful son). **I have never ignored your commandment"** but faithfully did everything his father asked. For all that, he pressed on, **"you have never given me** even **a goat** (making for a smaller feast than the fattened calf) **that I might be glad** and celebrate **with my friends. But when this your son came** (note that he refuses to call him "this my brother"), the very one who **has eaten up your life's *possessions* with prostitutes, you slaughtered for him the fattened calf!"** The elder brother felt totally unappreciated. The injustice of the whole thing rankled unbearably, and he stood there in front of his poor father, refusing his gentle entreaties.

ॐ ॐ ॐ ॐ ॐ

31 "And he said to him, 'Child, you *yourself* are always with me, and all that is mine is yours.
32 "'But it was necessary to be glad and to rejoice, for this your brother was dead and has *come to* life; and he was lost, and has been found.'"

This portrayal of the elder brother seemed too close to home. Everyone listening to the parable up to that point was rejoicing at the happy ending and the safe return of the lost son. Everyone could see how churlish and small the elder brother was being, despite his loud (and rudely unfilial) protestations of injustice. Now was indeed the time for rejoicing and feasting. All the Lord's listeners knew that the elder brother should just embrace his younger sibling and join the party.

The father gave voice to what everyone was feeling. Despite the disrespectful way the older boy addressed him (for he did not call him "Father"; compare v. 21), the father tenderly called him **child** (Gr. *teknon*), and assured him that as for the elder son (the **you** is emphatic in the Greek), he was **always with** the father and never far from his thoughts. All that belonged to the father was his too, and if he really wanted to celebrate with his friends, he could do that. But couldn't the boy see? **It was necessary** for them **to be glad and to rejoice**. They had no option but to celebrate like that. **For this your brother** (the father thus gently insists that the older boy not disown his younger sibling) **was dead** as far as they knew, **and has come to** life. **He was lost** to them, but now **has been found**. What else could they do but hold a great feast?

The parallel of the elder brother refusing to join the party for the returning lost son with the Pharisees refusing to join the joyful meal with the tax-collectors was painfully obvious. In the obvious churlishness of the elder brother, everyone could see reflected the attitude of the Pharisees. The Pharisees were not being zealous for righteousness, as they claimed. They were just being small-minded and sullen.

The Lord leaves the father's question unanswered, for it was up to the Pharisees and the scribes there to answer it. The lost son had come home, the tax-collectors and other sinners were returning. Would the Pharisees come eat with them and join the party? Or would they remain outside with the older brother, ignoring the entreating love of the Father?

§VI.17. Warnings on Wealth

§VI.17.i. Parable of the Unrighteous Steward

ॐ ॐ ॐ ॐ ॐ

16 1   Now He was also saying to the disciples, "There was a certain rich man who had a steward, and accusations were *brought* to this one of scattering out his possessions.

2   "And he called him and said to him, 'What *is* this I hear about you? Render an account of your stewardship, for you are no longer able to be steward!'

3   "And the steward said within himself, 'What will I do, since my lord is taking the stewardship away from me? I am not strong *enough* to dig; I am ashamed to beg.

4   "'I know what I will do, so that when I am removed from the stewardship, they will welcome me into their houses.'

5   "And he called to *himself* each one of his own lord's debtors, and was saying to the first, 'How much do you owe my lord?'

6   "And he said, 'A hundred baths of oil.' And he said to him, 'Take your bills, and sit quickly and write fifty.'

7   "Then to another he said, 'And you! How much do you owe?' And he said, 'A hundred kors of

> wheat.' And he says to him, 'Take your bills
> and write eighty.'
> 8 "And the lord praised the unrighteous steward
> because he had done prudently; for the sons of
> this age are more prudent as regards their own
> generation than the sons of light.
> 9 "And I *Myself* say to you, make friends for
> yourselves from the mammon of unrighteous-
> ness, that when it fails, they may welcome you
> into the eternal tents.

The Lord had other teaching for His **disciples** as well (it would seem as if this teaching was given at the same time as that of 15:1f). In order to teach them that money should be used to do good and not hoarded, He told them a parable.

In that parable, **there was a certain rich man**, a landowner, **who had a steward, and accusations were *brought* to this one of scattering out** and squandering his master's **possessions**. That is, the steward (who had complete control of his master's financial affairs, as all stewards did) was incompetent, and his master was suffering loss because of him. The master was incensed and loudly **called him** (the verb *called* is the Gr. *phone*, which often has connotations of high volume) **and said to him, "What *is* this I hear about you? Render an account of your stewardship, for you are no longer able to be steward!"** The steward was being fired, and the master demanded that he get the books in order so that he could pass on his job to someone else.

This left the steward with a dilemma regarding his future—he was **not strong *enough* to dig** and work as a common laborer, and was **ashamed to beg**. At last he came upon a solution (the verb **know** is in the aorist tense, indicating a sudden idea). He would use his final acts as steward to give unheard-of bargains and "sweetheart deals" to his master's debtors. As steward, he had full control of the household finances, so that bargains of these kind were legally within his power. This would ensure that those debtors would love him and would **welcome** him **into their houses**. He would use the money over which he had control to buy their friendship, so that he could henceforth stay with them!

He quickly put this plan into effect. To one debtor, he asked, **"How much do you owe my lord?"** and on learning that the man owed **a hundred baths of oil** (a bath was about 8½ gallons), he said, **"Take your bills** of debt, **sit quickly** (before anyone else sees you are getting such a bargain!) **and write fifty."** To the next man in line, he said, **"And you! How much do you owe?"** On learning that he owed **a hundred kors of wheat** (a kor was equal to about 11 bushels), he said, **"Take your bills and write eighty."** These were "sweetheart deals" indeed, for the amounts of rent in kind owed represented tremendous sums of money.

So it was that **the unrighteous steward** used money to provide himself with a secure future. When **the lord** of the steward learned of this, he **praised** him **because he had done prudently**. That is, he could not help but admire his worldly shrewdness. (Christ adds that very often **the sons of this age**, the worldlings, **are more prudent** and smarter in their use of money **than the sons of light**, the pious.) This grudging admiration on the part of the master is not to be taken as implying his unqualified approval of the way his steward acted. The steward was cited for his worldly prudence, not for his unrighteousness.

Christ then drew the final lesson of the parable: His disciples were to **make friends** for themselves using **the mammon of unrighteousness**, just as the steward did. For the steward, mammon (or money) was simply a means to an end. It was not to be hoarded away, but used—in this case, used to secure friendship so that when he left his master's house, his newly made friends would welcome him into theirs. In the same way, Christ's disciples should use money, giving it away in alms and befriending the poor. Then, after the money **fails** (that is, after they die and money can avail them no longer), they will have a welcome in heaven, as those poor whom they befriended and who died before are there to **welcome** them **into the eternal tents**, their everlasting dwellings.

ॐ ॐ ॐ ॐ ॐ

10 "He who is trustworthy in a very little *thing* is trustworthy also in much; and he who is unrighteous in a very little *thing* is unrighteous also in much.

11 "If therefore you have not been trustworthy in *the use* of unrighteous mammon, who will entrust true *riches* to you?

12 "And if you have not been trustworthy in *the use of* what is another's, who will give you what is your own?

13 "No house-*slave* can serve *as slave* to two lords; for either he will hate the one and love the other, or else he will give attention to one and despise the other. You are not able to serve *as slave* to God and mammon."

Christ continues to talk about the use of money in this age. Worldly wealth is **a very little *thing***, compared to the riches and glory of life in the age to come. God's bounty to us in that coming age is dependent on our use of money now. Any master knows that! For a servant **who is trustworthy in a very little *thing*** will be **trustworthy also in much**, in greater things; and the servant **who is unrighteous in a very little *thing*** will be **unrighteous also in much**. If a servant is slack or incompetent in doing small tasks, he will be the same in doing bigger ones as well.

In the same way, if we **have not been trustworthy in *the use* of** such a little thing as **unrighteous mammon** or money, how can we expect that God will **entrust** to us greater things, the **true *riches*** of eternal glory, in the age to come?

And if we **have not been trustworthy in *the use of* what is another's** (such as the money and resources lent to us by God in this life), who **will give** us **what is** our very **own** (the eternal riches of the Kingdom)? Thus, by our prudent use of money and almsgiving in this age, we prove ourselves fit to receive the unfailing glory of the age to come.

The use of money is therefore critical. For wealth is addictive, and like all addictions, its demands are total. Mammon, like God, will demand the absolute and total service of our lives; it will demand that all our energies be used in getting it, multiplying it, and keeping it. In this, it is like a lord or a master. And **no house-*slave* can serve *as slave*** (Gr. *douleuo*) **to two lords**. One has to choose. **Either** one **will hate the one and love the other**, or at the very least **give attention** to one's orders and **despise** the other, ignoring his orders. But unconditional and total loyalty cannot be given to both simultaneously. One is **not able to serve *as slave* to** both **God and mammon**, for both make total demands on the human heart. One must choose. Service to God therefore means a ruthless determination to keep mammon in its place and to treat it like a mere instrument in the service of God.

§VI.17.ii. Reply to the Pharisees

The passage that follows (vv. 14–18) is considered difficult by many. It is assumed that Luke composed this passage by pasting together sayings from previously existing written sources, and many puzzle over the apparent lack of connection between the verses. In particular, the mention of divorce in verse 18 seems to have no connection to what precedes it. I would suggest that St. Luke is indeed using a source here (whether written or oral) but that he is not so much pasting together disparate sayings as he is abbreviating a longer discussion.

I suggest that Luke makes use of a report (whether written or oral) of Jesus' debate with the Pharisees about the nature of the Law. The Pharisees had evidently reproached Jesus for His lack of proper respect for the Law (why else would He welcome sinners and generally ignore the tradition of the elders?—see Mark 7:5). Jesus responded to this by declaring that focus on the Law, since the days of John the Baptizer, has been replaced by the proclamation of the Kingdom, but that the Law still remains in effect.

Indeed, He says, it was the Pharisees who were flouting the Law by their externalism. Jesus was not flouting God's Law, but fulfilling its deepest intent. The Law, for example, forbade murder (Ex. 20:13), and Jesus penetrated to the root of murder by forbidding murderous anger. The Law forbade treating women like chattel, but insisted that in divorcing a woman, one give her a certificate of divorce, which prevented the man taking her back again on a whim (Deut. 24:1–4). Jesus penetrated to the root of the Law's intent by forbidding divorce entirely. The externalism of the Pharisees was not sufficient—if one was to enter the Kingdom, one's righteousness must exceed this externalism and fulfill the Law's true intent. (Matthew seems to have used material from this debate in his collection of sayings in Matt. 5:17ff.)

ॐ ॐ ॐ ॐ ॐ

14 Now the Pharisees, who were money-loving, were hearing all these things, and they were sneering at Him.
15 And He said to them, "You *yourselves* are those who justify yourselves before men, but God knows your hearts; for what is high among men is abominable before God.

The Pharisees (present, it would seem, since the beginning of Christ's discourse in 15:1ff) **were hearing all these things**. Possibly they felt targeted by Christ's reference to the religious people, the "sons of light," in His previous parable (v. 8). Certainly they were **money-loving** and took great exception to His teaching that the pious needed to give away money and refuse to serve mammon (vv. 9–13). They responded by **sneering at Him**. The Greek verb is *ekmukterizo*; literally, "to turn up the nose" (compare its use in 23:35). Their sneers were doubtless accompanied by the protests that *they*, at any rate, gave alms; *they* were righteous; *they* kept God's Law. It was Jesus, they said, who was not keeping God's Law—just look at the sinful company He was keeping.

In His reply, Jesus retorts that the Pharisees are **those who**

justify themselves **before men**. That is, their almsgiving and all their vaunted piety were just for show. It was as if they blew a trumpet before men to announce their almsgiving so that all could see it and applaud (Matt. 6:2). But **God knew their hearts** and how little love for the poor dwelt there. He was not fooled by their external almsgiving, but saw their hidden and overarching pride. **What was high** and haughty **among men** (such as that pride) was **abominable before God**. He demanded humility and true righteousness from men, not the mere external show of the Pharisees.

ॐ ॐ ॐ ॐ ॐ

16 "The Law and the Prophets were until John; since then the Kingdom of God is preached, and everyone is violently *entering* into it.

17 "But it is easier for heaven and earth to pass away than for one horn *of a letter* of the Law to fall.

18 "Everyone who dismisses his wife and marries another commits adultery; and he who marries one who is dismissed by *her* husband commits adultery.

The Pharisees had reproached Jesus for failing to preach the Law as they did. That was because they failed to discern the times. The time for proclaiming **the Law and the Prophets** was **until John** the Baptizer. Since his day, **the Kingdom of God is preached** (Gr. *euaggelizo*; cognate with *euaggelion*, "Good News," Gospel). The Scriptures, **the Law and the Prophets**, had this Kingdom as their goal, and with the coming of **John**, had fulfilled their purpose. John and Jesus did not come to proclaim Moses, but to proclaim the Good News that the Kingdom was at hand. Since they began preaching, **everyone** was **violently *entering* into** that Kingdom.

The phrase *to violently enter* is the Greek *biazomai*, which has the sense of "using force." The cognate noun *biastes* in Matthew 11:12 is translated "violent men"; the adjective *biaios* is used in Acts 2:2 to describe the violent rushing wind that filled the house on the Day of Pentecost. The thought here is of a stampede of men, impious sinners and desperadoes, crowding into the Kingdom in response to the preaching of Jesus and His Forerunner. The Pharisees thus should not look askance at the presence of sinners at table with Jesus—those sinners were part of the great stampede of common men who responded to the call with the enthusiasm of men storming a city.

That the Scriptures had as their goal the preaching of the Kingdom did not, however, mean that the Law could now be dispensed with. Jesus had not come to annul the Law or the Prophets. Rather He came to teach men how to fulfill them, for only by so doing could they enter the Kingdom (Matt. 5:17–20). The inner principles of the Law remained in force, for the Law was divine and eternal. Indeed, it was **easier for heaven and earth to pass away than for one horn of a letter** of the Law to fail. (This **horn** is the projection of a letter which distinguished one letter from another, like our crossing of an "l" to make a "t." The Law was authoritative down to each letter.)

Jesus was not the one making void the Word of God, the Pharisees were (compare Mark 7:13). For example, God in His Law made husband and wife to be a single, indissoluble unity, one flesh (Gen. 2:24), but the Pharisees allowed a man to divorce his wife for any reason at all. But the Law remained true, and **everyone who dismisses his wife and marries another** remains one with her still, so that he **commits adultery** against her. Furthermore, the man who **married** that wife **who was dismissed by *her*** first **husband** also **commits adultery**, for her first union with him remains. Such unions cannot be dissolved by the whims of man. It was the Pharisees who were not showing proper reverence for the Law!

§VI.17.iii. Parable of the Rich Man and Lazarus

ॐ ॐ ॐ ॐ ॐ

19 "Now there was a certain rich man, and he was clothing *himself* in purple and fine-linen, being glad every day, *feasting* brightly.

20 "And a certain poor man named Lazarus was cast at his gate, *covered with* sores,

> 21 "and desiring to be fed *to the full* with what
> was falling from the rich *man's* table; but even
> the dogs were coming and licking his sores.

The Lord then returned to His teaching on the dangers of hoarding money, and told a parable. In this parable, **there was a certain rich man**. He was habitually **clothing *himself* in purple and fine-linen**, wearing the robes of royalty and the softest underclothing. He was **glad** (compare its use in 12:19) and in high spirits every day, *feasting* **brightly**. (The Greek word rendered *brightly* is *lampros*; its cognate adjective *lampros* is used in Acts 10:30 to describe the gleaming apparel of an angel of God.) He was the perfect picture of luxury and contentment.

There was also **a certain poor man** who **was cast at his gate**, thrown there by society as one would throw away garbage. As the rich man was covered with purple and soft clothing, so Lazarus was *covered with* **sores**, and was so hungry that he **was desiring to be fed *to the full*** with anything, even the few crumbs **falling from the rich *man's*** **table** that were eaten by his dogs. His plight was ignored by the rich man (who could hardly miss seeing him every day). Moreover, **even the** lowly **dogs** were oppressing the poor wretch, **coming** up to his prostrate form **and licking his sores**, as if he were already dead, for he was too feeble to fight them off. The man is given a name, **Lazarus** (from the Heb. Eleazar).

This instance of giving a name to characters in a parable is unique among the Gospel parables. Why did Christ give him a name? Because it was important to show how the rich man knew the poor one by name (see v. 24) *and even then did nothing to help him*. The man starving at his very gate was not some nameless and unknown individual. He and the rich man were on speaking terms, and yet the rich man did not alleviate his suffering, but allowed him to die in hunger and misery before his very eyes.

> ৯৯ ৯৯ ৯৯ ৯৯ ৯৯
> 22 "Now it happened that the poor man died and
> was carried away by the angels to the bosom of

> Abraham; and the rich man also died and was buried.
>
> 23 "And in Hades he lifted up his eyes, being in torments, and sees Abraham far away and Lazarus in his bosom.
>
> 24 "And he called and said, 'Father Abraham, have mercy on me, and send Lazarus, that he may dip the tip of his finger *in* water and cool off my tongue, for I am pained in this flame!'
>
> 25 "But Abraham said, 'Child, remember that in your life you received your good things, and likewise Lazarus bad things; but now he is being comforted here, and you are *the one* pained.
>
> 26 "'And in *addition* to all these things, between us and you a great chasm has been established, that those wanting to come over from here to you are not able, and none may cross over from there to us.'

Then the scene shifts dramatically. At length **the poor man died** (evidently without proper burial; none is mentioned) and **was carried away by the angels** to Paradise, to a place at a festal table next **to the bosom of Abraham** himself. The rich man also died and was buried (doubtless with great magnificence). But he did not find himself at ease next to the patriarchs. Rather **in Hades** (the place of the dead) **he lifted up his eyes, being in torments, and sees Abraham far away—and Lazarus in his bosom**. (Compare 2 Esdras 7:85.) Here is an unexpected and dreadful reversal of fortune! In his agony he can only call out to them for help, begging the smallest favor and saying, **"Father Abraham, have mercy on me, and send Lazarus, that he may dip the tip of his finger *in* water and cool off my tongue, for I am pained in this flame!"** Note how the proud man is now humbled, and is forced to cry out like the beggars he once disdained, **"Have mercy on me!"** Note too, even more astonishingly, that he does not ask the great Abraham to come to his aid—such assistance had always been given to him in life by his servants, and

303

he asks *Lazarus* to do that servant's work even now. The rich man had never lifted a finger to help Lazarus when *he* was in misery, but he expects Lazarus to spring to his help when *he* is in distress! Even in Hades, the rich man has not changed, but still treats Lazarus as a mere servant.

Abraham replies with tenderness, calling him **child** (Gr. *teknon*), but he chides him all the same. There is no unfairness in the situation that calls for remedy—the rich man must **remember that in** his **life** he **received** his **good things, and likewise** then **Lazarus** received only **bad things; but now he is being comforted** and the rich man is *the one* **pained** (the **you** is emphatic in Greek). God has justly dispensed both fair fortune and foul. Things are as they should be! Besides, Abraham continues, as if to forestall any argument, **between** Abraham and his companions and the rich man **a great chasm has been established**, eternally separating the two. Lazarus could not come to his help even if he wanted to.

---

27 "And he said, 'Therefore I ask you, Father, that you send him to my father's house,

28 "'for I have five brothers, that he may testify to them, lest they also come to this place of torment.'

29 "But Abraham says, 'They have Moses and the Prophets; let them hear them.'

30 "But he said, 'No, Father Abraham, but if someone goes to them from the dead, they will repent!'

31 "But he said to him, 'If they do not hear Moses and the Prophets, neither will they be persuaded if someone rises from the dead.'"

The rich man then despairs for himself. But there is one favor, he thinks, that Lazarus could do, one service that he could yet render to his house. (See how he still thinks of Lazarus only in terms of what service he could provide.) He humbly **asks** Abraham for one more thing, calling him **Father** (the universal term of respect in antiquity).

Let him **send** Lazarus **to** his **father's house**, for there are his **five brothers**. (One thinks of the six godless sons of Herod the Great.) Let Lazarus, raised from the dead, **testify to them** and warn them of the error of their ways, **lest they also** hoard their wealth and spurn the poor and thus **come to this place of torment**.

Abraham is unmoved. He sees no need for such an extraordinary miracle. **They have Moses and the Prophets**, read every Sabbath. These adequately warn of the dangers of hoarding one's wealth (see Ex. 22:21f; Lev. 19:9f; Deut. 15:7f; Prov. 19:17; 21:13; Is. 3:13f; Amos 6:4f). **Let them hear them.** But the perishing soul will not give up. **"No, Father Abraham,"** he cries, perhaps remembering that the Scriptures were effectively ignored by himself. The Scriptures may not suffice—but **if someone goes to them from the dead, they will repent!**

Then comes Abraham's final reply, the masterstroke of the entire parable. **"If they do not hear Moses and the Prophets,"** Abraham replies, with the voice of doom, **"neither will they be persuaded if someone rises from the dead."** The rich man is left in his eternal torment as the parable ends.

For the Christians, reading this parable after Christ's Resurrection, the irony is superb—too superb, one supposes, to be coincidental. For Christ knew as He told this parable that He would rise from the dead. It is difficult not to suppose that He knew of the (at that time future) resurrection of His friend Lazarus too (John 11), and that it was for this reason that He chose the name Lazarus for the poor man in the parable. For Lazarus *did* rise from the dead—and even then, men did not repent (John 12:9–11).

§VI.18. Discipleship and Faith

ॐ ॐ ॐ ॐ ॐ

17 1 And He said to His disciples, "It is impossible *for* the stumbling blocks not to come, but woe *to the one* through whom they come!

2 "It would be better for him if a millstone were

> hung around his neck and he were thrown into
> the sea, than that he should cause one of these
> little ones to stumble.
>
> 3 "Pay attention to yourselves! If your brother
>   sins, rebuke him; and if he repents, forgive him.
>
> 4 "And if he sins against you seven *times* a day,
>   and turns back to you seven times, saying, 'I
>   repent!' forgive him."

St. Luke does not give any context for these sayings, but from the parallels in Matt. 18:6–7 and Mark 9:42, and from the content of this Lukan passage itself, it would seem that the disciples were arguing over their own importance. When they reached the place to which they were going (Peter's house in Capernaum; Mark 9:33), the Lord spoke to them about the necessity of maintaining peace among themselves (compare Mark 9:50). He said that given the work of Satan in the world, it was **impossible *for* stumbling blocks not to come**. Such things were inevitable—but **woe *to the one* through whom they** could **come!** The one who set such a stumbling block before his brother would suffer such wrath from God that **it would be better for him if a** great and heavy **millstone were hung around his neck and he were thrown into the sea**. Better he should die violently before having the chance to make his brother stumble and suffer the punishment due to that!

By **stumbling block**, Jesus means temptations to apostatize, which are ultimately the work of Satan. That is, if one of the **little ones**, the newer disciples of Jesus, suffers rejection from another disciple and leaves the fellowship of disciples because of it, the disciple who caused the defection will also suffer. Thus the disciples must **pay attention to** themselves, and not reject the humbler brother as if he were worthless. If one's **brother sins**, the disciple may indeed **rebuke him**, and **if he repents**, he should **forgive him**. This patience and desire for unity must be always maintained, so that even **if** the brother were to **sin seven *times* a day** and **turn back** in true penitence, **saying, "I repent!"** the disciple must **forgive him**. But he must never give up on him and reject him as worthless, no matter how bitter or prolonged the quarrel. For love believes all things, hopes all things, and endures all things (1 Cor. 13:7).

ॐ ॐ ॐ ॐ ॐ

5 The apostles said to the Lord, "Add to our faith!"

6 And the Lord said, "If you had faith like a mustard seed, you would say to *this* mulberry tree, 'Be uprooted and be planted in the sea'; and it would obey you.

7 "But who among you, having a slave plowing or tending *sheep*, will say to him when he has come in from the field, 'Come immediately and recline *to eat*'?

8 "But will he not say to him, 'Prepare something *that* I may sup, and gird yourself and serve me until I have eaten and drunk; and after these *things* you will eat and drink'?

9 "Does he thank the slave because he did the things he was directed *to do*?

10 "Thus you also, when you do all the things you are directed, say, 'We are useless slaves; we have done what we ought to have done.'"

St. Luke next relates an exchange regarding the faith needed for doing miracles. (It is possible that this exchange is placed here, immediately after the Lord's call to forgive in v. 4, in order to show how such forgiveness is also a great work of faith.) The disciples are called here **the apostles**, stressing their special status as the Lord's ambassadors, those chosen to proclaim His message and confirm it by doing miracles (9:1–2). It would seem that their cry to Christ that He would **add to** their **faith** was occasioned by some failure to perform a miracle—motivated perhaps by the desire of each apostle to win glory for himself.

The Lord replied that they did not require any further gift of faith, but simply needed to use the faith that they had. Not much faith was needed. Indeed, **if** they **had faith as** small as a tiny **mustard seed**, they could **say to *this* mulberry tree** (the mulberry was known for its deep roots), **"Be uprooted and be planted in the sea" and it would obey** them. Faith can accomplish anything, even such improbable wonders as planting a tree in the sea.

But they must beware of the desire for rewards, as if their service as apostles could place God in their debt. Their position before God was that of slaves before their Master. And **who among** them, **having a slave plowing or tending *sheep*, will say** to that slave **when he has come in from the field, "Come immediately and recline *to eat*"?** Rather, the slave will attend to the other tasks set by his master—he will first **prepare something** for the master to eat and drink, and will **gird** himself with the servant's garments to **serve** the meal. It is only after his master has eaten and drunk that he will then **eat and drink** himself. The master does not **thank the slave** because he did this extra work, for that is what slaves are for. Doing his assigned work does not entitle the slave to any great reward.

It was the same with the apostles. When they have done their apostolic work and performed their appointed miracles, they are still not entitled to vaunt themselves or to expect a reward as their right. They are to say (with the modesty characteristic of the east), **"We are useless *slaves*,"** and not think God is in their debt. Let their apostolic service be free of grasping desire for reward and of the hope of winning a greater place than their brothers.

§VI.19. Cleansing the Ten Lepers

---

11 And it happened, while He was going to Jerusalem, that He was passing through the middle of Samaria and Galilee.
12 And as He entered into a certain village, ten leprous men who stood at a distance met Him;
13 and they lifted their voices, saying, "Jesus, Master, have mercy on us!"

14 And when He saw *them*, He said to them, "Go, show yourselves to the priests." And it happened that as they were going, they were cleansed.

15 Now one of them, when he saw that he had been cured, turned back, glorifying God with a great voice,

16 And he fell on *his* face at His feet, giving thanks to Him. And he was a Samaritan.

17 And Jesus answered and said, "*Were there* not ten *who* were cleansed? But the nine—where *are they*?

18 "Was no one found who turned back to give glory to God but this foreigner?"

19 And He said to him, "Arise, go; your faith has saved you."

Luke next relates an encounter that occurred during one of Christ's journeys **to Jerusalem**. This one happened as **He was passing through the middle of Samaria and Galilee**—that is, as He was traveling along the frontier between the two regions. Because of His proximity to the two regions, **as He entered a certain village, ten leprous men met Him**, nine Jews (probably from Galilee) and one Samaritan. They stood at a distance as the Law prescribed (Lev. 13:45f) and **lifted their voices** so that Christ could hear, **saying, "Jesus, Master, have mercy on us!"**

With His customary compassion, Christ instantly sent out His healing power to them as soon as **He saw *them***, and **He said to them, "Go, show yourselves to the priests."** The priests were the ones to whom the Law gave the task of inspecting leprosy and of pronouncing the men clean and fit to return to society. The men were to hurry off to the priests to present their healed bodies for their inspection, so they could return once more to their families and loved ones. It was **as they were going** to the priests that **they were cleansed**.

Now **one of them, when he saw that he had been cured, turned back,** pausing on his joyful journey to the priests. He would go to the priests, but could not resist first returning to Christ to give thanks for his healing. When he saw his skin restored to normal, he began **glorifying God with a great voice**. Shouting out his praises to the God of Israel, he hastened back to Jesus and **fell on *his* face at His feet, giving thanks**. As the man lay there in prostrate joy, all could see (perhaps by his speech or his accent?) that **he was a Samaritan.**

Here was an unexpected sight! Samaritans had a reputation with the Jews for their impious heresy, and here was this Samaritan, putting his Jewish companions to shame by his piety! The Lord, however, was not surprised so much by the presence of the thankful Samaritan as He was by the absence of the nine Jews. With disappointed wonder, He responds to the sight by saying, **"*Were there not ten who were cleansed? But the nine—where are they*?"** The nine Jews had received healing for their bodies, but failed to **give glory to God** for this miracle of Jesus. Their leprosy was gone, but their souls remained untouched and unhealed. The foreigner, the lowly and despised Samaritan, however, by his thanksgiving received the fullness of God's gifts. Christ tells him briefly to **arise** and **go**. His **faith** had **saved** him and restored him to health. He could go to the priests, be certified as clean, and enter his new life with the blessing of God.

Luke relates the story with an eye upon the future Church. Christ had "filled Judea with His miracles" (the *Doxastikon* for Holy Friday Vespers), and yet the Jews remained unsaved. It was the foreigners, the Samaritans and the Gentiles, who would come and give thanks (Gr. *eucharisteo*) to Jesus, and who would find that their faith had saved them. The contrast between the nine Jews and the one Samaritan foreshadowed the displacement of the Jews by the Gentiles in the Church.

§VI.20. The Coming of the Kingdom

> ᎓ ᎓ ᎓ ᎓ ᎓
>
> **20 Now having been asked by the Pharisees as to when the Kingdom of God was coming, He**

> answered them and said, "The Kingdom of
> God is not coming with observation;
> 21 "nor will they say, 'Behold, here *it is*!' or,
> 'There *it is*!' For behold, the Kingdom of God
> is among you."

The Pharisees then asked Jesus **when the Kingdom of God was coming**. This was asked as a challenge, not a question. That is, these Pharisees did not pose the question because they wanted to be taught, but in order to refute our Lord's claim that the Kingdom of God was drawing near (Matt. 4:17; Luke 4:43). Drawing upon such traditions as those in 2 Esdras 5:1f (which speak of the sun shining at night and the moon shining during the day, of blood dripping from wood and voices coming from stones), the Pharisees ask where *are* such signs as these? If the Kingdom really *were* drawing near (as Jesus insisted), one should be seeing such signs abounding in the world. As it is, there were no such signs, and Jesus' claim, they said, must be rejected.

In reply, Jesus said that **the Kingdom of God** was not **coming with observation**. That is, its arrival would not be signaled by outward cosmic signs that one could observe. There would not be astonishing portents that could be seen in all the world, so that they **will say, "Behold, here *it is*!" or, "There *it is*!"** One should not be scanning the horizon for it, nor looking in this country or that for unmistakable signs of its coming. Rather, **the Kingdom of God** was **among** them already! Through the ministry of Jesus, through His words and deeds, that Kingdom had already broken into time and drawn near to men, without such cosmic fanfare.

> ৯৯ ৯৯ ৯৯ ৯৯ ৯৯
> 22 And He said to the disciples, "The days will come
> when you will desire to see one of the days of the
> Son of Man, and you will not see *it*.
> 23 "And they will say to you, 'Behold, there *it is*!
> Behold, here *it is*!' Do not go away, and do not
> pursue *them*.

24 "For just as the flashing lightning shines from *one part* under heaven to *the other part* under heaven, thus will the Son of Man be in His day.
25 "But first it is necessary *for* Him to suffer many things and be rejected by this generation.
26 "And as it happened in the days of Noah, thus it will be also in the days of the Son of Man:
27 "They were eating, drinking, marrying, being given in marriage, until the day Noah entered into the ark, and the flood came and destroyed all.
28 "Likewise, *it will be* as it happened in the days of Lot: they were eating, drinking, buying, selling, planting, *and* building;
29 "But on the day that Lot went out from Sodom, it rained fire and sulfur from heaven and destroyed all.
30 "It will be according to the same on the day the Son of Man is revealed.
31 "On that day, the one on the housetop and whose vessels *are* in the house, let him not go down to take them away; and the one in the field, likewise let him not turn back to the things behind.
32 "Remember Lot's wife.
33 "Whoever seeks to acquire his life will lose it, and whoever loses *it* will keep *it* alive.

Jesus then teaches His **disciples** about the nature of that Kingdom. Because of such opposition from the Pharisees, His disciples will encounter persecution also, and **the days will come when** they **will desire to see one of the days of the Son of Man, and will not see *it*.** By **the days of the Son of Man**, Jesus means the messianic age, the time when the Son of Man reigns in glory. The disciples, reeling from persecution, will earnestly long to find rest and to enjoy but **one of** those **days.** But they **will not see *it***; and the persecution will continue.

In that climate, they may be vulnerable to suggestions that rescue is at hand. Indeed, in the coming days of stress, when Jerusalem will be increasingly menaced by Rome, men **will say, "Behold, there *it is*! Behold, here *it is*!"** pointing to the rise of this or that messianic pretender as the sign that the final end is at hand. The disciples of Jesus should **not go away** to join them and **not pursue *them*** to swell their ranks. For such would-be deliverers will be but false-Christs. The final consummation that will bring the days of the Messiah will not come like that. The final triumph and **day** of **the Son of Man** will not come with the rise of a local Jewish revolutionary rallying his troops in the wilderness or in some hidden room. The true triumph of the Messiah will appear to all in a blinding cosmic flash of glory. It will be **just as the flashing lightning** which **shines from *one part*** under heaven to *the other part* under heaven—it will be instantly visible to all the land, and so suddenly overpowering as to be undeniable.

But that day must wait. Now is the time for patience—and for suffering. For **first it is necessary** for the Messiah to **suffer many things and be rejected by** that faithless **generation**. If the Master is to suffer, His servants must endure suffering too. For that is how they must prepare for the final Coming. It is through nonattachment to this age that Christ's disciples will be ready to meet the end.

For there will be no time to repent once Messiah reenters the world at His Second Coming. His return in glory will happen too suddenly to allow for any change of allegiance or any last-minute repentance. It will be as in **the days of Noah** (Gen. 7). Prior to the coming of the flood, there was nothing to indicate that all the world was to be suddenly swept away. They were **eating, drinking**, and all was proceeding as it had for centuries. Those **marrying** and **being given in marriage** doubtless thought they had their whole lives before them. All was normal, right up **until the day Noah entered into the ark, and the flood came and destroyed all**.

The final end will thus come suddenly, without any warning that will convince the people that time has run out. It will be just like in **the days of Lot** (Gen. 19), who survived the sudden destruction of **Sodom**. Right up until the very day Lot went out from Sodom, they were **eating, drinking, buying** with the thought of using what they bought, and **selling** with the thought of spending the money received. They were **planting** in hope of crops at a later season and **building** in hope of living in the buildings later. Without warning, **it rained fire and sulfur from heaven**, and instantly **destroyed all**. Such suddenness will characterize **the day** when **the Son of Man** will be **revealed** by God as the world's true King.

Now, therefore, is the time for loyalty to Christ and for serving Him heroically. The disciples must live in this age as if they belonged to the age to come, and sit but lightly on the attachments of this world. Worldliness must not tie them to this age, lest they be destroyed along with it. St. Luke borrows Christ's parabolic image of the man ready for instant flight to show the detachment needed to be ready for the final Coming. (That image was used originally, it would seem, in Christ's Olivet Discourse to describe the detachment needed to survive the crisis preceding the destruction of Jerusalem; compare Matt. 24:15–18; Mark 13:14–16.) Thus **the one on the housetop whose** valuable **vessels** *are* **in the house** must **not go down to take them away**; he must flee without a backward glance at his possessions if he would save his life. If **one** is **in the field** working when the call for flight comes, **let him not turn back** to find **the things** left **behind**, such as his cloak; let him likewise flee, with no thought of his former life. The disciples must **remember Lot's wife**, and how attachment to this world and lingering there meant her death (Gen. 19:26).

Thus, the timeless principle holds true: **Whoever seeks to acquire his life** by playing it safe, preferring the comforts and loyalties of this age, **will lose it** at the final Judgment, while **whoever loses** *it* by following Christ in renunciation of this world **will keep** *it* **alive** forever.

ॐ ॐ ॐ ॐ ॐ

34 "I say to you, on that night there will be two in one bed; one will be taken, and the other will be left.

35 "There will be two grinding at the same *place*; one will be taken, and the other will be left."

> 37 And answering they say to Him, "Where, Lord?" And He said to them, "Where the body *is*, there also will the vultures be gathered together."
>
> Note: Verse 36 is omitted in the best manuscripts; the few manuscripts that include it are influenced by its parallel in Matt. 24:40.

Once again, Christ assures His disciples of the swiftness of the coming judgment, and of how only one's internal heart will save one. Merely being Jewish will be of no avail. **Two** people may share the same race, the same family—even the same **bed**, and inherit two different fates. The situation envisioned is that of a farmer and his wife sleeping in their bed just before dawn. **On that night** of judgment, **one** of them **will be taken** in the flood of judgment, being swept away even as Noah's flood took away the wicked of the earth (Matt. 24:39), while **the other will be left**, as Noah was left behind to inherit a cleansed world. **Two** women might have arisen in that early light to do their early morning chores. They might be **grinding** together, one pouring the grain and the other turning the millstone to grind their daily bread: **one will be taken** in judgment, **and the other will be left**, safe and untouched. Safety is not found in keeping righteous company; it is only found in being spiritually prepared oneself.

As Jews who were trained all their lives to think that Israel enjoyed some kind of immunity in the final Judgment, the disciples found this alarming, and so **they say** to Jesus, **"Where, Lord?"** That is, where will such judgment fall? Surely not on Israel too? The Lord answers, **"Where the** dead **body *is*, there also will the vultures be gathered together."** Vultures inevitably find dead carrion to feed on, and sin will just as inevitably bring the judgment of God. Israel has no special immunity. If there is spiritual death, judgment will find them. Let the disciples not trust in their Jewishness to save them at the end, but even now renounce their rootedness in this world.

§VI.21. The Need to Pray: The Parable of the Unjust Judge

ॐ ॐ ॐ ॐ ॐ

18 1 Now He was telling a parable to them about *how* it was necessary *for* them always to pray and not to lose heart,

2 saying, "A certain judge was in a certain city *who* did not fear God and did not regard man.

3 "And a widow was in that city, and she was coming to him, saying, 'Avenge me against my opponent!'

4 "And for a time he was not willing, but after these *things* he said within himself, 'Even though I do not fear God nor regard man,

5 "'yet because this widow causes me toil, I will avenge her, lest in the end, by her coming she pound me *into exhaustion.*'"

6 And the Lord said, "Hear what the unrighteous judge says!

7 "Now *will not* God avenge His chosen ones who shout to Him day and night? And will He have patience regarding them?

8 "I say to you, He will avenge them quickly. However, when the Son of Man comes, will He find faith upon the earth?"

Because of the difficult times that are to characterize this age and because of the persecution they will experience (see 17:22), the disciples may be tempted to think that God has abandoned them and to give up on their faith. Christ therefore tells them **a parable about *how* it was necessary *for* them always to pray and not to lose heart**.

In this parable, there was **a certain judge in a certain city *who* did not fear God** or **regard man**. That is, he was both impious and corrupt, moved by considerations neither of conscience nor of reputation. What is envisioned is one of the secular city judges appointed by the government—men notorious for their willingness to accept a bribe. Their official Hebrew title was *dayyaney gezeroth*—"sentence judges," but they were popularly stigmatized as *dayyaney gezeloth*—"robber judges"!

In that same city, there was **a widow**, one poor, socially marginalized, and without the resources to provide the customary bribe which was her only hope with such a judge. It would seem that she had been defrauded by someone well able to pay the bribe. She kept **coming** to the judge time and again, insistently asking him to **avenge** her **against** her **opponent**—that is, to give her justice by getting back for her the money out of which she had been defrauded by her oppressor. Since she was not able to pay a larger bribe (and since the judge cared nothing for abstract justice), her case seemed hopeless.

Nonetheless, she refused to lose heart and give up. She came to the judge every morning, demanding that he vindicate her and end the unjust oppression. Day after day the judge refused and was **not willing** to hear her case. Then at last, **he said within himself, "Even though I do not fear God nor regard man, yet because this widow causes me toil, I will avenge her."** The judge did not have a change of heart; the woman just wore him down by her perseverance in asking. The judge thought that if he did not give her the justice she demanded, **in the end, by her coming, she** would **pound** him *into exhaustion*. The word translated *pound into exhaustion* is the Greek *upopiazo*; literally, to punch in the face and give the person a black eye. St. Paul uses the word as part of a boxing metaphor in 1 Corinthians 9:27; here it is used in a similarly metaphorical way. The judge feared that if he did not get rid of the woman, he would be worn down to nothing!

Jesus then draws the moral of the parable, inviting the disciples to **hear what the unrighteous judge says**. Even such an impious and corrupt judge as this one was prevailed upon by constancy in prayer. God is the righteous Judge of all the earth—will not He do even better than the unjust judge? Will **God** not **avenge His chosen ones**, His dear elect children?

If the unjust judge vindicated a woman for whom he cared

nothing, how much more will God vindicate His own? Especially as they **shout** in fervent and humble supplication **to Him day and night!** Will He **have patience regarding them**, placidly watching their adversaries persecute and destroy them? No, Christ assures His disciples, God **will avenge them quickly**, coming to their rescue. The final reference is to the Second Coming. Christ will at length come to end the world's oppression of His people and to vindicate them at the Judgment. They therefore should not cast away their faith or cease praying for the Kingdom to come.

Christ ends the teaching with a question, for the issue is not God's willingness to hear, but their willingness to persevere. At the end, **when the Son of Man comes** to consummate the Kingdom, **will He find faith upon the earth?** The final object of the question contains the definite article—literally, "will He find *the* faith upon the earth?" It seems that this is meant to call attention to the quality of their faith: Will the Son of Man find *that* faith, the faith embodied by the importunate widow, a faith that perseveres through all setbacks? God is ready to save. Are they willing to endure and keep on praying?

§VI.22. Trusting Our Own Righteousness: Parable of the Pharisee and the Tax-collector

ॐ ॐ ॐ ॐ ॐ

9 And He also told this parable to certain ones who put confidence in themselves that they were righteous, and disdained others:

10 "Two men went up into the Temple to pray, one a Pharisee and the other a tax-collector.

11 "The Pharisee stood and was praying with himself these *things*: 'God, I thank You that I am not as the rest of men *are*—robbers, unrighteous, adulterers, or even as this tax-collector.

12 "'I fast twice a week; I pay tithes of everything that I possess.'

13 "But the tax-collector, standing at a distance,

> was unwilling to lift up even his eyes to heaven,
> but was striking his breast, saying, 'God, be
> merciful to me, the sinner!'
> 14 "I say to you, this one went down into his house
> justified *rather* than that one; for everyone who
> exalts himself will be humbled, but he who
> humbles himself will be exalted."

Luke next narrates Christ's parable of the tax-collector (or publican, from the Latin, *publicani*, since they paid into the public treasury) and the Pharisee. St. Luke perhaps places the parable here to show how prayer must be offered in humility, not in pride. It is possible that when Christ told this parable, there were many Pharisees present, those **who put confidence in themselves that they were righteous and disdained others**. Certainly the Pharisaical attitude of despising the common man for his laxity was well known (see John 7:49).

In approaching this parable today, we must remember that the Pharisee was then commonly thought to be the one most likely to win God's approval, while the publican or tax-collector was universally despised as an impious scoundrel. We must not let our modern Christian condemnation of the Pharisees cause us to forget that the Lord's original hearers would have sided with the Pharisee as "the good guy" of the story. (One modern equivalent, for example, might be "The Monk and the Drug Addict.")

The parable begins with **two men** going **up into the Temple to pray** and offer their respective prayers in hope of winning God's favor and forgiveness. One was **a Pharisee** and the other **a tax-collector**. The contrast between them could not have been more stark.

The Pharisee was obvious to all, clothed as he was in his broad phylacteries and long tassels at the ends of his garments (Matt. 23:5). He **stood** (the universal posture for prayer in antiquity) and **was praying with himself** (that is, he took his stand for prayer a little apart from the rest, as if to save himself from contamination by them).

The Lord gives us a sample of his long prayer: **"God, I thank You**

that I am not as the rest of men *are*—**robbers** and swindlers, ever
on the lookout to take what is not theirs, **unrighteous** and impious
who never fast, tithe, or pray, **adulterers**—(here we may think he
looks around at the crowd to spy the tax-collector behind him)—**or
even as this tax-collector."** The note of superiority and scorn is
unmistakable. Unlike them, the Pharisee continues, **"I fast twice a
week; I pay tithes of everything that I possess"**—a notable feat, for
the Law required tithes only of crops, not of all that one acquired.

This is not the end of his prayer. Jewish prayer ended with some
ascription of glory to God. Christ turns from the Pharisee in the
middle of his prayer, as if to say, "You get the general idea."

The Lord turns His attention next to **the tax-collector**. He had
come into the Temple courts, but, keenly aware of his unworthiness to be in God's Presence, was **standing at a distance**, towards
the back of those courts. Prayer was offered with uplifted eyes and
uplifted hands, but the tax-collector **was unwilling to lift up even
his eyes to heaven**—never mind lifting up his hands. Instead, he
was striking his breast in anguished self-loathing. All he could bring
himself to say was, **"God, be merciful to me, the sinner!"** (Literally, "be propitiated for me, the sinner"; Gr. *ilaskomai*; compare its
use in Heb. 2:17.)

Note the definite article: He knew himself to be worse than all,
and of all those people around him, he felt that he alone was **the
sinner**. He could no longer stand himself, and came into the Temple
courts to offer his repentance to God.

Jesus then comes to the parable's surprise ending: Contrary to
what all expected from the prayers of such men, He assures His
listeners that **this one**, the tax-collector, **went down into his house
justified** and forgiven that day, *rather* **than that one**, the Pharisee.
The Pharisee went from the Temple unforgiven and unblessed.

Why? Because **everyone who exalts himself will be humbled**
by God, **but he who humbles himself will be exalted** by Him.
The Pharisee, by his pride, spent his whole life and all his prayer
exalting himself, confident as he was in his own righteousness. The
tax-collector humbled and abased himself, knowing that his only
hope was the divine mercy. This is the principle built by God into

all spiritual life: Humility brings His blessing, while pride cuts men off from God. The Pharisee's life was built on a foundation of unreachable, exalted pride—and thus his prayer was not acceptable to heaven. Let all who would follow Jesus hearken and offer their persevering prayer in humility!

§VI.23. Christ Blesses the Children

> ॐ ॐ ॐ ॐ ॐ
>
> 15 And they were bringing to Him even their infants that He might touch them, but when the disciples saw *this*, they were rebuking them.
> 16 But Jesus called for them, saying, "Let the children come to Me, and do not forbid them, for to such belongs the Kingdom of God.
> 17 "Amen I say to you, whoever does not welcome the Kingdom of God as a child will never enter into it."

As a contrast to the pride of the Pharisees, St. Luke next relates Christ's blessing of the children. The Pharisees may have delighted in their spiritual status, but the children approached Christ in complete and utter simplicity, without depending on any supposed accumulated merit. As such, they were a fitting image of true discipleship.

It was the custom to bring children to any famous rabbi for him to lay hands on them and bless them. It was hoped that this would have good effects on the children's future lives. The mothers of the area were doing this, **bringing to Him** not only young children but **even their infants**. **When** Jesus' **disciples saw** the women approaching with their children, **they were rebuking them** (probably repeatedly, striving to overcome the will of determined mothers). It would seem likely that this occurred at the end of a long and exhausting day of teaching, and that the disciples were concerned to protect their Master from (as they thought) trivial and unnecessary interruption. Let Jesus get some much-needed rest!

But when Jesus became aware of this, He **called for** the children, saying to the disciples, **"Let the children come to Me, and do not forbid them, for to such belongs the Kingdom of God."** Children indeed have no status in the eyes of the world. But **the Kingdom of God** belongs to such as these, since they are able to receive it in simplicity, as a gift. Adults who are battered by the hardness of the world (such as the Pharisees) think they have to earn God's favor, but these little ones come to Jesus with open hearts and open hands, expecting to be welcomed simply because Jesus is good and loving. This is the essence of true discipleship and of saving faith. If one wants to inherit the Kingdom of God, one will have to **welcome** that Kingdom **as a child**, receiving it as a gift, apart from any considerations of merit. The proud heart that insists on its hard-earned status will **never enter into it.**

§VI.24. The Rich Young Ruler and the Kingdom of God

18 And a certain ruler asked Him, saying, "Good Teacher, what shall I do to inherit eternal life?"

19 And Jesus said to him, "Why do you call Me good? No one *is* good but God alone.

20 "You know the commandments, 'Do not commit adultery, do not murder, do not steal, do not bear false witness, honor your father and mother.'"

21 And he said, "All these things I have kept from my youth."

22 And when Jesus heard this, He said to him, "One *thing* is still lacking for you; sell as much as you have, and give *it* away to the poor, and you will have treasure in heaven; and come, follow Me."

23 But when he had heard these things, he became very sorrowful; for he was extremely rich.

24 And Jesus saw him and said, "How difficult it

> will be for those who have properties to enter into the Kingdom of God!
>
> 25 "For it is easier for a camel to enter through the opening of a needle than for a rich *man* to enter into the Kingdom of God."
>
> 26 And they who heard it said, "Then who is able to be saved?"
>
> 27 But He said, "The things impossible with men are possible with God."

As a contrast to the children who come to Christ in simplicity, Luke next relates how the rich man came to Him asking what pious achievement he could pursue to merit the Kingdom. This was a **ruler**, an official of the local synagogue. He came to Christ with extravagant praise, flattering Him with the unusual title **Good Teacher**, asking what mighty work or mitzvah could he **do to inherit eternal life**.

The Lord responded first to this extravagant and unparalleled compliment, for it revealed that the man had too easy and superficial an idea of goodness. Jesus answers his question with a question of His own: **"Why do you call Me good?"** In saying this, Jesus is not denying that He is good. The focus of the query is not on Jesus and whether or not He is good; it is on the man's idea of goodness. Christ would have him know that true goodness is transcendent and otherworldly, so that **no one *is* good but God alone**. That is, only God is absolutely good, and if the ruler is to find his way to salvation, he must recognize this and drop any pretension he has to being good. The man doubtless considered himself a good man, one who came to ask advice from another good man. Christ stops him from pursuing this false trail any further, calling him to recognize the transcendence of true goodness and his own spiritual poverty.

Only then does Christ answer the ruler's question, calling him back to what God had revealed in His Law. **"You know the commandments,"** Christ tells him, quoting a selection of them (compare Ex. 20:12–16). Let the man keep these, loving God by loving man made in His image. If he will do this, he will indeed inherit eternal life on the Last Day.

The man had already done this, affirming that **all these** commandments he had **kept from** his **youth**, when he first took upon himself the yoke of the Law. The Lord did not contradict this answer. But He could see into his heart and knew that there was a void hidden there, an emptiness which was a desire to experience the Kingdom here and now. There was **one *thing* still lacking** for him, one thing the ruler needed to do to enter the Kingdom now: **sell as much** as he had and **give *it* away to the poor** so that he would **have treasure in heaven**. Thus liberated, he could **come, follow** Jesus.

Here was the call to a deeper obedience, a call to become Jesus' disciple and experience the power of the Kingdom now. The man was at the crossroads, poised between the Kingdom and this world. Alas, he chose the world. **When he had heard these things**, his face fell and **he became very sorrowful, for he was extremely rich**. This was not the counsel he expected. He expected Jesus would bid him do some great work, and yet leave the fabric of his life and routine intact. He was unwilling to break the mold of his pleasant life for the uncertainty and adventure of following Jesus in poverty, and he wordlessly went away. As Jesus watched him go, he commented to His disciples, **"How difficult it will be for those who have properties** and great wealth **to enter into the Kingdom of God!"** Indeed, it was **easier for a camel to enter through the opening of a needle than for a rich *man* to enter into the Kingdom of God**. Becoming Jesus' disciple and entering the Kingdom in this age meant willingness to renounce comfort and popularity for the sake of the Gospel, and those who had such wealth would find such a sacrifice all but impossible.

The disciples who **heard it** were astonished, for contemporary thought regarded wealth as a sign of God's favor. If even the rich had such difficulty entering the Kingdom, **then who** was **able to be saved?** Christ did not relent when He saw them stumble at this, nor did He modify His words, as if wealth were *not* always dangerous to the human soul. Rather, He simply referred this to the divine power, saying **the things impossible with men** (such as wealthy men renouncing their wealth or using it for the Kingdom) were **possible with God.** (The history of monasticism would later prove this truth, and the desert would later be full of many such camels who had gone through the eye of the needle.)

꽃 꽃 꽃 꽃 꽃

28 And Peter said, "Behold, we have left our own *homes* and followed You."

29 And He said to them, "Amen I say to you, there is no one who has left house or wife or brothers or parents or children, for the sake of the Kingdom of God,

30 "who will not receive manifold as much at this time, and in the age to come, eternal life."

Peter, speaking for the rest, was anxious for a reassuring word. Like them, he had **left** his **own *home*** with all its security and **followed** Jesus. The rich ruler had been unwilling to renounce the world's comforts and popularity—but the disciples had done so. Peter does not here speak boastfully, but with the plaintive nervousness of a child, unsure of his acceptance. And Christ does indeed reassure them, prefacing His promise with His customary **Amen I say to you**. Not just the Twelve would be rewarded, but there was **no one who** had **left house or wife or brothers or parents or children for the sake of the Kingdom of God who** would **not receive manifold as much at this time, and in the age to come, eternal life**. Every single person who chooses discipleship to Jesus over the claims of family loyalty and the comforts of home will be amply rewarded, both in this age and in the next.

§VI.25. Third Passion Prediction

꽃 꽃 꽃 꽃 꽃

31 And He took aside the Twelve and said to them, "Behold, we are going up to Jerusalem, and all things which are written through the

---

> prophets about the Son of Man will be fulfilled.
> 32 "For He will be delivered *up* to the Gentiles,
>   and will be mocked and abused and spat upon,
> 33 "and after they have scourged Him, they will
>   kill Him; and the third day He will rise."
> 34 And they had insight into none of these *things*,
>   and this word was hidden from them, and they
>   did not know the things that were said.

St. Luke next relates the third prediction of the Passion. Christ **took aside the Twelve** to prepare them privately for the trauma to follow. Since 9:51, Luke has been stressing Jerusalem as the focus and goal of Christ's ministry, and here Jerusalem is once again revealed as the culmination of His journeying. He and His disciples are **going up to Jerusalem**, where the city will show itself the fulfillment of prophecy, the City of the Passion. It is there that **all things which are written** of Christ **through the prophets will be fulfilled** (e.g. Is. 50:6; 53:3f). For **He will be delivered *up* to the Gentiles, mocked, abused** and slapped **and spat upon**. After having Him **scourged** (the usual prelude to crucifixion), they will **kill Him**. The **third day** will see Him **rise**.

The disciples **had insight into none of these *things***. All their Jewish understanding had trained them to think of Messiah only in victorious terms, as the conquering hero. Such talk of defeat, degradation, and death had no place in their scheme of things. Jesus must have been speaking parabolically, as He often did. **This word** or saying **was hidden from them** in that God had not yet given them the understanding necessary to see how a suffering Messiah would fulfill the Scriptures (9:45).

§VI.26. Healing the Blind Man

> ࿔ ࿔ ࿔ ࿔ ࿔
> 35 And it happened that as He was coming near
>   to Jericho, a certain blind *man* was sitting by
>   the way, begging.

36 Now hearing a crowd going by, he was inquiring what this might be.

37 And they declared to him that Jesus the Nazarene was going by.

38 And he shouted out, saying, "Jesus, son of David, have mercy on me!"

39 And those going before *him* were rebuking him, that he should be silent, but he was crying out all the more, "Son of David, have mercy on me!"

40 And Jesus stood *still* and ordered him to be led to Him; and when he had come near, He asked him,

41 "What do you want Me to do for you?" And he said, "Lord, that I may see again!"

42 And Jesus said to him, "See again; your faith has saved you."

43 And immediately he saw again, and was following Him, glorifying God; and when all the people saw *this*, they gave praise to God.

Our Lord now approaches Jericho as part of His final approach to Jerusalem. Concerning His stay here, Luke relates stories about two men: a blind beggar and a tax-collector named Zacchaeus. Luke's account is interesting because he situates the healing of the blind beggar as Christ **was coming near to Jericho**, whereas Matthew and Mark both situate the healing when Christ was *leaving* Jericho (Matt. 20:29; Mark 10:46). Moreover, Luke (with Mark) mentions only one beggar, whereas Matthew mentions two (Matt. 20:30). Further, just as Luke is the only one of the three evangelists to locate the healing as Christ approaches Jericho, so is he the only one who narrates the story of Zacchaeus.

I would offer the following possible reconstruction. As Jesus enters Jericho, He is hailed by a beggar, one notable enough to be named (the name, Bartimaeus, is preserved in Mark 10:46). At that time, Bartimaeus remains lost in the crowd as Christ goes in to stay overnight in the home of Zacchaeus. The next day, having learned of

Christ's whereabouts from the considerable grumbling of the crowd about that very thing (19:7), Bartimaeus repositions himself outside the house of Zacchaeus and is joined by the second beggar. As Christ leaves Zacchaeus' home and the city, He meets Bartimaeus and his companion and heals them both. All three evangelists telescope the events, retaining only whatever is relevant to their purposes.

Whatever the precise geography, there was **a certain blind *man*, sitting by the way, begging**. As a blind man, he had no means of life but begging. He **heard** the large **crowd** that perpetually accompanied Jesus **going by** and **was inquiring what this might be**. When they **declared to him that Jesus the Nazarene was going by**, he recognized that this was his one and only opportunity to be healed. The famous wonder-working prophet was reputed to have healed the blind—and even, by some, to be the Messiah. In order to get Christ's attention in that noisy throng, **he shouted out, saying, "Jesus, son of David, have mercy on me!"** Such a clear confession of Jesus' messiahship was indeed unusual and sure to bring attention.

It did, but not quite the attention the blind man hoped for. Possibly because his relentless shrieking was an irritant, the crowd, long hardened to the plight of beggars, **were rebuking him, that he should be silent**. The blind man knew, however, that with every moment and with Jesus' every step, all hope was fading for him, and he refused to be silenced. Rather, **he was crying out all the more**.

When He heard him, **Jesus stood *still*** in the road **and ordered him to be led to Him**. Upon coming near, Jesus asked him, **"What do you want Me to do for you?"** The need was obvious enough, yet Christ asked the question to preserve the man's dignity. He could have healed him without first asking him to say what he wanted, as if what mattered was just the healing. But Christ cared not just for the healing of the ailment, but for the man himself who was healed. Though the blind man was "just a beggar" (as many thought), Jesus dealt with the man as with an equal and allowed him the dignity of being patiently heard. The man excitedly responded, **"That I may see again!"** (Gr. *ina anablepso*). Christ gave him exactly what he asked for, saying, **"See again"** (Gr. *anablepson*), adding that his **faith** had **saved** him.

The man then became an image of the Christians, who receive spiritual sight through Christ in the waters of baptism and who are saved by faith. Like them, the blind beggar began **following Him** on the road to Jerusalem, **glorifying God** all the while in ecstatic joy. **When all the people saw *this*** miracle, **they gave praise to God**—which outpouring of praise was itself also a sign of the coming Kingdom of God.

§VI.27. Zacchaeus

19 1 And He entered and was coming through Jericho.

2 And behold! a man called by the name of Zacchaeus, and he was a chief tax-collector, and he *was* rich.

3 And he was seeking to see who Jesus was, and he was not able because of the crowd, for he was little in stature.

4 And he ran before to the front and went up upon a sycamore that he might see Him, for He was about to come through that *way.*

5 And as He came to the place, Jesus looked up and said to him, "Zacchaeus, hurry and come down, for today it is necessary for Me to remain at your house!"

6 And he hurried *and* came down, and welcomed Him with joy.

7 And all who saw *this* were grumbling on, saying, "With a sinful man He has entered to get lodging."

8 And Zacchaeus stood and said to the Lord, "Behold, Lord! the half of my possessions I will give to the poor, and if I have oppressed anyone *out* of anything, I render fourfold!"

9 And Jesus said to him, "Today salvation has come to this house, because he also is a son of Abraham.

> 10 "For the Son of Man has come to seek and to save the lost."

St. Luke brings his story of Christ's journeying to Jerusalem (begun in 9:51) to a climax with the story of the salvation of Zacchaeus. In Luke's narrative, a man bursts suddenly onto the scene (signaled with a characteristic **behold!**), appearing before Christ as He **was coming through Jericho**. The **name** of the man is given as **Zacchaeus** (Heb., *Zakkay*, an abbreviation of Zechariah).

This in itself reveals the importance of the story for Luke, for he rarely gives the names of those whom Christ saves, preferring to leave the spotlight on the Lord alone. (In the case of the blind beggar Bartimaeus, Luke even omits his name when it was present in his Markan source.) Here, however, the spotlight is allowed to fall on the one healed as well, for Zacchaeus, a great sinner, is an image of all the godless and **the lost** that **the Son of Man came to seek and save**—such as the godless and lost Gentiles.

The character of Zacchaeus is sketched in a few strokes: **he was a chief tax-collector** (that is, he was also in charge of other tax-collectors), and **he *was* rich**. That wealth doubtless came from the well-known tax-collector habit of oppressing the poor out of their money, defrauding them by collecting more than was due. We also learn that **he was little in stature**.

It would seem that Zacchaeus was not a man who liked himself. How many nights did his conscience strive with his better self and keep him awake? How often did he secretly yearn to be accepted and loved, and to know the favor of God? It would be because of these secret desires, we may think, that he felt driven to look into the face of the prophet from Nazareth as He was passing through—this wonder-worker who was reputed to love sinners and even to eat with them (compare 7:34). It was out of the question to try to meet Him, especially in such a public way, and perhaps Zacchaeus even felt a bit apprehensive about the possibility of such a meeting; did not Jesus have harsh denunciations for heartless rich men like him (see 6:24–25)? Nonetheless, he was determined at least to see Jesus. His desire must have been overwhelming, for he decided to climb up into a roadside tree outside of town to see Him, and in that culture, adult men would never have made themselves ridiculous by climbing a tree—or by running in public. Yet Zacchaeus was willing to do both to catch a glimpse of Jesus.

So it was that the little publican **ran before to the front** of the crowd and **went up upon a sycamore** (a tree with low branches for easy climbing and broad leaves to hide behind) **that he might see Him** as He **came through that** *way*. As Jesus **came to the place** where Zacchaeus was and from which he looked down into Jesus' face, **Jesus looked up** at him. The two men locked eyes, and for a moment, Zacchaeus's world stood still. Perhaps Zacchaeus expected some rebuke for his sin, or at least a word of gentle mockery. To his great astonishment, the Lord addressed him by name—an example of His supernatural knowledge (compare such knowledge in John 1:47f). Better yet, instead of the expected rebuke, the Lord said, **"Zacchaeus, hurry and come down, for today it is necessary for Me to remain at your house!"** That is, Jesus was taking the initiative to seek him out, to accept his hospitality, and to make him His equal friend. (Such was **necessary** for Christ not just because those were the preferred lodgings given the size of His entourage, but also because Christ came to do the Father's will and search out His lost sheep. It was thus **necessary** to stay with Zacchaeus, because that was how He could call him home.)

Christ told Zacchaeus to **hurry and come down**, and Luke reports the publican's response using the same words: **he hurried** *and* **came down**. That is, he obeyed, and **welcomed Him with joy** into his home. **All who saw** *this* (most of whom, we may imagine, had suffered at the hands of the tax-collector) **were grumbling on** (Gr. *diagogguzo*, a more intensive form of *gogguzo*, "to grumble"), saying, **"With a sinful man** Jesus **has entered to get lodging** for the night." The words *with a sinful man* stand at the head of the sentence in the Greek, to emphasize the crowd's indignation at Jesus' choice of host. Instead of any of the respectable and pious people in Jericho, He chose Zacchaeus!

Zacchaeus, however, was not fazed, but exulted in his newfound acceptance. As they reclined at supper that evening, **Zacchaeus**

stood up and announced to Jesus and to all the assembled guests his new resolve. **"Behold, Lord!"** he began, announcing his sudden and new determination, **"the half of my possessions I will give to the poor, and if I have oppressed anyone *out* of anything, I render fourfold** back to him!" It is an impressive change of life, for he had doubtless oppressed a number of people, and this was a generous restitution. In the Law, restitution in such cases of fraud was set at a return of the original amount plus one-fifth (Lev. 6:1–5). To restore it **fourfold** was more in keeping with the more extreme crime of cattle theft (Ex. 22:1). Zacchaeus felt keenly his guilt and was determined to make it good.

Such generosity was evidence of a truly changed heart, and the Lord exulted with him, pronouncing, **"Today salvation has come to this house!"** God had rescued His lost sheep and brought him home. Men might despise Zacchaeus and give up on him, treating him as if he were a Gentile, but God had not given up on him. Zacchaeus **also** was **a son of Abraham** and heir to the mercies of God. Jesus had been sent to recover the lost sheep of the house of Israel (Matt. 15:24), and this included such men as Zacchaeus.

The story of the recovery of Zacchaeus forms the culmination of Luke's narrative of Christ's journeying to Jerusalem (the parable that follows in vv. 11–27 is related as part of Christ's table conversation in the house of Zacchaeus). Why does it have such an importance for Luke?

The answer: In the case of Zacchaeus, *Christ took the initiative*. In many other stories, the sick and needy came to Christ, and He responded to their requests. In this instance, Zacchaeus made no request (though his location up the tree did witness to his internal openness to Christ). Christ sought him out and uttered the first word—a word that was eagerly welcomed. It was the perfect example of how **the Son of man** had **come to seek and to save the lost**. Zacchaeus was not so much seeking Christ as *Christ was seeking him*, even before there was any indication of repentance or piety on the part of Zacchaeus. The publican's repentance and change of heart were not the cause of Christ's seeking him out; they were the fruit of it.

In this Zacchaeus was the perfect symbol of the Gentiles (and the Church's mission to the Gentiles was a great concern to Luke, himself a Gentile). For Christ sought the Gentiles even before they were aware of His love, while they were still worshipping idols. As St. Paul would later write (quoting Is. 65:1–2), God "was found by those who sought Him not, and became manifest to those who did not ask for Him" (Rom. 10:20). Christ's seeking for and saving Zacchaeus was an image and promise of how He would later seek and save all the nations of the world.

§VI.28. The Kingdom Coming: The Parable of the Minas

ॐ ॐ ॐ ॐ ॐ

11 And while they were hearing these things, He proceeded to tell a parable, because He was near Jerusalem, and they supposed that the Kingdom of God was about to appear immediately.

12 He said therefore, "A certain nobleman went to a distant region to receive a kingdom for himself and return.

13 "And he called ten of his slaves and gave them ten minas, and said to them, 'Do business until I come.'

14 "But his citizens hated him and sent an embassy after him, saying, 'We do not want this one to reign over us!'

15 "And it happened that when he came back after receiving the kingdom, he had the slaves called to whom he had given the silver, that he might know what business-gain they had made.

16 "And the first arrived, saying, 'Lord, your mina has earned ten minas.'

17 "And he said to him, 'Well *done*, good slave! Because you have been faithful in the smallest *thing*, be in authority over ten cities.'

18 "And the second came, saying, 'Your mina, lord, has made five minas.'

19 "And he said to this one also, 'And you *yourself* are to be over five cities.'

20 "And the other one came, saying, 'Lord, behold your mina, which I laid up in a neckerchief!

21 "'For I was afraid of you, because you are an exacting man; you take what you did not lay down and harvest what you did not sow.'

22 "He says to him, 'Out of your *own* mouth I will judge you, you evil slave! Did you know that I *myself* am an exacting man, taking what I did not lay down and harvesting what I did not sow?

23 "'Then why did you not put my money upon a *banker's* table, and having come, I *myself* would have collected it with interest?'

24 "And he said to the bystanders, 'Take the mina from him, and give *it* to the one who has the ten minas.'

25 "(And they said to him, 'Lord, he has ten minas!')

26 "'I tell you, that to everyone who has will more be given, but from him who does not have, even what he has will be taken.

27 "'But these enemies of mine who did not want me to reign over them, bring them here before me and slaughter them down.'"

The following parable was told by Christ at the supper given for the guests at the house of Zacchaeus as **they were hearing these things** about the publican's repentance and salvation. (That this was a different parable from that of the talents, which Christ told privately to His disciples on the Mount of Olives and which was recorded in Matt. 25:14–30, is apparent from a comparison of the details. St. John Chrysostom affirms that these are two different parables in his *Homily 78* on Matthew's Gospel.)

Christ was **near** to His **Jerusalem** destination (about seventeen miles away), and many supposed that He would declare Himself as military king and rout the Romans, and that **the Kingdom of God** in its fullness **was about to appear immediately**. The Lord therefore told this **parable** to show that the Kingdom was *not* to appear immediately in its fullness, but that now was the time for faithfulness in service. It was only after a long time that he would **receive** the **Kingdom** and **return** to reign on the earth.

Jesus' parable is based loosely on the well-known example of Archelaus. His father Herod had willed to him the kingdom, and Archelaus went to distant Rome for the Romans to ratify his possession of his kingdom. Some in Israel protested this arrangement, sending an embassy to try to have it overruled.

In the Lord's parable, **a certain nobleman went to a distant region to receive a kingdom**, so that there was a long time between his departure and his return in triumph. This was an image of this age, the time between Christ's Ascension and His return at the Second Coming. Before the nobleman left, **he called ten of his slaves** and left them in charge of his affairs. This would ensure that his household and place in the country he left would be intact upon his return. To each of them he gave a mina, a sum equal to about three years' wages for the working man. The sum was not so much a legacy as a test of faithfulness. Each of the slaves was commanded to **do business** and trade with the mina **until** the master **came** back. Christ adds, as a secondary detail of His parable, that the master's **citizens hated him and sent an embassy**, a delegation, to protest to the nobleman's lord this future arrangement, saying to him, **"We do not want this one to reign over us!"** That is, the delegation attempted to have the nobleman's lords overturn the arrangement.

Their protest was ineffectual, so that the lord **came back, after receiving the kingdom** he had been promised. His first order of business after returning was to find out how his slaves had managed his affairs. He **called** those **to whom he had given the silver** to receive their reports.

The first arrived (Gr. *paraginomai*, suggesting that he did not merely come into his lord's presence, but swept into his presence, exultant with his success). He announced, **"Lord, your mina has earned ten minas,"** and his master responded by commending him, **"Well *done*, good slave! Because you have been faithful in the smallest *thing*, be in authority over ten cities."** The reward is out of all proportion to the gain accomplished by the slave—an image of the immensity of the weight of glory waiting for us in comparison to our paltry service and sufferings (compare 2 Cor. 4:17).

The second came (Gr. *erchomai*; indicating a less dramatic entrance than his predecessor—perhaps he felt a bit dispirited at accomplishing only half as much). He reported, **"Your mina, lord, has made five minas."** He also was rewarded out of all proportion to his service (though admittedly less than the first slave) as his master replied, **"And you *yourself* are to be over five cities."** We are left to imagine similar reports and rewards for another seven slaves who came to give an accounting of their work.

Then came the last slave. Note that he is not called "the tenth" or "the last," but rather **the other**, for his surly disobedience set him apart from all his comrades. This one reported, **"Lord, behold your mina, which I laid up in a neckerchief! For I was afraid of you, because you are an exacting man; you take what you did not lay down and harvest what you did not sow."** That is, the slave had completely refused to obey his master's command to do business until he came. He had simply laid up in a neckerchief the original mina—not even keeping it in a very safe place! He accused his lord of being **an exacting man**, one who would **take what** he **did not lay down and harvest what** he **did not sow**, unfairly demanding a high return, and the slave professed to be **afraid** that he would lose the original mina if he traded with it as he was ordered. He therefore refused to obey and simply returned the mina that was given to him.

It was an astonishing speech for a slave to make to his master, and a terrible accusation. Quite fittingly, the master decided that **out of** his own **mouth** and on the basis of his own words he would **judge** his **evil** (that is, worthless) **slave**. Did the slave think that his master was as hard as all that? Then on even the slave's own figuring he should have **put** the **money upon a *banker's* table** and invested it, that when the master **came** he **would have collected it with interest**. Even such a small effort would have produced some gain!

By his not doing so, it was apparent that the slave was not motivated by fear of losing his master's mina, but by simple disobedient laziness. He had not done all he could, but was simply negligent, even by his own standards.

The master angrily said to the bystanders (probably those of his retinue), **"Take the mina from him and give *it* to the one who has the ten minas."** In the parable, this was not so much a reward for the first servant who had produced ten minas (after all, he had just been rewarded with ten *cities*, and the addition of a single mina would be a small reward in comparison). Rather, it was an angry judgment on the lazy slave. He would not have gotten to keep the mina anyway, since he was returning it to his master. The master's action constitutes his stripping the slave of whatever he had in his hands and of all entrusted responsibility.

The choice of the one to whom the mina was given provoked an involuntary protest from the onlookers (probably the onlookers in the parable). He **has ten minas** already and is standing there, weighted down with the silver, already amply rewarded. It seemed to them a bit much that one so greatly rewarded should be the master's favorite in this matter too. The master, however, refused to relent, assuring them (**I tell you**) that **to everyone who has will more be given, but from him who does not have, even what he has will be taken**. That is, the one who has God's blessing upon him in this age for his obedience will be given even more in the age to come, whereas the one who does *not* know God's blessing now will have even less in the age to come, for he will suffer the loss of everything in the lake of fire.

Then, after dealing with his slaves, the nobleman who received his kingdom turns next to those of his subjects who did all they could to prevent it. Those declared **enemies** of his must now suffer the doom they expected if their rebellion failed. The new king commands that his soldiers **bring them here before** him and **slaughter them down** (Gr. *katasphazo*, a more intensive form of *sphazo*, "to slaughter"). By having the execution carried out in his presence, the king is sure to root out all trace of rebellion against his rule.

The horrific image (of a not unusual practice in the ancient world) witnesses to the doom that awaits all those who persevere in their hatred and resistance to Christ. The Last Day will for them be a time of divine wrath.

❧ VII ☙

MINISTRY IN JERUSALEM
(19:28—21:38)

§VII.1. Entry into Jerusalem

§VII.1.i. Triumphal Entry

☙ ☙ ☙ ☙ ☙

28 And after He had said these things, He was
going on before *them*, going up to Jerusalem.

29 And it happened that when He drew near to
Bethphage and Bethany, near the mountain
that is called *the Mountain* of Olives, He sent
two of the disciples,

30 saying, "Go into the village opposite, in which
as you enter you will find a colt tied, on which
not one man has ever yet sat; loose it and
bring it.

31 "And if anyone asks you, 'Why are you loosing
it?' thus will you speak, 'The Lord has need
of it.'"

32 And those who were sent went away and found
it just as He had told them.

At last the Lord was entering the Holy City of Jerusalem, the
goal of His journeying and of His ministry. **After He had said these
things** (i.e. that the glory of the Kingdom was not imminent, but
must be preceded by the Cross, 19:11–27; compare 18:31–33), He
then made preparations to enter the City in which He would die.

As if hurrying to an appointed consummation, **He was going on before *them***, not shrinking from the inevitable collision with His foes, but striding boldly in the front of His disciples as they walked **to Jerusalem**.

It was **when He drew near to Bethphage** (a suburb of Jerusalem) **and Bethany** (a village outside of Bethphage, just one mile or so from Jerusalem) that He made His final preparations to enter the City in triumph. Staying the night in Bethany (at the home of Lazarus; see John 12:1), **He sent two of the disciples** to Bethphage to find the animal that He had prearranged to be ready for Him.

This was the way in which He would proclaim to the Holy City that He was the Messiah—and reveal what kind of Messiah He was. For He would not come into the City riding upon a warhorse, as if He were a military Messiah. Rather, He would come in lowliness and in peace. Moreover, that it was the Holy Messiah who was to use the colt was shown by its never having been used before; **not one man had ever yet sat** upon it. (Compare Num. 19:2, which says that a heifer used for sacred service must be one that had never been used before.)

Jerusalem, however, still swarmed with His foes, who were looking for any opportunity to arrest Him. He therefore had arranged for this secretly beforehand. The animal would be tied up in the open street, so that they would find it as soon **as** they **entered** the village. This is the one they should **loose and bring** to Him. If anyone challenged them, they were to identify themselves with the password, **"The Lord has need of it."** The saying was ambiguous and a fit password in such a dangerous climate, for the words **the Lord** could be taken to refer to the animal's owner, giving the impression to listening bystanders that the owner was simply claiming his own. (We note similar precautions for secrecy taken in the choice of a place to eat the Passover meal; 22:8–13.)

ॐ ॐ ॐ ॐ ॐ

33 And while they were loosing the colt, its lords
    said to them, "Why are you loosing the colt?"
34 And they said, "The Lord has need of it."

35 And they led it to Jesus, and they threw their garments upon the colt, and mounted Jesus on *it*.

36 And while He was going, they were spreading out their garments in the way.

37 And as He was now drawing near to the descent of the Mountain of Olives, the whole multitude of the disciples began rejoicing, praising God with a great voice for all the works of power which they had seen,

38 saying, "Blessed *is* the King who comes in the Name of the Lord; peace in heaven and glory in the highest!"

39 And some of the Pharisees from the crowd said to Him, "Teacher, rebuke Your disciples!"

40 And He answered and said, "I tell you, if these keep silent, the stones will cry out!"

It all happened just as the Lord Jesus said. **While** His disciples **were loosing the colt, its lords** (that is, its owners) asked them what they were doing, and upon receiving the prearranged reply, they freely gave it to them. Thus **they led it to Jesus, and threw their garments upon the colt, and mounted Jesus on *it*.** Christ rode the last bit of distance into the City in humble triumph, visually proclaiming to all that He was Israel's Messiah and Savior. All knew what His entry meant, and the whole city went wild with enthusiasm. **They were spreading out their garments in the way** before Him, shouting loudly and **rejoicing, praising God with a great voice for all the works of power which they had seen** Jesus do. That is, all His previous miracles (including the recent raising of Lazarus; John 12:17–18) had built up His reputation as Messiah, and the people responded to what they took for His confirmation of their faith in Him. Hailing Jesus as the Messiah, they shouted, **"Blessed *is* the King who comes in the Name of the Lord,"** that is as God's regent, to do God's will and establish His Kingdom. They expected Jesus to rout the Romans and end their occupation. Thus there would be **peace in heaven**, as the angels and saints with God above smiled with contentment upon their liberated comrades on earth (their anguished cry of "How long?" being finally answered), and God would have **glory in the highest** heaven.

Some of the Pharisees were present that day, and they were indignant at such a display. They vigorously denied that Jesus was the Messiah, and claimed that it was a scandal for Him to permit such public acclamation. They bade Him therefore **rebuke** His **disciples** and tell them to stop saying such things. Jesus refused. He simply answered that, of a certainty (**I tell you**), **if these** in the crowd were to **keep silent**, then **the stones** along the way themselves **would cry out** and say the same things. As the triumphant Messiah, His coming to Jerusalem must be acclaimed, for so the Scripture had prophesied (Zech. 9:9)—if not by men, then by the normally mute and lifeless stones!

§VII.1.ii. Weeping over the City

> ॐ ॐ ॐ ॐ ॐ
>
> 41 And when He drew near, He saw the city and wept over it,
>
> 42 saying, "If you had known in this day, even you, the things that make for peace! For now they have been hidden from your eyes.
>
> 43 "For the days will come upon you, when your enemies will throw up a palisade against you, and encircle you around, and hem you in from all *sides*,
>
> 44 "and will raze you *to the ground*, you and your children within you, and they will not leave *one* stone upon *another* stone within you, because you did not know the time of your visitation."

Jesus was not misled by the demonstration into thinking that Jerusalem was about to repent of its historically hardhearted ways. Even as He **drew near** to the city and its resplendent Temple (perhaps during His descent down the Mount of Olives, when He first beheld all the city spread out before Him), **He saw** also its rebellious heart and the divine judgment it would bring, and He **wept over it**. The Lord's great heart loved the city, and He had long yearned to gather its citizens together in love and keep them safe in the Father's care (13:34). Despite the enthusiastic shouts that day, Christ knew that His mission was being misunderstood, and that they would ultimately reject Him. They **did not know the time of** their **visitation**, or recognize that God, through Jesus, was visiting them in blessing, and so they would not respond by accepting Jesus as Messiah. Despite their present acclamation, by that Friday they would disown Him to a Roman cross.

Such faith and repentance were **the things that make for peace** and were alone what could bring the favor of God. But the judgment of God had come upon them, bringing spiritual blindness as a punishment for long years of their own refusal to see, and now such things were **hidden from** their **eyes**. Having chosen blindness for so long, now they found themselves unable to see.

Such persistent rebellion (which would culminate in their rejection of Christ) made the final wrath of God inevitable. Within one generation, **the days would come upon** them **when** their **enemies**, the Romans, would **throw up a palisade against** them as part of their siege. The Roman armies would **encircle** Jerusalem **around and hem** them in **from all** *sides*, allowing no escape. In AD 70 they would **raze** the site *to the ground*, both the current generation of Jerusalemites and their **children within** the besieged city. In their ferocity the Romans would not cease until they had **not left** *one* **stone upon** *another* **stone**. Some of the children there that day would grow up to experience this tremendous outpouring of wrath. No wonder the Lord wept over their coming fate!

§VII.1.iii. Cleansing the Temple

ॐ ॐ ॐ ॐ ॐ

45 And He entered into the Temple and began to
   cast out those who were selling,

> 46 saying to them, "It is written, 'And My House
> will be a house of prayer,' but you *yourselves*
> have made it a thieves' cave."

Having entered the city in triumph, He also **entered into the Temple** to take charge of it as its true Lord. In the courts of the Gentiles (the only place there where the Gentiles from all the nations could come and pray), there had been set up another set of tables for selling doves and changing money into the only coinage allowed for Temple use. (There were markets on the nearby Mount of Olives for that purpose as well.) These tables transformed that area into an oriental bazaar, making prayer for the visiting Gentiles all but impossible. Yet God had said through Isaiah, **"My House will be a house of prayer"** (Is. 56:7), and so **those who were selling** there were in clear violation of God's written will. From being a house of prayer for those who sought God in all the world, it had been transformed into a **thieves' cave**, a place where the unrighteous huddled and hid in safety, intent on avoiding detection and punishment for their misdeeds (the reference to the thieves' cave is drawn from Jer. 7:11). Christ therefore **began to cast** them **out** and to restore the sanctity of His Father's House.

§VII.1.iv. Teaching in the Temple

> ॐ ॐ ॐ ॐ ॐ
>
> 47 And He was teaching daily in the Temple, but
> the chief-priests and the scribes and the first
> *men* of the people were seeking to destroy Him,
> 48 and they were not finding what they might do,
> for all the people were hanging on Him, hearing
> *Him.*

Having restored the Temple, Jesus began to make it His own, using it for the purpose for which it had been built—for the glory of God. He **was teaching daily in the Temple**, instructing the multitudes that flocked there during the Passover season. **All the**

people were spellbound by His teaching and **were hanging on Him**, drinking in His every word.

This enraged **the chief-priests and the scribes** who had charge of the Temple, as well as **the first *men* of the people**, the heads of the leading families. They were furious that Jesus had presumed to cast out those whom they had permitted to sell in their courts, and all the more furious that He was using the Temple to spread His teaching. They **were** thus **seeking** day after day **to destroy Him** but **were not finding what they might do**. As long as He was surrounded by enthusiastic crowds, arresting Him was out of the question, for those attempting such an arrest would be stoned or torn to pieces (compare a similar fear of the crowd should John the Baptizer be denounced; 20:6). They were forced to keep silent and to bide their time.

§VII.2. Chief Priests Challenge Jesus' Authority

§VII.2.i. Challenge of the Cleansing of the Temple

After relating how Christ's entrance into Jerusalem and His cleansing of the Temple enraged the Temple authorities (19:39, 45–48), Luke then relates a series of their challenges to Jesus' authority. The Temple authorities bitterly resented Jesus' presence there and His popularity, and they did all they could to counteract it.

ॐ ॐ ॐ ॐ ॐ

20 1   And it happened that on one of the days while He was teaching the people in the Temple and preaching *the Good News,* that the chief-priests and the scribes with the elders came up,

2   and they spoke, saying to Him, "Tell us by what authority You do these things, or who is the one who gave You this authority?"

3   And He answered and said to them, "And I *Myself* will also ask you a word, and you tell Me:

> 4 "the baptism of John—was it from Heaven or
>   from men?"
> 5 And they reasoned among themselves, saying,
>   "If we say, 'From Heaven,' He will say, 'Why
>   did you not have faith in him?'
> 6 "But if we say, 'From men,' all the people will
>   stone us down, for they are persuaded that John
>   was a prophet."
> 7 And they answered that they did not know
>   where it was from.
> 8 And Jesus said to them, "Neither will I tell you
>   by what authority I do these things."

By taking over the Temple courts and using them as the locale for His teaching without first getting their blessing, Jesus was implicitly claiming a higher authority than theirs. What *was* this authority? Was it rabbinic authority, such as teachers possessed? Was it military authority, obtained from the Romans? Was He claiming messianic authority? When Jesus first entered Jerusalem, the display of messianic fervor from the crowds (19:36–38) took Jesus' foes by surprise. Now they had regrouped and were ready with a counter-challenge.

They had prepared their challenge well. **On one of the days while He was teaching** (probably in the colonnade, on the way to give His daily teaching; compare Mark 11:27), an impressive delegation of **chief-priests** and **scribes** with **elders** accosted Him with their question. Boldly they demanded that He **tell** them **by what authority** He was **doing these things, or who** was **the one who gave** Him **this authority**. If He were to declare that His authority came from God, they would ask Him to prove it by doing a sign, and they felt sure that He would refuse this further demand, for He had consistently refused it before (Mark 8:11–12). This refusal would cause Him to lose face, and He would forfeit His right to override their authority and teach in the Temple.

They put their question to Him with great directness, confident of the result. To their surprise, however, He answered with a counter-question. If they wanted Him to answer their question, they must first answer a question of His. That seemed only fair. Then, if they answered it, He would indeed answer their question. And Jesus' question to them was simple: **The baptism of John—was it from Heaven** (that is, from God) **or from men?** Did John the Baptizer truly possess divine authority, or was he simply pretending to have an authority which God had not in fact given him? Jesus was not asking them to prove their answer, just to give their verdict.

This was a problem for Jesus' foes. Retreating from the pressing crowd around them, **they reasoned among themselves, saying, "If we say, 'From Heaven,' He will say, 'Why did you not have faith in him?'"** That answer was obviously out, for they would thereby be proving themselves to be unfit judges of divine authority. But the other possible answer, **"From men,"** was equally unacceptable. If they repudiated John as a deceiver, **all the people** around them would **stone** them **down** (Gr. *katalithazo*, a more intensive verb than *lithazo*, "to stone," indicating stoning to death), **for they were persuaded that John was a prophet**.

Emerging from their huddle, they therefore reported that **they did not know where** John's authority **was from**. (In other words, "No comment!") In saying this, they proved themselves unworthy of hearing a straight answer from Jesus. If they were not able to recognize the authority of John, they could certainly not recognize the authority of Jesus, for both came from the same source.

In posing His counter-question as a condition of answering their question, Christ was not simply extricating Himself from their trap. He was revealing their hearts and giving them the opportunity to hear the truth. If they courageously took a stand according to their own conscience, risked the wrath of the crowd, and said, "From men," that at least would be a straight answer (even if it was the wrong one). By following their consciences whatever the risk of personal injury, His foes would show themselves as men interested in truth. They would thereby prove themselves worthy of hearing the truth from Jesus. As it was, they showed themselves less interested in speaking the truth than in their own safety, and were thus unworthy of hearing the truth. The Lord refused to cast His pearls before such men (see Matt. 7:6).

§VII.2.ii. Parable of the Vineyard

ॐ ॐ ॐ ॐ ॐ

9   And He began to tell the people this parable: "A man planted a vineyard and rented it out to farmers, and left home for a considerable time.

10   "And at the *appointed* time he sent a slave to the farmers that they might give him some of the fruit of the vineyard. But the farmers beat him and sent him out empty.

11   "And he proceeded to send another slave; and that one they beat also and dishonored, and sent him out empty.

12   "And he proceeded to send a third, and this one also they wounded and cast out.

13   "And the lord of the vineyard said, 'What will I do? I will send my beloved son; perhaps this one they will respect.'

14   "But when the farmers saw him, they were reasoning with one another, saying, 'This is the heir; let us kill him that the inheritance may become ours!'

15   "And they cast him out of the vineyard and killed him. What, therefore, will the lord of the vineyard do to them?

16   "He will come and destroy these farmers and will give the vineyard to others." And when they heard *this*, they said, "May it never be!"

17   But He looked at them, and said, "What therefore is this that is written, 'The stone which the builders rejected, this has become the head of the corner'?

18   "Everyone who falls on that stone will be broken *to pieces*; but upon whomever it falls, it will crush him."

> **19 And the scribes and the chief-priests sought to lay hands upon Him that very hour, and they were afraid of the people; for they knew that He spoke this parable against them.**

The Lord **began to tell the people** around them **this parable** (perhaps as soon as He reached His destination in the Temple). It was about **a man** who **planted a vineyard and rented it out to farmers**. (St. Luke omits the details about the vineyard itself given in Mark 12:1, for these details are echoes of a similar parable in Is. 5:1–7, and Luke's Gentile readers could not be expected to pick up on such a reference.) Such situations were common enough in Galilee, with absentee landlords renting out their lands to tenant farmers. After planting his vineyard, the man **left home for a considerable time**. (Vineyards when first planted were not ready to yield crops for at least four years.)

At the *appointed* time, when the crop was ready, the man **sent a slave to the farmers that they might give him some of the fruit of the vineyard** as the agreed-upon due. To the owner's shock, the farmers **beat** the slave **and sent him out empty**. The lord of the vineyard did not instantly retaliate for such an outrage, but **proceeded to send another slave**, hoping the farmers would change their mind and give this one the required crop. But **that one they beat also and dishonored** with insults and defiance, **and sent him out empty** as well. With extraordinary patience, the owner **proceeded to send a third**. But the farmers' rebellion was increasing. This one they not only beat but **wounded**.

The lord of the vineyard was running out of options, for whatever slaves he sent would obviously fare no better than the ones already sent. After much thought, therefore, he decided to **send** his **beloved** and only **son**, thinking **perhaps this one they will respect**. Doubtless the presence of his son would command more respect than that of slaves.

It was not to be. Rather than respecting the owner's son, **when the farmers saw him, they** began **reasoning with one another,**

"This is the heir; let us kill him that the inheritance may become ours!" If they killed this one, the land would be left legally ownerless, and upon the death of the father, they would inherit it for themselves. So it was that **they cast him out of the vineyard and killed him**.

Christ's foes were doubtless horrified by this turn of events—and all the more so since, as Jews, they would catch the reference to the parable in Isaiah 5 about the rebellious leaders in Israel. In that parable, the leaders of Israel had continually rejected God's prophets, and in Jesus' parable, the chief-priests, as their successors, were now rejecting God's beloved Son, Jesus. **They knew that He spoke this parable against them**.

So it was that when Christ asked the final question, "**What, therefore, will the lord of the vineyard do to them?**" with its inevitable answer shouted from the crowd (Matt. 21:41), **"He will come and destroy these farmers and will give the vineyard to others,"** Christ's foes were aghast. They sputtered out, **"May it never be!"** for they recognized themselves in the Lord's parable and realized that Jesus had proclaimed that God would reject them as leaders over His People. (The **others** to whom the vineyard of the faithful in Israel was to be given were Christ's disciples—His Church.)

Despite His adversaries' furious opposition to His teaching, Christ did not back down. **He looked at them** intently, aiming His reply directly at them. Relentlessly Jesus sealed the application of His parable with a citation of Scripture, **"The stone which the builders rejected, this has become the head of the corner"** (Ps. 118:22). His foes were appalled at the application of such judgment against them. They thought it impossible that they could act the part of the rebels in the parable, for they were pious. Jesus had spoken this parable against them to refute their opposition to Him, but they felt they could not be wrong in this opposition. By citing Psalm 118:22, Jesus showed how David himself had prophesied that his messianic descendant would indeed be rejected by the builders and leaders in Israel. The chief-priests could indeed be wrong in their opposition to Christ, for this was exactly what the Scripture prophesied.

There were other scriptural references as well. Isaiah had spoken of a stumbling stone that many would stumble over and be broken (Is. 8:14–15), and Daniel had spoken of a stone cut from a mountain which would strike the nations of the earth and crush them to dust (Dan. 2:34–35). Building on such references, Christ promised judgment to those who would reject Him. **Everyone who falls on that** messianic **stone** would be **broken *to pieces*; upon whomever it fell, it would crush him** to dust. That is, divine judgment would be total and final to anyone who rejected Jesus as Messiah as they were doing.

At this extended reply to their question, **the scribes and the chief-priests sought to lay hands upon Him that very hour**. They would have loved to have Him arrested on the spot. They were unable to do so, however, for **they were afraid of the people**. The crowd that was prepared to stone them for a public denunciation of John was at that time not about to tolerate a public arrest of Jesus (compare Mark 14:1–2).

§VII.2.iii. Question about Taxes to Caesar

ೋ ೋ ೋ ೋ ೋ

20 And they kept *watch* on Him, and sent spies who pretended to be righteous, that they might take hold of *Him in* His word, so as to deliver Him up to the rule and authority of the governor.

21 And they asked Him, saying, "Teacher, we know that You speak and teach correctly, and You do not receive a face, but teach the way of God in truth.

22 "Is it permissible for us to pay tax to Caesar, or not?"

23 But He detected their craftiness and said to them,

24 "Show Me a denarius. Whose image and inscription does it have?" And they said, "Caesar's."

25 And He said to them, "Then render to Caesar the

> things that are Caesar's—and to God the things
> that are God's."
> 26 And they were not strong enough to take hold of
> Him in His word before the people, and marvel-
> ing at His answer, they were silent.

Later on (possibly that same day), they **sent spies who pretended to be righteous** (the word translated *pretended* is the Gr.
upokrinomai, cognate with *upokrisis*, "hypocrisy"). These were sent
that they might take hold of *Him in* His word and ensnare Him
in something He said. Their aim was not, as before, simply to have
Jesus lose face before the crowd, but **to deliver Him up to the rule
and authority of the governor**. Their aim was not to overthrow
His popularity, but to have Him arrested and handed over to the
Romans. Jesus' foes **sent spies** instead of coming themselves, for if
they came themselves, their hostile intent would be obvious from
the start. They had to send people not immediately recognizable as
Jesus' opponents who could pretend to be His followers.

They decided that the easiest trap to set was on the issue of
Roman taxation. The Romans collected tribute tax from every
Israelite, as they did from all they conquered. This tribute was thus
a sign of Rome's sovereignty over Israel and was bitterly resented
by every patriotic Jew. It seemed to many (such as the Zealots)
that to pay the tax was to give to Rome one's ultimate allegiance,
which belonged to God alone. (Indeed, the tax's introduction was
accompanied by rioting.) For the Romans, refusal to pay the tax
was equivalent to treasonous rebellion, and they were prepared to
punish to the limit any man who seemed to stir up the masses to
such rebellion.

The question Jesus' foes decided to ask was this: **"Is it permissible for us** Jews **to pay tax to Caesar, or not?"** That is, is the payment of such tribute contrary to God's Law? It was a clever trap,
for if Jesus answered, "We must pay the tax to Caesar," He would
lose popularity before the people, for all hated the tax. He would be
compared unfavorably to John, for the Baptizer, while not forbidding the payment of the tax, did stand up to the secular authorities

at the cost of his life. If, however, Jesus answered, "True piety is not consistent with paying the tax," then they had Him, for this was a treasonous utterance, and they could hand Him over to the Roman authorities.

Jesus' opponents remembered how He had evaded their last trap and were determined that He would answer this question. They prefaced their question with an elaborate bit of flattery. **"Teacher,"** they began deferentially, **"we know that You speak and teach correctly, and do not receive a face** (a rendering of the Semitic *nasa panim*, meaning "to show partiality"), **but teach the way of God in truth."** That is, Jesus did not water down the truth for the sake of partiality before the powerful, but always gave a straight answer. By giving such a preface, they made it impossible for Him to refuse to answer their question (as He did the last time; v. 8), lest He seem to be indeed showing that partiality before the powerful.

Then they asked their question, pretending to be asking a rabbi for a ruling about the Law so that they could follow that ruling. The trap was sprung.

Jesus, however, **detected their craftiness** and knew they were only asking in order to ensnare Him. He asked them to **show** Him **a denarius**, the coin with which the tribute tax was to be paid. (The tribute tax had to be paid in Roman coinage, just as the Temple tax had to be paid in Temple coinage.) Holding it up to them, He asked, **"Whose image and inscription does it have?"** They had no choice but to state the obvious: **"Caesar's,"** for it bore an image of Caesar wearing a laurel wreath and the abbreviated inscription, "Tiberius Caesar, son of the divine Augustus, Augustus." Christ handed the coin back to them, giving them His requested ruling: **"Then render to Caesar the things that are Caesar's—and to God the things that are God's."** The coin had Caesar's face and title on it, so it obviously belonged to him. If it was his, then let people give it to him! But let them take care to give him no more than his humble due. Ultimate allegiance belonged not to Caesar, but to God.

It was a staggering answer, cutting to the core of many complex spiritual and political issues in a few words. Jesus' foes had tried to **take hold of Him in His word** and ensnare Him in what He said

(v. 20), but **they were not strong enough** for that. Their calculated cleverness was no match for the wisdom of the Son of God. **Marveling at His answer**, they had no choice but to be **silent** in their defeat.

§VII.2.iv. Question about the Final Resurrection

ॐ ॐ ॐ ॐ ॐ

27 Now there came to Him some of the Sadducees (who say *there is* not to be a resurrection),

28 and they asked Him, saying, "Teacher, Moses wrote for us that if one's brother dies, having a wife, and this one is childless, his brother should take the wife and raise up seed to his brother.

29 "Therefore there were seven brothers, and the first took a wife, and died childless;

30 "And the second,

31 "And the third took her; and likewise all seven did not leave behind a child, and they *all* died.

32 "Finally the woman died also.

33 "In the resurrection, therefore, which one's wife will she become? For all seven had her *as* wife."

34 And Jesus said to them, "The sons of this age marry and are given in marriage,

35 "but those who are *judged*-worthy to attain to that age and the resurrection from the dead neither marry nor are given in marriage;

36 "for neither are they able any longer to die, for they are equal-to-angels and are sons of God, being sons of the resurrection.

37 "But that the dead are raised, even Moses reported in *the passage* about the bush, where he calls the Lord the God of Abraham, and the God of Isaac, and the God of Jacob.

38 "Now He is not the God of the dead, but of the living, for all live to Him."

39 And some of the scribes answered and said,
"Teacher, You have spoken well."
40 For no longer were they daring to ask Him
anything.

The next challenge came from **the Sadducees**. These were a sect
consisting of the high priestly family and other leading aristocratic
families in Jerusalem. They were known to disagree with the Pharisees
in that they held that ***there is* not to be a** final **resurrection** of the
dead. They believed that the dead no longer existed in such a way
as to be reunited with their bodies and raised up at the Last Day.
They also did not acknowledge the present supernatural ministries
of angels (Acts 23:8). Further, they recognized only the five books
of Moses as true Scripture, rejecting the other books of the Hebrew
Scriptures as merely human invention.

The Sadducees also approached Jesus with feigned deference,
calling Him **Teacher** and asking Him to give a rabbinical ruling on
a point of Law. They proposed a scenario based on the Law of **Moses**
which said that **if one's brother dies, having a wife, and this one
is childless, his brother should take the wife** as his own **and raise
up seed** or children **to his brother**. The law is found in Deuteronomy 25:5f and is motivated by a desire to have a man's ancestral
inheritance stay with his family. The children of the union therefore
would be legally the children of the dead man and would inherit
his property, thus preserving the name of the family within Israel.

Given this law, the Sadducees present the following situation:
**There were seven brothers, and the first took a wife, and died
childless**. In conformity to the Law, **the second** brother then married the widow, but he also died childless. He was followed by **the
third**, and likewise, at length, **all seven**. All married the woman in
turn, but **did not leave behind a child** before dying. **Finally the
woman died also**. It was apparent by now that this was not based
on a real-life situation, but upon literary precedents (such as the
story in Tobit 3:8, where seven men married the same woman one
after another). Then came the Sadducees' question: **In the resurrection, therefore, which one's wife will she become?** Polyandry (or

having the woman shared by seven husbands) was obviously out of the question. Which of the seven should be chosen as her husband (with all the conjugal rights this presupposed) in the age to come?— **for all seven had her *as* wife**.

It was not a frivolous question, nor one aimed simply at stumping Jesus so that He could not reply. Rather, it was an attempt to show the incompatibility of a belief in the final resurrection with the world presupposed by the Mosaic Law. For (they argued) if one tried to combine that Mosaic worldview with a belief in the final resurrection, then such insoluble and absurd situations as this arose. One could not sensibly apply the Law to situations envisaged by the world of the resurrection. Therefore, since the Law was divine, *that world of the resurrection did not exist*. The Sadducees were trying to show that the world presupposed by the Law was a naturalistic one, not a supernaturalistic one, with its beliefs in the resurrection.

Jesus answered their question by revealing that the world of resurrection, the age to come, is radically unlike this world and age. **The sons of this age marry and are given in marriage**; they begin families and raise them, with all the conjugal exclusivity implied by that. But such social institutions as marriage and procreation are to pass away and have no place in the age to come. **Those who are *judged*-worthy to attain to that age** to come **and the resurrection from the dead neither marry nor are given in marriage**. Marriage and procreation are necessary to repopulate the earth during this age when people die. But in the age to come, there will be no death, and the saved can **die** no more. **They are equal-to-angels** (Gr. *isaggelos*), being immortal and deathless, engaged continually in the ceaseless adoration of God. Like the angels, they are counted **sons of God** (compare Job 1:6; 38:7), sharing His immortal deathlessness, since the saved are **sons of the resurrection**.

Christ had yet more teaching for the Sadducees. He wanted them to know **that the dead are raised** and to be certain of it as revealed in the Scriptures. He could not appeal to such Scripture passages as Daniel 12 (which spoke clearly of the resurrection), for the Sadducees did not recognize the Book of Daniel to be Holy Scripture. Only the five books of Moses were genuine Scripture as far as they were concerned.

In His mercy, Christ does not argue that they should accept the rest of the Old Testament as Scripture. Rather, He bends to their infirmity and proves His point about the resurrection from the Mosaic Law itself, which they did accept. For **even Moses reported, in *the passage* about the** burning **bush** (Exodus 3), that the dead were raised. For in that passage, Moses **calls the Lord the God of Abraham, and the God of Isaac, and the God of Jacob**. To be someone's God meant to be their protector, and God in this passage was proclaiming Himself as the protector of Abraham, Isaac, and Jacob. To be the protector of the dead is a contradiction in terms. **He is not the God of the dead**. That would be absurd and unworthy of God. Rather, He is the God **of the living**, protecting and caring for the Patriarchs still, for none are beyond His reach, but **all live to Him**. This being so, men do not perish at death to vanish from the care and purposes of God. Rather, they remain in the palm of His hand, enjoying His love, awaiting His timing—and anticipating the final resurrection.

It was another extraordinary answer, and even some of the scribes of the Pharisees (who believed passionately in the resurrection and had opposed the Sadducees on this point) admitted, **"Teacher, You have spoken well."** Never had the Sadducees been so thoroughly refuted with their own Scriptures or beaten at their own game. Seeing that Jesus was obviously equal to any challenge, **no longer were** His foes **daring to ask Him anything** or to attempt His public humiliation with their traps and tricks.

§VII.2.v. Jesus' Reply about the Son of David

ॐ ॐ ॐ ॐ ॐ

41 And He said to them, "How is it that they say the Christ is *the* son of David?

42 "For David himself says in the Book of Psalms,

> 'The Lord said to my lord, "Sit at My right
> hand,
> 43 ""until I put Your enemies as a footstool for
> Your feet."'
> 44 "David therefore calls him 'lord,' and how is
> He his son?"

After Jesus had dealt with all the challenges from His opponents, He came forward with a challenge of His own. **"How is it that** men **say the Christ is *the* son of David?"** He asked. What Christ was objecting to was not the Davidic lineage of the Messiah. The title meant more than simply that. As it was used then, it implied that Messiah was to be a military hero as David had been—a revolutionary like David, one who would liberate Israel from the Romans. The Davidic Kingdom of God, according to this line of thinking, was to be an earthly one.

This was all wrong. The Kingdom of God was not of this world (John 18:36), but was heavenly and supernatural. The Messiah was not to be a military figure, like David, but a transcendent one.

This was apparent, Jesus said, from what **David himself says** in his own writings, **in the Book of Psalms**. There David writes, **"The Lord said to my lord, 'Sit at My right hand, until I put Your enemies as a footstool for Your feet'"** (Ps. 110:1). In this passage, the first **Lord** was God; the second **lord** whom God addressed was the Messiah. This much was uncontroversial, for all Jesus' hearers accepted this psalm as Davidic and as a prophecy of Messiah.

Then came the revelation: Jesus points out that **David calls** the Messiah **lord**, so **how is** that Messiah David's **son**? That is, David himself acknowledged that his messianic descendant (in whom the hope of the psalm would be fulfilled) was superior to himself, and so far above David that David addresses Him as his **lord**. Obviously that Messiah could not be derivative from David, but must be greatly beyond him. What Christ was rebuking here was a *politicized understanding* of the Messiah. Messiah was no revolutionary hero. He was no chip off the old Davidic block. Messiah was a heavenly Lord and His Kingdom a heavenly Kingdom.

§VII.2.vi. Jesus' Denunciation of the Scribes

> ॐ ॐ ॐ ॐ ॐ
>
> 45 And while all the people were hearing, He said to the disciples,
> 46 "Beware of the scribes, who want to walk *about* in robes, and love greetings in the marketplaces, and first-seats in the synagogues, and first-places at suppers,
> 47 "who eat up widows' houses and for pretense pray long; these will receive more judgment."

Luke then relates other things Christ publicly taught during that week, mentioning the bad example of the scribes and the good example of the poor widow.

Christ warned His **disciples**, those who looked to Jesus for guidance, to **beware of the scribes** and to avoid their hypocritical ways, for their pride was dangerous to any real spirituality. The scribes of the Pharisees liked to **walk *about* in robes**. These robes were not liturgical vestments (only priests of the Temple could wear those), but rather the clothes one would normally wear for outdoor daily living. The scribes made a point of wearing long flowing white robes (white clothes were a mark of distinction) in order to stress their high social rank. Also, they **loved** respectful **greetings** as they passed through **the marketplace**, delighting as people stood up and bowed to them, addressing them as "Rabbi," "my Master," "my Father."

Further, they coveted **first-seats in the synagogues**, up at the front and facing the people, where all could admire their importance. At **suppers** and banquets also, they loved to occupy the **first-places** as their right (for one's seat at such meals was allotted according to one's relative importance).

Thus, pride suffused all their social actions, and it was this pride that Jesus rebuked. The mere wearing of long robes or being greeted respectfully or occupying a head table was not the problem. The problem was the scribes' proud delight in and insistence on these outward marks of honor.

For although they gave out that they were better than others, this outward show masked an interior greed and vanity. They would **eat up widows' houses**, sponging off pious widows until all their resources were gone. They would **pray long** in public all **for pretense** and to convince others of how holy they were. True holiness, rooted in compassion for the poor and in humility, was far from them, and on the Last Day, they would **receive more judgment** than others, a greater condemnation. The scribes might offer themselves to the people as models of piety, but let the people beware!

§VII.2.vii. Jesus' Commendation of the Widow

ॐ ॐ ॐ ॐ ॐ

21 1 And He looked up and saw the rich casting their gifts into the treasury.

2 And He saw a certain needy widow casting in two leptas.

3 And He said, "Truly I say to you, this poor widow cast in more than all;

4 "for they all cast into the gifts from their abundance, but she cast in from her lack, all her living."

Finally, Luke counterbalances Jesus' denunciation of the scribes with His commendation of the poor widow. In the outer Court of the Women (so-called because it was accessible to all Jews, including the women), there were thirteen trumpet-shaped receptacles placed against the wall. It was into these that the people would place their gifts. When Jesus **looked up**, He **saw the rich casting their gifts into the treasury** (doubtless with a great flourish). He also **saw a certain needy widow casting in two leptas**. A *lepta* was the smallest coin then used, and its value was 1/128 of a denarius. Since a denarius was a day's wage for the working man, the two *leptas* were a small offering indeed. Many present might have thought nothing of her gift, saving their acclaim for the largest gifts put in by the rich.

But God does not value as men value, for He sees the intents of the heart. Jesus recognized and assured His disciples (saying **truly I say to you**) that **this poor widow cast in more than all** the others. The others **cast into the gifts from their abundance**; they could well afford the contributions they made. This widow cast in all her living, all that she had to survive on. Having two *leptas*, she could have cast in only one and kept back the last one for herself—but she did not. In her devotion to God, she put in every bit she had. And in those days, when widows had no social assistance to fall back on, such giving was piously reckless indeed. This was the example Jesus held up to His disciples to be imitated—the total devotion to God that sacrifices everything out of love for Him and trusts Him for daily bread. Here was love for God and true faith.

§VII.3. The Olivet Discourse

ॐ ॐ ॐ ॐ ॐ

5   And as some were talking about the Temple, that it was adorned with beautiful stones and votive-offerings, He said,

6   "These things which you are observing—the days will come in which there will not be left *one* stone upon *another* stone which will not be torn down."

7   And they asked Him, saying, "Teacher, when therefore will these things be? And what *is* the sign when these things are about to happen?"

As the culmination of His ministry in Jerusalem, Christ predicts the city's desolation as the fulfillment of the long-awaited and prophesied wrath of God (21:22). The prophetic discourse is occasioned by remarks of His disciples. It was as He and His disciples were leaving the Temple site that they were enthusing to Him about the glory of the buildings, and about how it **was adorned with beautiful stones and votive-offerings**. Well they might enthuse, for the Temple site was one of the wonders of the ancient world. The Temple itself was made of huge white stones, each about 25 cubits long, 8 cubits high, and 12 cubits wide. (A cubit was about 18 inches.) It was also covered with gold plates, so that it shone with blinding brilliance in the sun.

Jesus, however, could see beneath its outward glory to the diseased pride which lurked hidden in its heart, and He knew that such pride would inevitably result in their rejection of Him and in the final judgment of God. He responded to His disciples' enthusiasm by saying, **"These things which you are observing** with such excitement—**the days will come in which there will not be left *one* stone upon *another* stone which will not be torn down."**

The disciples were stunned at this response, and as they left the Temple site and went eastward across the Kidron Valley (Mark 13:3), they thought of what His words could mean. As Jews, they had assumed that the Temple of God would endure to the end of the world. It seemed to them therefore as if Jesus might be speaking about the end of the world, and at last **they asked Him, saying, "Teacher, when therefore will these things be? And what *is* the sign when these things are about to happen?"** (Luke omits the detail present in Mark 13:3 that the question was asked privately, possibly because he wants to avoid the impression of Jesus giving secret, subversive teaching; compare his report in Acts 26:26 of Paul saying that the Christian movement was not something "done in a corner.")

꒷ ꒷ ꒷ ꒷ ꒷

8 And He said, "Watch out that you are not deceived; for many will come in My Name, saying, 'I am *He*,' and 'The *appointed* time has drawn near'; do not go after them.

9 "And when you hear of wars and tumults, do not be alarmed, for it is necessary that these things happen first, but the end is not immediately."

10 Then He was saying to them, "Nation will be raised against nation, and kingdom against kingdom,

11 "and there will be great earthquakes, and in

> *various* places pestilences and famines, and
> there will be terrors and great signs from heaven.

In response, Jesus is concerned both to answer their question about the destruction of the Temple (for that was what was meant by "these things"), and also to warn them about the end of the world (which they wrongly assumed would coincide with the destruction of the Temple).

He begins by telling them to **watch out** that they **are not deceived** by the events that will soon take place. **Many** will **come** in Christ's **Name**, false Christs who will arise, claiming messianic authority. They will promise that **the *appointed* time** for divine deliverance for the city has **drawn near**. They are not truly from God, and none should **go after them**, trusting that God will spare the city. The disciples will **hear of wars and** riotous **tumults**, as all worldly stability seems to be collapsing around them. Surely these will be signs of the approaching end of the world! Yet it is not so, and they should **not be alarmed** by those wars and tumults. It is **necessary that** they **happen first,** for God has so decreed it, but **the end** of the world is **not immediately** to follow.

Indeed **nation** will **be raised** by God **against nation** (note the passive voice, indicating that these events come by the hand of God), and even **kingdom against kingdom**, as wars spread throughout the world. There will be **great earthquakes, and in *various* places** throughout the earth **pestilences and famines**. There will be **terrors** and other **great signs from heaven** (Josephus, writing about that time, mentions a comet appearing for a long time over the city in the form of a sword). All of these may seem to herald the end of the world, but it is not to be so.

ॐ ॐ ॐ ॐ ॐ

12 "But before all these things they will lay their hands on you and will persecute you, delivering you to the synagogues and prisons, bringing you before kings and governors for My Name's sake.

13 "It will turn to *an opportunity* for you to witness.
14 "Therefore set your hearts not to study-beforehand to defend *yourselves*;
15 "For I *Myself* will give you a mouth and a wisdom which all who oppose you will not be able to withstand or contradict.
16 "But you will be delivered up even by parents and brothers and relatives and friends, and they will put *some* of you to death,
17 "And you will be hated by all because of My Name.
18 "Yet a hair from your head will never perish.
19 "By your perseverance you will acquire your souls.

There will be other things to cause the disciples to think that the end is soon at hand. **Before all these** other **things**, their foes **will lay their hands** upon the disciples **and will persecute** them, **delivering** them **to the synagogues and prisons**. In the decades following the crucifixion, their fellow Jews will persecute them for being disciples of Jesus, bringing them to trial for heresy in their local courts, and beating them with the customary thirty-nine lashes for their stubbornness (compare 2 Cor 11:24). They will even **bring** them **before kings and governors** because they confess the **Name** of Jesus, as St. Paul was later brought.

This will **turn to *an opportunity*** for them **to witness** to their faith, so they should not fear. A fearful person might think himself abandoned by God and use the time in prison to **study-beforehand** how **to defend** himself, getting the best legal counsel available. But they should not worry, but **set** their **hearts** at rest and rely on God's ever-present help. For it will be Jesus Himself (the **I** is emphatic in the Greek) who will **give** them **a mouth and a wisdom** that **all who oppose** them will **not be able to withstand or contradict**. Jesus will make them true prophets in that hour and use them to proclaim His Word.

This does not mean that they will be reprieved or that they will not suffer. Indeed, they will **be delivered up even by parents and brothers and relatives and friends**. Their closest and dearest, those on whom they can normally depend for help in desperate situations, will turn against them and denounce them to the authorities. In this time of testing, some of the disciples will be **put to death**, and all of the disciples **will be hated by all** the world **because** they are loyal to Jesus' **Name**. They should not fear, though, for a single **hair from** their **head** will **never** ultimately **perish**. God is with them to preserve them intact throughout their time of trial, and He will bring them safely into the Kingdom. They must persevere in their faith, for it is **by** that **perseverance** that they will **acquire** their **souls** and win life in the age to come.

꒛ ꒛ ꒛ ꒛ ꒛

20 "But when you see Jerusalem encircled by armies, then know that her desolation has drawn near.
21 "Then let those who are in Judea flee to the mountains, and let those who are in the midst of her go out from *her*, and let not those who are in the country enter into her;
22 "for these are days of avenging, that all things written may be fulfilled.
23 "Woe to those having *a child* in the womb, and to those nursing *babes* in those days, for there will be great distress upon the land and wrath to this people,
24 "and they will fall by the mouth of the sword and will be led captive into all the nations, and Jerusalem will be trampled by the nations until the *appointed* times of the nations be fulfilled.

The Lord then answers their original question about when the destruction of the Temple will occur and what will be the sign when it is about to occur (v. 7). In Matthew's and Mark's versions of this section, Jesus speaks of the abomination of desolation standing where it ought not to, in the holy place (Mark 13:13; Matt. 24:15). Such words would have been incomprehensible to Luke's Gentile audience, and so he paraphrases Christ's words, explaining that Jesus was referring to **Jerusalem** (the holy city and its sacred environs) being **encircled by armies**. This is the sign the disciples have requested to know, which shows that **her desolation** and judgment from God have **drawn near**. It is the sign that Jerusalem, having been abandoned and left defenseless by God, is about to fall. **Those who are in** the surrounding area of **Judea** should **flee to the mountains** around for safety (and not into the city, as was customary during siege); **those who are in the midst** of the city should **go out from her**. **Those who are in the country** area around her should **not enter into her**, thinking the city is a place of refuge.

For there is to be no refuge within her, **for these** will be **days of** divine **avenging** of all the blood of the prophets shed from the foundation of the world (11:50). It was written in the Scriptures that God would avenge such rebellion (e.g. Deut. 28:49–68), and **all** that is **written** will at last **be fulfilled**.

Christ therefore has no choice but to pronounce **woe** upon **those having *a child*** in **the womb in those days** of siege and terror, and upon **those nursing *babes***, for such will be unable to run far enough to escape. And such flight will be the only way out, for there will be **great distress** and calamity **upon the** whole **land** and **wrath to** all **this people**. To remain is to fall to defeat.

Many false prophets will arise to predict what all Jews hope for in their hearts—that God will defend Zion in the end, and that the Holy City of Jerusalem will remain inviolable, with no strangers passing through her any more (see Joel 3:17). Such hopes are false. The people will **fall** as **the mouth of the sword** devours them and will **be led captive into all the nations**. **Jerusalem** will not know the glory and international sovereignty she hopes for. She will be the tail, not the head (Deut. 28:44–45). She will not be honored by the nations, but will **be trampled by the nations** and treated with contempt **until the *appointed* times of the nations are fulfilled**, and the kingdom of this world becomes the kingdom of God and of His Christ (Rev. 11:15).

Christ's words found their terrible fulfillment in the decades after He uttered them. In the days leading up to AD 70, there were indeed wars and earthquakes and famines. Jewish nationalism became more intense and apocalyptic, as many false prophets arose to predict Zion's future victory and the coming of the messianic age. Persecution of Jewish Christians raged in Palestine, and some were put to death.

Then in October of AD 66, the Roman armies of Cestius Gallus marched against Zion and encircled her. The Christians there remembered Christ's words and fled to the mountain city of Pella. In AD 70, the Roman armies returned under Titus and laid siege to Jerusalem again. The city put up a valiant fight, even though starvation reduced them to cannibalism. Finally the city fell, and the Temple was burned to the ground, with scarcely one stone left upon another. Its inhabitants were butchered, and those who were left were led captive into all nations. That generation was indeed to see days of avenging and of great distress upon the land. (The story of Jerusalem's fall and the Christians' escape is told by Eusebius in his fourth-century work, *History of the Church*, 5.5–8.)

> ৡ৸ ৡ৸ ৡ৸ ৡ৸ ৡ৸
>
> 25 "And there will be signs in sun and moon and stars, and upon the earth anguish of nations, in perplexity at the noise of the sea and the waves,
> 26 "men stopping-breathing from fear and the expectation of the things coming upon the world, for the powers of the heavens will be shaken.
> 27 "And then they will see the Son of Man coming in a cloud with power and much glory.
> 28 "But when these things begin to happen, unbend *yourselves* and lift up your heads, because your redemption draws near."

Finally, the Lord teaches about the end of the world, about which they had asked, thinking that it would accompany the destruction of the Temple. After the tribulation of the days of that age, when the appointed times of the nations are finally over, there will be **signs in**

sun and moon and stars, the sun darkening, the moon not giving its light, and the stars falling from the sky (compare Matt. 24:29). And under the heaven, there will be **upon the earth anguish of nations**, as all tremble **in perplexity**, at a loss to understand **the** roaring **noise of the sea and** its ever-rising **waves**. All fear the rising tumult of the sea will engulf them.

The **powers of the heavens will be shaken**, as the orderly fabric of the cosmos seems to be coming unhinged. Christ does not describe further the terror of those days, but simply says that brave men will be **stopping-breathing** (Gr. *apopsucho*, either fainting from lack of breath or dying) **from fear and the expectation of the things coming upon the world**. We are left to imagine the terrors of those days, as the natural world turns unnatural. Such an apocalyptic picture is well-painted by chapters in the Book of Revelation.

The terror of those days will not last for long. For **then they will see the Son of Man coming in a cloud with power and much glory**. The **cloud** speaks of Christ's heavenly descent as He comes with all the glory of God (compare the cloud as an image of heavenly glory in Dan. 7:13). Christ does not elaborate on this Second and glorious Coming, for the reality will transcend all words. St. Peter speaks of that day as a time when "the heavens will pass away with a roar and the elements will be destroyed with intense heat" (2 Pet. 3:10), indicating that all the images we may use will pale before the power of the actual event.

The important thing, **when these things begin to happen** and when the world cowers and is bent double in fear, is for His disciples to **unbend** themselves and straighten up. They have nothing to fear. They should **lift up** their **heads** in joyful anticipation, **for** their **redemption draws near**. All throughout this long age, they have suffered the rigors of slavery (compare Rom. 8:23), but the moment of liberation is at hand!

ॐ ॐ ॐ ॐ ॐ

29 And He told a parable to them: "Behold the fig tree and all the trees!

> 30 "When they put out *leaves* already, you see *it* and know for yourselves that already summer is *now* near.
> 31 "Thus you *yourselves* also, when you see these things occurring, know that the Kingdom of God is near.

To encourage His disciples not to faint with fear during those final days before the end, Christ **tells a parable to them**. They should **behold the fig tree and all the trees**. They can all remember how the fig tree stands out from those trees in particular with its bare branches throughout the winter. It **puts out** its *leaves* later than the other trees and is thus a sign that **summer** is *now* **near**. In the same way, when the disciples **see these things occurring** (i.e. the powers of the heaven being shaken, vv. 25–26), they can similarly **know that the Kingdom of God is near**. The world will be trembling with terror, expecting worse things to come, but the disciples, seeing the example of the fig tree, should expect the good things of the coming Kingdom.

> ॐ ॐ ॐ ॐ ॐ
> 32 "Amen I say to you, this generation will by no means pass away until all things occur.
> 33 "Heaven and earth will pass away, but My words will never pass away.

As the Lord concludes His discourse, He adds a word about the certainty of His predictions. He promises that **this generation** (the adulterous generation then living and resisting Him— compare the use of the term in 7:31; 9:41; 11:29–32, 50–51) **will by no means pass away** (the negative is emphatic) **until all things occur**. That is, the entire sequence of events Jesus has described will begin to happen before that generation has died out. This is not to say that all those things, including the Second Coming, will *occur* within that generation—indeed, much of the Lord's teaching here is aimed against the idea that the end is imminent (e.g. vv. 8–9). The concern here is not with *timing*, but with *certainty*: Christ says here that they will not have to wait for proof of the certainty of His words, for their fulfillment will begin within that generation.

The Lord's words proved true, for He spoke these words on Mount Olivet no later than AD 33, and within one generation, Jerusalem lay in ruins. His words were not the words of men, but of God, and would therefore abide forever. **Heaven and earth will** one day **pass away, but** His **words will never pass away**. They remain forever and will find their speedy fulfillment.

ॐ ॐ ॐ ॐ ॐ

34 "Pay attention to yourselves, lest your hearts be burdened with dissipation and drunkenness and the worries of life, and that day come on you suddenly like a snare;

35 "for it will come upon all those sitting on the face of all the earth.

36 "But keep awake at all times, beseeching that you may have strength to flee away from all these things that are about to happen and to stand before the Son of Man."

Luke ends the discourse with Christ's warning. The words of the Lord were not given so that men could speculate with their heads, but so they might keep purity in their hearts. The final and practical outcome is therefore ethical and is manifested in how the Christian lives daily life. Throughout this age there will be spiritual stress (compare 2 Tim. 3:1–5) as the world, the flesh, and the devil conspire to separate us from life in the Lord. This will be increasingly so as this age reaches its climax before the Coming of the Lord.

The disciples must therefore **pay attention** to themselves and take care not to let the world squeeze them into its mold. If their **hearts** are **burdened** with sins such as **dissipation and drunkenness** as an attempted escape from **the worries of life**, then **that**

day of judgment will **come** on them **suddenly like a snare**. That is, it will catch them unawares, and there will be no time for saving repentance. They must not think they can relax their guard and still be safe, for the day of judgment **will come upon all those sitting on the face of all the earth**, revealing the state of every man's heart and how well he endured the final temptations. One may flee from the judgment overtaking Jerusalem, but not from this judgment! This will overtake all the children of men, wherever they live.

The word rendered *dissipation* is the Greek *kraipale*, and it means both intoxicated carousing and the hangover that follows it; thus it comes to mean dizziness, staggering, when the head refuses to function. The warning here is not simply a warning against the sin of drunkenness, but also against a spiritual thoughtlessness and hedonism, an attitude that seeks to lose itself in mindless and numbing pleasure.

Because of the increasing challenges of this age, Christ commands His disciples to **keep awake at all times**. The word translated *keep awake* is the Greek *agrupneo*, cognate with the word *agrupnia* in 2 Corinthians 6:5, "sleepless nights, vigils." The thought here is that Christ's disciples must never doze off spiritually, for there is no time during which danger will sleep. Instead, they must **beseech** God continually that they may **have strength to flee away from all these things** and **to stand before the Son of Man**.

To **flee away** (Gr. *ekpheugo*) from all the challenges and trials does not mean to avoid them or not experience them. Rather, it means to emerge from them and from the arena of trial unscathed, standing blameless before the judgment of the Son of Man. St. Paul uses the word *ekpheugo* in this way in 1 Thessalonians 5:3, saying that those spiritually unprepared for the Coming will find sudden ruin and "will not flee away." The word is used in the same way in Hebrews 2:3; 12:25, warning that apostates will not be able to "flee away" from God's judgment. We should not expect immunity from challenges and temptations. If God did not spare His Son sufferings and trials, He will not spare us! We are to beseech God, not for immunity from trials, but rather for strength to endure them blamelessly.

§VII.4. Summary of Jesus' Jerusalem Ministry

ॐ ॐ ॐ ॐ ॐ

37 Now *during* the days He was teaching in the Temple, but *during* the nights He would go out and stay on the mountain that is called *the Mountain* of Olives.

38 And all the people would get up early *to come* to Him in the Temple to hear Him.

Luke concludes His account of Jesus' ministry in Jerusalem with a summary of how He spent His time. **During the days, He was teaching in the Temple, but *during* the nights He would go out** from the sacred precincts and **stay on *the Mountain* of Olives**.

It would seem as if this **stay** on Mount Olivet refers not to Jesus' spending the night (though some Passover pilgrims did encamp in the open). Jesus' friends Mary, Martha, and Lazarus lived in nearby Bethany, and it would seem that this was where He slept during this final week in Jerusalem (see Mark 11:11; Matt. 21:17). Certainly the City itself, swarming with His enemies intent on arresting Him, would be too dangerous to overnight in, especially if He slept defenselessly out in the open.

Rather, it seems that Luke means by this that Jesus would resort to the Mountain of Olives for prayer every night, praying in the garden there. Luke mentions this detail now to prepare for the future detail in 22:39, saying that Judas knew that Jesus could be found on Mount Olivet on the night that He was arrested, for that was where He went every night to pray.

๛ VIII ๛

THE PASSION
(22:1—23:56)

§VIII.1. Judas' Plan to Betray Jesus

๛ ๛ ๛ ๛ ๛

22 1   Now the Feast of the Unleavened *Bread*, which is called the Passover, was drawing near.

2   And the chief-priests and the scribes were seeking how they might destroy Him, for they were afraid of the people.

3   And Satan entered into Judas who was called Iscariot, being of the number of the Twelve.

4   And he went away and spoke with the chief-priests and captains how he might deliver Him up to them.

5   And they rejoiced and agreed to give him money.

6   And he consented and was seeking an opportunity to deliver Him up to them apart from the crowd.

Luke next relates Judas' plan to betray Jesus. (St. Luke omits the account of the anointing at Bethany which is found in Mark 14:1–11, since he has already recorded a similar anointing earlier in Jesus' ministry in 7:36–50.) Here he simply relates Judas' intention to betray Jesus into the hands of His enemies around the time when the Feast of the Unleavened Bread was **drawing near** (popularly called **the Passover** by the Jews, because the Passover meal began the week-long feast; Deut. 16:1–8).

All the time that Jesus was in Jerusalem, **the chief-priests and the scribes** were furious at Him over His teaching in the Temple, and all the more so since they were consistently unable to refute Him. They were therefore **seeking how they might destroy Him**. That is, they could not simply have Him arrested, for **they were afraid of the people** and of the riot Jesus' arrest would cause. Accordingly, they were on the lookout for some way to seize Him when He was out of the public eye.

Such an opportunity came with the defection of one of the inner circle, **of the number of the Twelve.** Judas in his heart had long been alienated from his Lord (see John 6:70). Nothing so inflames hatred like the necessity of keeping it secret and of having to cover it with an outer cloak of insincere love. Judas' inner hostility to Jesus at last reached its peak (Christ's rebuke of him in favor of the woman of Bethany was the last straw; Mark 14:1f; John 12:1f), and he decided to side with Jesus' foes. Luke, alive to the forces of spiritual conflict behind the scenes (compare 4:13; 22:31); stresses that Judas' defection was also the result of **Satan entering into** him.

Having succumbed to darkness, Judas **went away** from his apostolic companions and secretly **spoke with the chief-priests and captains** (that is, the Temple police, the ones who would do the arresting), **how he might deliver** Jesus **up to them. They rejoiced** at this unexpected defection, which alone made His arrest possible, and **agreed to give him money**. Luke mentions the financial aspect of their agreement to show how low were Judas' motives. He was not acting out of loyalty to any great principle, but out of envy and greed, like the lowest of traitors. Having made his bargain, Judas from then on was **seeking an opportunity to deliver Him up to them apart from the crowd**. He would not have long to wait.

§VIII.2. The Last Supper

ॐ ॐ ॐ ॐ ॐ

7   Then the day of Unleavened *Bread* came, on
    which it was necessary to sacrifice the Passover.

8   And He sent Peter and John, saying, "Go and

> prepare the Passover for us, that we may eat *it*."
>
> 9 And they said to Him, "Where do You want *us* to prepare *it*?"
>
> 10 And He said to them, "Behold, when you have entered into the city, a man will meet you bearing a jar of water; follow him into the house into which he enters.
>
> 11 "And you will say to the house-master, 'The Teacher says to you, "Where is the lodging-room where I may eat the Passover with My disciples?"'
>
> 12 "And that one will show you a large upper room spread; prepare *it* there."
>
> 13 And they departed and found *it* just as He had told them; and they prepared the Passover.

Having narrated Judas' secret meeting in the early part of Christ's final week, St. Luke then leaps ahead to narrate Christ's Last Supper with His disciples, the night in which He was actually betrayed. The final **day of Unleavened *Bread* came**, when the priests of the Temple would **sacrifice the Passover** (i.e. the Passover lamb). As devout Jews, Jesus and His disciples would have a lamb offered and would eat the Passover meal within the confines of the Holy City. This arrangement would have to be handled carefully, for the city was swarming with Jesus' foes, who were anxious to arrest Him secretly. While overnighting with His friends in Bethany, He was safe (Mark 11:11), but His Passover meal in Jerusalem must be taken in secrecy, with its location unknown to His foes.

So it was that the advance arrangements were carefully made. A brave resident in Jerusalem (perhaps the Mary mentioned in Acts 12:12) offered secret hospitality to the Galilean, and the disciples were sent to check the arrangements. Christ **sent Peter and John** for this purpose. They were told that **when** they **had entered the city, a man** would **meet** them, **bearing a jar of water**. This was unusual, for water jars were usually carried by women, and so the carrying of a water jar by a man could function as the prearranged sign. They should **follow him into the house into which he enters**, for that was the place. (It seems that when these arrangements were first made, the place had not yet been chosen.) The disciples should **say to the house-master, "The Teacher says to you, 'Where is the lodging-room where I may eat the Passover with My disciples?'"** At this prearranged word, he would recognize them as sent by Jesus and would **show** them **a large upper room spread** with rugs and cushions. Peter and John should **prepare** the meal **there**, by arranging for the lamb, unleavened bread, wine, and other Passover dishes. So it was that **they departed and found *it* just as** Jesus **had told them**.

We note that the prearranged password exchange of verse 11 contains no names; no spying adversary of Jesus overhearing the conversation would be able to learn of Jesus' Passover whereabouts and inform the chief-priests and the scribes. (For this reason also the disciples were to wordlessly follow the man bearing the water jar.) We note too that none of the Twelve knew of the location in advance. Doubtless the Lord took this last precaution to conceal the location from Judas until the last moment, thus preventing him from having Him arrested before His final meal with His own. That final meal was of crucial importance to the future saving purposes of God for His People, for at it the Eucharist was to be instituted.

ॐ ॐ ॐ ॐ ॐ

14 And when the hour had come, He reclined, and the apostles with Him.

15 And He said to them, "I have desired with desire to eat this Passover with you before I suffer,

16 "for I say to you, I will never eat it until it is fulfilled in the Kingdom of God."

17 And when He had received a cup and given thanks, He said, "Take this and divide *it* up among yourselves;

18 "for I say to you, I will not drink from the fruit of the vine from now on until the Kingdom of God comes."

When the hour for the Paschal meal **had come**, Jesus **reclined** at the table for the meal, **and the apostles** with Him. (Luke's reference to the Twelve as **the apostles** reveals that the following events have definitive significance for the apostolic Church.) Christ began the evening by assuring them that He had greatly **desired** (literally, **desired with desire**, a construction found in the Greek Septuagint; e.g. Gen. 31:30) **to eat this Passover with** them **before** He **suffered**, for this was the last time of joy and fellowship He would ever share with them on earth. When next He would feast with them, it would be when the Passover joy found its **fulfillment in the Kingdom of God**. The Cross was very close. And the meal was not valued simply for sentimental reasons. Rather, as mentioned above, the meal would be the setting for the Eucharist's institution, which sanctified His coming death not merely as a martyrdom, but as a saving and eternal Sacrifice.

Luke stresses Jesus' foreknowledge of His future Passion, showing that this suffering was not an involuntary defeat, but a voluntary self-sacrifice. To further underscore Jesus' foreknowledge, Luke narrates how when **He had received a cup** of wine, and **given** the customary **thanks** and ritual blessing over it, **He said, "Take this and divide** *it* **up among yourselves, for I say to you, I will not drink from the fruit of the vine from now on until the Kingdom of God comes."**

Which cup of wine was this that Jesus was forgoing? At the Passover meal, there were four cups of wine. The meal would begin with the head of the house chanting a blessing over the first cup (the "cup of *Kiddush*" or sanctification), setting apart the meal that followed as a sacred time. Each then drank that cup, and then the meal itself would be brought in. (The meal consisted of the Passover lamb, unleavened bread, bitter herbs, greens, and a dish of stewed fruit.) The host would then dip some of the bitter herbs in a sauce and hand them to each one present, as a kind of appetizer.

A second cup of wine was filled and blessed (the "cup of *Haggadah*" or storytelling), and the story of the Exodus was recounted. The first part of the Great Hallel was sung (Psalms 113–114) and the second cup drunk.

The head of the house then took the unleavened bread, chanted a blessing over it, broke the bread, and distributed it. The bitter herbs were eaten, the host dipping them into the stewed fruit dish. This began the meal proper, which went on for some time. The meal would end with the third cup of wine (the "cup of blessing"). The entire evening ended with the drinking of the fourth and final cup (the "cup of *Hallel*," or praise), over which was sung the rest of the Great Hallel, Psalms 115–118. Thus the night ended on a note of joy as devout Jews looked to the final redemption.

As we have seen before, Luke has little concern for sequential order (thus he narrates Christ's beating in 22:63–65 before he narrates His trial and condemnation in 22:66–71, although the beating almost certainly followed the condemnation, as Mark 14:64–65 and Matt. 27:65–68 say). Luke's concern is more thematic and dramatic than it is chronological.

I would therefore suggest that this cup Christ told His apostles to drink without Him was the fourth cup. It could not have been the first cup, for there was little sense in Christ's abstaining from the first cup of wine if He was going to drink the other cups (which He certainly did, for there is no sense here that He did not drink at all during the supper). It made sense, however, for Him to abstain from the fourth cup, for this was a cup of joy, and He was now setting Himself to embrace not joy, but suffering. The apostles could finish the meal with joy, but His time of sorrow had come, and He was bracing Himself for the contest. The time of joy for Him would be in **the Kingdom of God**. In verse 18 Luke places this abstinence from future drinking as a counterbalance to Christ's abstinence from future eating in verse 16. Both sayings show Christ knew the end was at hand.

We note too Luke's stress on the Kingdom of God in these verses (unique among the Gospel writers), for he reports our Lord's saying that the Passover meal (which looked forward to the redemption of Israel) was soon to be **fulfilled in the Kingdom of God** (v. 16), and also His saying that He will no longer drink wine **until the Kingdom of God comes** (v. 18). Luke is in many ways *the* theologian of the Kingdom, for he tells us not only how the Kingdom's fullness will be delayed (19:11), but also how it is experienced even now in the Church (compare his relation of Philip's preaching the good news "about the Kingdom of God," Acts 8:12). In speaking of the final hours of Christ, Luke emphasizes how the Lord's actions are bringing in the Kingdom of God. The Eucharist (to be related in vv. 20–21) is set in this Kingdom context.

> ૐ ૐ ૐ ૐ ૐ
>
> 19 And when He had taken bread and given thanks, He broke *it* and gave to them, saying, "This is My Body which is given for you; do this for My memorial."
> 20 And likewise the cup after they had supped, saying, "This cup *is* the new covenant in My Blood which is poured out for you.

St. Luke next relates the institution of the Eucharist itself. **When Jesus had taken bread** to begin the meal proper, **He broke *it* and gave to them**. This was not unusual, but was the normal way in which any meal began. What was unusual is that the Lord said as He gave it to them, **"This is My Body which is given for you; do this for My memorial."** The disciples were doubtless bewildered. What could Jesus mean? We may think that as they ate, they felt the unnamed and ominous shadow of the Cross fall on them, perhaps remembering the Lord's earlier words about eating His Flesh (John 6:51, 53–58).

The meal continued as usual, as all ate the Passover lamb and the other dishes. Then, at the end of the meal **after they supped**, at the third cup of wine, the Lord again said something unusual: **"This cup *is* the new covenant in My Blood which is poured out for you."** Once again, the significance of these words could not have been grasped then. Only later would they understand, in the light of His Sacrifice on the Cross. For this meal had prepared them to offer a memorial before God of that Sacrifice. It prepared them for what they would do ever after, so that God would remember Christ's sacrificial death and make its power present among them. By eating that bread and drinking that cup, they would eat His Body and drink His Blood, and live forever.

> ॐ ॐ ॐ ॐ ॐ
>
> 21 "But behold, the hand of the one delivering Me up *is* with Me on the table!
> 22 "For indeed, the Son of Man is going as it had been appointed; but woe to that man through whom He is delivered up!"

Luke also narrates Christ's prediction of the betrayal, saying that **the hand of the one delivering** Him **up** was **with** Him **on** that very **table. The Son of Man was going** to His death even **as it had been appointed** by God, but the fact that this had been prophesied did not excuse the treachery of the traitor. **Woe to that man through whom** the Messiah **was delivered up!**

Luke tells the story of the betrayal with great economy of words, not even narrating Judas' actual leaving of the table and going to fetch the arresting party. Though it appears from Mark and Matthew's narratives (Mark 14:17–22; Matt. 26:20–26) as well as from the narrative of John (John 13:21–31) that Judas' (secret) identification and departure happened *before* the fellowship of the meal itself began, Luke narrates it here, *after* mentioning the institution of the Eucharist. As we have seen, Luke's concern is more dramatic than chronological. Luke narrates the prophecy of Judas' betrayal at this spot to place that betrayal within the providential and saving purposes of God (and as a bridge to the quarrel of the disciples). By narrating the institution of the Eucharist first, Luke shows how God was acting to save men through the death of Christ, and using the treachery of Judas to fulfill this purpose. Once again, Christ's arrest is seen not as part of an unforeseen defeat, but as the prophesied plan of God.

> ॐ ॐ ॐ ॐ ॐ
>
> 23 And they began to debate among themselves which one of them it might be who was about to do this.

> 24 And it happened *that there was* also a conten-
> tion among them as to who of them was sup-
> posed to be greater.
> 25 And He said to them, "The kings of the Gentiles
> lord it over them; and those who have authority
> over them are called 'benefactors.'
> 26 "But with you *it is* not to be thus, but the one
> who is the greater among you, let him become
> as the youngest, and the one leading as the one
> serving.
> 27 "For who is greater, the one who reclines, or the
> one who serves? *Is it* not the one who reclines?
> But I *Myself* am in the midst of you as the one
> who serves.

The Lord's word about hidden disloyalty led to **a contention** among the disciples **as to who of them was supposed to be greater**. As they were approaching Jerusalem, they had quarreled over the places that would be assigned to them in the Kingdom (Mark 10:35–45), and the Lord had at that time told them to beware that they did not act like the Gentile rulers in their approach to author-ity. Earlier that very evening, the Lord had to once again exhort them to humility (see John 13:3–17). Now again, as they **began** to **debate among themselves which one of them it might be who was about to do this**, they fell to mutual recrimination, as fear of a hidden traitor made them distrustful and disdainful of each other.

The Lord therefore had to repeat His word about avoiding the ways of **the kings of the Gentiles**. In the godless world of the nations, such rulers would **lord it over** their subjects and heap up self-aggrandizing titles, styling themselves **benefactors** of the people. (The example of Ptolemy III of Egypt comes to mind, or that of Antiochus VII of Syria.) The concern of such men was for their own honor.

With the disciples of Jesus, however, *it is* **not to be thus**. Rather, **the one who** would prove **the greater** must take on the humble tasks of service usually assigned to **the youngest**. The **one leading**

must behave **as the one serving**. They have Him as their example.
Who is greater: the one who reclines at table to eat the meal, **or
the one who serves** him the meal? The master or the slave? Surely
the one who reclines and is served! Yet Jesus was **in the midst** of
them, all through His ministry, **as the one who serves**. Just that
night, He had risen from reclining at table and girded Himself with
a towel to wash their feet, taking the part of a slave who serves (John
13:4–5). That was the conclusive proof that to be truly great, one
must take the part of the servant. Their quarreling over who was
the greater had to stop.

> ৵৵ ৵৵ ৵৵ ৵৵ ৵৵
>
> 28 "And you *yourselves* are those who have
>   remained on with Me in My trials.
> 29 "And I *Myself* decree to you that, as My Father
>   has decreed to Me a Kingdom,
> 30 "that you may eat and drink at My table in My
>   Kingdom, and you will sit upon thrones judg-
>   ing the twelve tribes of Israel.

They need not fear—they will all be rewarded well enough. They
are the ones out of all Israel (the pronoun **you** is emphatic in the
Greek) who have **remained on with** Him **in His trials**. Many others
have proven themselves fickle, but they have stood by Him, despite
the dangers they have endured even to that present hour. Thus He
decrees to them that, **as** His **Father has decreed a Kingdom** and
glory for Him as Messiah, so they will share that glory. They will **eat
and drink at** His **table in** His **Kingdom** (that is, share His place
of honor), and will **sit upon thrones judging the twelve tribes of
Israel**, ruling under Him in the age to come.

> ৵৵ ৵৵ ৵৵ ৵৵ ৵৵
>
> 31 "Simon, Simon, behold, Satan has demanded
>   to sift you *all* as wheat.
> 32 "But I *Myself* have besought about you, that
>   your faith may not fail, and you, when once

> you have turned back, establish your brothers."
> 33 And he said to Him, "Lord, with You I am
> prepared to go both to prison and to death!"
> 34 And He said, "I say to you, Peter, the rooster
> will not sound today until you have *completely*
> denied three times that you know Me."

Before that glory, however, there will come times of trial, testing, and challenge. Addressing Peter as the leader of the group, He forewarns him of the test of suffering that is about to engulf them all. Calling him tenderly by name, **"Simon, Simon,"** Jesus reveals that **Satan has demanded** and received from God permission to **sift** them all (the **you** is plural in the Greek) as thoroughly **as wheat**. That is, Satan is going to be allowed to persecute them all, for the hour and authority of darkness are at hand (22:53). This will reveal what is in the disciples' hearts, and whether they are wheat or chaff, whether they will be faithful or will fall away.

Peter need not fear, for Jesus Himself (the **I** is emphatic) has **besought** God **about** him, that his **faith** ultimately **may not fail**. Though Peter may falter, at the end he will **turn back** to his apostleship and to faith. He must then **establish** his **brothers** and strengthen them in return. Peter's leadership among the Twelve is assumed. His lapse will not be fatal, for Christ, the Mediator between God and men, has prayed for him, and will return him again to his former position of leadership. In Christ's concern for Peter (and through Peter, for the rest of the brothers), we see Christ's abiding care for all His beloved children who stumble. Through His love, no fall need be final.

Peter, however, is indignant at the thought of failing. Still thinking himself superior to his brothers (compare Mark 14:29), he assures his **Lord** that **with** Him he is **prepared to go both to prison and** even **to death** if need be! The Lord knows, however, what is in Peter's heart. He assures Peter in reply that **the rooster will not sound** that day **until** he has *completely* **denied three times** that he even **knows** Him (the word rendered *completely deny* is the Gr. *aparneomai*, a stronger verb than *arneomai*, "to deny"). The roosters began their crowing in Palestine at this time of year about 1:00 or 2:00 A.M. Within a few short hours, Peter was to prove how little constancy he had in him.

ॐ ॐ ॐ ॐ ॐ

35 And He said to them, "When I sent you out without purse and bag and sandals, did you lack anything?" And they said, "Nothing."

36 And He said to them, "But now, let the one who has a purse take *it*, likewise also a bag, and let the one not having one sell his garment and buy a sword.

37 "For I say to you that it is necessary that this which is written be fulfilled in Me, 'And He was reckoned with the lawless ones,' for indeed that *which is* about Me has a fulfillment."

38 And they said, "Behold, Lord, here are two swords!" And He said to them, "It is sufficient."

Difficult times indeed are coming, and Christ forewarns His disciples of the dangers to come. He asks them to compare the time **when** He **sent** them **out without purse and bag and sandals** (9:1f) to the coming days. In those earlier times of mission, **did they lack anything?** They answered, **"Nothing"**—they had all they needed, being supplied by the hospitality they encountered. **But now**, things will be different. They cannot count on receiving hospitality or help but must rely solely on themselves. Persecution, not welcome, would be the order of the day. **The one who had a purse** must **take** *it* along on the journey, and **likewise also a bag**. Indeed, **the one not having one** should **sell** even his outer **garment** (a necessity for cold nights) in order to **buy a sword**. (The sword was carried by travelers for self-defense against robbers.) The point of the Lord's parabolic utterance is that His disciples must now provide for their own needs and not rely on receiving a friendly welcome.

This is inevitable, it **is necessary** that the **written** prophecy of the

Scriptures **be fulfilled** in Him, which said, **"And He was reckoned with the lawless ones"** (Is. 53:12). Israel will come to regard Jesus as a lawless apostate and a deceiver, and will crucify Him, for **indeed** everything written **about** Him **has a fulfillment**. All the Scriptures have Him as their fulfillment, goal, and end, including this final act of hostility towards Him. This hostility cannot but affect the apostles too, for if Israel persecutes Him, they will persecute His followers also (John 15:20).

On hearing of the need for a sword, the disciples (with their customary literal minds) find two such weapons and say, **"Behold, Lord, here are two swords!"** Literally speaking, two swords among eleven disciples are nothing and will be quite inadequate to defend them against actual armed attack. But Jesus was not referring to actual armed combat, but to their using their own resources in reliance on the power of God. Therefore He answers, **"It is sufficient,"** for even such small resources are sufficient if accompanied by faith in God. God can multiply a mere five loaves and make them more than adequate to feed a multitude of thousands (9:13f), and He can use the paltry resources of the apostles (imaged by the two swords) to defend them also. Let the apostles trust in God in the dark days ahead. Whatever wisdom and courage they have in them will be enough.

§VIII.3. Gethsemane on the Mount of Olives and Jesus' Arrest

ॐ ॐ ॐ ॐ ॐ

39 And He came out and went as was His custom to the Mountain of Olives, and the disciples also followed Him.

40 And when He arrived at the place, He said to them, "Pray that you may not enter into testing."

41 And He withdrew from them about a stone's throw, and bent the knees and was praying,

42 saying, "Father, if You desire *it*, remove this cup from Me; but not My will, but Yours be done."

> *43 Now an angel from heaven appeared to Him,*
> *strengthening Him.*
> *44 And being in agony, He was praying more*
> *earnestly; and His sweat became as drops of*
> *blood, falling down upon the earth.* *
> 45 And when He arose from prayer, He came to
> the disciples and found them sleeping from
> sorrow;
> 46 and said to them, "Why do you sleep? Arise
> and pray that you may not enter into testing."
>
> (*Verses 43–44 are absent from some manuscripts and are
> probably not original to Luke's Gospel.)

Luke then relates the arrest of Jesus and how **He came out** of the upper room where He ate the Paschal meal with His disciples and **went as was His custom to the Mountain of Olives**. The specific location on Mount Olivet was the garden of Gethsemane (Mark 14:32), an enclosed garden of olive trees which Jesus was in the habit of using for prayer throughout the evening (21:37). Judas, like the other apostles, was aware that this was Jesus' custom during His time in Jerusalem. He knew that Jesus would resort to this place after the Paschal supper, and so it was to this location that he summoned those who would arrest Jesus.

When Jesus **arrived at the place, He said** to the disciples, **"Pray that you may not enter into testing."** He had come to Olivet to pray and to brace Himself for the final hours of His life, but even so He did not forget His own. In the midst of His own agony, He was concerned that His disciples survive spiritually as well, and bade them pray, not for Him, but for themselves. In particular, He told them to pray that they **might not enter into testing**. The word translated *testing* is the Greek *peirasmos*, sometimes rendered "temptation." The thought here is not that they might be spared the psychological experience of temptation, but that they might emerge from the onslaught of the Enemy with their faith intact. This testing was the special work of Satan, a trial that would sift them thoroughly

(22:31). Christ wanted them to avoid being overwhelmed by the sufferings ahead, lest they entirely fall away.

He then **withdrew from them about a stone's throw** (that is, a few paces, just far enough to be by Himself) and **bent** His **knees** and began praying. This posture was significant, for the normal posture for prayer was standing. Prayer on bended knee indicated great humility and urgency. (As His prayer continued with greater fervency, Jesus further humbled Himself and fell on the ground; Mark 14:35.) The substance of His prayer (overheard by the disciples nearest to Him before they dozed off) was that if His **Father desired it**, He might **remove this cup** of suffering from Him.

It is impossible for us to know into what dark depths the Son of God descended while He prayed in the garden and while the long shadows of the coming Cross began to fall over His heart. The subjective experience of God incarnate as He wrestled with sin and death will remain forever hidden from the mere children of men. For it was not simple physical pain that was looming before Him, but also the unfathomable desolation of becoming sin for our sake and of bearing away the sins of the world (2 Cor. 5:21; John 1:29). What we can know is that He aligned His human **will** with the will of the **Father**, so that if there was no other way to redeem the world except through His drinking this proffered cup of suffering, He would still do it. Here was the path blazed for all the martyrs to follow, a relentless determination to do the will of God no matter what the cost.

In many manuscripts, there follows at this point a description of the intensity of Christ's prayer and how **an angel from heaven appeared to Him, strengthening Him** (possibly by assuring Him that such a cup was indeed the will of the Father). Knowing this to be the Father's will, He continued **praying more earnestly** that He might do it, even though **in agony** of heart. Such was the agony of heart and the corresponding intensity of prayer that **His sweat became as drops of blood falling down upon the earth**. His prayer was so great that His sweat was no mere beads running lightly down His skin, but fell thickly from Him, as drops of blood would fall. Such sweat does not simply show how hard Jesus prayed, it also foreshadows the shedding of His Blood in the hours to come.

As mentioned above, verses 48–49 are in many manuscripts, but many manuscripts omit them, and the textual evidence for omission is strong. If the verses were original to Luke, their omission would be hard to account for. (Though Epiphanius argues that the verses are original, and that they were omitted by those who were uncomfortable with the thought that Jesus seemed to need an angel, I do not find Epiphanius's argument convincing.) Some manuscripts insert the verses after Matthew 26:39. I would suggest that these verses constitute a genuine apostolic tradition about Jesus' agony in the garden, and so early found their way into this place in Luke's Gospel, but that they were not original to Luke. For this reason they are printed in italics in the above text.

After praying for Himself, Jesus **arose from prayer** and **came to the disciples and found them sleeping**. Luke adds that they were asleep **from sorrow**, worn by the stress of the past days. Christ wakes them, saying, **"Why do you sleep? Arise and pray that you may not enter into testing."** Time was limited and was better spent in praying for the coming crisis than in dozing. Let the apostles pray as they were told to do! (The disciples dozed off three times and three times were awoken by Christ. Luke, in his abbreviated account, omits this detail, which is found in Mark 14:37–41.)

ॐ   ॐ   ॐ   ॐ   ॐ

47 While He was yet speaking, behold, a crowd! And the one called Judas, one of the Twelve, was going before them; and he drew near to Jesus to kiss Him.

48 But Jesus said to him, "Judas, do you deliver up the Son of Man with a kiss?"

49 And when those who were around Him saw what was going to be, they said, "Lord, should we strike with the sword?"

50 And a certain one from them struck the slave of the chief-priest and took off his right ear.

51 But Jesus answered and said, "Leave off

> *going* this far!" And He touched his ear and
> cured him.
> 52 And Jesus said to the chief-priests and captains
> of the Temple and elders who had come against
> Him, "Have you come with swords and wooden
> *clubs* as against a thief?
> 53 "When daily I was with you in the Temple,
> you did not stretch out your hands against
> Me. But this is your hour, and the authority
> of darkness."

Luke's account then goes straight to Christ's arrest. The sudden-ness of Judas appearing with **a crowd** is signaled by the word **behold!** Without any warning, the arresting party burst in upon them (all the more sudden if they were dozing), with **the one called Judas going before them**, his position at their head showing how he had now sided with Jesus' foes. Judas is described again as **one of the Twelve** to stress his place in Christ's inner circle, and to make the defection all the more heinous. Judas **drew near to Jesus to kiss Him**, the customary respectful greeting, while the crowd hung back. The arresting party was taking no chances of getting the wrong man in the darkness of the unlit garden and the confusion of trying to find Jesus in the midst of eleven other men. The kiss from Judas was meant as the sign that this was the man they should arrest.

The irony of giving a respectful and deferential kiss to someone while betraying him was not to pass without its fitting rebuke. Using his name **Judas** in a loving appeal to friendship and future repentance, Jesus asked His former apostle, **"Do you deliver up the Son of Man with a kiss?"** Jesus was not simply calling attention to the hypocrisy of the act, He was also appealing to Judas to forswear such hypocrisy, for this was Judas' only chance of future repentance.

The crowd had come with weapons and torches, ready to meet armed resistance. (The Lord Himself said that if His kingship were earthly, His disciples would indeed fight that He might not be given up to His foes; John 18:36.) The **captains of the Temple** (i.e. the Temple police) and the Roman cohort accompanying them (mentioned in John 18:3) were armed **with swords**, and the others with them with **wooden *clubs***. Why such a show of force? I suggest that there was something else present in their minds besides the possibility of armed resistance from the disciples. The Jews among them doubtless remembered the fiery fate of those sent to arrest Elijah (2 Kin. 1:9–10), when God struck down those who opposed His prophet. Jesus was also held to be a great prophet, and they feared lest perhaps this was true after all. The weapons therefore expressed this unnamed fear that lurked in their hearts.

When the disciples around Jesus saw what was going to be, and that His arrest was imminent, they leaped to His defense. Scrambling to their feet, they said, **"Lord, should we strike with the sword?"** Christ had earlier spoken of the need for a sword (v. 36), and they mistakenly thought this was what He was referring to. **A certain one from them** (Peter, as we learn much later from John 18:10) **struck the slave of the chief-priest** who was in the crowd **and took off his ear**. (Luke, ever with a physician's eye, notes that it was his **right** ear.) No doubt Peter was aiming at taking off his head, not just his ear. But Peter, after all, was a fisherman, not a soldier.

In all the confusion, fear, shouting, and scrambling, one voice rang out above the din—the voice of the Master, commanding peace. **Jesus answered** the disciples' question with the command, **"Leave off *going* this far!"** Armed rebellion (as Luke the apologist is quick to record) was not what He was about. Such armed violence must cease. Luke (again showing himself ever the physician) notes that Jesus **touched** the **ear** of the wounded slave **and cured him**. For He did not come to destroy men's lives but to save them (9:56). By recording this healing, St. Luke shows his Roman audience that the Christian faith was not seditious and dangerous as people had said. It was about forgiveness and peace, not violence.

Christ surrenders to His captors, but not without a word of challenge. He points out to them the evil and illegitimacy of the whole arrest. He asks them, **"Have you come with swords and wooden *clubs* as against a thief? When daily I was with you in the Temple, you did not stretch out your hands against Me."** That is, if I was such a criminal indeed, why did you not arrest Me earlier when you had the chance? The fact that this arrest is taking place secretly, hidden from the public eye, testifies to the fact that it is illegitimate. But He will not resist, for **this** is their **hour** to act with impunity. It is time for **the authority of darkness** to triumph.

§VIII.4. Jesus' Trial

The events of Christ's trial before the Jewish Sanhedrin (or Council) and of Peter's denial are told very quickly. After taking Jesus into custody, they brought Him into the place where the trial was to be held that night.

Strictly speaking, such night trials were illegal, but the Sanhedrin, the Jewish supreme court, felt that they had no choice. As a volatile and occupied territory, Israel did not have the right to inflict the death penalty. That right was jealously guarded by the Romans, and they alone had authority to sentence someone to death. If Jesus were to be executed, he must be found guilty of a capital offense by a Roman court—that is, by the governor, Pontius Pilate. And if Jesus' foes were to avoid a riot by a mob of His supporters, this must be done quickly. That meant He must be tried before Pilate first thing in the morning, at dawn. And *that* meant He must be found guilty of a capital offense by the Jewish court *before* daybreak. Hence the necessity of the night trial.

Assuming He was arrested after 11:00 P.M., it would have been almost midnight when He appeared before the Great Sanhedrin or supreme council. After a quick appearance before Annas (the former chief-priest and real power behind the high-priestly throne; John 18:13, 19–24), Jesus was led to His actual trial.

> ॐ ॐ ॐ ॐ ॐ
> 54 And having taken Him, they led *Him* and brought *Him* into the house of the chief-priest, but Peter was following from a distance.
> 55 And after they had kindled up a fire in the middle of the courtyard and had sat together, Peter was sitting in the middle of them.

56 And a certain servant-girl, seeing him as he sat in the light and staring at him, said, "This one was also with Him!"

57 But he denied, saying, "Woman, I do not know Him."

58 And after a little, another saw him and said, "You *yourself* also are from them!" But Peter said, "Man, I am not!"

59 And after about one hour had gone, a certain other man began to insist, saying, "Truly this one also was with Him, for he also is a Galilean!"

60 But Peter said, "Man, I do not know what you are saying!" And immediately, while he was still speaking, a rooster sounded.

61 And the Lord turned and looked at Peter. And Peter remembered the word of the Lord, how He had told him, "Before a rooster sounds today, you will *completely* deny Me three times."

62 And he went out and wept bitterly.

It appears that the trial took place at **the** palatial **house of the ruling chief-priest** Caiaphas. After his initial panic and flight, **Peter** had recovered himself and **was following from a distance**. This distance was not due solely to cowardice. Peter was determined to avoid arrest himself, for then he could be of no help to his Lord.

When Jesus was taken into the house of Caiaphas, Peter, not being one of the Sanhedrin, waited outside in the courtyard with others. It was now about 1:30 A.M., and the night air was cold. All there **had kindled up a fire in the middle of the courtyard** and now **sat together**, huddling together for warmth. Peter was cold too, and desperate not to draw attention to himself (which he would if he sat apart from them). So **Peter was sitting in the middle of them**, trying to blend in, thinking of his next move. Sitting **in the light** of the fire was his undoing. **A certain servant-girl** there (possibly put up to it by her friend, the servant-girl who kept the door; John 18:17) sits **staring at him** and then bursts out, **"This one was also with Him!"** He should be arrested too! This was the second time he had been identified that night (see John 18:17), and once again he was quick to deny everything. **"Woman,"** he shot back (or "Madam," we would say today), **"I do not know Him."**

After a little, when he had moved off to what he hoped would be a safer location, another servant girl (Mark 14:69) identified him and raised the cry, joined by others. These jumped all over him, saying, **"You *yourself* also are from them!"** and Peter, addressing himself to the loudest one there (a man) says, **"Man** (or sir), **I am not!"**

After about one hour had gone, Peter returned to the charcoal fire. It was now about 2:30 in the morning. There **a certain other man began to insist, saying, "Truly this one also was with Him** in the garden, **for he also is a Galilean!"** Galileans spoke with a peculiar accent, pronouncing their gutturals differently than Judeans did, and Peter's previous denials had given the man opportunity to recognize Peter's Galilean accent. Most of Jesus' disciples were Galileans, he thought—surely this man was one of them.

Peter denied it again, and **immediately, while he was still speaking** and calling curses down on his head if ever he knew Jesus (Mark 14:71), **a rooster sounded**. From where He was, **the Lord turned** around and **looked at Peter**, staring at him (Gr. *emblepo*, a more intensive verb than "to look," *blepo*). The look went right into Peter's heart as he **remembered the word of the Lord**, how He had predicted his denials not many hours before. Peter **went out** of the courtyard in haste and **wept bitterly**.

---

৯৭ ৯৭ ৯৭ ৯৭ ৯৭

63 And the men who were hemming Jesus in were mocking Him, beating Him,

64 and having covered around His *face*, they were asking Him, saying, "Prophesy; who is the one who hit You?"

65 And they were saying many other things against Him, blaspheming.

Luke now relates the mocking and beating of Jesus by the officers of the Council. No doubt the officers, frustrated by their powerlessness to arrest Him in the Temple before, handled Him roughly and with verbal abuse as soon as He was brought in. As mentioned above, though, most of the abuse and the real beating occurred *after* His condemnation, not before. Nonetheless, St. Luke relates all of the abuse here, *before* the condemnation, to show how the verdict was decided in advance. This was not to be a real trial at all, but a farcical show, leading up to a predetermined end.

Thus, Luke relates that **the men who were hemming Jesus in** (Gr. *sunexo*, the same verb used for the crowd hemming Jesus in during the healing of the woman with the flow of blood; 8:45) **were mocking Him**. He was supposed to be a prophet and to have supernatural knowledge as the prophets did (compare 2 Kin. 5:25–26). They would see about that! **Having covered around His** *face* so that He could not see them, they began taking turns **beating Him**, **asking Him** to **prophesy** and identify **the one who hit** Him. There were other insults as well, but Luke will only say that **they were saying many other** insulting **things against Him, blaspheming** (that is, reviling).

ॐ ॐ ॐ ॐ ॐ

66 And as it became day, the elders of the people assembled, both chief-priests and scribes, and they led Him away to their Council, saying,

67 "If You *Yourself* are the Christ, tell us." But He said to them, "If I tell you, you will never believe *it*;

68 "and if I ask *you*, you will never answer.

69 "But from now on the Son of Man will be sitting at the right of the Power of God."

70 And they all said, "Are You Yourself therefore the Son of God?" And He said, "You *yourselves* say I am *the one*."

71 And they said, "Why do we still have need of witnessing? For we have heard it ourselves from His own mouth."

Jesus' trial is then reported. Once again, Luke gives a very abbreviated account. He omits the Markan details of many false witnesses coming forward, and of their testimony even so being found inconsistent (Mark 14:55–59). Since it was legally necessary for such testimony to prove consistent, and since Jesus Himself refused to speak at His trial (and thus provide them with ammunition), the proceedings dragged on for some time, lasting throughout the night.

Indeed, it was not until about daybreak that the impasse was broken. **As it became day** (that is, as the sun was beginning to dawn), there was at last an exchange between Jesus and His accusers. (This is the only part of the trial reported by Luke, who telescopes the trial into this one exchange.) They asked Him, if He was **the Christ**, the long-awaited Messiah, to **tell** them. He was reluctant to engage them, for it was pointless to do so. If He would tell them anything about Himself, they would **never believe** *it*, and if he **asked** them a question to defend Himself, they would **never answer**. Questions and answers alike were fruitless for such closed minds, so why should He speak? Nonetheless, He would tell them the truth.

Quoting Psalm 110:1, Jesus affirmed that **from now on** He, **the Son of Man,** would be **sitting at the right of the Power of God**, sharing all the authority of God as His Messiah. (Luke expands the Jewish circumlocution of the Name of God by the term "the Power" for the sake of his Gentile audience, so that they will know which "power" Jesus was referring to; compare Matt. 26:64.) Now Jesus stood in their midst as a helpless criminal, but soon He would sit enthroned beside God as Judge of all.

And so that his readers would have no doubt about Jesus' claim, Luke records Jesus' answer to the court's inquiry about whether He was **the Son of God**: **"You** *yourselves* **say that I am** *the one.***"** (Both pronouns are emphatic in the Greek.) In English, the reply might be thought ambiguous (i.e. "that's what *you* say, not I"), but there was no such ambiguity. It simply means, "You have answered your own question," and was the usual respectful way to answer affirmatively. (From Matthew and Mark's Gospels, we learn that this affirmation was made by Christ only after the high priest adjured Him in the Name of God to either confirm or deny that He was the Messiah.)

After such an unequivocal admission that He did claim to be the Messiah, the trial was over. Such a pretension from (as they thought) a mere man, and a Sabbath-breaker at that, was blasphemous and worthy of death. All concluded that they did not **still have need of witnessing** and of testimony from others. They had **heard** the blasphemy themselves **from His own mouth**. A guilty verdict was the only possibility.

Luke paraphrases their words (recorded in Mark 14:63) about not needing any further "witnesses" (Gr. *martures*) to a vaguer statement that they need no further **witnessing** (Gr. *marturia*), for he omits the Markan details about them striving to find a consistent witness. This is part of Luke's general practice of paraphrasing the narrative as he abbreviates it.

ॐ ॐ ॐ ॐ ॐ

23 1 Then the whole multitude of them arose and led Him before Pilate.

2 And they began to accuse Him, saying, "We found this one perverting our nation and forbidding *us* to pay taxes to Caesar, and saying that He Himself is Christ, a king."

3 And Pilate asked Him, saying, "Are You *Yourself* the King of the Jews?" And He answered him and said, "You *yourself* say."

4 And Pilate said to the chief-priests and the crowds, "I find no guilt in this man."

Very little time is spent narrating the Jewish trial, because St. Luke would concentrate more on Christ's trial before the Romans. The Christian movement at the time of Luke's writing was under great suspicion of being seditious—not surprising, since its Founder was executed for sedition, and riots often attended the spread of the movement (compare Acts 17:6–7). Luke is therefore concerned to show how Christ was found by Pilate to be not guilty of any sedition.

After the Jews had extracted an admission from Jesus that He was the Messiah, **the whole multitude of them arose and led Him before Pilate** once the Roman courts were open after daybreak. Once there, **they began to accuse Him**, mixing half-truths with outright falsehoods. We can almost see the crowd of them standing around Pilate, each one adding another accusation. They began by declaring that they had **found** through examination that **this one** (the refusal to use His Name is a sign of their distaste for Him) was **perverting** their **nation**. The nature of the perversion and fraud was that He was declaring Himself to be **Christ** (explained by them, for Pilate's sake, to mean **a king**). For good measure, they added that Jesus was also **forbidding** pious Jews **to pay taxes to Caesar**. In reporting this, Luke expects his readers to detect the outright falseness of this accusation (from 20:20–25) and to see it as characteristic of all their false accusations.

The accusation of being a king was serious, for to Roman ears this constituted rebellion and a call to overthrow the Romans in Palestine. **Pilate asked** Jesus about the charges, **saying, "Are You** *Yourself* **the King of the Jews?"** The pronoun **You** is emphatic in the Greek, as if Pilate could scarcely believe that this one standing before him in humility was a dangerous rebel. Jesus, though not *that* kind of king, was nonetheless the Messiah, the true King of Israel (John 1:49), and so **He answered him** affirmatively, saying, **"You** *yourself* **say,"** the normal polite method of affirmation. Pilate (we may think) then questions Jesus further. Luke only relates his verdict at the end of it all, when he announces **to the chief-priests and the crowds, "I find no guilt in this man."** This is no private opinion, but an official verdict of "not guilty."

ॐ ॐ ॐ ॐ ॐ

5 But they were *growing* strong *in their demands*, saying, "He stirs up the people, teaching throughout the whole of Judea, starting from Galilee, as far as here."

6 But when Pilate heard *it*, he asked if the man was a Galilean.

7 And when He really-knew that He was from

> Herod's authority, he sent Him to Herod, who himself also was in Jerusalem in these days.
>
> 8 Now Herod rejoiced much when he saw Jesus, for he had wanted to see Him for a considerable time, because he had been hearing about Him and was hoping to see some sign done by Him.
>
> 9 And he was asking Him with many words, but He answered him nothing.
>
> 10 And the chief-priests and the scribes were standing *there*, accusing Him vigorously.
>
> 11 And Herod with his soldiers, after disdaining and mocking Him, clothed Him in bright garb and sent Him back to Pilate.
>
> 12 Now Herod and Pilate became friends with each other that very day, for before they had been at enmity among themselves.

This verdict of "not guilty" is not what the Jewish rulers had stayed up all night to accomplish, and they continued their barrage, **growing strong in their demands**. They insisted that **He stirs up the people, teaching** His rebellious stuff **throughout the whole** Roman province **of Judea, starting from Galilee** (a well-known hotspot of Jewish rebellion) and extending **as far as here** in Jerusalem. This was no small local sensation, they insisted, but a real threat to Roman sovereignty throughout the land.

They expected this to change Pilate's mind so that he would reconsider his verdict. But mention of Galilee gave Pilate another idea. **When he really-knew** and had confirmed that Jesus **was from Herod's authority** (for Herod had authority over Galilee), **he sent Him to Herod**, who was in Jerusalem for the Passover. The motivation seems to have been to shift some of the responsibility for the verdict onto Herod, brought in as a supposed expert in Jewish matters. Pilate, though a callous anti-Semite, still had a Roman sense of justice and knew that Jesus was innocent of sedition. It was highly inexpedient politically, however, to antagonize this powerful Jewish lobby, who might find a way to get him into trouble at Rome (see

John 19:12). Better to spread the responsibility around if he could!

Herod rejoiced much when the delegation arrived unexpectedly at his residence in Jerusalem (probably the old Hasmonean palace just west of the Temple). **He had wanted to see** Jesus **for a considerable time**, to check out His reputation as a miracle-worker. (Perhaps he still wanted to confirm that He was not John the Baptizer raised from the dead; see Matt. 14:1–2.) For a long time **he was asking** Jesus questions, trying to get Him to answer him and discuss His case. Herod, however, was no seeker after truth, but simply a low and cunning fox (13:32) who had long wanted to eliminate Jesus as a cause of political trouble. Christ therefore answered him nothing. **The chief-priests and the scribes** who accompanied Jesus from Pilate when He was sent to Herod also **were standing** *there*, **accusing Him vigorously**. (Luke stresses the many accusations thrown at Jesus to show that, despite all these accusations, Jesus was still found not guilty.)

When it was apparent they would get nowhere, **Herod** with his bodyguard of **soldiers**, **after disdaining and mocking Him** (that is, after heaping verbal insults upon Him), showed their superiority over Him in a show of mockery. Was Pilate sending Jesus to him so that he could see the celebrity for himself? Jesus didn't look much like a celebrity! Let Him go back to Pilate looking the part! They **clothed Him in bright garb** before they **sent Him back to Pilate**. Herod had nothing more to offer Pilate than to return his lunatic back to him.

The words rendered *bright garb* are the Greek *estheta lampran*. The words are the same used to describe the garments of the angel in Peter's vision of Acts 10:30. It is probable that these were white garments, used in mocking imitation of the white garments of Roman dignitaries.

Luke adds that this event led **Herod and Pilate** to **become friends with each other**. **Before** this, they had been **at enmity**, sullenly maintaining an icy separation, but when Pilate solicited Herod's opinion in this dilemma, a new closeness developed. (Luke mentions this alliance because he would later refer to it when reporting in Acts 4:25–28 how it fulfilled ancient prophecy.)

The visit to Herod is narrated only in Luke's Gospel. It is part of Luke's purpose to multiply the number of people to hear Jesus' case and refuse to find Him guilty (23:15). For by sending Jesus back to Pilate in this way, Herod was not only showing his contempt for Jesus. He was showing he did not take Him seriously as a military threat.

꒰ ꒰ ꒰ ꒰ ꒰

13 And Pilate called together the chief-priests and the rulers and the people

14 and said to them, "You brought this man to me as one who misleads the people, and behold, having investigated *Him* before you, I *myself* have found in this man no guilt of which you accuse Him.

15 "Neither *did* Herod, for he sent Him back to us. And behold, nothing worthy of death has been done by Him.

16 "I will therefore discipline Him and release Him."*

18 But they cried out all together, saying, "Away with this one, and release Barabbas to us!"

19 (*He* was one who had been cast into prison for a certain riot happening in the city and for murder.)

20 And Pilate called to them again, wanting to release Jesus,

21 but they kept on calling out, saying, "Crucify, crucify Him!"

22 A third *time* he said to them, "Why, what wickedness has this one done? I have found in Him no guilt *unto* death; I will therefore discipline Him and release *Him*."

23 But they were pressing *on him* with great voices, asking that He be crucified. And their voices were overpowering *Pilate's*.

24 And Pilate *gave* judgment that their request should be done.

25 And he released the one they were asking for, who had been cast into prison for riot and murder, but Jesus he delivered up to their will.

* Verse 17 should be omitted as not original to Luke, but rather added by later scribes who wanted to bring it into conformity with Matt. 27:15 and Mark 15:6.

Pilate then addresses the assembled crowd of **chief-priests, rulers** (that is, members of the Sanhedrin), and others from **the people** to confirm his verdict. Though they had **brought this man** to him **as one who misleads the people** and incites rebellion, **having investigated** and examined Him, he himself (the pronoun is emphatic) had **found in this man no guilt** concerning the things of which they accused Him. This finding (the second time Pilate declared Jesus to be not guilty) was backed up by **Herod** too, for **he sent Him back** in such a way as to show that he found the charges ludicrous. Pilate proposed to **discipline Him** by scourging (to punish Him for being a nuisance) and then **release Him** as one who was innocent of capital offense. (We learn from John's Gospel that this scourging was carried out, and that Christ was displayed to the crowd afterwards in hope that the sight would elicit sympathy; John 19:1–5.)

Pilate brought up the custom of granting a Passover amnesty (John 18:39), with the suggestion that Jesus should be the one given the amnesty. This suggestion enraged the crowd. Seeing Jesus humiliated by the Romans, they easily believed the slanders of His foes that He could not be the Messianic Conqueror, but was a deceiver. **They cried out all together, saying, "Away with this one, and release Barabbas to us!"** (Luke adds that Barabbas **had been cast into prison for a certain riot happening in the city and for murder**.) Barabbas was probably a Zealot, or at least of Zealot sympathies, and the riot was an anti-Roman demonstration. He appeared to the crowd to be just the sort of revolutionary they had hoped Jesus would be.

Pilate's attempt at manipulating the crowd was backfiring badly. He **called to them again, wanting to release Jesus, but they kept calling out, saying, "Crucify, crucify Him!"** Despite Pilate's declaring for the **third** *time* that Jesus had done nothing deserving death, and that he would therefore **discipline Him and release** *Him*, the crowd was insistent that He be executed. They were **pressing** *on* Pilate **with great voices**, chanting for Barabbas and shouting that Jesus should be crucified. Another riot was in danger of breaking out. **Their voices were overpowering** *Pilate's*, and he bowed before the inevitable. **He released the one they were asking for** (Luke stresses to his Roman readership that this one **had been cast into prison for riot and murder) but Jesus he delivered up to their will**. The sense of flagrant injustice is brought to the fore in the narrative—a murderer was released, and an innocent man was sentenced to death.

§VIII.5. Jesus' Crucifixion

26 And when they led Him away, they laid hold of a certain Simon of Cyrene, coming in from the country, and laid on him the cross to carry after Jesus.

27 And there were following Him a great multitude of the people, and of women who were lamenting and bewailing Him.

28 But Jesus, turning to them, said, "Daughters of Jerusalem, do not weep for Me, but weep for yourselves and for your children.

29 "For behold, the days are coming when they will say, 'Blessed *are* the barren, and the wombs that did not bear, and the breasts that did not nourish!'

30 "Then they will begin to say to the mountains, 'Fall on us!' and to the hills, 'Cover us!'

31 "For if they do these things when the wood *is* moist *and green*, what will happen when it *is* dry?"

> **32** And two others also, who were evil-workers, were being led away with Him to be destroyed.

When **they** (i.e. the Roman soldiers) **led** Jesus **away** to be crucified, Luke relates that **they laid hold of a certain Simon of Cyrene**. Simon was evidently a Jew from the Diaspora, in Jerusalem for the Passover. He was **coming in from the country**, having entered Jerusalem from where he was lodging in the countryside surrounding the overcrowded city during the Passover season. Perhaps Luke mentions this geographical detail to make clear that Simon was not part of the mocking crowd, but was an innocent bystander who just happened to be there at that time. It is possible too that Simon is identified as **of Cyrene** in deference to the large number of Cyrenian Christians in the later Jerusalem church (compare Acts 6:9; 11:20).

It was customary for the condemned to carry his own cross (that is, the horizontal bar onto which his hands would be nailed) to the place of execution. It would seem that Jesus, having been scourged after a night of beating and abuse, was unable to complete this final duty. So it was that the soldiers laid on Simon **the cross to carry after Jesus**, conscripting him to finish this work for Him.

Also **there were following** Jesus a **great multitude of the people**, including some **women who were lamenting and bewailing Him**, making the customary mourning that accompanied the dying and dead. **Jesus,** stopping and **turning to them, said, "Daughters of Jerusalem, do not weep for Me, but weep for yourselves and for your children."** Even in His final pain, Jesus took thought for others who would suffer. As He looked at His own Cross, He could see the future days when thousands of His countrymen would be nailed to such crosses in the horrifying aftermath of the fall of Jerusalem in AD 70. So terrible would those days be that men would invoke a blessing on **the barren**, and say, **"Blessed are the wombs that did not bear and the breasts that did not nourish!"** Usually those who were barren were thought accursed, and children were thought a blessing. In the days to come, however, such terrible things would befall children that the childless would be thought blessed in comparison.

In those days, such disasters would strike that people would **say to the mountains, "Fall on us! and to the hills, "Cover us!"** (The panicked cry is from Hos. 10:8.) Better that the mountains and hills should fall on them and destroy them than that they should live to further experience the suffering of those days. For if the Romans could permit such **things** as the crucifixion of the innocent Christ **when the wood** *was* **moist** *and green* (that is, when Israel was *not* rebelling against Rome), what retributions would they exact when the wood was **dry** (that is, when Israel *was* rebelling against Rome)? If a fire could occur in the moist forest—what kind of conflagration could be expected in the dry woods?

As Jesus staggered onward, **two others also, who were evil-workers, were being led away with Him to be destroyed**. Jesus was not alone. He suffered the further indignity of being classed with true criminals.

ॐ ॐ ॐ ॐ ॐ

33 And when they came upon the place called the Skull, there they crucified Him and the evil-workers, one on the right and the other on the left.

34 *But Jesus was saying, "Father, forgive them; for they do not know what they are doing."** And they cast lots, dividing up His garments.

35 And the people stood by, observing. And the rulers also were sneering at Him, saying, "He saved others; let Him save Himself if this one is the Christ of God, the Chosen One."

36 And the soldiers also mocked Him, coming up to Him, offering Him vinegar,

37 and saying, "If You *Yourself* are the King of the Jews, save Yourself!"

38 Now there was also an inscription over Him, "This one is the King of the Jews."

39 And one of the evil-workers who were hanged was blaspheming Him, saying, "Are You

---

> *Yourself* not the Christ? Save Yourself—and us!"
>
> 40 But the other answered and, rebuking him, said, "Do you *yourself* not fear God, since you are under the same judgment?
>
> 41 "And we *ourselves* indeed righteously, for we are receiving things worthy of what we have done, but this one has done nothing improper."
>
> 42 And he was saying, "Jesus, remember me when You come into Your Kingdom!"
>
> 43 And He said to him, "Amen I say to you, today you will be with Me in Paradise."
>
> * Some manuscripts omit this part of the verse, making it likely that it is not original to Luke. There is no reason to doubt, however, that it is a genuine reminiscence of Christ's words on the Cross.

At length **they came upon** the customary site for executions, appropriately named **the place called the Skull**, since it was a place of death. It was **there they crucified Him**, nailing His forearms to the crossbeam and crossing His ankles to drive a single nail through them into the wood of the upright. He was in the midst of two other criminals, classed as no better than they. It was usual for such men to spend their final breath cursing their tormentors and calling down the vengeance of God upon them. **Jesus**, however, **was saying, "Father, forgive them; for they do not know what they are doing."** The Roman soldiers who drove in the nails were simply doing their job, and Christ bore them no malice. Instead, He prayed for their repentance and forgiveness before God on the Last Day. (That the soldiers are the primary object of the prayer is indicated by the present tense: **what they are doing**—compared to what the Jewish rulers did in the past.) This prayer sets the tone for all Christians who suffer persecution, showing that martyrs should still seek the salvation of all, even of those who slay them (compare the example of Stephen, Acts 7:60). The soldiers, for their part, were oblivious to the divine generosity extended to them: they continued to plunder Jesus of all He had, even **casting lots, dividing His**

garments among them. Some garments were valued more than others, and lots had to be cast to assign which garments would fall to which soldier. Luke relates the plundering of His garments to stress that Jesus was robbed of every final shred of dignity. He was mocked and derided by all—by aristocratic Jewish rulers, by rough and ready Roman soldiers, even by dying criminals.

After He was nailed to the Cross, **the people stood by**, observing His agony and reviling Him. **The rulers** of Israel were also there, **sneering at Him**. Jesus had claimed (as they thought) to be **the Christ of God, the Chosen One** of Heaven, the one who would lead Israel to victory over the Romans. His hanging on the Cross was final and irrefutable proof that those claims were false, and that He was a deceiver. They therefore derided Him, saying, **"He saved others** and rescued them from their afflictions; **let Him** now **save Himself** if He is who He claims to be!" Jesus did not respond to their challenge by coming down from the Cross and saving Himself, and this seemed to them the conclusive proof that He was not the Messiah.

Even **the soldiers mocked Him**, joining in the derision. They were **offering Him vinegar** (that is, the sour wine usually drunk by laborers; compare Ruth 2:14). This was the common drink of soldiers too, but their offering Jesus some of their drink formed part of their mockery: "Would the King like a drink from the royal cup?" (We learn from John 19:28–29 that this was offered in Christ's final moments.) Throughout those terrible hours they echoed the challenges they heard from those around them, and said to Jesus, **"If You *Yourself*** (the pronoun is emphatic) **are** truly **the King of the Jews** (as the charge above you reads), then **save Yourself!"** What kind of a king are You?

For **there was an inscription over Him** which read, **"This one is the King of the Jews."** The inscription delineated the charge against the one crucified, identifying the criminal as "thief" or "murderer." This was all that Pilate would allow to be said, refusing the request of the Jews to make clearer their view that Jesus was falsely claiming such a kingship (John 19:19–22). The mockery of soldiers (v. 37) was suggested by this inscription.

Luke then relates an exchange between the two criminals crucified on either side of Christ. Both had joined with the crowd
in deriding Jesus (Mark 15:32), but one felt compunction for his
insults and repented. As **one of the evil-workers who were hanged**
continued **blaspheming** Jesus and challenging Him, saying, **"Are
You *Yourself* not the Christ? Save Yourself—and us!"** the other
thought better of it. He began rebuking his fellow, saying, **"Do you
yourself not fear God, since you are under the same judgment**
of death as Jesus and will soon go to God for His sentencing? **And
we *ourselves* righteously** and justly, for we are simply receiving our
just recompense. **This one**, however, **has done nothing improper."**

The penitent thief knew that he could reasonably expect only
condemnation from God for his sins. Despite Jesus' apparent defeat,
however, the wise thief still believed that **Jesus** would be received
with honor by God and would still **come into** His **Kingdom** as
Messiah. It was, given the circumstances, an astonishing act of faith.
God had revealed Jesus' messiahship to Peter (Matt. 16:17), and He
had revealed the same to this criminal also. The thief still expected
Jesus to triumph as Messiah in the age to come. Jesus responded
to the doomed man by saying, **"Today you will be with Me in
Paradise."** As a thief, the man might have expected condemnation
from the righteous God, but in a single moment, the man's faith
had justified him and made him worthy of the Kingdom (compare
the Exaposteilarion of Holy Friday Matins). When the man's eyes
closed in death that day, he could expect to share paradisal bliss with
Christ in Abraham's bosom.

---

44 And it was now about the sixth hour, and
   darkness was over the whole land until the
   ninth hour,
45 the sun having failed, and the veil of the Sanctuary was split in two.
46 And Jesus, calling with a great voice, said,
   "Father, into Your hands I commit My spirit!"
   And having said this, He expired.

> 47 Now when the centurion saw what had happened, he was glorifying God, saying, "Certainly this man was righteous!"
> 48 And all the crowds who came together for this sight, when they saw what had happened, were returning, striking their breasts.
> 49 And all His acquaintances and the women who were following with Him from Galilee were standing at a distance, seeing these things.

At **about the sixth hour**, or noon, **darkness was over the whole land until the ninth hour**, or 3:00 P.M., for **the sun failed** in its light. This was no normal eclipse, but an expression of the Creator's horror at the injustice done under the sun. Like one hiding his face from an unbearable crime, the sun hid its face from the sight of God being crucified by His creatures. **The veil of the Sanctuary** (that is, the large curtain separating the Sanctuary from the forecourt, visible to all in the Temple) was split in two. This was clearly a supernatural rending, as if God Himself were rending His garments in grief. The tearing of the holy sanctuary veil constituted a profanation of the Temple and a prophecy that God had abandoned His House. Henceforth, there could only be judgment—a judgment that would come in AD 70 with the final destruction of the Temple and the effective end of the Jewish state.

At the moment of death, Jesus **was** heard **calling with a great voice** and saying, **"Father, into Your hands I commit My spirit!"** (From John 19:30, we learn that the great shout was, "It is finished!") His final utterance was thus not one of defeat, but of triumphant faith. Immediately upon saying that He surrendered His life into the Father's hands, **He expired**, showing that His death was entirely voluntary. Here was no involuntary demise, no killing of an unwilling victim, but the serene self-offering of one in control of life and death.

This was not lost on **the centurion** in charge of the execution. **When** he **saw what had happened** and the way Jesus died, he began **glorifying God** by declaring, **"Certainly this man was righteous!"** That is, Jesus was no criminal, but was innocent. Jesus had claimed to be the Son of God, and the pagan soldier could only agree. Luke paraphrases the man's confession that Jesus was indeed the Son of God as He claimed (recorded in Mark 15:39) as saying that He was innocent, because Luke wants to stress that Jesus (and His followers) were innocent of any charge of sedition.

Even **all the crowds who came together** to drink in the **sight** of His execution, when they saw the circumstances of His death, **were returning** to their homes **striking their breasts** in grief over the death of an innocent man. In anticipation of their further actions, St. Luke relates that **all His acquaintances**, including **the women who were following with Him from Galilee, were standing at a distance, seeing these things**. They were there to witness His death and burial (v. 55) and would be in a position to witness also to the fact that His tomb would soon be empty.

§VIII.6. Jesus' Burial

ॐ ॐ ॐ ॐ ॐ

50 And behold, a man named Joseph, being a councilor, a good and righteous man—

51 (this one had not assented to their intention and practice), from Arimathea, a city of the Jews, who was anticipating the Kingdom of God,

52 this one came to Pilate and asked for the body of Jesus.

53 And he took *it* down and wrapped it up in a linen *cloth*, and laid it in a rock-hewn tomb, where no one had yet lain.

54 And it was the Day of Preparation, and the Sabbath was dawning.

55 Now the women who had come with Him from Galilee followed after, and observed the tomb and how His body was laid.

56 And they returned and prepared aromatic *spices* and perfumes. And on the Sabbath they were quiet according to the commandment.

Luke then relates the burial of Jesus, but does so in such a way as to set the stage for His Resurrection. After Christ's death on the Cross, **a man named Joseph** took the lead. He is described by Luke as being **a councilor** (that is, a member of the council, or the Sanhedrin), but who was nonetheless **a good and righteous man**. He is further described as from **Arimathea** (that is, Ramathaim-Zophim, about twenty miles northwest of Jerusalem, described by Luke for his Gentile audience simply as **a city of the Jews**) and as one who **was anticipating the Kingdom of God**, like other pious Jews (compare 2:25, 38). Luke adds that though he was a member of the Sanhedrin, **this one had not assented to their intention** and decision to kill Jesus, and that he had nothing to do with that **practice** and deed. It is likely that he was not even present for the Lord's farcical trial the night before.

Joseph was therefore a man of some standing in Israel, one well up to the task of **coming to Pilate and asking for the body of Jesus**. This was an unusual request, for the bodies of those crucified were usually given to their families, but not so with those crucified for sedition. Such was Joseph's devotion to Jesus that he was willing to risk the displeasure of the governor—to say nothing of the displeasure of his colleagues in the Sanhedrin.

Joseph **took** the body **down** from the Cross **and wrapped it up in a linen *cloth*, and laid it in a rock-hewn tomb**. Luke adds that **no one had yet lain** in that tomb (such tombs had space for the burial of several persons), for he wants his readers to be assured that no mistake was possible later when the women could not find His body in the tomb. His was the only body laid there, and there was no possibility of a mix-up of bodies. This all occurred on the **Day of Preparation** (that is, the day before the Sabbath, Friday in our calendar), and **the Sabbath** was just **dawning**.

The Greek word rendered *dawning* is *epiphosko*, often used for the dawning of day (thus Matt. 28:1). Here the reference is probably to the shining of the first star of the evening, signaling that the Sabbath was beginning. It was Friday evening, and soon all pious Jews would rest **on the Sabbath**, being **quiet** and inactive **according to the commandment**. Not only did Joseph therefore have to make the burial arrangements hastily, so did **the women who had come with** Jesus **from Galilee** and who now observed from a distance the noble Joseph's work in the tomb.

In the trauma and chaos of those hours, they quickly decided to all meet back at the tomb as soon as they could, to perform a final anointing of their own. **They** therefore **returned** to their respective abodes and **prepared aromatic** *spices* **and perfumes** for that task. (From Mark 16:1, we learn that at least some of the women did not have the necessary materials and had to buy them after the Sabbath ended. In the hasty minutes before the Sabbath fell, all began the task of assembling what was needed for anointing, a task some had to complete after the Sabbath.)

Luke stresses that the women **observed the tomb and how** Jesus' **body was laid**. There was no possibility that they would later go to the wrong tomb.

It may be asked why the women decided to anoint the body of Jesus, since they observed Joseph burying Him, and Joseph performed an anointing himself, albeit a hasty one (John 19:38–40). Here we begin to plumb the depths of the human heart. The women felt a sense of powerlessness all throughout that terrible day, watching the Lord they loved condemned, nailed to a cross, and dying before their eyes. They must have felt that they needed to do something for Him as a final expression of love—even if that thing (the funerary anointing) had already in some measure been done. A second anointing may not have been demanded by the social customs of that time, but it was demanded by the love of their suffering hearts.

❧ IX ☙

THE RESURRECTION
(24:1–49)

§IX.1. The Empty Tomb

❧ ❧ ❧ ❧ ❧

24 1 But on the first *day* of the week, at early dawn, they came to the tomb, bringing the aromatic *spices* which they had prepared,

2 and they found the stone rolled away from the tomb,

3 but when they went in, they did not find the body of the Lord Jesus.

4 And it happened that while they were perplexed about this, behold! two men stood by them in flashing garb;

5 and as they were afraid and bowed their faces to the earth, *the men* said to them, "Why do you seek the living one among the dead?

6 "He is not here, but was raised. Remember how He spoke to you while He was in Galilee,

7 "saying that it was necessary for the Son of Man to be delivered into the hands of sinful men and be crucified and the third day rise."

8 And they remembered His words,

9 and returned from the tomb and declared all these things to the Eleven and to all the rest.

10 Now they were Mary Magdalene and Joanna

and Mary *the mother* of James; and the rest
with them were telling these things to the
apostles.
11 And these words appeared before them as nonsense, and they disbelieved them.*

* The following verse, v. 12, should be omitted as not original
to Luke. Though in most manuscripts, it seems to have been
added by a later scribe, to harmonize this account with v. 24
and with that of John 20:3–10.

The story of Christ then reaches its climax with His appearances
to His own after He had been raised from the dead. It begins **on the
first *day* of the week at early dawn**, at the first available moment.
The women **came to the tomb, bringing the aromatic *spices* they
had prepared**, ready to anoint the body despite the decay which
(they thought) would have set in. Though a great stone had been
rolled in front of the tomb (Mark 15:46), unexpectedly **they found
the stone rolled away from the tomb. They went in** to the tomb,
trembling and eager to perform their planned anointing, but **did
not find the body of the Lord Jesus**.

While they were perplexed about this and trying to think of
where the corpse might be, **behold**, to their great shock, **two men**
suddenly **stood by them in flashing garb**. (The word translated
flashing, Gr. *astrapto*, is the same word used in 17:24 to describe
the flashing of lightning from one part of the sky to the other. The
garb with which the men were clothed was no earthly garments,
but shone with the blinding light of heaven.) The women **were
afraid** (Gr. *emphobos*, a stronger word than *phobos*, "fear," indicating
a greater terror) and so **bowed their faces to the earth**, cowering
before the two men.

The two men (angels, we are meant to understand) said to them,
"Why do you seek the living one among the dead?" The living
are not customarily found in tombs—and Jesus is living, so why
look for Him here? (It would seem that angels also have an ironic
sense of humor!) **He is not here, but was raised**. Could they not
remember how He spoke to them often, even **while He was in**

Galilee, and how He predicted this (9:22, 44; 18:31–33)? They should have recalled this themselves, and so not have come to the tomb on such a fruitless mission! So prompted, **they remembered His words**. They also **returned from the tomb** (Mark reveals that they in fact "fled" from the tomb; Mark 16:8) to find **the Eleven and all the rest** of the disciples still in Jerusalem, to whom they **declared all these things**.

Comparing this account with that of John's Gospel, we learn that Mary Magdalene had come to the tomb earlier than the other women, had found it empty, and had already fled to tell this to Peter and John (John 20:1–2). It was while Mary was running to find Peter and John that the other women arrived, to be greeted by the angels.

Luke, with his sense of the importance of eyewitnesses (1:2), records the names of those who reported all this: **Mary Magdalene and Joanna and Mary _the mother_ of James**, along with **the rest** of the women who could confirm this story. **These words appeared before** the apostles, however, **as nonsense**, as mere twaddle, as stupid women-talk, and **they disbelieved** the women. An empty tomb was one thing, but a story of angels was quite another! St. Luke records the reluctance of the apostles to believe the story to set in greater relief the final proof that convinced them. The apostles were no credulous dreamers, quick to believe any tale of the supernatural, but men of the world who needed to be convinced. If the apostles therefore believed that Christ was risen, all men could take it as certain!

§IX.2. The Emmaus Appearance

ॐ ॐ ॐ ॐ ॐ

13 And behold! two from them were going that same day to a village which was about sixty stadia distant from Jerusalem, which _is_ named Emmaus.

14 And they were conversing with one another about all these things which had occurred.

15 And it happened that while they were conversing

> and debating, Jesus Himself drew near and was going with them.
>
> 16 But their eyes were held from really-knowing Him.
>
> 17 And He said to them, "What *are* these words that you exchange with one another as you walk?" And they stood *still*, *looking* gloomy.

One of Christ's appearances to two of His disciples is now related. In relating this appearance, Luke shows the disciples did not immediately recognize Jesus, but had to be convinced. (The story was also chosen because, as said above in an Excursus, St. Luke centers his story on Jerusalem and its environs.) Luke stresses the unexpected nature of the appearance by beginning the story with the word **behold!** At that time, **two from** the body of the disciples **were going that same** first **day** of the week **to a village which was about sixty stadia distant from Jerusalem** (a mere seven miles). Luke, reporting the details as one building a case from eyewitness detail, mentions both the name of the village, **Emmaus**, and the name of one of the men, Cleopas (v. 18, probably his source for the story).

This Emmaus is probably the village Mozah, some 55 *stadia* from Jerusalem. (It was close enough to the neighboring colony of Roman soldiers a little over a mile away that Josephus could refer to the colony as Emmaus in his *Wars of the Jews*, 7,6,6.)

The men on the way there **were conversing with one another** about all the events which had occurred. They had been shocked and traumatized by Jesus' arrest and execution, like all of His disciples, and were "debriefing" with one another as they walked.

While they walked, they were **conversing and debating** (the word rendered *debating* is the Gr. *suzeteo*, sometimes meaning "arguing," as in 22:23). Were they arguing over who was to blame for what, as their own parts in the debacle played out over and over in their heads? Or possibly over what to make of the women's story? Whatever their talk, it was during this that **Jesus Himself drew near and was going with them**. Despite it being Jesus,

their eyes were held and prevented **from really-knowing** and recognizing Him. (It seems that His Resurrection form differed somewhat from His previous earthly appearance; compare John 21:12.) They received the stranger as part of their group, though it seems that they stopped their conversation when He arrived. That was only to be expected, since being His disciple was still very dangerous, and the disciples would lock their doors for fear of the Jews when they met (John 20:19).

As their conversation stopped when He arrived, **He said to them, "What *are* these words that you exchange with one another as you walk?"** It seems to have been an animated and fascinating conversation—what were they talking about? At this question, **they stood *still*** in the road, ***looking* gloomy** and depressed. Did they look at one another for mutual assurance before deciding to trust this Stranger with their conversation?

ॐ ॐ ॐ ॐ ॐ

18 And one *of them*, Cleopas by name, answered and said to Him, "Are You the only one sojourning in Jerusalem who also does not know of the things which have happened in her in these days?"

19 And He said to them, "What things?" And they said to Him, "The things about Jesus *the* Nazarene, who was a prophet powerful in work and word before God and all the people—

20 "how the chief-priests and our rulers delivered Him up to the judgment of death and crucified Him.

21 "But we *ourselves* were hoping that it was He who was about to redeem Israel. But also, with all these things, it is the third day since these things happened.

22 "But also some women from us amazed us. When they were at the tomb early,

23 "and did not find His body, they came, saying

417

> that they had also seen a vision of angels, who said that He was alive.
>
> 24 "And some of those who were with us went to the tomb and found *it* thus, just as the women also had said, but Him they did not see."

Cleopas takes the lead and responds by asking if their new companion is **the only one sojourning in Jerusalem who also** did **not know** of the recent news. That is, their companion must surely be a visitor, a festal pilgrim newly arrived that day, not to know of the events that have turned the whole city upside down. Indeed, he must be **the only one** in the whole city who is unaware of those things.

It would seem they need to vent, and when Jesus asks, **"What things?"** the information just pours out of them. They both answer the question (note the plural of v. 19 after the singular **Cleopas** in v. 18), one adding to the responses of the other. It was all about **Jesus** *the* **Nazarene, who was a prophet powerful in** miraculous **work** and in insightful **word** of teaching. In classic Old Testament tradition, He was mighty **before God**, approved by Him as His own prophet, and also acclaimed by **all the people**. It was all about **how the chief-priests and rulers delivered Him up to the judgment** and sentence **of death** at the hands of the Romans, and through them, **crucified Him.**

Here they confess their own perplexity. We can almost see their enthusiasm falter and their expressions change as they admit that they, for their part (the pronoun is emphatic), **were hoping that it was He who was about to redeem Israel**. They had thought that Jesus was the Messiah and that, when He entered Jerusalem just scant days before, the final Messianic deliverance was at hand. But such was obviously not the case, for it was **the third day since these things happened**, and the Romans were still firmly in charge.

But also, as if things were not perplexing enough on the emotional rollercoaster they had been on, **some women from** their group **amazed** them. (The verb rendered *amazed* is the Gr. *existemi*, which is also used to indicate being out of one's senses, as in Mark 3:21.

This was no mild surprise, but a complete mind-blowing shock.) For **they came** and reported that they **had seen a vision of angels, who said that He was alive. Some** of them **went to the tomb** to confirm the story. They **found** the tomb **thus, just as the women also had said**, empty of the body, but Jesus **they did not see** (though the angels the women reported seeing said He was alive). It is all so incredible, and now they do not know what to think.

ॐ ॐ ॐ ॐ ॐ

25 And He said to them, "O mindless ones and slow of heart to believe all that the prophets have spoken!

26 "Was it not necessary for the Christ to suffer these things and to enter into His glory?"

27 And beginning with Moses and with all the prophets, He interpreted to them the things in all the Scriptures about Himself.

28 And they drew near to the village where they were going, and He made as though He would go farther.

29 And they prevailed upon Him, saying, "Remain with us, for it is toward evening, and the day has already declined." And He went in to remain with them.

30 And it happened that when He had reclined with them, He took the bread and blessed *it*, and breaking *it*, was giving *it* to them.

31 And their eyes were opened-up and they really-knew Him; and He vanished from them.

32 And they said to one another, "Were not our hearts burning in us while He was speaking to us on the way, while He was opening-up the Scriptures to us?"

33 And they arose that same hour and returned to Jerusalem, and found the Eleven collected and those who were with them,

34 saying, "The Lord has risen indeed, and has
     appeared to Simon!"
35 And they were explaining the things on the way,
     and how He was made known to them in the
     breaking of the bread.

The Stranger responds to their perplexity in typical Jewish fashion, by quoting the Scriptures. Were they perplexed because they thought Jesus was the Messiah and yet He had been killed? How **mindless** they were (Gr. *anoetos*, here having the sense of bumbling; compare its use in Gal. 3:1 in Phillips translation, "you dear idiots"). How **slow of heart to believe all that the prophets had spoken!** For the prophets had predicted that **the Christ** must **suffer these things** and only then **enter into His glory**. If they knew the Scriptures, they would have expected this to happen to Jesus. His suffering does not prove that He was *not* the Messiah, but that He *was*!

They listened to the Stranger with dumbfounded fascination as, **beginning with Moses and with all the prophets, He interpreted to them the things in all the Scriptures** pertaining to Messiah. (He did not, of course, identify Himself as that Messiah as He spoke.) Previously these things in the Scriptures were not completely understood, but now that Christ had fulfilled them, all was clear.

All too soon **they drew near to the village where they were going, and He made as though He would go farther**, bidding them farewell. (This is ever the Lord's way, for He will not come where He is not invited.) They couldn't get enough of His words, however, so **they prevailed upon Him** to **remain** with them for the night, since daylight was starting to fail. The word translated *prevail upon* is the Greek *parabiazo*, related to *biazo*, "to use force" (compare its use in Deut. 22:25). The disciples would not take "no" for an answer! So it was that **He went into** their house **to remain with them** that night.

It was during the evening meal that something happened. **When He had reclined** at table with them, the Stranger, though supposedly their guest, assumed the role of their host and Master. For He **took the bread and blessed** *it*, **and breaking** *it*, **was giving** *it* **to them**—exactly as their Master Jesus had done so many times before.

Their world turned around as **their eyes were opened-up and they really-knew** and recognized **Him** as their beloved Master of old. No sooner had this occurred than **He vanished from them**.

Everything then fell into place. Of course it had been Jesus! **Were not** their **hearts burning in** them **while He was speaking** to them **on the way, opening-up the Scriptures?** Who else could do that but the Lord? Despite the lateness of the hour (they had thought it too late for their companion to travel further that night), **they arose that same hour and returned to Jerusalem** to report this to the apostles. There they **found** all of them with exciting news of their own. **The Eleven** had **collected** themselves and the rest of **those who were with them** in Jerusalem to report that **the Lord had risen indeed, and had appeared to Simon**. Before appearing to the disciples on the road to Emmaus, He had appeared to Simon as well (compare 1 Cor. 15:5), for time and space were now no barrier to Him. The two of them spent the evening **explaining the things** that occurred **on the way** to Emmaus, and **how** Jesus **was made known to them in the breaking of the bread** once they had reached there. (For Luke, as a member of the Church, this resonates with eucharistic references as well, since it is at the eucharistic breaking of the bread that the Church knows the Presence of her risen Lord.)

❧EXCURSUS
ON THE IDENTITY OF THE TWO EMMAUS DISCIPLES

The name Cleopas is a contraction of Cleopatros (compare Antipas as a contraction of Antipatros) and is a Hellenistic name. It is not to be confused with the Clopas of John 19:25. The "o" in the name Clopas is the Greek letter *omega*, and if the "eo" in the name Cleopas were contracted, it would more naturally contract into "ou," not *omega*. Thus the Cleopas of our Emmaus story is not to be identified with the Clopas of John 19:25.

It would seem that Cleopas was a resident of Emmaus and a disciple of Jesus. Luke mentions his name not only (we think) to state who his source for the story was, but also because Cleopas continued to be a person of some importance in the Jerusalem church.

Who was the other unnamed man? One tradition (reflected in a prayer said over those traveling) identifies him as no less a person than Luke himself, the author of the Gospel. This, however, is unlikely, for tradition makes Luke a native of Antioch and a Gentile, and it is unlikely that such a person would be resident in Emmaus. Besides, Luke himself says that he consulted eyewitnesses in writing his Gospel (1:1–4), and this would be a strange thing to say if he were himself such an eyewitness. Lastly, when Luke is a part of the narrative action (such as in Acts 16:10–17; 20:5–15; 21:1–8; 27:1—28:16), he signals his presence by using the pronoun "we"—which is not the case here.

We must be content to leave this disciple in the anonymity intended by Luke. He was connected with Cleopas, probably as a close friend. It seems he was going with Cleopas to his home (or was Cleopas going to *his* home?) to share a meal for the night. In the trauma and confusion that befell Jesus' disciples following His Passion, friends clung together for mutual support.

§IX.3. Final Appearances and Words

36 And *while* they were speaking these things, He Himself stood in the midst of them.

37 But they were alarmed and afraid and thought that they were observing a spirit.

38 And He said to them, "Why are you shaken, and why do questionings arise in your heart?

39 "See My hands and My feet, that I am Myself; touch Me and see, for a spirit does not have flesh and bones as you observe that I have."*

41 And while they were still disbelieving from the

> joy and were marveling, He said to them, "Have
> you some food here?"
> 42 And they gave Him a part of a broiled fish,
> 43 and He took *it* and ate *it* before them.
>
> * Verse 40, which relates how Jesus showed the disciples His
> hands and His feet, should probably be omitted as not original
> with Luke. It seems to have been added by a scribe for the
> sake of clarity, stating what was implied in v. 39, based on
> John 20:20.

The visit of the two men from Emmaus to the apostles and others
in Jerusalem took place the evening of the first day of the week. During this excited exchange of information, *while* **they were speaking
these things**, Christ **Himself stood in the midst of them**. One is
given the impression of a sudden, supernatural appearance. (John,
when relating this same event in John 20:19–23, mentions that the
doors were indeed securely closed where the disciples were, so that
Jesus appeared supernaturally in the room with them.) To His risen
form, things such as locked doors were no obstacle.

This was the first time the apostles as a group had seen the risen
Lord, and they were startled at such an appearance. (Since, as John
20:19 says, they were nervous enough to lock the doors for the fear
of the Jews, their startled reaction is all the more explicable—they
were jumpy enough *before* the Lord appeared!) They were **alarmed
and afraid** (Gr. *emphobos*, used for an intense fear) and their first
thought was that **they were observing a spirit**, a ghostly phantasm.

Christ soon calmed their fears. Gently, He asked them **why**
such **questionings** and doubts were **arising in** their **hearts**. Did
they think He was a ghost? Then He offered to show them His
hands and His **feet**, so they might observe where the nails had
pierced His holy flesh—the marks were still imprinted on His
glorified and risen form as a testimony of God's eternal love for us.
By seeing this they could know that it was truly Jesus Himself. Let
them not shrink in fear—let them boldly come! Condescending to
their weakness, Christ invited them to come right up and **touch
Him and see** the wounds up close—then they would know He

was no ghost, for **a spirit** did **not have flesh and bones** as He did.

The word rendered *touch* is the Greek *pselaphao*, "to grope" (compare its use in Acts 17:27). Christ invited them not just to touch Him gingerly, but to lay hold of Him, so they could be sure He was real. For this was a real tangible body of **flesh and bones**. He was no hallucination, but was truly risen!

Such was their **joy** in having their beloved Lord back, they could not help **disbelieving** for a moment. It was too much, too wonderful, to take in all at once. As they stood silently **marveling**, scarcely daring to believe in case it proved to be nothing but a wonderful dream, **He said to them, "Have you some food here?"** And then, to prove He was tangible and real, He **ate before them** the **part of a broiled fish** that was on hand and had formed part of the meal they had eaten. (A few manuscripts add that He also ate a honeycomb, but this is a later addition, probably reflecting church liturgical practice, for honey was sometimes given the newly baptized.) Once again, Luke shows how the initially incredulous disciples were convinced by irrefutable proofs (compare Acts 1:3).

In Luke's narration of this resurrection appearance, we can detect an escalating volume of proof. In verses 1–11, the women find the Lord's tomb empty, but do not meet the Lord. Then in verses 13–31, two disciples meet the Lord, but He vanishes from among them as soon as they recognize Him. Here in verses 36f, the Lord reveals Himself to all the Eleven, proving to their senses that He was alive and solid. The proofs of His Resurrection thus become ever more certain as time advances.

A final note may be added about the nature of Christ's risen body. It was, as St. Paul describes it in 1 Corinthians 15:44, "a spiritual body," but this does not mean that it was ghostly or unsolid. Rather, this means that His body is now liberated from the limitations of time and space and from the laws of physics. It is now part of the greater realm of the Spirit, which is why Christ could appear and disappear at will and over several miles, and why things such as locked doors were no limitation to Him. The risen body is still one of flesh and bones and of solid corporeality, but this corporeality lives by the laws of the age to come.

ॐ ॐ ॐ ॐ ॐ

44 And He said to them, "These are My words which I spoke to you while I was still with you, that it was necessary that all things which are written about Me in the Law of Moses and the Prophets and Psalms be fulfilled."

45 Then He opened-up their mind to have insight into the Scriptures,

46 and He said to them, "Thus it is written, that the Christ should suffer and arise from the dead the third day,

47 "and that repentance for forgiveness of sins should be heralded in His Name to all the nations, beginning from Jerusalem.

48 "You *Yourselves* are witnesses of these things.

49 "And behold, I *Myself* am sending forth the promise of My Father upon you, but you *yourselves* are to stay in the city until you are clothed with power from on high."

Luke now relates Christ's words on a later occasion. As is his custom, Luke telescopes Christ's teaching throughout the forty days following His Resurrection into one long discourse. (Compare a similar telescoping of the lengthy events of Christ's trial in 22:66–71.) We know that the words of verses 44–49 belong to a later discourse near the end of the forty days because the apostles went to Galilee during that time (Matt. 28:16; Mark 16:7), and yet here Christ tells them not to leave Jerusalem (24:49); therefore, the trip to Galilee must have occurred before this. Even apart from the witness of the other Synoptic Gospels, we know that the words of verses 44–49 must have been uttered at a later date, for the appearance of verses 36f. took place on the first day of His Resurrection (compare verses 1, 13, 36). Immediately after this present discourse of verses 44f., the Lord leads the disciples out as far as Bethany and then ascends to the Father (verses 50f.), which Luke later says occurred at the end of forty days (Acts 1:3f.). Thus the discourse of verses 44f. could not have been given at the same time as the other discourses, but Luke has telescoped all the post-Resurrection discourses into one.

In this present discourse, Christ reveals to them how all was predicted and happened just as God willed. He refers the disciples back to the **words which** He **spoke to** them **while** He **was still with** them in the flesh (that is, during His ministry, for He now was with them in a new and risen form). Back then, He told them that He must suffer and die, and only afterward be raised to glory (9:22). This is exactly what happened, for **it was necessary that all things written about** Him **in the Law of Moses and the Prophets and Psalms be fulfilled** (i.e. the Psalms and the other writings of the tripartite Scriptures; compare the prologue of Sirach, which speaks of the Law and the Prophets and the other books). After this, **He opened-up their mind to have insight into the Scriptures**, explaining passage by passage how those Scriptures found their fulfillment in Him. (It follows from this that the Hebrew Scriptures cannot be understood apart from their fulfillment in Jesus Christ.)

At last He summed up all His teaching by saying that **thus it was written** throughout the Scriptures, **that the Christ should suffer and arise from the dead the third day.** More than that, His disciples had a part in this long-prophesied plan as well: **repentance** leading to **forgiveness of sins should be heralded in His Name** by them **to all the nations, beginning from Jerusalem.** The world lay in bondage to sin, guilt, and death, but forgiveness and release was now possible for all. The Kingdom was thus not just for Jews, but for all the world. Let all men repent of their sins and trust in the saving Name of Jesus (Acts 4:12), and this forgiveness and liberation could be theirs. This was the message the disciples were called to take as God's heralds into all the earth.

They were thus commissioned by Christ as **witnesses of** all **these things** they had seen. (The pronoun **You** is emphatic—they had seen, and so they were called to give their testimony.) But they would not be left unaided in their work of witness. **Behold** (the drama of the sending forth is expressed in this word), Jesus Himself would be **sending forth the promise of** His **Father upon** them, the

Holy Spirit. The Spirit would empower them to be His witnesses in all the world (Acts 1:8). The Holy Spirit is called **the promise of** the **Father** because God had promised in the Scriptures to pour out His Spirit upon His people (see Joel 2:28–29; Acts 2:15–18).

This age-old promise was now near to fulfillment, and the disciples would soon be sent out **to all nations, beginning from Jerusalem**. They must therefore wait in Jerusalem for the Holy Spirit to come, for it was from that city that they would soon be sent out. The time was near; let them not leave the city any more! Rather, let them **stay in the city** until they were **clothed with power from on high**, for once they had that power, they could begin their work. The receiving of the Spirit is compared to being **clothed**, for that is the classic Old Testament image (compare the Spirit of the Lord clothing Gideon in Judg. 6:34). Like the saints of old, the disciples would receive **power** from heaven to do mighty exploits.

❦ X ❧

THE ASCENSION
(24:50–53)

🙿 🙿 🙿 🙿 🙿

50 And He led them out as far as near Bethany, and He lifted up His hands and blessed them.
51 And it happened that while He was blessing them, He went away from them and was being taken up into heaven.
52 And they returned to Jerusalem with great joy,
53 and were continually in the Temple, blessing God.

After this, Christ **led them out as far as near Bethany**, on the eastern slope of the Mount of Olives. That is, He did not take them far from the city in which He had told them to stay, just far enough out so as to have solitude with them for His departure. **He lifted up His hands** as the high priest lifted his hands in blessing (compare Sirach 50:20) and **blessed them** one final time. It was during this final blessing that **He went away from them**, being slowly **taken up into heaven**. (The gradual nature of the ascension is expressed in the imperfect tense, as it says that Christ **was being taken up**.) This heavenly blessing shows the Church how Christ continues to bless us from heaven as we worship Him on earth. By allowing the disciples to observe His Ascension (rather than simply vanishing and not appearing to them any more), Christ revealed that He now was to sit at the right hand of God.

After this, they obediently **returned to Jerusalem with great joy and were continually**, day after day, visiting **the Temple, blessing**

God. Thus St. Luke's Gospel ends where it began, in the Temple of God. It ends on a note of **joy**, as the disciples spend their days **blessing God**. This, for Luke, is the hallmark and result of the Gospel—it causes men to bless God for His goodness and for the joy He gives.

Luke is the only evangelist to narrate the Ascension (Mark 16:19 is a later addition to Mark's original Gospel.) This is significant, for Luke wants to stress the heavenly nature of Christ's Kingdom. Jesus the King is not an earthly revolutionary, threatening the political power of Rome. He is a heavenly Lord, and His Kingdom is not of this world.

It is with this heavenly ascension that Luke ends his Gospel (the first of a two-volume work; see Acts 1:1–2). Christ came to preach good news to the poor of all the world. In all the earth, the poor and hopeless were looking for a Savior. The apostles were soon to be sent forth with the news that that Savior had come.

About the Author

Archpriest Lawrence Farley currently pastors St. Herman of Alaska Orthodox Church (OCA) in Langley, B.C., Canada. He received his B.A. from Trinity College, Toronto, and his M.Div. from Wycliffe College, Toronto. A former Anglican priest, he converted to Orthodoxy in 1985 and studied for two years at St. Tikhon's Orthodox Seminary in Pennsylvania. In addition to the books in the Orthodox Bible Study Companion series, he has also published *The Christian Old Testament: Looking at the Hebrew Scriptures through Christian Eyes; A Song in the Furnace: The Message of the Book of Daniel; Unquenchable Fire: The Traditional Christian Teaching about Hell; A Daily Calendar of Saints: A Synaxarion for Today's North American Church; Let Us Attend: A Journey Through the Orthodox Divine Liturgy; One Flesh: Salvation through Marriage in the Orthodox Church; The Empty Throne: Reflections on the History and Future of the Orthodox Episcopacy;* and *Following Egeria: A Visit to the Holy Land through Time and Space.*

ANCIENT FAITH RADIO

Visit www.ancientfaithradio.com to listen to Fr. Lawrence Farley's regular podcast, "The Coffee Cup Commentaries."

A Complete List of the Books in the Orthodox Bible Study Companion Series

The Gospel of Matthew
Torah for the Church
• Paperback, 400 pages, ISBN 978-0-9822770-7-2

The Gospel of Mark
The Suffering Servant
• Paperback, 280 pages, ISBN 978-1-888212-54-9

The Gospel of Luke
Good News for the Poor
• Paperback, 432 pages, ISBN 978-1-936270-12-5

The Gospel of John
Beholding the Glory
• Paperback, 376 pages, ISBN 978-1-888212-55-6

The Acts of the Apostles
Spreading the Word
• Paperback, 352 pages, ISBN 978-1-936270-62-0

The Epistle to the Romans
A Gospel for All
• Paperback, 208 pages, ISBN 978-1-888212-51-8

First and Second Corinthians
Straight from the Heart
• Paperback, 319 pages, ISBN 978-1-888212-53-2

Words of Fire
The Early Epistles of St. Paul to the Thessalonians and the Galatians
• Paperback, 172 pages, ISBN 978-1-936270-02-6

The Prison Epistles
Philippians – Ephesians – Colossians – Philemon
• Paperback, 224 pages, ISBN 978-1-888212-52-5

Shepherding the Flock
The Pastoral Epistles of St. Paul the Apostle to Timothy and Titus
• Paperback, 144 pages, ISBN 978-1-888212-56-3

The Epistle to the Hebrews
High Priest in Heaven
• Paperback, 184 pages, ISBN 978-1-936270-74-3

Universal Truth
The Catholic Epistles of James, Peter, Jude, and John
• Paperback, 232 pages, ISBN 978-1-888212-60-0

The Apocalypse of St. John
A Revelation of Love and Power
• Paperback, 240 pages, ISBN 978-1-936270-40-8

Other Books by the Author

The Christian Old Testament
Looking at the Hebrew Scriptures through Christian Eyes

Many Christians see the Old Testament as "the other Testament": a source of exciting stories to tell the kids, but not very relevant to the Christian life. *The Christian Old Testament* reveals the Hebrew Scriptures as the essential context of Christianity, as well as a many-layered revelation of Christ Himself. Follow along as Fr. Lawrence Farley explores the Christian significance of every book of the Old Testament.

• Paperback, 200 pages, ISBN 978-1-936270-53-8

A Song in the Furnace
The Message of the Book of Daniel

The Book of Daniel should be read with the eyes of a child. It's a book of wonders and extremes—mad kings, baffling dreams with gifted interpreters, breathtaking deliverances, astounding prophecies—with even what may be the world's first detective stories added in for good measure. To argue over the book's historicity, as scholars have done for centuries, is to miss the point. In *A Song in the Furnace*, Fr. Lawrence Farley reveals all the wonders of this unique book to the receptive eye.

• Paperback, 248 pages, ISBN 978-1-944967-31-4

Let Us Attend
A Journey Through the Orthodox Divine Liturgy

Fr. Lawrence Farley provides a guide to understanding the Divine Liturgy, and a vibrant reminder of the centrality of the Eucharist in living the Christian life, guiding believers in a devotional and historical walk through the Orthodox Liturgy. Examining the Liturgy section by section, he provides both historical explanations of how the Liturgy evolved and devotional insights aimed at helping us pray the Liturgy in the way the Fathers intended.

• Paperback, 104 pages, ISBN 978-1-888212-87-7

A Daily Calendar of Saints
A Synaxarion for Today's North American Church
Popular biblical commentator and church historian Fr. Lawrence Farley turns his hand to hagiography in this collection of lives of saints, one or more for each day of the calendar year. His accessible prose and contemporary approach make these ancient lives easy for modern Christians to relate to and understand.
• Paperback, 304 pages, ISBN 978-1-944967-41-3

Let Us Attend
A Journey Through the Orthodox Divine Liturgy
Fr. Lawrence Farley provides a guide to understanding the Divine Liturgy, and a vibrant reminder of the centrality of the Eucharist in living the Christian life, guiding believers in a devotional and historical walk through the Orthodox Liturgy. Examining the Liturgy section by section, he provides both historical explanations of how the Liturgy evolved and devotional insights aimed at helping us pray the Liturgy in the way the Fathers intended.
• Paperback, 104 pages, ISBN 978-1-888212-87-7

One Flesh
Salvation through Marriage in the Orthodox Church
Is the Church too negative about sex? Beginning with this provocative question, Fr. Lawrence Farley explores the history of the Church's attitude toward sex and marriage, from the Old Testament through the Church Fathers. He persuasively makes the case both for traditional morality and for a positive acceptance of marriage as a viable path to theosis.
• Paperback, 160 pages, ISBN 978-1-936270-66-8

The Empty Throne
Reflections on the History and Future of the Orthodox Episcopacy
In contemporary North America, the bishop's throne in the local parish stands empty for most of the year. The bishop is an honored occasional guest rather than a true pastor of the local flock. But it was not always so, nor need it be so forever. Fr. Lawrence Farley explores how the Orthodox episcopacy developed over the centuries and suggests what can be done in modern times to bring the bishop back into closer contact with his flock.
• Paperback, 152 pages, ISBN 978-1-936270-61-3

Following Egeria
A Visit to the Holy Land through Time and Space
In the fourth century, a nun named Egeria traveled through the Holy Land and wrote an account of her experiences. In the twenty-first century, Fr. Lawrence Farley followed partially in her footsteps and wrote his own account of how he experienced the holy sites as they are today. Whether you're planning your own

pilgrimage or want to read about places you may never go, his account will inform and inspire you.
• Paperback, 160 pages, ISBN 978-1-936270-21-7

Three Akathists:
Akathist to Jesus, Light to Those in Darkness
• Staple-bound, 32 pages, ISBN 978-1-944967-33-8

Akathist to the Most Holy Theotokos, Daughter of Zion
• Staple-bound, 32 pages, ISBN 978-1-944967-34-4

Akathist to Matushka Olga Michael
• Staple-bound, 32 pages, ISBN 978-1-944967-38-3

For complete ordering information, visit our website: store.ancientfaith.com.

Other Books of Interest

The Orthodox Study Bible: Old and New Testaments

Featuring a Septuagint text of the Old Testament developed by outstanding Orthodox scholars, this Bible also includes the complete Orthodox canon of the Old Testament, including the Deuterocanon; insightful commentary drawn from the Christian writers of the first ten centuries; helpful notes relating Scripture to seasons of Christian feasting and fasting; a lectionary to guide your Bible reading through the Church year; supplemental Bible study articles on a variety of subjects; a subject index to the study notes to help facilitate Bible study; and more.
• Available in various editions. Visite store.ancientfaith.com for more details.

The Names of Jesus
Discovering the Person of Jesus Christ through Scripture
by Fr. Thomas Hoko

In this book based on his popular podcast series of the same name, the late Fr. Thomas Hopko shares meditations on over 50 different names and titles used for Jesus in the Bible. Learn what each name uniquely has to tell us about the character of the Son of God, His role in our salvation, and the relationship we can choose to cultivate with Him.
• Paperback, 400 pages, ISBN 978-1-936-70-41-5

The Rest of the Bible
A Guide to the Old Testament of the Early Church
by Theron Mathis

A beautiful widow risks her life to defend her people while men cower in fear. A young man takes a journey with an archangel and faces down a demon in order to marry a woman seven times widowed. A reprobate king repents and miraculously turns back toward God. A Jewish exile plays a game of riddles in a Persian king's court. Wisdom is detailed and exalted. Christ is revealed.

These and many other stories make up the collection of writings explored in this book—authentic books of the Bible you've probably never read. Dubbed "Apocrypha" and cut from the Bible by the Reformers, these books of the Greek Old Testament were a vital part of the Church's life in the early centuries, and are still read and treasured by Orthodox Christians today. *The Rest of the Bible* provides a brief and intriguing introduction to each of these valuable texts, which St. Athanasius termed "the Readables."
• Paperback, 128 pages, ISBN 978-1-936270-15-6

Christ in the Psalms
by Patrick Henry Reardon

A highly inspirational book of meditations on the Psalms by one of the most insightful and challenging Orthodox writers of our day. Avoiding both syrupy sentimentality and arid scholasticism, *Christ in the Psalms* takes the reader on a thought-provoking and enlightening pilgrimage through this beloved "Prayer Book" of the Church. Which psalms were quoted most frequently in the New Testament, and how were they interpreted? How has the Church historically understood and utilized the various psalms in her liturgical life? How can we perceive the image of Christ shining through the psalms? Lively and highly devotional, thought-provoking yet warm and practical, *Christ in the Psalms* sheds a world of insight upon each psalm, and offers practical advice for how to make the Psalter a part of our daily lives.

• Paperback, 328 pages, ISBN 978-1-888212-21-7

Christ in His Saints
by Patrick Henry Reardon

In this sequel to *Christ in the Psalms,* Patrick Henry Reardon once again applies his keen intellect to a topic he loves most dearly. Here he examines the lives of almost one hundred and fifty saints and heroes from the Scriptures— everyone from Abigail to Zephaniah, Adam to St. John the Theologian. This well-researched work is a veritable cornucopia of Bible personalities: Old Testament saints, New Testament saints, "Repentant saints," "Zealous saints," "Saints under pressure" . . . they're all here, and their stories are both fascinating and uplifting. But *Christ in His Saints* is far more than just a biblical who's who. These men and women represent that ancient family into which, by baptism, all believers have been incorporated. Together they compose that great "cloud of witnesses" cheering us on and inspiring us through word and deed.

• Paperback, 320 pages, ISBN 978-1-888212-68-6

The Trial of Job
Orthodox Christian Reflections on the Book of Job
by Patrick Henry Reardon

"The Book of Job always constituted essential and formative reading about the ways of the soul. This has always been the conviction of the spiritual classics through the centuries. Yet, for some reason, the figure of Job is elusive to us—possibly because he seems so comfortably distant; or perhaps because he seems so frightfully close. What Fr. Patrick Reardon achieves with this book is to render Job comprehensible (to those of us who are still lay readers of Scripture), tangible (to those who have not yet tasted the way of darkness and despair), and accessible (to those who have already experienced any form of brokenness and broken-heartedness). Ultimately, all of us identify with one or another aspect of Job's life. As life inevitably informs and as this book intuitively confirms, one cannot sing Psalms without having read Job!"—Fr. John Chryssavgis, author of *Light Through Darkness* and *Soul Mending*

• Paperback, 112 pages, ISBN: 978-1-888212-72-3

For complete ordering information, visit our website: store.ancientfaith.com.

Ancient Faith Publishing hopes you have enjoyed and benefited from this book. The proceeds from the sales of our books only partially cover the costs of operating our nonprofit ministry—which includes both the work of **Ancient Faith Publishing** and the work of **Ancient Faith Radio**. Your financial support makes it possible to continue this ministry both in print and online. Donations are tax-deductible and can be made at **www.ancientfaith.com**.

To view other books by Ancient Faith,
please visit our website: **store.ancientfaith.com**

 ANCIENT FAITH RADIO

Bringing you Orthodox Christian music,
readings, prayers, teaching, and podcasts
24 hours a day since 2004 at
www.ancientfaith.com

CPSIA information can be obtained
at www.ICGtesting.com
Printed in the USA
BVHW030221290719
554553BV00001B/53/P